THE DINAH SHORE COOKBOOK

THE
DINAH SHORE
COOKBOOK

DINAH SHORE

DOUBLEDAY & COMPANY, INC.
Garden City, New York
1983

DESIGNED BY LAURENCE ALEXANDER

Library of Congress Cataloging in Publication Data

Shore, Dinah, 1920–
The Dinah Shore cookbook.

Includes index.
1. Cookery.   I. Title
TX715.S55873   1983   641.5   80–2436
ISBN 0–385–15928–5

CONTENTS

ACKNOWLEDGMENTS

This is a hard one. There are so many people responsible for helping me get the book together. The list goes back not only for the two years I've spent getting this final manuscript together, but the dozens of years I've spent lovingly experimenting with new foods, borrowing from friends, relatives, and chefs who've allowed me to hover over them while they were trying to get out the meals for the evening and luncheon and even breakfast diners. (The interminable questions they answered! "What was that?"; "How much would you say you used?"; "Can they buy it in Tupelo as well as Boston?"; "How many will that serve?"; "How can we cut that down?" and so on . . . and on.) The gracious restaurateurs, chefs and cooks, writers and friends, who sent me their favorites, translated to measurements for the ordinary kitchen with hardly an error. The weary ones who sent the ones without a specific ingredient or directions—and you know who you are! (I still can't believe one famous chef makes his famous marinated herring with mayonnaise—but that was a rare exception.) Thank you all.

Thanks, specifically, to Pauline, my darling Pauline Bumann, who labored beside me day after day testing long, complicated "masterpieces." We pasted our recipes on the cupboards above us—her idea—laid out our ingredients below them in a line in the order in which they'd have to be used, and plowed ahead, as well as retesting the one we'd done for years to be sure we had the ingredients and measurements exactly the way they had to be so you could reproduce the "masterpiece" with optimum results.

To my dearest sister, my only sister, Bessie, who tested and proofread and even drafted my favorite brother-in-law, Maurice Seligman, for typing and proofreading—and on whose extraordinary vocabulary I pulled from time to time for a new descriptive phrase; I began to run out of mine.

To the Shirleys, Schroer and Hunt, "Laverne and Shirley," who not only typed some eighteen hours a day toward D-day—Delivery of manuscript date—but tested and tasted in their homes and here, and would give their eyeteeth for a plain old bowl of chili and beans at this point.

To Carl Sontheimer, my wonderful friend who is a bottomless pit of knowledge about food and causes and effects of why something did or didn't work, and was one of the first really encouraging voices from the outside world. We knew what we were trying to accomplish, but Carl spurred me on when it seemed it might never happen.

To the innumerable friends who tasted our testings, and Bee, who tested some for me, as well as twelve-year-old Katie, both Korshaks. Katie later came through with the Macaroni Red Devil testing when I wanted to see how practical these recipes might be for semi-experienced cooks. Of course Katie's exceptional, but she proved that if you can read and follow exactly what is written, you don't have to have attended the Cordon Bleu School to use our book.

To Liliana, who chopped and cut and cleaned up and even tested a few, so that I could find out if great and curious potential cooks with a limited knowledge of the language could use our book. She could. Her Guatemalan Chilies Rellenos in Chapter 9 is an example of her own expertise and creativity.

To Gloria, who performed the same function at the beach and came through with the Mexican Pork Roast in Chapter 8 and the Mexican Rice in Chapter 10.

To my editor Ferris Mack, who has waited patiently—sort of—for the delivery of this book since November two years ago.

To Jeremy Tarcher, who kept all lines of communication open to keep Ferris confident that he was going to get this book and me confident that it could really be done.

To Millie Loeb, who claims her role was The Nudge, but who did a lot more than that. She made notes on my notes. I believe her favorite phrase was, "I don't understand this." Or, "Tempt me further into trying it." She moved me further into writing and with fervor when the muse moved slower than my typewriter.

To Judi Kaufman, who tried to keep me organized on paper anyway.

To Larry Alexander, who laid out our book so skillfully we didn't have to make that devastating 500-page cut!

To Steve Kral, who typed till all ungodly hours during the rainy and sunny season till we could get through with it.

To Odile Muñoz, my dressmaker, who kept altering my wardrobe—I gained a pound a month (truly) when we started serious work on the book.

To the cameramen, who began to photograph me from the shoulders up as I began to develop Junoesque proportions—or pear-shaped, if you want to get less lyrical about it.

To Mike Abrams, with whom I spent much time in heavy exercise as he dictated the routines and lectured nonstop about the virtues of slimness and strict dieting, and drove me to it by forcing me to get on that scale.

To the Scarsdale, Stillman, Grapefruit, Asparagus, Lettuce, Mozzarella, Tomato, Cambridge, Princeton, Pritikin, Duke, Vogue, Harpers, Golden Door, ad infinitum diets I started constantly and stopped when a new batch of recipes came in to be tried.

To my Adidas running shoes that I fondly thought were helping me take it off—they did the best they could with the load they were carrying.

INTRODUCTION

Most people go sightseeing, seek out historical monuments, or go antique shopping when they visit a new place. I go restaurant hopping. I get to know more about those people and places historically, socially, and culturally by their cuisine and attitude toward it than in almost any other way.

Food is people to me, sharing and socializing on the most convivial and most comforting level. Dining together—breaking bread, as they used to say—is a personal way to get to know someone better.

It seems to me we are eating better and more adventurously, more exotically, all over America today. Maybe it's because we have become more open to new cultures, new customs, and new ideas, and consequently, new cuisines. People from all over the world are landing on our shores and borders daily. We don't learn their language. They learn ours just as our parents and grandparents all the way back had to do when they landed in this strange new world. But we do learn their food, and through this kind of cultural exchange we have accomplished what all our efforts at legislation have not been able to do—building toward understanding and respect.

We're trying all kinds of new culinary sensations and still holding on to the plain old down home, all American cooking indigenous to each area—our own heritage. We couldn't change it if we wanted to, which we don't. It gets right down to where "down home" is or was. Living in middle America near a river or lake is quite different from living near a seacoast. Living in cattle, sheep, wheat, or dairy country helps determine how we eat. We use those things best which are readily available in our terrain. It's fascinating to me how we carry our first food preferences all over America with us. They are like my blue blanket, and maybe you feel that way too. That's what people who come here from all over the world are doing—carrying their "down home" cooking with them. It is in part the why and how-it-came-about of this book.

I believe that an attitude toward food begins at home in childhood. My father was a meat-and-potatoes man, but Mother was adventurous. She was influenced and delighted by every new recipe she came upon in Winchester and Nashville. It seems to me her table was always pretty. The tablecloth was sparkling white, the crystal gleamed, and the food was lusciously and lovingly prepared by Mother and Ya Ya (real name Lillian, which gives you an idea how long she had been with our family. I couldn't say Lillian when she first came to us). Even at breakfast, which was always eaten in a hurry. (There has always been a problem in our family about promptness. I hope it's not in the genes, but nobody—not Mother, Daddy, nor my sister Bessie—ever started to go anywhere early enough to get there on time.) Back to breakfast—even in the rush to get to school on time, I don't ever remember a milk carton or a cereal box on the table or a biscuit that wasn't made from scratch. Just one exception: Mother loved golf and on one Sunday morning a month would take off early for the golf course. One of the first memories I have was Aunt Jemima's Buckwheat pancake mix, which I proudly cooked for Daddy's breakfast. You just had to mix it with water and cook the pancakes on the griddle, but you had to remember to heat the syrup and the butter and always serve them on a warm plate. For dinner at noon it was fried chicken, mashed potatoes, creamed corn or succotash in the summer, or chicken-fried steak with biscuits and crisply grated fried potatoes, or chicken and dumplings, etc. Supper was something else wonderful, probably with hot corn bread and homemade ice cream. Food was never incidental in our home. I've crisscrossed this country many times doing concerts and benefits and TV shows, but a couple of summers ago just before launching our concert tour, we called food critics, food editors, personal friends, restaurant devotees, professional and amateur, for their recommendations for the "best food in the area." The response was an eye opener—a new French bistro—terrific! Another, a splendid Italian restaurant—*mamma mia!* A magnificent Chinese with new and unusual specialties, Czechoslovakian, Mexican, Middle Eastern, Spanish, Thai, Swedish, Vietnamese—all in the same town! And then the food of the locale—long established beloved home cooking indigenous to the area. We tried as many as we could, and when I say we—I mean my troop of musicians, singers, technical people, P.R. folk, and agents. It was a great, satisfying experience.

The concerts went really well, so I began to rationalize that those great performers of another era lived and sang with purity and gusto in direct proportion to how happily and well they had dined the night before. They moved from one city to another sharing their talents with the whole country—their reputation for excellent performance exceeded only by their girth. I know why. I only ate that one meal a day; otherwise I'd have been singing in caftans and mumus. I was popping hooks and zippers all over the place. But I learned about us and food, and that is what you'll find in this book.

I give small dinner parties fairly often. Sometimes when my home looks especially pretty and the flowers are still fresh, two nights in a row are easier than a week apart. So—a few words about parties.

A nervous hostess makes nervous guests. It's kind of like going into a lion's den. Fear gives off scents and makes the lion react in unpredictable ways. If you're calm, he's comfortable. So enjoy your own party. Easier said than done, but plan all of it well ahead, from menu to seating arrangements, and leave as little as possible for that very last moment. If it's really an important new guest whom you must impress—your spouse's boss, yours, the famed critical perfect hostess—make it easy on yourself. Don't try that brand new twelve-step-assemble-as-guests-are-seated headline maker. Look up your standbys—the ones you've cooked before successfully and comfortably.

Plan your menu definitely and be prepared to change it when you go grocery shopping the day before the dinner party and find some wonderful in-season something.

Don't be fooled into thinking the simple broiled steak, chicken, or fish is the answer. Those must be done at the very last minute and perfectly, and fish can be as temperamental and demanding as a soufflé. Whereas a long-cooking roast or stew can be set out twenty minutes ahead of serving and not suffer for it.

I do my table in the morning. I set out the platters and utensils for serving with a little slip of paper as a reminder of what each is supposed to hold. If I can, I copy the recipes out of my source and stick them up on the cupboard door with tape for easy checking. Or at least keep the book handy on the counter.

No more big, expensive clumps of flowers for centerpieces for me. I put those in the living room. I use five or six or even eight small vases of different heights and shapes, holding one or two flowers at most—long, medium, and short-stemmed. I place candles inside, between, and around the flowers or I use a beautiful scattering of the prettiest fruit and vegetables in season set on something—a small platter or large leaf—so they won't stain my table or cloth. If you have small art objects you may not even have noticed for ages around the house, such as little crystal animals or birds, these can be scattered in between. Be sure your guests can see each other over and through the flowers and candles. People look and feel prettier by candlelight. Turn off the overhead chandelier, no matter how prized it is. Take it from us show folk that overhead lighting is a shadow maker—in the wrong areas.

Just a word about your guest list. We're all a little clannish and sometimes it's more comfortable not to have to stretch beyond that same three couples you see two or three times a week. But if you're like me, you really don't want a group much larger than eight people, so there you are with six already and you've limited yourself to two new faces. Try to condition your friends, neighbors, and family to the idea that you don't want to start out with the basic six. You'd like to hear some new ideas and thoughts every once in a while—and so might they. They may have some hurt feelings for a day or so, but as long as they're not excluded from too many, they'll love you for it in the long run. Don't forget, you've relieved them from having to invite you to every single small gathering.

I keep a notebook with a complete record of menus and who dined on them. This keeps me from repeating myself too often. I even try to keep track of who I seated next to whom. You might be suspected of attempted matchmaking if you've repeated that coupling too often.

When buffet time comes, to keep the line from getting too long and the food from getting cold, I've reverted to one of my favorite chauvinistic attitudes. Instead of having everyone line up along the buffet table I say, "Ladies, please take two plates, one for yourself and one for the gentleman on your left," or conversely, "Gentlemen, please take two plates, one for yourself and one for the lady on your left." Just make sure he gets you some of everything—not just what he thinks you should have.

I supervise the serving of the food to make sure the sauce goes on the right thing in the right proportion and the vegetables as well as the beloved mashed potatoes or their equivalent go on every plate.

By the way, line up your buffet table in a logical order—warmed dinner plates, main course, sauce and/or condiments beside it, starch and vegetables.

If I've baked bread, I pass it hot right after they've filled their plates. Someone gave me a few of those little Lucite bread boards. I place a small loaf and a knife with a serrated edge on each Lucite bread board between two guests and let them hack away. An individual portion of butter there for the two of them saves a lot of reaching.

I keep referring to table settings, but if you don't have that kind of setup, not to worry. Put place mats, napkins, knives, forks, spoons, wine and water glasses on coffee tables. It makes dining more comfortable. Guests should not have to juggle plate, glasses and utensils on their laps, make conversation, and slice and bite simultaneously.

If people are bound and determined to help out by bringing plates back into the kitchen, let them. Just pile them in one spot near the dishwasher and don't worry about really cleaning up until everybody leaves. You've got those glasses to collect and ashtrays to empty post-party anyway.

Just as it's difficult to make the first part of your party a success without a few special articles, plates, platters, silverware, and serving utensils, it's impossible to cook well for yourself, two people, or twelve without the proper kitchen tools and equipment. Pots with matching tight lids, mixing bowls, measuring cups, spoons, spatulas—rubber and metal—molds, cookie sheets, roasting pans, cake pans and so on. You have less chance of cutting yourself instead of the vegetables if you depend on a good set of sharp knives and *then* there's the food processor! It has literally revolutionized cooking today. It's a time, food, bowl, and soul saver. My favorite phrase when I really want an excuse for buying something for *me* that isn't in the budget is "You owe it to yourself!" I feel that way about my Cuisinart. If you're going to buy a processor, save up until you can buy the best. There are other fine ones, I'm sure, but the Cuisinart really does it all dependably, from mayonnaise to carrots julienne to thick-sliced potatoes to pureed soups to breads, sauces, etc. If dog is man's best friend, surely that Cuisinart is in there somewhere as the cook's.

We've tested every recipe in this book in our kitchen and a lot more that didn't make it. It's put a heavy load on friends in every sense of the word. They have needed discriminating palates, open minds, honest opinions, and stomachs of iron.

When I ran out of local talent for tasting our testings, I drafted a few out-of-town friends. There was some bewilderment at first when they were greeted with these variegated menus. (How about five hors d'oeuvres, six entrées, seven vegetables, four first courses, four or five salads, and six to eight desserts!) They accepted the small plates that separated each dish from the previous one. There is no way one could give a true appraisal of a real Indian curry and its condiments on the same plate as red enchiladas and then a green enchilada and a collection of salsas for each. But soon they began to get used to the idea and recognized themselves for the guinea pigs they were.

Incidentally, after a while you could certainly begin to separate the steadfast diehard true tasters from the faltering, fragile, fainthearted, by the skeptical reluctance or eagerness in their voices when I called.

One who stuck by me all through this was Art Buchwald. After all, he and Annie didn't live out here so they weren't on draft duty daily or weekly, but he finally hinted (rather snidely, I thought) that there was *no* book in the works. It was just an excuse to have parties and see how far down the garden path I could lead these laboratory mice. Well, here you are, Art Buchwald—my real, live, something-for-us-all cookbook. I have left out a lot of my favorites, among them chili dogs and double hamburgers and french fries and pepperoni pizza, but that's for the next one.

'Tis an ill cook that cannot lick his own fingers.

WILLIAM SHAKESPEARE
Romeo and Juliet

I am loath to trust that cook who maintains she constantly practices her craft and gaineth never a pound.

DINAH SHORE

Chapter 1

BASICS

This chapter could be called "A Few of My Favorite Things," but it would only describe a small portion of its value to the rest of the book. It contains a large variety of recipes, techniques, and methods I think you should know about—from time savers, dish savers, shortcuts sometimes taken for granted by people who cook constantly, to complete recipes. It contains those all-important stocks—chicken, beef, and fish—which can be kept in the freezer for weeks at a time, alongside that essential brown sauce. There's everything here, from a variety of piecrusts to duxelles, *beurre manié* to mayonnaise. You'll find many of the shortcuts, sauces, and enhancers listed with a specific recipe in other parts of the book, but we've tried to minimize the number of cross-references for one seemingly simple recipe; if you need it by itself, chances are you'll find it in this chapter.

There are recipes for those precious home-canned relishes, pepper jellies, conserves, and chutneys, as well as those great snacks we always keep in plastic containers for quick lunches, sudden drop-ins who've come to expect the Special Pimiento Cheese Spread or Mother's Chicken Salad—almost always there—made from every salvageable scrap of chicken, leftover roast turkey, or roast chicken chicken. Did I mention seasoned salts, seasoned flours, roux for sauce bases? They're in here too. Most are basic, useful, constantly ready in my refrigerator, freezer, or cupboard for preparation of a special something on a moment's notice. It makes it a little harder to cook in somebody else's kitchen, so let's have the party at my house—I love it!

BÉCHAMEL (CREAM) SAUCE MAKES 1 CUP

This is what was always simply called cream sauce at home or white sauce everywhere else. It is so basic and so necessary in cooking of all kinds, and there are so many lovely variations, you can hardly cook successfully without some knowledge of it.

2 tablespoons unsalted butter	Salt and freshly ground white or black pepper
2 tablespoons flour	per
1 cup heated milk	

In heavy saucepan, melt butter over low heat; add flour and stir until the roux of flour and butter is well blended. Stirring constantly over low heat, cook about 3 to 4 minutes to lose the floury taste. Do not let the roux brown. (See Note.)

Add heated milk slowly, stirring constantly with wire whisk or wooden spoon until it thickens.

Season to taste with salt and pepper.

NOTE This roux can be made in large quantities and stored at this point after cooling. It will keep in the refrigerator for weeks in a covered jar. When you need a Béchamel, Velouté, or any comparable sauce, take 2 to 4 tablespoons of the roux, soften in a 1 1/2-quart saucepan with a heavy bottom, and add the milk, broth, or stock and proceed as above.

CHEESE SAUCE

To 1 cup Béchamel, add 1/2 cup or more of grated Cheddar, Monterey Jack, or Gruyère cheese and, if desired, a dash of cayenne pepper. Heat until cheese is melted.

MORNAY SAUCE

To 1 cup Béchamel, add 1/2 cup Gruyère and 1/4 cup Parmesan cheese and an extra tablespoon of butter. Simmer for 3 minutes.

For extra flavor or richness, in addition to the butter add 2 tablespoons cream or 1 tablespoon dry sherry before cheeses are added.

This sauce can be used over warmed slices of leftover turkey, or chicken breasts placed on crisply toasted buttered English muffins, with Parmesan cheese sprinkled over all and placed under the broiler until it bubbles.

EGG SAUCE

To 1 cup Béchamel Sauce, add 2 hard-boiled eggs, chopped, and at the last minute 1 beaten egg yolk into which you've stirred a little of the hot Béchamel (to keep yolk from cooking too soon when it comes into contact with the hot sauce). The addition of 1/4 teaspoon of Dijon mustard gives this an extra dimension.

SAUCE SUPRÊME

Add 1/4 to 1/3 cup cream to Béchamel. Simmer 3 to 4 minutes. Blend a tablespoon of the hot sauce into 2 beaten egg yolks, then stir egg yolk mixture into the Sauce Suprême. Finally, beat in 2 to 3 tablespoons cold butter, 1 tablespoon at a time, until melted and well blended.

VELOUTÉ SAUCE

To the basic roux for Béchamel Sauce, add 1 cup heated chicken broth or veal broth instead of milk. If you want it richer, add 1/2 cup half and half or heavy cream and stir until warmed through. Blend a tablespoon of the hot sauce into 2 beaten egg yolks, then pour egg yolk mixture into Velouté Sauce and stir over lowest heat until slightly thickened, about 1–2 minutes.

TOMATO SAUCE   MAKES 1 QUART

1/4 cup olive oil
2/3 cup finely chopped yellow onions
2/3 cup finely chopped carrots
2/3 cup finely chopped celery
4 pounds fresh ripe plum tomatoes *or* 4 cups canned Italian plum tomatoes, including juice

3 whole cloves garlic
2 tablespoons fresh basil, finely chopped, *or* 2 teaspoons dried basil
1/2 teaspoon sugar
2/3 tablespoon chopped parsley
3 teaspoons salt, or salt to taste

In 3- or 4-quart saucepan, heat olive oil until light haze forms over it. Add onions and sauté over medium heat until they are just translucent, but not browned. Add carrots and celery and sauté for another minute.

Add tomatoes, garlic, basil, sugar, parsley, and salt. Reduce heat to medium and simmer, uncovered, for 20 minutes. Stir from time to time while cooking. If sauce gets too thick or dry, add chicken broth or tomato juice to desired consistency. Remove garlic cloves before serving.

FRESH TOMATO BASIL SAUCE   MAKES ABOUT 2 CUPS

1 tablespoon olive oil
1 cup finely minced onions
2 cloves garlic, minced
1/2 teaspoon sugar
3 large tomatoes, peeled and coarsely
   chopped

1/2 cup water
1/4 cup fresh basil, coarsely chopped
1/4 cup parsley, coarsely chopped
Dash cayenne pepper
Pinch of oregano
Salt and pepper to taste

Heat oil in large skillet. Add onion and garlic and sauté until very lightly browned. Add sugar and mix well. Add tomatoes and water. Bring to boil, then cover and reduce heat. Let simmer until sauce is blended.

Add basil, parsley, cayenne pepper, oregano, salt, and pepper. Simmer about 10 or 15 minutes, until flavors are well blended.

MARINARA SAUCE   MAKES ABOUT 2 CUPS

2 tablespoons olive oil
1/2 cup finely chopped onions
6 large tomatoes, peeled, seeded, and
   chopped or 8 canned Italian plum tomatoes, cut into 2 or 3 pieces, plus 1/4 cup of
   juice
3 tablespoons tomato paste

2 cloves garlic, cut in half
1 tablespoon fresh basil, finely chopped, or 1
   teaspoon dried basil
3/4 teaspoon sugar
1/3 tablespoon parsley
Freshly ground black pepper
1/2 teaspoon salt

Using a 2- or 3-quart saucepan, heat olive oil until light haze forms over it. Add onions and cook over moderate heat until they are soft but not browned.

Add tomatoes, tomato juice, tomato paste, garlic, basil, sugar, parsley and pepper. I add salt after almost 20 minutes of cooking.

Reduce heat to medium and simmer for 30 to 40 minutes, stirring occasionally, until tomatoes are soft and shapeless. Remove garlic cloves and taste sauce for seasoning. Remove from heat and set aside.

BARBECUE SAUCE

2 onions, cut in quarters
8 cloves garlic, cut in half
4 tablespoons chili powder
1 cup oil
1 1/4 cups white vinegar
1 cup tomato catsup

4 8-ounce cans tomato sauce
10–12 little red chili peppers
Salt to taste
1 tablespoon paprika
2 heaping teaspoons prepared mustard
1 teaspoon freshly ground black pepper

Combine all ingredients. Cook for a minimum of 1 hour; 2 is better. This sauce keeps for ages in the refrigerator.

BEURRE MANIÉ

This is simply a mixture of softened butter and flour to be added at the last minute of cooking to thicken a sauce or gravy slightly.

The proportions are usually one to one. That is, 2 tablespoons softened butter to 2 tablespoons flour. If the sauce you're trying to thicken is rich, use 1 tablespoon softened butter to 2 tablespoons flour. Mix with your fingers to blend thoroughly. Roll into small balls and toss one or two at a time into the sauce; turn heat to low, and beat with a wooden spoon or wire whisk to blend into sauce. Don't add too many at one time, as sauce may get too thick. You can always add more.

CLARIFIED BUTTER

The recipe that follows isn't really a recipe; it's a cooking technique. I suggest clarifying a whole pound of butter because it keeps so nicely in the refrigerator. It's helpful to use clarified butter to prevent burning when you are pan-frying or sautéing.

In a saucepan with a heavy bottom, melt 1 pound butter, cut into chunks, over lowest possible heat. Use an asbestos pad between pan and burner if your heat isn't low enough, as butter must not brown. Let butter melt slowly until the milky residue sinks to the bottom and foam rises to the top. Skim off foam and carefully pour out the clear yellow liquid into a small saucepan. The clear liquid is clarified butter.

HOLLANDAISE

6 egg yolks
1/4 cup lemon juice
1 teaspoon salt

Dash of cayenne
1/2 pound (2 sticks) butter, cut up

In bowl of food processor fitted with the steel blade, place egg yolks, lemon juice, salt, and cayenne. Switch processor on and immediately off.

Heat butter until bubbling. With motor running, pour hot butter through feed tube in a slow, steady stream. Turn off food processor as soon as all butter has been poured through the feed tube.

Pour sauce into top of double boiler and keep it warm over hot but not boiling water. If sauce curdles, whisk in 2 tablespoons hot water, 1/2 teaspoon at a time.

CRÈME FRAÎCHE

This is a version of Crème Fraîche. There are many, but dear Julia (Child) recommends this one instead of the sour cream–heavy cream mixture, and she wouldn't steer you wrong. She wouldn't know how.

1 cup heavy cream

1 teaspoon buttermilk

Mix cream and buttermilk well and keep at room temperature 12 to 24 hours (8 hours when the weather is warm). Stir, cover, and refrigerate.

BROWN SAUCE

6 tablespoons clarified butter or rendered
    chicken fat
2 onions, coarsely chopped
1 small carrot, coarsely chopped
3 tablespoons diced bacon or ham, rendered
1/2 cup flour
8 cups hot Beef Brown Stock
2 stalks celery, including tops

Herb Bouquet (tie in cheesecloth bag):
    3 sprigs parsley
    1 bay leaf
    1 garlic clove
    1/4 teaspoon thyme
1/4 cup tomato sauce or 1/2 cup tomato
    puree

In large, heavy 3-quart saucepan heat butter or chicken fat. Cook onions and carrots 5–10 minutes. Add bacon or ham.

Blend flour into vegetables. Cook over moderate heat, stirring until flour, carrots, and onions are rich brown. Add 3 cups hot Beef Brown Stock, celery, and the herb bouquet and cook the mixture, stirring frequently, until it thickens.

Add 3 more cups stock and simmer sauce slowly, stirring occasionally, for 1 to 1 1/2 hours, or until it is reduced to about one half. As it cooks, skim off fat that rises to surface.

Add tomato sauce or tomato puree, cook for a few minutes, and strain the Brown Sauce through a fine sieve. Add 2 more cups brown beef stock and continue to cook slowly for about 1 hour, skimming surface from time to time, until sauce is reduced to about 4 cups. Strain sauce and let cool.

Freeze in ice cube trays, then put 4 to 6 frozen cubes in plastic bags for storage in freezer. They keep for months and you use only what you need to strengthen a sauce. This is the difference between plain flour gravy and a great sauce. It's worth the effort because you don't have to do it more often than every six months or so.

BEEF BROWN STOCK

MAKES 2 1/2 TO 3 QUARTS

3–4 pounds meaty beef and veal bones
2 onions, peeled and stuck with 3 cloves
2 carrots, cubed
3 stalks celery
2 teaspoons salt
3 quarts cold water

Herb Bouquet (tie in cheesecloth bag):
  1 bay leaf
  6 sprigs parsley
  1/2 teaspoon thyme
  2 cloves garlic, unpeeled
  1 teaspoon black peppercorns

Preheat oven to 400°F.

Crack bones into small pieces. Place cracked bones, onions, and carrots in shallow pan and brown very well in oven, turning bones and vegetables occasionally so they will brown evenly. It should take 30–40 minutes. Be sure onion is very brown, almost burned; this gives color to sauce.

In large kettle place bones, onions, carrots, celery, salt, and herb bouquet. Add cold water to cover by 2 to 3 inches.

Bring water slowly to a boil, skimming fat from surface when necessary. Cook stock slowly at least 4 hours, adding more water if necessary. Taste stock after 4 hours; if it tastes weak, let it simmer down to evaporate some of the water. Strain stock into bowl and refrigerate. (I freeze it in small containers. If kept in the refrigerator, it must be brought to the boiling point every 4 days so it will not spoil.)

CHICKEN STOCK OR BROTH

MAKES ABOUT 2 1/2 QUARTS

1 whole chicken (3–4 pounds)
2 pounds chicken necks, backs, and wings
3 quarts water *or* water to cover
1 whole onion, unpeeled
2 or 3 stalks celery, including tops

1 carrot, cut in half
1 bay leaf
4 sprigs parsley
6 peppercorns
2 teaspoons salt

Place whole chicken and extra parts in deep stockpot. Use everything except the liver. Add water to cover by 3 inches.

Let come to a boil; skim off scum as it rises to the top and discard.

When clear, lower heat and add onion, celery, carrot, bay leaf, parsley, peppercorns, and salt. Bring to the boiling point again and skim again, if necessary. Add more hot water so the chicken is still covered by 3 inches.

When whole chicken is tender—about 1 hour—remove and set aside for other uses. Continue cooking stock for another 30 minutes.

Strain broth into a large bowl and cool thoroughly. Place in the refrigerator.

When broth is cold, remove the layer of fat on the surface. Freeze stock in pint containers, leaving at least 1 inch air space at top.

FISH STOCK

MAKES ABOUT 3 QUARTS

1 pound mild fish (sole, snapper, or bass)
and extra fish bones if available
3 stalks celery, including tops
2 whole carrots
5 sprigs parsley

1 small whole onion
6 peppercorns, crushed
3 quarts water or to cover
Salt to taste

In a large uncovered saucepan, combine all ingredients and bring to boil. Lower heat and simmer for 1 hour.

Strain stock into a large bowl and cool thoroughly. Refrigerate. Freeze in 1-pint containers leaving 1 inch air space at top.

VEGETABLE STOCK

MAKES ABOUT 6 CUPS

6 cups water
4 stalks celery, including tops
1 onion
1 small green pepper

2 carrots
4 sprigs parsley
6 lettuce leaves
Salt and pepper to taste

Combine all ingredients, cover, and bring to a boil. Reduce heat and simmer 45 minutes to an hour until well blended. Strain, cool, and refrigerate or freeze in small containers.

MAYONNAISE

MAKES 1 1/2 CUPS

2 egg yolks
1/4 cup lemon juice or vinegar
1 teaspoon dry mustard
1/2 teaspoon salt

1/4 teaspoon cayenne pepper
Pinch of sugar
1 1/4 cups vegetable or olive oil

Put all ingredients except oil in bowl of food processor fitted with steel or plastic blade. Process for a few seconds. Turn machine off and scrape down sides of bowl. With machine running, add oil through feed tube in a very thin stream. Blend until thick. Refrigerate.

DILL MAYONNAISE

MAKES 1 1/2 CUPS

1 cup homemade mayonnaise
3 teaspoons lemon juice
3 tablespoons chopped fresh dill *or* 3 tea-

spoons dried dill weed
1/4 teaspoon Worcestershire sauce
Dash of Tabasco sauce

Mix until all ingredients are well blended. Chill.

BASIL MAYONNAISE

MAKES 1 CUP

2 eggs
1/2 cup fresh basil leaves
2 tablespoons white vinegar or lemon juice
1 tablespoon Dijon mustard
1 scant teaspoon salt

1/2 teaspoon dry mustard
1/4 teaspoon cayenne pepper
1/8 teaspoon minced garlic
Scant 1/4 cup oil (I use peanut oil)

Place all ingredients except oil in bowl of food processor fitted with the metal blade. Blend all ingredients well. With motor running, add oil through feed tube in thinnest stream until mixture is the consistency of thin mayonnaise. Chill.

MUSTARD MAYONNAISE

MAKES 1 CUP

1 cup homemade mayonnaise
2 teaspoons lemon juice
2 tablespoons Dijon mustard

1/4 teaspoon Worcestershire sauce
1/8 teaspoon Tabasco sauce

Mix all ingredients until well blended. Chill.

BASICS

9

SAUCE VERTE

1 medium cucumber, peeled and seeded
1 cup homemade mayonnaise
1/2 cup watercress

1/3 cup parsley
1/2 green pepper, cut into chunks
Salt and pepper to taste

Shred cucumber with shredding disc of food processor. Remove cucumber to a colander and drain very well, pressing with a tea towel to remove excess liquid.

Add remaining ingredients to the same bowl, but fitted with the steel blade. Blend until smooth. Fold in shredded cucumbers by hand.

TARTAR SAUCE

1 teaspoon Dijon mustard
1/8 teaspoon pepper
1 teaspoon powdered sugar
1/4 teaspoon salt
2 teaspoons grated onion
2 egg yolks

1/2 cup olive oil
3 tablespoons vinegar
1 tablespoon chopped olives
1 tablespoon capers
1 tablespoon chopped dill pickle
1 tablespoon chopped parsley

In small bowl combine mustard, pepper, sugar, salt, grated onion, and egg yolks. Beat well.

Drop by drop, add olive oil and vinegar as you would in making mayonnaise. This may be done in your blender or food processor.

When mixture is thick, add olives, capers, pickle, and parsley. If parsley is omitted, the sauce will keep for weeks in your refrigerator.

CUCUMBER SOUR CREAM

1/2 cucumber, peeled and sliced
1/2 teaspoon salt
2 tablespoons vinaigrette or French dressing
1 tablespoon chopped fresh dill *or*
   1 teaspoon dried dill weed

3 tablespoons sour cream
1 teaspoon chives, chopped, *or*
   1 scallion, finely chopped including green part

Sprinkle salt on cucumber and let stand for 15 minutes to drain. Pat dry.

In bowl, combine dressing, dill weed or fresh dill, sour cream, and chopped chives or scallion. Mix well to blend. Fold in cucumbers. Chill.

BASIC FRENCH DRESSING

MAKES 1 1/2 CUPS

12 tablespoons light vegetable oil
8 tablespoons white vinegar or lemon juice
2 teaspoons salt
1 1/2 teaspoons pepper
2 teaspoons Dijon mustard
2 teaspoons sugar

1 teaspoon paprika
3/4 teaspoon dried basil, crushed
3/4 teaspoon dried tarragon, crushed
3 cloves garlic, mashed slightly but left in
   cloves

Put all ingredients into a jar with a good lid and shake well. Keeps in refrigerator.

FRESH HERB DRESSING

MAKES 3/4 CUP

1/2 cup salad oil
1/4 cup tarragon vinegar
1 tablespoon snipped chives
1 tablespoon snipped fresh dill weed *or* 1
   teaspoon dried dill weed

1/2 clove garlic, crushed
1 teaspoon sugar
1 teaspoon salt
Dash of pepper

Combine all ingredients in jar with tight-fitting lid; shake well. Refrigerate until well chilled—at least 1 hour.

OUR SEASONED SALT

MAKES ABOUT 1 CUP

1 cup salt
1 tablespoon Spanish paprika
1 teaspoon ground black pepper
1/4 teaspoon ground white pepper

1/4 teaspoon celery seed
1 clove garlic, finely minced
1/4 teaspoon red pepper flakes

Mix all ingredients together and store in a tightly sealed jar.

CREOLE MEAT SEASONING

MAKES 3 3/4 CUPS

I use this on many dishes. As the preseasoning for beef, lamb, or pork roasts, stews, chickens, and heavy-fleshed fish. Don't cut down on the amount of the peppers. They are part of its charm and melt into the meat with a memorable piquancy.

1 1/2 cups salt
3/4 cup finely minced garlic
3/4 cup black pepper

1/2 cup cayenne pepper
1/4 cup cumin seed

Combine all ingredients and mix thoroughly. Pour into large glass jar with a tightly fitting lid. Keeps indefinitely.

FOUR SPICES

1 cup ground white pepper
1 1/2 tablespoons powdered cloves

3 1/2 tablespoons powdered ginger
4 tablespoons freshly grated nutmeg

Mix all ingredients together. Place in jar with tightly fitting lid. Keeps well. (Available under Spice Islands label as Spice Parisienne.)

DUXELLES

MAKES 3 CUPS

2 pounds mushrooms
1/2 pound (2 sticks) unsalted butter

3 shallots, finely chopped
Salt and freshly ground black pepper to taste

Wipe mushrooms with damp cloth. Chop very fine, stems and all. Place in a tea towel and gently squeeze dry.

Melt butter in a heavy skillet. Add mushrooms and shallots and cook very slowly over low heat, stirring occasionally, until mixture becomes thick and dark. Season to taste with salt and pepper.

This mixture may be stored in the refrigerator for up to 10 days and may be frozen for up to 1 month.

I use duxelles to add flavor to sauces, gravies, fillings, such as a filling for Filet Mignon en Croûte or for chicken, for dressing up a plain braised celery or any kind of simple braised vegetable.

BREAD CRUMBS

MAKES ABOUT 2 CUPS

1 loaf stale bread

Cut bread into chunks and process in food processor for 2 or 3 minutes to have perfect bread crumbs. Spread the crumbs out in a pan to dry overnight or place in a moderate oven for a few minutes.

TWICE TOASTED BREAD

10 slices very thin white, wheat, or rye
  bread

Butter, softened

Preheat oven to 200 degrees.

    Butter one side of bread slices or both sides if desired. Cut into squares, triangles, rectangles, etc. Bake for 2 to 4 hours, or until bread is golden brown. Stored in a covered container, these twice-toasted slices will keep for weeks.

SPECIAL PIMIENTO CHEESE SPREAD

MAKES ABOUT 2 1/2 CUPS

2 cups sharp Cheddar cheese, grated medium
  fine
4-ounce jar pimiento pieces
1/2 teaspoon Tabasco sauce

Pinch of salt
1 teaspoon Worcestershire sauce
1/2 cup mayonnaise
2 jalapeño peppers, finely chopped (optional)

Mix all ingredients together until well blended. Spread on thin white bread circles or wedges. Keep covered in plastic container in refrigerator.

MOTHER'S CHICKEN SALAD

SERVES 8 TO 10

This is chicken salad as my mother used to make it. It is unusually good, and I use it often. It keeps well for a week.

2 2 1/2–3 pound cooked chickens, cut into
  chunks
2 cups celery, chopped
1/2 cup chopped green peppers
4 hard-boiled eggs, chopped
2 teaspoons grated onion

Salt and pepper to taste
1 tablespoon Worcestershire sauce
Dash of Tabasco sauce
3/4 cup chopped nuts, preferably pecans
2/3 cup mayonnaise (more if needed)
1 teaspoon capers

Place cooked chicken meat in a large bowl. Add celery, peppers, chopped eggs, onions, and salt and pepper to taste. Stir gently over and over to mix well, then add Worcestershire, Tabasco, nuts, mayonnaise, and capers. Stir gently to mix well. P.S. If you have leftover roast chicken or turkey, it will not be as moist as boiled chicken so marinate it in Basic French Dressing for 30 minutes before adding other ingredients.

APRICOT-GINGER CONSERVE

MAKES ABOUT 10 6-OUNCE GLASSES

1 pound dried apricots
2 quarts water
1 cup candied ginger, chopped fine
1 tablespoon grated orange rind

1/2 cup lemon juice
5 1/2 cups sugar
1 cup almonds, coarsely chopped

Soak apricots in water overnight. In same water, simmer apricots for 30 to 40 minutes or until tender.

Place in food processor bowl and puree. Return to pot and add ginger, orange rind, lemon juice, and sugar. Cook 20 minutes or longer, stirring often and lowering heat as mixture begins to thicken and your thermometer reaches jelly level (220°–230°F.).

Add almonds and cook 5 minutes more. Pour into scalded jelly glasses and seal.

PEACH AND PLUM CHUTNEY

MAKES ABOUT 3 CUPS

3/4 cup dark brown sugar, firmly packed
1/2 cup red wine vinegar
3/4 cup water
9 fresh peaches, peeled and diced
3 plums, peeled and diced
1/2 cup golden raisins
1/2 cup minced onions
1/2 cup minced red peppers
2 tablespoons fresh lemon juice

1 tablespoon finely chopped crystallized ginger
1 teaspoon minced fresh ginger root
2 teaspoons curry powder
1/2 teaspoon mustard seed
1/2 teaspoon red pepper flakes
1 1/2 teaspoons salt
1/4 teaspoon pepper

In a large saucepan combine sugar, vinegar, and water; cook mixture over low heat, stirring, until sugar is dissolved. Bring syrup to a boil and boil for 5 minutes.

Add peaches and plums and simmer for 10 minutes. With a slotted spoon, transfer peaches and plums to bowl.

Add remaining ingredients to saucepan. Bring liquid to a boil and boil it, stirring occasionally, for 10 minutes, or until it is very thick.

Add peaches and plums and any juices that have accumulated in the bowl. Bring mixture to a boil and simmer, stirring, for 5 minutes, or until syrup is very thick.

Transfer chutney to a serving bowl. Let it cool and chill it, covered, for 2 days.

HOT PEPPER JELLY

WARNING: *Be careful when handling hot peppers. Make sure not to rub your eyes before washing your hands well.*

36 small hot jalapeño peppers
1/3 cup water
3 cups white vinegar
5 pounds sugar

2 6-ounce bottles fruit pectin (Certo) *or*
    4 3-ounce packages liquid fruit pectin
    (Certo)
Drop green food coloring

Wash and remove stem and bottom from peppers. Combine peppers with seeds and water in food processor or blender and blend until peppers are mashed.

Place peppers, vinegar, and sugar in large kettle. Stirring constantly, bring to a boil and boil rapidly 5 minutes.

Strain or not, as desired, and return to kettle. Stir in fruit pectin and bring to a full rolling boil. Boil hard for 1 minute, stirring constantly. Remove from heat and skim off foam. Add food coloring.

Pour into hot, sterile 8-ounce jars. Seal with paraffin. Cover with lids and store in cool place.

Serve with cream cheese and crackers as an hors d'oeuvre or with lamb instead of mint jelly.

PICKLE RELISH OR TENNESSEE CHOW CHOW

MAKES A LOT
(START SAVING YOUR PINT JARS)

4 quarts green tomatoes
1 dozen red peppers
1 dozen green peppers
1 medium head cabbage
10 large onions

3 tablespoons salt
3 cups sugar
3 cups vinegar
3 tablespoons mustard seed
1 teaspoon turmeric

Finely chop green tomatoes, red peppers, green peppers, cabbage, and onions. Add salt and let stand overnight.

Drain vegetable mixture and mix well with remaining ingredients. Boil for 20 minutes. Pour into jars and seal.

PICKLED BEETS

1/2 cup white vinegar
1/2 cup water
1/2 cup sugar
1 teaspoon salt

1/8 teaspoon freshly ground black pepper
2 cups thinly sliced freshly cooked or canned
  beets

In stainless steel or enamel 2-quart saucepan, combine vinegar, water, sugar, salt, and pepper. Bring to a boil, stirring until sugar is dissolved, and boil briskly for 2 minutes.

Meanwhile place sliced beets in a deep glass, stainless steel, or enamel bowl. Pour hot marinade over beets and let them cool, uncovered, to room temperature.

Cover bowl with plastic wrap and refrigerate for at least 12 hours, stirring every few hours to keep slices moist.

PICKLED CUCUMBERS

MAKES APPROXIMATELY 2 QUARTS

2 teaspoons kosher salt
1 teaspoon celery seed
7 cups sliced cucumbers
1 green pepper, finely chopped

1 onion, finely chopped
2 cups sugar
1 cup vinegar

Sprinkle salt and celery seed over cucumbers, then over peppers and onions. Mix well. Chill.

Mix sugar and vinegar and stir while heating to a simmer, but do not boil. Let cool, then chill in refrigerator.

Add to cucumbers and mix together gently. Put in two quart jars and refrigerate 5–6 weeks before serving. Should keep 5–6 months.

BASIC OMELET

SERVES 1–2

3 eggs
1/2 teaspoon salt

Pinch of freshly ground white pepper
1 tablespoon butter

Beat eggs lightly in bowl with fork until foamy. Add salt and pepper.

Place 9-inch or 10-inch omelet pan over moderate to high heat. Pan is ready when drops of water flicked into pan bounce. Add butter and swirl around in pan.

Pour egg mixture into pan. Make circular swishes with fork to see that eggs cover bottom of pan. Shaking pan by its handle with one hand, continue to make swirling motions with fork, lifting egg mixture slightly with each swirl.

When eggs are cooked but still soft in the center, pour desired filling on upper half of omelet. Tilt pan up on one side and let eggs slide down to the other, using fork to flip them over like an envelope while they're sliding. Slip omelet out of pan upside down onto a warmed plate. Serve at once.

FILLINGS

FOR FRESH TOMATO OMELET:

TOMATO SAUCE

1 tablespoon finely chopped green pepper
1 tablespoon butter
1 slice baked ham, cut into small cubes, *or* 2 strips cooked bacon, crumbled
1 tomato, peeled and finely chopped
2 tablespoons leftover vegetable, finely chopped (string beans, peas, or zucchini)
Salt and pepper to taste
1 teaspoon sugar
Pinch sweet basil
Pinch thyme

Sauté green pepper in butter until a little soft. Add ham or bacon, tomatoes, vegetable, salt, pepper, sugar, basil, and thyme. Reduce heat and simmer until sauce is well blended. Taste for seasoning.

When omelet is cooked but still soft in center, pour 2 tablespoons of tomato sauce on upper half of omelet. Garnish with remaining tomato sauce.

FOR CHEESE OMELET, add

1 cup Monterey Jack or Cheddar cheese, coarsely grated

FOR AVOCADO-CHILI OMELET, add

1/2 avocado, diced
4 strips bacon, fried and crumbled
4-ounce can jalapeño chilies, drained, seeded, and cut into strips
1/2 cup Monterey Jack cheese, coarsely grated

FOR OMELET GRAND-MERE, add

1 teaspoon chopped chives
1 teaspoon chopped parsley
Dash Tabasco sauce
2 tablespoons bacon, fried and crumbled
1 boiled potato, cut into 1/4-inch cubes and crisply fried
2 tablespoons Gruyère, coarsely grated

Add chives, parsley, and Tabasco to eggs. Add bacon when egg mixture is in pan. When omelet is cooked but still soft in center, place potatoes down center and sprinkle cheese over top of potatoes.

GREAT CRÊPES

Crêpes are a necessity. They're light and can be used in many different ways. They share almost as many purposes as an omelet, adapting to sauces and fillings of many varieties. They can be used as the main course, first course, or dessert. And they're easy; you can make the batter ahead for a large number of crêpes. They freeze perfectly. Wrap in foil or plastic wrap in batches of six, separated by waxed paper. They defrost easily and quickly. I've been convinced that they are more nutritious than most breads or rolls.

1 cup cold water	1/2 teaspoon salt
1 cup milk	2 cups sifted flour
4 eggs	1/4 cup clarified butter
2 teaspoons sugar	

In food processor bowl, place water, milk, eggs, sugar, and salt, then add flour. Process for 3 minutes or so, until really smooth. Let sit for a minimum of 30 minutes at room temperature; as long as 2 hours if you have time.

Brush crêpe pan with clarified butter. Heat crêpe pan. Ladle 1/4 cup batter into skillet. Tilt until bottom and sides of skillet are covered. Cook 1 or 2 minutes, shaking pan; then loosen gently with spatula, flip over, and cook other side. They do not have to be brown, just cooked. Slip out onto a clean dishtowel. Wrap in foil and freeze in packages of 4 or 8, separated with waxed paper. They thaw out quickly.

NOTE Crêpe pan should be a special heavy-weight 6- to 8-inch pan. Don't use it for anything else and don't wash it. Wipe after using and hide it so nobody will use it for bacon and eggs or anything other than crêpes.

SIMPLE SYRUP

4 cups sugar	4 cups water

Place sugar and water in saucepan and stir until sugar is dissolved. Simmer 5 minutes, then cool to room temperature. Refrigerate in a covered jar.

STIFFLY BEATEN EGG WHITES THE NEW WAY

1 tablespoon white vinegar	6 *fresh* egg whites at room temperature
1 tablespoon water	

Combine vinegar and water in small bowl. Set aside.

Place egg whites in food processor bowl and process with steel blade about 8 seconds. Turn processor on again and, adding vinegar-water mixture through feed tube, continue to process 1 minute, or until egg whites are very stiff.

PÂTE BRISÉE I, OR PIECRUST

MAKES 8 TARTS OR ONE 10-INCH PIECRUST

1 3/4 cups flour
10 tablespoons (1 1/4 stick) cold unsalted
    butter, or 5 tablespoons butter and 5 table-
    spoons lard, or 5 tablespoons cold, unfla-
vored, unsalted rendered chicken fat
1 teaspoon salt
2 to 3 tablespoons ice-cold water

Put all ingredients except water in processor fitted with the metal or plastic blade. Process until mixture has texture of coarse cornmeal. With motor running, add water a tablespoon at a time until dough gathers in a ball around blade. If you need more water, add 1 teaspoon at a time, very gradually. Do not overprocess. Remove from bowl, wrap loosely in waxed paper, flatten slightly, and chill in refrigerator 30 minutes or up to 2 hours.

FOR TARTS

Preheat oven to 375 degrees.

Remove waxed paper, place dough on floured board and whack with rolling pin. Roll dough out about 1/8 inch thick. Cut in circles large enough to fit into tart pans or to cover cups on reverse side of large muffin tins.

Bake 10–15 minutes. Cool before filling.

FOR PIECRUST

Remove waxed paper, place dough on floured board and whack with rolling pin to flatten. Roll dough out to about 1/4 to 1/8 inch thick and a good 2 to 3 inches larger than your pie plate.

Flour rolling pin. Loosen dough on board with spatula and lift end nearest you onto rolling pin. Roll dough over pin gently and place over center of plate and unroll. Crimp edges attractively with fingers. Lift pie plate and with sharp knife trim all excess dough.

For baked pie shell (to be used only when specifically called for in a recipe), prick dough all over with tines of fork. Cover dough with waxed paper and put beans or pie weights on top of the waxed paper to keep shell from puffing up or collapsing. Bake for 10 minutes, then remove paper and weights carefully and continue to bake until shell is golden, about 10 minutes longer.

PÂTE BRISÉE II

1 1/2 cups all-purpose flour
1/2 cup (1 stick) cold sweet butter, cut in
  quarters
1/4 cup shortening

1 tablespoon powdered sugar
1/4 teaspoon salt
2 to 3 tablespoons ice-cold water

Place flour, butter, shortening, sugar, and salt in food processor. Using steel blade, process with several quick on/off turns until mixture looks like coarse meal. (This may also be done by hand using a wire pastry blender.)

With motor running, add water through feed tube, 1 tablespoon at a time, until dough forms ball around blade. (If done by hand, add water while turning dough with fork, just until mixture holds together.) Remove dough and press into flattened ball. Chill until easy to roll, about 1/2 hour.

Roll dough out into a 12-inch circle about 1/8 inch thick. Fold into quarters to pick up, and carefully lay in 10-inch Pyrex pie plate. Unfold and arrange loosely in pie plate, being careful not to stretch the dough. Turn over edge and flute.

Bake as directed for Pâte Brisée I.

CREAM CHEESE PASTRY

2 cups sifted all-purpose flour
1 teaspoon salt
1/2 cup shortening

3-ounce package cream cheese
3 tablespoons ice water

Sift flour and salt together in mixing bowl. Cut in shortening with a pastry blender until mixture is like coarse cornmeal. Cut in cream cheese until mixture is again like coarse cornmeal.

Gradually sprinkle with ice water, 1 tablespoon at a time, while tossing with fork.

Shape into a ball and flatten slightly with palm of hand. Divide in half and wrap loosely in waxed paper. Then place in refrigerator to chill 30 minutes or more.

Remove dough from refrigerator. Place on lightly floured board and roll out each half between 2 sheets of waxed paper into an 11-inch circle. Fit one circle into a 9-inch pie pan. Add desired filling.

Moisten rim of lower crust, place top crust on filled pan and tuck rim of top beneath edge of undercrust and flute with fingers, making tight seal.

Bake as directed for filling used.

PÂTE SUCRE I

1 3/4 cups flour
10 tablespoons (1 1/4 sticks) cold unsalted
    butter, or 6 tablespoons butter and 4 table-
    spoons lard, or 4 tablespoons cold, unfla-
vored rendered chicken fat
4 tablespoons sugar
2 to 3 tablespoons ice water

Put all ingredients except water in processor bowl fitted with the steel or plastic blade. Process until mixture has a mealy texture. Add water, a tablespoon at a time, and process briefly until dough gathers in ball around blade. If you need more water, add 1 teaspoon at a time, very gradually. Remove dough from bowl and chill in refrigerator for 2 hours.

Place dough on lightly floured pastry cloth or board, pat in all directions with floured rolling pin, and roll from center out in all directions. Roll into a round 1/8 inch thick and larger than the top of the pie pan.

Fold dough into quarters to pick up, place in pan, and unfold. Fit dough into pan loosely. Trim edge slightly larger than pie pan. Flute dough along edge with fingers.

Add filling and bake as directed for filling used.

For a baked pie shell: Follow baking directions for Pâte Brisée I, only bake in preheated 400-degree oven 8 to 10 minutes, then remove weights and bake for an additional 5 to 8 minutes, until lightly browned.

PÂTE SUCRE II

8 tablespoons unsalted butter (1 stick), or 6
    tablespoons (3/4 stick) unsalted butter and
    2 tablespoons chicken fat
1 1/2 cups cake flour (if you don't have cake
    flour, sift regular flour, measure, and re-
move 2 tablespoons from it)
1/4 cup sugar
1 whole egg
4 egg yolks

Place flour and shortening in bowl of food processor. Using metal blade, blend until mixture becomes crumbly. Add whole egg and egg yolks and blend again until ball forms on blade. Chill in waxed paper for a minimum of 1 hour.

Remove and roll into 1/8-inch-thick rectangle, at least 17 × 8 inches, on lightly floured surface. Drape dough over rolling pin and unroll it on 14 × 4 1/2-inch flan pan with removable bottom. Fit dough firmly into pan and cut off the excess, leaving a 1 1/2-inch overhang. Fold dough inward, push it up 1/4 inch over edge, and crimp edge decoratively. Prick bottom of shell all over with fork and chill for 1 hour. Add filling and bake as directed.

For a baked pie shell: Follow baking directions for Pâte Brisée I, only bake in preheated 400-degree oven 8 to 10 minutes, then remove weights and bake for an additional 5 to 8 minutes, until lightly browned.

Chapter 2

OPENERS

Openers are the teasers—little samples foretelling the wonders to follow. But like teasers, they shouldn't give away the plot or nobody has to stay for the show—or the dinner. They are meant to be light and comfortable accompaniments to whatever it is your guests are sipping, from designer water and wine to mixed drinks.

I don't believe in a cocktail hour. An hour, that's too long. If dinner is for 8:00 P.M., 7:15 P.M. is plenty of time for arrival and greetings and a drink or two. If you serve promptly at the hour you've designated, friends will get the idea pretty soon that if they arrive 30 to 45 minutes late, you will already have started without them. If they persist in being late, you have a couple of alternatives—don't invite them or, if they have a really good excuse like coming from the airport, the office, or the studio (that only counts out here), serve everybody else and save the main portion of their dinner, keeping it warm or reheating it in the radar range for a couple of minutes. Of course, if they're your only guests, relax and watch TV and try to remember, it's only a whole day's work.

In serving your hors d'oeuvres, keep in mind your weight watchers. Give them a break by serving crudités—raw vegetables—along with your favorite hot dip, such as Green Chilies with Cheese (in this chapter), or a cold one. Individual bite-sized hot hors d'oeuvres are great, but if they're larger than bite size or have sauces that may be drippy, have little plates, napkins, and small forks readily available.

The perfect openers are easy to serve and easy to eat. Remember the comfort of your guests and the cover on your couch and your carpet. Try not to duplicate any part of your dinner menu. Chicken for dinner—no chicken hors d'oeuvres; a piecrust or fresh bread for dinner—no quiche or pastry-enclosed hors d'oeuvres. A hot one and a cold one are nice if it's for a group of more than six.

Be sure you spend as much time as possible greeting, getting everybody comfortably introduced and settled before you take off for the kitchen and the last finishing touches of the real business of the evening—the dinner. Serve openers that can either be ready to serve when your guests are in the door, or ready to pop into the oven or heat on the stove as they are arriving. Appoint a drink-and-hors d'oeuvres replenisher. Some of these tidbits can be larger than bite-size to serve as your first course, such as the Stuffed Lebanese Meat Balls, the Duck Liver Pâté, or the Lobster Spring Rolls, all in this chapter, but unless your help has help that evening, I'd serve them in the living room, especially if you've planned a buffet-style dinner. It sure saves a lot of hopping up and down from dining chair to buffet line. See the Introduction for my suggested relief from this little potential traffic congestion. If it doesn't make you nervous or reveal your grand surprise, let your guests stand around in the kitchen. Most of my friends love to do that, and help out too.

CHICKEN FRITTER CROQUETTES

SERVES 6 AS AN APPETIZER

I've loved chicken croquettes for as long as I can remember. These are tiny and satisfying, especially with the tangy sauce for dipping. If you want, pour a light layer of sauce on the bottom of the warmed serving dish and lay the little morsels right on top, with the remaining sauce in an extra little bowl on the side.

1 egg	1/2 teaspoon salt
1/4 cup milk	1 1/2 cups chicken, cooked and chopped
1 cup flour	Bread crumbs
1 teaspoon baking powder	Oil for deep frying

In bowl, lightly beat egg and add milk.

Sift flour together with baking powder and salt. Stir into egg mixture. Fold in chicken. Chill in refrigerator for 30 minutes. Form into 1 1/2-inch balls and roll in bread crumbs.

Drop the balls, a few at a time, into deep oil heated to 375°F. and deep-fry for 1 minute, or until golden brown. Transfer fritters with a slotted spoon to paper towels to drain. Serve with Brown Sugar Sauce.

BROWN SUGAR SAUCE

MAKES 1 CUP

1/2 cup catsup	1/4 cup minced onions
1/3 cup water	2 tablespoons cider vinegar
1/4 cup brown sugar	1 teaspoon cornstarch

Combine all ingredients in a small saucepan. Bring mixture to a boil and simmer it over moderately low heat, stirring until it is thickened. Serve sauce hot.

SNOW PEAS STUFFED WITH CRAB

SERVES 6 AS AN APPETIZER
MAKES ABOUT 24

This is as pretty a finger food as you'll find. It does not go a long way, as even dedicated weight watchers usually have 3 or 4. It's delicately toothsome.

1/2 pound fresh snow peas

Wash and clean snow peas. Split peas on top side, leaving bottom intact to form a little boat. Blanch in lightly salted boiling water for 10 seconds, then submerge in cold water for a moment. Remove and drain. Set aside to cool.

Stuff generously with crab meat filling, about 1 heaping teaspoonful for each snow pea. Chill in refrigerator until ready to serve.

Serve these on your prettiest, simplest tray. They need very little extra garnish.

CRAB FILLING

12 ounces crab meat, well drained
2 hard-cooked eggs, finely chopped
4 scant tablespoons mayonnaise, or more if
   needed

3 dashes Tabasco
1 teaspoon capers
3 tablespoons celery, finely chopped

Mix all ingredients very gently so as not to break up crab meat.

DOLMA

MAKES ABOUT 2 DOZEN

One evening, Millie "Editor" and Judi "Organizer" decided it would be a terrific idea to have twenty or thirty new faces and palates test and taste some of our potential entries for the book. So I anxiously handed over some of my precious hoard—like letting your child go to a strange new school for the first time. Everybody had to test one—and, if they were bringing a date, mate, spouse—two. That way we could make a dent in the stack and get moving. Judi did the allocating and assigned herself two, including this one. The Shirleys, Schroer and Hunt (Laverne and Shirley for short) volunteered two each, Millie did two, and Pauline and I did five (Wouldn't you know I'd get stuck with the Feijoada Completa!)

I was warned that some of the guests were experienced cooks, some were so-so, and some were relative but enthusiastic novices. Randy (see page 247 for the Black Pasta he brought in that night as a brand-new entry) did the tables and flowers and helped lay out the buffet, which of course by now stretched three fourths of the way around the kitchen and onto the stove. Everybody wanted some of everything, and even with all that food we had hardly a scrap left over. It was a huge success and fun. We held a little post-dining, open-critique seminar and decided on the list of yeses, noes, and definite maybes. This recipe, obviously, was a definite yes.

It's another recipe from Mrs. A. D. Kadafar, who also sent us the Hummus, on page 44, which we tested the same night. It, too, was a definite yes.

2 large onions, chopped
1/2 cup olive oil
3 cups cooked rice
1/2 cup pine nuts
2/3 cups tomato puree
1/2 cup currants
1/3 cup tightly packed fresh mint leaves,
   chopped; or 2 tablespoons dried mint,

crumbled
1 teaspoon allspice
1 teaspoon freshly ground black pepper
Salt to taste
8-ounce jar grape leaves
1 cup water
1 tablespoon lemon juice
Yogurt Cucumber Sauce

In a medium-heavy skillet, sauté onions in oil over medium heat, stirring constantly, until soft, about 8 minutes. Add rice and pine nuts; sauté for 5 minutes. Add tomato puree, currants, mint, allspice, pepper, and salt. Cook, covered, for another 15 minutes, then cool.

Drain grape leaves and unroll carefully. Spoon about 2 tablespoons onion-rice mixture onto each of 24 grape leaves and wrap. Line a large, heavy skillet with grape leaves. Fill with Dolmas.

Combine water and lemon juice. Pour into skillet and bring to a boil over high heat. Cover and reduce heat; simmer 25–30 minutes or until liquid is absorbed. Serve with Yogurt Cucumber Sauce.

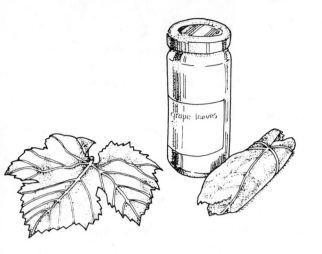

Carefully remove grape leaves from jar. Unroll and place stem side up.

Spoon 2 tablespoons mixture onto leaf near stem. Fold sides over, then roll into cylinder.

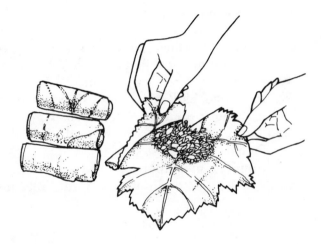

Line large, heavy skillet with over-lapping grape leaves. Add Dolma.

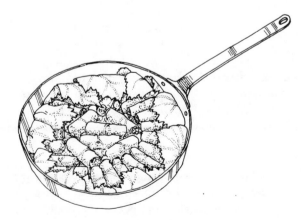

YOGURT CUCUMBER SAUCE

1 cup yogurt
1/2 cup sour cream

1/3 cup diced cucumber
3/4 teaspoon dried dill weed

Combine all ingredients. Allow to blend 2–3 hours in refrigerator before serving.

MUSHROOM AND SAUSAGE QUICHE

MAKES 24 SMALL QUICHES

The hotter the sausage the more macho this becomes, refuting the theory that real men don't eat quiche. I believe real men do eat it. They're just bored to the bones with having been served the bland, fluffy, ever popular ladies' luncheon saver. This will wake them up.

3/4 pound fresh ground pork sausage, *or* hot
   Italian sausage, *or* link sausage *or* any
   spicy sausage
1 tablespoon oil
1/4 pound fresh mushrooms, thinly sliced
1 tablespoon butter
1 tablespoon finely chopped onion
1 small clove garlic, minced
1 1/2 cups heavy cream

4 eggs, lightly beaten
3 tablespoons Dijon mustard
1/2 teaspoon salt
1/8 teaspoon freshly ground black pepper
3/4 cup grated Swiss cheese
24 unbaked small tart shells, approximately
   1 1/2 inches in diameter (Cream Cheese
   Pastry, page 20)

If sausage is in casings, slit casings and remove meat. Discard casings. Brown sausage meat in a heavy skillet in the oil, stirring occasionally to crumble, until cooked. Remove to paper towels to drain.

In another skillet, sauté mushrooms in butter until nearly all moisture is absorbed, about 5 minutes. Add onion and garlic and cook until onion is transparent. Add heavy cream and cook until thickened. Cool slightly.

Preheat oven to 375°F.

Combine mushrooms and sausage with remaining ingredients. Pour into tart shells. Bake 35–40 minutes, or until knife inserted in center comes out clean.

FALAFEL

MAKES ABOUT 30 1-INCH BALLS
SERVES 4–6 AS AN APPETIZER

These are marvelous also as a luncheon dish in toasted pockets of pita bread on top of shredded lettuce with a mixture of well-seasoned tomatoes, onion, and green pepper, all finely chopped and sprinkled on top of Falafel balls. On second thought, why limit it? It's a great light early dinner dish. I'd have them for breakfast, lunch or . . .

1/2 cup fine bulgur (cracked wheat)
1 1/2 cups coarsely crumbled pita bread, *or*
   substitute 1 1/2 cups coarsely crumbled
   homemade-type white bread
1 1/2 cups dried garbanzos, soaked, cooked,
   and drained, *or* 2 cups canned, drained
   and rinsed under cold water
1/4 cup fresh lemon juice

2 tablespoons finely chopped parsley
2 tablespoons finely chopped fresh cilantro
3 teaspoons finely chopped garlic
2 teaspoons crushed red pepper
2 teaspoons ground cumin
1 teaspoon salt
Freshly ground black pepper
Vegetable oil or shortening for deep frying

Place bulgur in a small bowl; pour in enough cold water to cover completely. Let wheat soak for about 15 minutes, then drain thoroughly in sieve or colander.

Meanwhile, drop crumbled bread into another bowl, add cold water to cover, and soak for 15 minutes or so. Drain water from bread and vigorously squeeze pieces completely dry. Set bulgur and bread aside.

In a blender or food processor, combine garbanzos, lemon juice, parsley, cilantro, garlic, red pepper, cumin, salt, and a few grindings of black pepper. Blend at high speed for 1 minute, or until mixture is reduced to a smooth puree. Transfer to a deep bowl.

Stir wheat and bread into garbanzo puree. Moistening your hands occasionally with cold water, shape mixture into balls 1 inch in diameter. Arrange these on waxed paper or a plate and let dry at room temperature about 1 hour.

In a heavy 10- to 12-inch skillet or electric skillet or deep fryer, heat 2 to 3 inches of oil or shortening until it reaches 375°F. Fry balls in batches, turning gently once or twice, for 2 to 3 minutes, or until golden brown. Transfer with slotted spoon to paper towels to drain while you fry remaining Falafel.

Regulate heat if necessary to keep oil at 375°F. during entire cooking process.

Mound Falafel on a heated platter and serve hot as an accompaniment to drinks or as first course.

BISCUITS WITH COUNTRY FRIED HAM

SERVES 10

This is a staple around here, especially right after Christmas when we are lucky enough to receive country hams from Tennessee and Virginia. Everything has to be hot—and be careful not to have too many biscuits on hand for that first go around as you'll spoil their dinner.

2 cups flour, sifted	1 cup plus 2 tablespoons milk
2 teaspoons baking powder	20 small squares country ham
1/2 teaspoon salt	2 tablespoons butter
1/2 cup shortening	

Preheat oven to 400°F.

Sift dry ingredients together. Add shortening and cut into flour mixture with 2 knives until the texture of very coarse meal. Stir mixture gently while adding milk sparingly until dough is sticky and not dry.

Lift dough out to floured board, pat gently, and cut with floured 1-inch biscuit cutter. After first batch is cut, pinch dough together, trying not to mix too much flour into it during the process, and cut out remaining biscuits.

Place on greased cookie sheet so that biscuits don't touch. Bake for 10 minutes until nice and brown.

Take sliced squares of country ham (cut approximately same size as biscuit), fry in a little butter, and place between split, buttered hot biscuits.

LOBSTER SPRING ROLLS

There is no more popular first way to greet favorite guests for the predinner toast to the sunset than with these beautiful, crispy and succulent egg rolls. Substitute shrimp if you like, but do try them as they are not all that hard to do. The filling can be made in the morning and the wontons rolled ready to fry; then they can be kept in the refrigerator for hours before the guests arrive. They can also be frozen in packages.

1/2 pound pork, shredded

3 teaspoons cornstarch

4 3/8 cups peanut oil

2 scallions, finely chopped

1 teaspoon finely chopped ginger root

3 tablespoons light soy sauce

2 teaspoons sugar

1/2 pound lobster, chopped (lobster tail is fine)*

2 1/2 teaspoons salt

2 tablespoons dry sherry or Chinese rice wine

1 head Chinese cabbage, shredded

1/2 cup bamboo shoots, shredded

5 to 6 dried Chinese mushrooms (remove heavy stem from center and discard; soak mushroom caps for 20 minutes in hot water to soften) shredded

3 stalks bok choy, blanched for 1 minute, drained and coarsely chopped

1/2 cup water chestnuts, chopped medium fine

1 pound bean sprouts

40 wontons or egg-roll wrappings (available in frozen food or produce section of your market)

2 teaspoons water

Mix pork with 1 teaspoon of the cornstarch and set aside.

Heat 2 tablespoons of the oil in wok. Add scallions and ginger and stir-fry until aroma is released. Add pork mixture and stir-fry. It should change color from pink to gray in a minute or so.

Add 1 tablespoon of the soy sauce and the sugar and continue to cook for 1 minute. Remove from wok and set aside. If it needs draining, place on several paper towels to absorb oil.

Mix lobster with 1 teaspoon salt and 1 teaspoon cornstarch. Add to wok and stir-fry very quickly. When it starts to turn pink, add sherry or rice wine. Stir-fry 1 second and remove to bowl.

Heat 2 tablespoons oil in wok. Stir-fry cabbage, bamboo shoots, mushrooms, and bok choy very quickly, not more than 1 1/2 to 2 minutes. Remove from wok and add water chestnuts to wok. Stir-fry 1 minute and remove from wok.

Add 1 tablespoon oil to wok and stir-fry bean sprouts 1 minute only. Combine pork, lobster, and vegetable mixtures in wok. Add 1 teaspoon salt and 2 tablespoons soy sauce. Taste for seasoning. If needed, add an additional 1/2 teaspoon salt. Stir-fry until heated through. Remove to colander. Drain liquid and let mixture cool. This is your filling and it is now ready to put into wontons or egg-roll wrappings.

FINAL ASSEMBLY

If you find your wontons not as thin as you would like, roll them out a little with a rolling pin.

Place 2 heaping tablespoonfuls of meat mixture on each wonton or wrapping. Roll lengthwise into envelopes.

*Shrimp may be substituted.

Place 2 heaping tablespoons filling on each wonton wrapper.

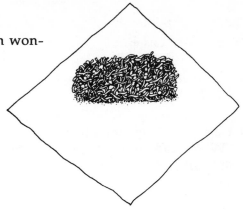

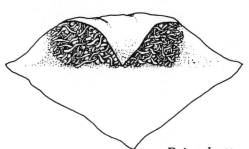

Bring bottom of wrapper up and over filling and
tuck point under filling.

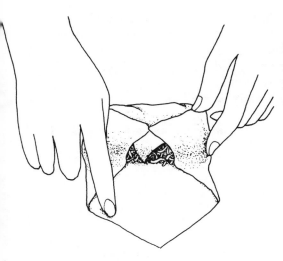

Bring sides of wrapper up and over
roll at right angles so that it now
resembles an open envelope. Moisten
edges of remaining flap.

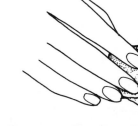

Roll lengthwise into spring roll shape,
sealing flap.

Mix water with 1 teaspoon cornstarch. Seal wrapping with cornstarch mixture.
(Everything up to this point may be prepared in advance.)

When you are ready to serve, heat 4 cups oil to 375°F. in wok. Deep-fry 3–4
minutes until golden brown and crisp.

Serve with Dipping Sauce.

These may be frozen before frying. I lay 6 wontons gently on a large sheet
of heavy foil and fold carefully over the top to seal. Label with cooking instructions
as given above. Or fry lightly and then freeze. To refry, let thaw. Heat oil to 375°.
Fry two or three at a time until deep golden brown and crisp. For baking after freezing, let thaw and bake in preheated 375°F. oven until golden brown, about 15
minutes.

DIPPING SAUCE

1/2 cup tomato catsup

4 teaspoons dark soy sauce

Mix ingredients in small bowl.

2 teaspoons dry hot mustard

1/2 teaspoon water

Mix ingredients in small bowl.

    When ready to serve, place 1 tablespoon of catsup mixture in each individual small bowl with 1/2 teaspoon of mustard mixture gently placed on top of catsup at side of bowl.

CHICKEN WINGS IN OYSTER SAUCE

As you may have gathered, the Chinese dishes are simple, fun, and wonderfully satisfying (not to mention delicious, nutritious, etc.) if a few simple procedures are done ahead. I line up the whole group of ingredients in the order in which they'll be used on a tray or cookie sheet, using small bowls for finely chopped ingredients, sauce ingredients and marinade, and with the main ingredient—in this case, the chicken wings in their marinade—in a larger bowl.

    I've listed below the ingredients that can be placed together in small bowls until you're ready to assemble the whole dish in your wok.

    Have a cookie sheet lined with paper towels to drain the fried wings, and a warmed platter nearby for your spinach and, finally, the whole luscious dish.

18 chicken wings

MARINADE

2 tablespoons soy sauce
1 1/2 tablespoons rice wine
1 tablespoon cornstarch

1/2 teaspoon salt
1/4 teaspoon freshly ground pepper

1 tablespoon chicken broth
2 teaspoons rice wine
1 teaspoon minced garlic
1/2 teaspoon salt

1 pound spinach, washed, trimmed, and well drained
1 tablespoon minced scallions
2 teaspoons peeled and minced ginger root

SAUCE

1 1/2 cups chicken broth
1 1/2 tablespoons oyster sauce
1 tablespoon soy sauce

2 teaspoons rice wine
1 1/2 teaspoons sugar

1 tablespoon water
1 1/2 teaspoons cornstarch

4–6 cups peanut oil
1 teaspoon sesame seed oil

Remove tips from chicken wings, reserving them for making stock. Halve wings at second joint.

In a large, shallow bowl combine marinade ingredients. Add wings, tossing them to coat with mixture, and let them marinate for at least 30 minutes. Drain chicken wings.

Place the following in separate small bowls ahead of time and then set bowls aside.

    a. Combine chicken broth, rice wine, minced garlic and salt.

    b. Combine minced scallions and ginger root.

    c. Combine sauce ingredients.

FINAL ASSEMBLY

Heat wok over high heat until it is very hot. Add 1 tablespoon of the peanut oil and swirl it around hot wok. Add garlic mixture and spinach. Stir-fry mixture for 1 minute, or until spinach is wilted. Remove and arrange spinach-garlic mixture around edge of heated large serving platter and set aside.

In wok heat 4–6 cups peanut oil until very hot (400°F.), or until green scallion top turns brown within 30 seconds after being dropped in. Fry the chicken wings in batches for 3 minutes, or until golden brown. Lift out with slotted spoon or Chinese strainer and drain on paper towels.

Remove all but 1 tablespoon of oil from wok. Reheat wok over high heat until it is very hot. Add scallion mixture and stir-fry 30 seconds until aroma is released.

Stir sauce mixture into wok and then add wings. Bring mixture to a boil and simmer, partially covered, for 15 minutes.

Now mix the cornstarch and water. Add to wok and stirring, cook mixture 1–2 minutes, no more. The sauce will be thick. Sprinkle sesame seed oil over all and toss lightly. Arrange mixture in center of platter, surrounded by spinach-garlic mixture.

NOTE I suggest keeping your cornstarch handy in a small bowl so you won't forget to use it in combination with water at the last minute.

CHICKEN WINGS WITH SPICY APRICOT SAUCE
SERVES 6–10 AS AN APPETIZER

The Reverend Billy Graham enjoys a right good meal whether at home or on his frequent worldwide tours. He paid us a visit on our show and I found out ahead of time that this was one of his favorite dishes. The China Trader out near Hollywood's NBC does this delicacy about as well as any restaurant in this country. The chef and maitre d' and I had a few conferences and kitchen consultations. I think I polished off a couple of platters—all in the interest of research. Dr. Graham polished off a few too on the show, as I remember.

SPICY APRICOT SAUCE

1 cup dried apricots (about 1/3 pound)
1 cup water
1/2 cup cider vinegar
1/4 cup sugar
2 tablespoons honey

1 teaspoon Chinese chili paste with garlic *or*
   3/4 teaspoon cayenne pepper or Tabasco
   sauce
1/4 teaspoon salt

In a heavy 1 to 1 1/2-quart saucepan, combine apricots and water and bring to a boil over high heat. Reduce heat to its lowest possible point, cover pan tightly, and simmer for about 30 minutes or until apricots are soft and have absorbed almost all of the liquid (watch carefully for any signs of burning).

Puree apricots in food processor or blender, or put through a food mill. With rubber spatula, scrape apricots into a bowl. Add vinegar, sugar, honey, paprika, and salt, and beat vigorously with a spoon or wire whisk until mixture is smooth. Cover tightly and refrigerate until ready to use.

CHICKEN WINGS

1 cup cornstarch
2 teaspoons baking powder
1/2 teaspoon salt
1/4 teaspoon pepper
Pinch of sugar

2 dozen chicken wings, prepared for frying*
2 eggs, beaten
Peanut oil for frying
Sesame seeds

Combine cornstarch, baking powder, salt, pepper, and sugar.

Dip chicken wings in beaten eggs, then roll in cornstarch mixture. Fry in deep hot (375°F.) peanut oil 8–10 minutes or until golden brown. This can be done ahead. Just before serving, refry in hot oil until golden brown, then drizzle sauce over and sprinkle with sesame seeds.

*To prepare chicken wings for frying: Each chicken wing consists of thin wing tip, a middle section, and large meaty section. Cut off wing tips and second sections (use these to make chicken stock). With a knife, pare meat on large section down toward large end of bone, leaving meat attached at large end. Pull meat down over bone knob where it's attached, so that each wing will resemble a drumstick.

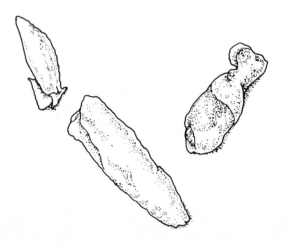

To prepare wings for frying, cut off wing tips and second sections and reserve for another use.

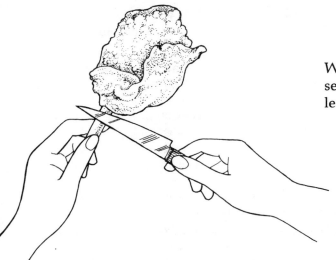

With knife, scrape meat on remaining section toward large end of bone, leaving meat attached.

The cooked wings ready to serve.

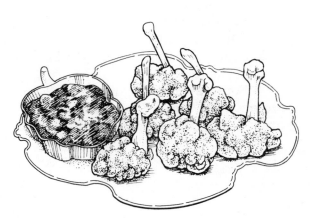

CAVIAR IN PETITE POTATO SKINS

SERVES 4

Credit my friend Mollie Chappellet with introducing me to this one. We were dining on their patio in Napa Valley one glorious summer evening. I was so busy with my contributions to the party, I hardly got around to seeing what Mollie was up to. She used that rare Sacramento River caviar, but it works well with the imported stuff too—what wouldn't work with any kind of fresh caviar? Incidentally, she dug the petite potatoes right out of her glorious garden in front of the patio.

12 very small new potatoes
Oil for deep frying

3–4 tablespoons caviar
2–3 tablespoons sour cream

Preheat oven to 350°F.

Wash potatoes and bake for 25 to 35 minutes or until done. Remove from oven and let cool. Scoop out a small amount of the potato pulp.

Heat oil in deep fryer or wok to 375°F. Deep-fry potato skins until golden. Remove and drain on paper toweling.

Fill with a little caviar and serve with a dollop of sour cream on the top. Serve immediately.

KADIN BUDU "LADY MEAT BALLS"

I think these are called Lady Meat Balls because they're more delicate than lusty and can be handled with hardly a flutter from a cocktail napkin.

1 pound lean lamb or beef, ground
1/2 cup finely chopped onions
1/4 cup long- or medium-grain rice, uncooked
1 tablespoon salt

1/2 teaspoon freshly ground black pepper
2 cups water
1 cup olive oil or vegetable oil
2 eggs, lightly beaten

Combine meat, onions, rice, salt, and pepper in a deep bowl. With a large spoon or your hands, mix ingredients together and knead vigorously until they are well blended.

Roll mixture into balls about 1 inch in diameter and shape into egg-like ovals.

In a heavy 12-inch skillet, bring water to a boil over high heat. Add meat balls and return water to boil. Reduce heat to low and simmer uncovered 30 minutes; add boiling water if necessary to keep balls covered. With slotted spoon, transfer meat balls to plate.

Pour water from skillet, add oil, and heat over moderate heat until light haze forms. With tongs, dip balls in beaten eggs and drop them into hot oil. Fry meat balls over high heat 5–8 minutes until brown on all sides. Drain on paper towels and serve.

STUFFED LEBANESE MEAT BALLS

There's no such thing as "One Meat Ball." I have a few examples here that put that canard to rest for a while. Count on 2 or 3 or 4 meat balls per person, depending on the length of your predinner hour or the breadth of your dinner guests. They are simple, can be made in quantity, and can be kept in the freezer quite a while. The use of spices, herbs, and grain in combination with meat gives each Middle Eastern delicacy its own character. In one restaurant the entire first course was an array of 8 or 10 varieties served with pickles (sweet, sour, or dill), pickled beets, and chopped cold combinations of tomatoes, onions, peppers, and cilantro. Then they brought on dinner!!

COLD FILLING

3/4 pound ground lamb
3/4 pound ground beef
3 onions, chopped
1/2 teaspoon sugar
1/2 cup chopped green pepper
1/2 cup chopped parsley

1/4 teaspoon allspice
1 teaspoon salt
1/2 teaspoon black pepper
1/2 teaspoon paprika
2 tablespoons pine nuts

Cook meat on low heat 7 minutes until it loses its pink color. Sprinkle onions with sugar, then add to meat. Add peppers. Stir and cook 25 minutes. Add parsley, allspice, salt, pepper, paprika, and pine nuts and mix thoroughly. Cool.

TO MAKE KUFTA

1 1/4 pounds twice-ground leg of lamb
Scant 3/4 pound bulgur (fine)
Salt and pepper to taste

1/2 cup chicken broth
1 egg, lightly beaten

Mix lamb and bulgur with salt and pepper. Knead very well, adding chicken broth and egg to keep mixture soft and pliable.

FINAL ASSEMBLY

2 cups chicken broth
1 cup water

8-ounce can tomato sauce

Make 1-inch balls by rolling in palm of your hand. With thumb make hollow in each ball, pressing walls out.

Stuff with cold filling and seal lamb-bulgur mixture.

Bring chicken broth, water, and tomato sauce to a boil and simmer balls 10 minutes in this liquid. Remove very carefully with slotted spoon to warmed serving platter. You may have to cook in 2 or 3 batches.

BATTER-FRIED STUFFED MUSHROOMS

SERVES 8–10

Stuffed mushrooms, like quiche, have become so popular we're liable to get as turned off of the former as some people seem to be of the latter. This one is different. The recipe looks difficult perhaps because of its length, but much of it can be prepared ahead. Your batter will be better for having waited around an hour or even more, since you're frying the whole thing. Anyway, you can prepare your filling in the morning or even a day ahead. If you don't have a deep fryer, not to worry—a good heavy-bottomed saucepan with a wire basket or your skimmer works fine. I love this as a luncheon dish. A well-seasoned medium-thick Béchamel sauce with a teaspoon of finely chopped onion, pimiento, and green pepper sautéed before adding flour to Béchamel gives it a substantial look.

BATTER

1 cup light cream
1 cup beer
2 eggs, lightly beaten

Salt and pepper to taste
1 1/2 cups flour

In bowl combine light cream and beer, eggs, and salt and pepper to taste. Slowly beat in flour, beating until batter is smooth and has the consistency of thick cream. Let the batter stand, covered, 1 hour.

FILLING

1/4 cup minced shallots
2 tablespoons butter
1/2 pound twice-ground lean beef
2/3 cup fresh bread crumbs
1/4 cup heavy cream
1 egg, lightly beaten

2 tablespoons snipped chives
1 tablespoon finely chopped apple
1 tablespoon chopped almonds
1/4 teaspoon tarragon
Salt and white pepper to taste

In a small skillet cook shallots in butter over moderate heat, stirring, 5 minutes until softened.

Transfer to bowl. Add ground beef, bread crumbs, heavy cream, egg, chives, apple, almonds, tarragon, and salt and white pepper to taste. Mix well.

FINAL ASSEMBLY

36 large mushrooms, stems removed (reserve stems for another use)

4 cups oil for deep-frying

Wipe mushroom caps with dampened paper towels. Fill each cap with heaping tablespoon of stuffing, smoothing the top.

Dip stuffed mushrooms in batter. Fry in deep fryer in hot deep fat (375°F.) for 4 minutes or until golden brown.

With a skimmer or slotted spoon, transfer mushrooms as they are done to paper towels to drain. Sprinkle with salt and keep warm in a 300°F. oven, leaving door ajar.

MUSHROOM CROUSTADES   MAKES ABOUT 48 CROUSTADES

Buy day-old sandwich bread. It is easier to slice than fresh bread and gives thinner slices.

1 loaf thinly sliced white bread
6 tablespoons clarified butter
1 1/2 pounds fresh mushrooms
3 to 4 shallots, chopped
2 tablespoons flour
1 cup cream (more if needed)

Salt and freshly ground white pepper
Cayenne pepper
1 tablespoon lemon juice
2 tablespoons chopped parsley
2 tablespoons chopped chives
Parmesan cheese, freshly grated

Preheat oven to 400°F.

Cut 2 to 3 rounds from each slice of bread, using 2-inch biscuit cutter. Using very sharp knife, slice the rounds again, as bread must be very thin. Butter both sides of rounds with clarified butter. Mold into small (1 1/2-inch diameter) muffin tins. Bake 8–10 minutes or until lightly browned. (These can be made ahead of time and frozen.)

Brush or clean mushrooms with dampened paper towels, but do not wash. Shred in food processor.

In a skillet, sauté shallots in 1 tablespoon of clarified butter until soft. Add mushrooms and sauté until most of juice cooks away. Remove from heat and set aside.

Melt 2 tablespoons butter in saucepan and add flour. Stir for a minute or two and then add cream, stirring constantly until mixture thickens. When thickened, gently stir in mushrooms and shallots. Add salt, pepper, and cayenne pepper to taste. Add lemon juice, parsley, and chives. This mixture may be kept for 24 hours if refrigerated.

Just before serving, preheat oven to 350°F.

Fill toasted shells with mushroom mixture, mounding slightly. Sprinkle Parmesan cheese on top and bake 10–12 minutes in muffin tins until heated through and lightly browned.

STUFFED PRAWNS

SERVES 8 AS AN APPETIZER

A splendid one-to-a-customer hors d'oeuvre. Or, as a separate course in a Chinese dinner, prepare the amount of stuffing for serving two or three people and use medium shrimp instead of large prawns.

STUFFING

4 ounces ground pork
4 ounces fresh small shrimp, shelled, deveined, and rinsed in cold water, patted dry, and minced into paste
1/4 cup water chestnuts, chopped
1 scallion, minced (including green part)

1 teaspoon thin soy sauce
1/2 teaspoon salt
1/4 teaspoon sugar
1 big pinch freshly ground black pepper
1 egg white, slightly beaten until foamy

BATTER

1 egg, slightly beaten until foamy
2 tablespoons flour
1/4 teaspoon 5-spice powder (available in most supermarkets in gourmet section or with Chinese foods)

1 tablespoon water
1/8 teaspoon salt
2 teaspoons cornstarch
1/2 teaspoon baking powder

SOY-VINEGAR DIP

1/2 cup Chinese red vinegar or cider vinegar   4 tablespoons thin soy sauce

Mix stuffing ingredients in bowl and set aside. Mix batter ingredients in bowl and set aside. Mix dip ingredients in bowl and set aside.

FINAL ASSEMBLY

8 large fresh prawns, shelled, deveined, and butterflied

1 egg yolk
4 cups peanut oil

Brush split side of prawns with egg yolk. Then spread stuffing generously on egg-yolked side of prawns.

Heat oil in wok to deep-fry temperature (400°F.). Gently dip stuffed prawns into batter. Fry until golden brown. Drain on paper towels. Serve hot with Soy-Vinegar Dip.

To shell and devein prawns:

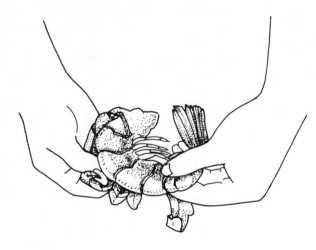

Carefully pull away shell of prawn so as not to tear flesh.

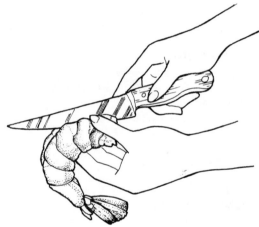

With sharp knife, score center of outer curve to make an incision about 1/16 inch deep, the length of the prawn.

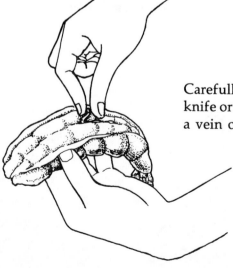

Carefully remove vein with tip of knife or fingertips. Some prawns have a vein on underside as well.

SAUERKRAUT CROQUETTES MAKES ABOUT 28 CROQUETTES

One evening while we were testing recipes for this book I made half this recipe and hedged my bet with another sure-fire previous winner just in case my guests had this burning emotion against sauer-kraut. I could have doubled it! They hardly touched my handy-dandy, sure-fire, ever-ready goody and went after these like the Cookie Monster on a spree. P.S. Nobody asked for the Di-Gel. As a matter of fact, Pauline and I, both sauerkraut lovers, had to make another batch the next day so we could taste them.

16-ounce can sauerkraut
1/3 cup minced scallions
3 tablespoons butter
3 tablespoons flour
2/3 cup scalded milk
1/2 pound boiled ham, minced
1/3 cup fine day-old bread crumbs

Salt and cayenne pepper to taste
Flour
1 egg, lightly beaten with 1 teaspoon water
Pinch of salt
Additional bread crumbs
2 cups oil for deep-frying

Rinse sauerkraut in colander under cold running water and drain it. Place sauer-kraut in a large saucepan with water to cover. Bring to boil, and continue to boil for 10 minutes. Drain sauerkraut in colander, squeeze out any moisture, and chop well.

In a large saucepan sauté scallions in 2 tablespoons of the butter over moderate heat for 2 minutes. Stir in flour and cook mixture, stirring, for 3 minutes. Remove pan from heat, add scalded milk in a stream, whisking mixture until thick and smooth.

Add sauerkraut and cook mixture over low heat, stirring occasionally, for 10 minutes. In a skillet sauté ham in 1 tablespoon butter over moderately high heat until it is just heated through, and stir in bread crumbs.

Fold ham mixture into sauerkraut mixture. Add salt and cayenne pepper to taste and simmer, stirring, for 3 minutes.

Spread mixture 1/2 inch thick on well-buttered cookie sheet and chill it, covered with foil or plastic wrap, for at least 4 hours.

Form tablespoons of mixture into 1 1/2-inch cork shapes. Dust croquettes with flour, coat them with egg-water mixture and pinch of salt, and roll them in bread crumbs. Refrigerate croquettes, covered, for 1 hour.

In a deep fryer, fry croquettes a few at a time in hot deep fat (375°F.) 3–4 minutes until golden. With skimmer or slotted spoon transfer to paper towels to drain. Arrange croquettes on heated serving dish.

SHAO MAI

These may be prepared completely in advance and resteamed. Or you may freeze them prior to steaming, and then steam 30 minutes before serving.

4 water chestnuts (fresh if possible), chopped
   fine
1 scallion, chopped fine
1 tablespoon sherry
1/2 teaspoon salt
1 pound ground beef, ground pork, or
   chopped shrimp

1 egg
2 tablespoons light soy sauce
24 wonton wrappings, rolled thin
1 teaspoon cornstarch
2 teaspoons water
Red wine vinegar
Light soy sauce

In food processor, chop water chestnuts. Then add scallions, sherry, and salt. Add ground beef or pork or shrimp. Add egg. Blend not more than 10 seconds—let it keep a little texture. Add soy sauce.

Put 1 tablespoon of filling in center of each wonton wrapping. Gather sides of each wrapping around filling. Squeeze center gently. Leave edges of dough shirred. Seal with cornstarch dissolved in water.

Line steamer tray or vegetable steamer with a wet cloth. Place Shao Mai on tray over boiling water. Steam 15–20 minutes, covered. Remove Shao Mai to platter at once to prevent sticking. May be served with red wine vinegar or a combination of equal parts of red wine vinegar and light soy sauce.

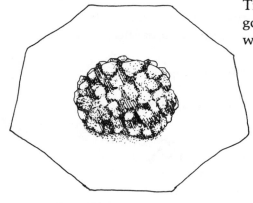

Trim large wonton wrapper so that it is an octagon. Put 1 heaping tablespoon filling in center of wrapper.

Gather sides of wrapper around filling. Squeeze center gently, leaving edges of dough shirred.

Shao Mai, ready to be steamed.

OPENERS

CHINESE SLICED PORK

This comes straight from my friend at the beach, Patti Pritchett, who is about as big as a minute and a half and can pack it away like a weight lifter or a truck driver. She's a great cook and here's proof.

If you're unable to get the small pork tenderloins, buy the large one and ask your butcher to cut it into two or three 2 1/2-inch strips lengthwise. Be sure not to overcook it, as it should be tender and juicy. Cook to 160°F. maximum on the meat thermometer.

2 1-pound boneless pork tenderloins (eye of
   the loin)

MARINADE

3/4 cup prune juice
1/4 cup soy sauce
3/4 cup catsup

3/4 cup white sugar
1 1/2 teaspoons salt

With tines of large fork, pierce pork in several places.

Mix marinade in glass dish and marinate pork for 24 hours.

Preheat oven to 350°F.

Remove pork from marinade and place in roasting pan. Roast uncovered in oven, basting with marinade every 10 minutes and removing grease from bottom of pan from time to time. Roast for 35 minutes or more (about 17 minutes per pound) until pork is done—160° on a meat thermometer. Cool to room temperature.

Slice very thin and serve with Dipping Sauce.

DIPPING SAUCE

1/2 cup chili sauce or catsup
1 tablespoon soy sauce

1/2 teaspoon chili paste with garlic (optional)

Mix all ingredients together and place in bowl.

1 tablespoon dry mustard

1 teaspoon water or enough to make a medium-thin paste

Mix together and place in one corner of sauce bowl.

3 tablespoons sesame seeds (optional)

Dip pork in sauce and then in sesame seeds for an extra treat.

CURRIED CHICKEN BALLS

Around here everybody cooks. Shirley Schroer—no relation, but might as well be, we've worked together for so long now—came through with this one as well as a lot of testings for this book. This was a big hit at one of our parties. She served it on a large round platter with all the parsley left in the San Fernando Valley. It was beautiful and received raves. There was only one left by the time I got through being hostessy and insisting, "No, no—you go ahead. We have plenty."

8-ounce package cream cheese
2 cups cooked chicken, chopped
1 cup walnuts, coarsely chopped
1/4 cup mayonnaise

1 tablespoon prepared mustard
1 teaspoon dried dill weed
2 1/2 teaspoons curry powder
1 cup grated coconut

In large bowl, combine all ingredients except coconut. Roll into balls and then roll into coconut. Chill at least 4 hours or even overnight.

SHIRLEY SCHROER

JAMES COCO'S CHEESE SPREAD
MAKES 2 1/2 CUPS

Jimmy Coco is one of the funniest, finest comedians around. He always seemed to be on a diet when I first knew him. He has it licked now, but I hope he hasn't given up this pre-party maker in the process. If you've misplaced the recipe, Jimmy, here it is the way you did it on the TV show—everybody loves it!

8 ounces cream cheese, softened
3 ounces bleu cheese, grated
1/2 cup pitted dates, chopped

1 cup chopped walnuts (reserve 1/2 cup)
1/2 cup dry sherry

Combine all ingredients, blend well together. Form into ball. Roll in reserved walnuts. Chill and serve with crackers.

HUMMUS AND PITA TOASTS
MAKES ABOUT 2 3/4 CUPS

I first tasted Hummus—this cool, mysterious mixture of chick peas, or garbanzos, and herbs—on a trip to the Middle East. It is a popular and regular part of the diet in every country in the area regardless of politics. I tried many times and places to find a recipe that measured up to my memories of it, so you can imagine how pleased I was when this one came my way. I went to dinner one evening at Anne and Kirk Douglas's and met Mrs. A. D. Kadafar and her husband. When she learned I was doing this book, we talked food all evening, naturally. This is her recipe. Try it with the Pita Toasts accompanying it.

2 cups (1 16-ounce can) canned chick peas
   (garbanzo beans), drained
2/3 cup taheeni (sesame paste)
3/4 cup lemon juice
2 cloves garlic, finely minced

1 teaspoon salt
1/4 cup finely minced parsley leaves
1/2 teaspoon sesame seed oil
1 tablespoon minced parsley, for garnish
Pita Toasts

Place chick peas, taheeni, lemon juice, garlic, and salt in food processor or blender and blend until pureed.

Remove to bowl, add parsley and sesame seed oil, and mix well. Chill for several hours. Before serving, garnish with parsley. Serve with Pita Toasts.

PITA TOASTS

MAKES 48 TOASTS

3/4 cup (1 1/2 sticks) butter, softened
2 tablespoons minced parsley
1 tablespoon snipped chives, minced
1 tablespoon lemon juice

1 large clove garlic, minced
1/8 teaspoon salt
1/8 teaspoon white pepper
6 rounds of pita bread

Preheat oven to 450°F.

Cream together butter, minced parsley, chives, lemon juice, garlic, salt and pepper and let mixture stand, covered, for at least 1 hour.

Halve each pita bread horizontally, separate each half into 4 pieces, and spread the inside of each piece with butter mixture. Arrange pita on greased baking sheet in one layer and bake in top third of oven 5 minutes until lightly browned and crisp. Transfer toasts to bread dish.

CHEESES—HOT AND COLD

It's hard to resist a bargain. In this recipe you get two for one. Served hot with cold apple slices or crisp celery sticks, it has an entirely different flavor and look and appeal than when served cold with crisp crackers, wheat crackers, or melba toast. I can't decide which version I like better and I doubt your visitors will know they came out of the same batch of ingredients.

1 package (3 ounces) cream cheese, softened
1 cup grated sharp, yellow Cheddar cheese
1 cup grated Muenster cheese
2 tablespoons Dijon mustard

1 medium clove garlic, crushed
1 small onion, finely minced
1/8 cup finely chopped parsley
1/8 cup finely chopped chives

Preheat oven to 375°F.

Mix all ingredients thoroughly. Divide recipe in half.

To serve cold: Roll one half of mixture into a ball and then roll in parsley and chives and serve chilled.

To serve hot: Place one half of mixture in a small ovenproof baking dish. Bake for 15 minutes. Serve with apple slices, celery sticks, and crackers of your choice.

BAGNA CAUDA AND CHILI CON QUESO

Crudités, as the French call them—raw, fresh vegetables, as we call them—crunchy and crisp, served with a dip, are popular because no one feels overfed before the real food fest starts. Here are two suggestions for dips, both hot and as different from each other as the countries from which they come. You couldn't quite say that Bagna Cauda was the Chili con Queso of Rome any more than you could say the Chili con Queso is the Bagna Cauda of Mexico City, but they serve the same comfortable predinner purpose. Of course, these dips can be served with their traditional accompaniments as mentioned.

BAGNA CAUDA (HOT GARLIC AND ANCHOVY DIPPING SAUCE)

YIELD 1 1/2 CUPS

2 slices white bread, crusts removed
1 cup heavy cream
8 anchovy fillets, rinsed and patted dry

4 garlic cloves, crushed
3/4 cup olive oil
1/2 stick butter (1/4 cup)

In a shallow dish, soak bread in 1/4 cup of the cream until it is absorbed. Bring remaining 3/4 cup cream to a boil to scald.

In a food processor puree bread, anchovies, and garlic. With motor running, add olive oil in a thin stream; continue to puree mixture until it is the consistency of a thick sauce.

Melt butter in a heavy saucepan, add anchovy puree and 3/4 cup scalded cream in stream. Beat mixture until it is thick and well combined.

Simmer sauce, stirring, for 5 minutes or until it is heated through, but do not let it boil. Transfer sauce to heatproof serving bowl set over brazier or warming candle and serve it hot with raw vegetables.

CHILI CON QUESO (GREEN CHILIES WITH CHEESE)

SERVES 8 AS AN APPETIZER

4 tablespoons finely minced onion
2 tablespoons butter
2 cups solid-pack canned tomatoes, drained (reserve juice) and slightly mashed
1 1/2 cups chopped canned peeled green chilies
Salt and pepper

1 pound Monterey Jack cheese *or* 1/2 pound Monterey Jack cheese and 1/2 pound sharp Cheddar cheese, cubed
1/2 cup half-and-half
1/2 cup reserved juice from tomatoes, or more if needed

Sauté onions in butter until translucent.

Add tomatoes, chilies, salt and pepper to taste, and simmer for 15 minutes. Then add cubed cheese. When cheese begins to melt, add half-and-half and tomato juice. Taste. You may want to add more chilies. I love this picante.

It's wonderful for a cocktail dip with Tostaditas.

TOSTADITAS

12 flat round unfried corn tortillas
Vegetable oil for frying

Salt (optional)

Cut corn tortillas into eighths.

In large frying pan heat vegetable oil until very hot.

Fry tortillas until crisp. Drain on paper towels. Salt if desired and use instead of store-bought variety.

DUCK LIVER PÂTÉ (MADE WITH CHICKEN LIVERS)   MAKES 1 2-POUND LOAF OR 8 SMALL PÂTÉS

Narsai David was my dinner partner at a food- and wine-tasting party at the famous Scandia Restaurant. I was out of my depth on the exquisite wines, so my escort, Wayne Rogers, who really knows his vinos, conducted my seminar on the subject and in between sips and sighs David and I talked food. He sent me this recipe from his marvelous restaurant in Napa Valley.

It calls for duck livers, but in the whole city of L.A. I could not find any ducks willing to part with their livers. Chickens don't seem to mind nearly as much, so here's David's Duck Liver Pâté made with eager chicken livers.

1 cup sliced onions
1 1/4 cups butter
1 small tart green apple, cored, peeled, and sliced
1 pound chicken livers cut in half

1/4 cup applejack or sherry
1/4 cup heavy cream
1 teaspoon lemon juice
1 1/2 teaspoons salt
Port Wine Aspic

Sauté onions in 1/2 cup of the butter until lightly browned. Add apples and cook 3 to 4 minutes until apples start to soften. Add chicken livers and sauté over high heat until pink.

Transfer to blender. Deglaze pan with applejack or sherry and add to blender with heavy cream. Blend well. Remove from blender, cool to lukewarm.

Add remaining 3/4 cup of butter (cut into chunks) to blender and whip until creamy. Beat butter slowly into still warm pâté along with lemon juice and salt.

Pour Port Wine Aspic into terrine to a depth of about 1/8 inch. Let set. Pack pâté in. I use only half my aspic and pour the remainder over top of individual molds.

PORT WINE ASPIC

2 teaspoons unflavored gelatin
1 cup port wine
2 tablespoons sugar

1 tablespoon water
3 tablespoons red wine vinegar
1/2 teaspoon tarragon

Soften gelatin in 1/4 cup port wine. Set aside.

Dissolve sugar in water. Cook rapidly while stirring until sugar melts and reaches medium-dark caramel color. Add vinegar, remaining 3/4 cup port wine, and tarragon. Simmer for 2 minutes. Add gelatin to hot mixture and stir until dissolved. Spoon through strainer into terrine or molds to a depth of 1/8 to 1/4 inch. Chill until set, then fill with soft pâté. Refrigerate until time to serve.

NOTE On gas stoves, the port will probably ignite and burn for a while.

MUSHROOM PÂTÉ

This is a great one to keep on hand for drop-ins. Serve the pâté with rye toast points. As a first course, serve 2 thin slices on a lettuce leaf with 5 or 6 cornichons and crusty, warmed French bread slices or chunks—or crisply toasted rye slices, cut into 4 pieces. As a buffet dish, place a sharp knife on the platter and leave pâté whole with 3 or 4 thin slices cut to indicate that guests continue to treat it gently and, hopefully, sparingly. (It ain't exactly chopped liver where you just dig in.) Place a couple of perfect outer lettuce leaves under the pâté and a small perfect center cup-shaped lettuce leaf to hold the absolutely necessary cornichons (that French sour pickle). If they are unavailable or too expensive, slice slender 2-inch substitutes out of your favorite delicatessen's best sour pickle.

10 shallots, minced
1/4 cup butter
4 cups coarsely chopped mushrooms, including stems
3/4 pound chicken livers, trimmed and cut in half if they are large

1 pound ground chuck
1/2 cup heavy cream
1/2 cup fresh bread crumbs
2 eggs, lightly beaten
3 tablespoons cognac

1/4 cup dry vermouth
1/4 teaspoon fennel seed, crushed
3 tablespoons green peppercorns, crushed slightly
Salt to taste

Salt and pepper to taste
3/4–1 pound sliced bacon
1 pound button mushrooms, wiped with dampened paper towels and stems removed

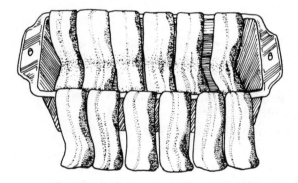

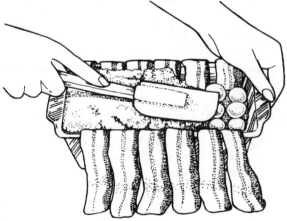

Line a 2-quart terrine or loaf pan with sliced bacon placed across width of pan, leaving enough overhang to fold over top.

Cover mushroom layer with remaining meat mixture, being careful not to disturb mushrooms.

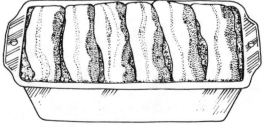

Fold overhanging bacon neatly over pâté.

In large, heavy skillet cook shallots in butter over low heat, stirring, 5–7 minutes until softened.

Add chopped mushrooms and cook until some of liquid has evaporated, then add livers and cook mixture over moderate heat 5–6 minutes, or until livers are lightly browned on outside but still pink within.

Add vermouth, fennel seed, green peppercorns, and salt to taste. Bring liquid to boil. Remove skillet from heat and let mixture cool.

In food processor or blender, grind mixture in batches until livers are minced.

In a large bowl combine mixture with ground chuck, heavy cream, fresh bread crumbs, eggs, and cognac. Season well with salt and pepper.

Preheat oven to 375°F.

Line 2-quart terrine or loaf pan with sliced bacon, covering bottom and sides and leaving enough overhang to fold over top. Fill terrine with half of meat mixture, cover mixture with button mushrooms and sprinkle them with salt and pepper. Add remaining meat mixture, being careful not to disturb mushrooms, and rap terrine sharply on counter to expel any bubbles. Smooth top with spatula and fold overhanging bacon over pâté.

Put terrine in baking pan, adding enough hot water to outer pan to reach halfway up sides of terrine. Bake pâté covered with foil and a lid or with a triple layer of foil for 2 hours. Transfer terrine to rack and let it stand for 30 minutes. Return terrine to empty baking pan. Weight the pâté with 2-pound weight, by using plate or pan the shape of the pâté with a 2-pound can of any food placed on top of plate. Chill in refrigerator overnight. Remove weight, foil, and lid, and run sharp knife around edges of terrine. Place platter over terrine, invert, and slide pâté onto platter.

MARINATED SHRIMP   SERVES 15–20

Peggy Greenbaum, my Palm Springs friend, is from Louisiana. The discrimination of her palate is a reflection of the good food to which she has been exposed to all her life. Here's a shrimp dish for a large group that calls for a few special ingredients that definitely permit a few shortcuts in preparation. The Shrimp and Crab Boil is available in your fish market or they will get it for you, and the gardiniera I found in the Italian delicatessen of one of our supermarkets.

1 box (3 ounces) Shrimp and Crab Boil
5 pounds fresh shrimp, peeled and deveined
1 large onion, thinly sliced
2 cups red wine vinegar

2 12-ounce jars gardiniera (Italian mixed vegetables)
1/3 cup oil

Fill large soup pot with water until 2/3 full. Add Shrimp and Crab Boil, bring water to a boil, and cook 20–30 minutes. Add shrimp and cook until light pink. Drain immediately.

Pour hot shrimp into deep bowl. Add onions, vinegar, Italian mixed vegetables, and oil. Marinate in refrigerator at least 24 hours.

PEGGY GREENBAUM, PALM SPRINGS

GRAVAD LOX (MARINATED SALMON)

SERVES 10–12

Some wonderful days the fish counter seems to be overflowing with beautiful fresh salmon. Instead of just poaching or broiling or croquetting it, try this elegant and delicious way the Danes have served it for generations.

Some maintain that freezing the salmon before preparing your gravad lox makes it more porous. I don't think this is necessary. If you score it and follow the recipe as described, it will be perfect—how much better do you want it to be? Fresh dill is usually in when salmon is plentiful, and most produce markets carry winter dill. If they don't have it on hand they'll get it for you with a little notice—mine did.

The recipe came to us from Le Bistro in the Marc Plaza Hotel in Milwaukee.

5 pounds salmon fillets (have fish dealer fillet salmon)
2 tablespoons kosher salt
2 tablespoons crushed black peppercorns
1 cup sugar

1 cup fresh dill, coarsely chopped
1/2 cup fennel seeds
4 cups salad oil
1 cup aquavit

Remove skin from salmon fillets. Cut slits with sharp knife at 4- or 5-inch intervals on top and bottom of fillets to allow the marinade and seasonings to be absorbed.

Place fillets in a deep dish, just large enough to hold them. Sprinkle fish with salt, crushed peppercorns, sugar, dill, and fennel seeds. Press these ingredients into flesh of fish to let spices seep through.

Pour salad oil and aquavit over all. Cover tightly with foil or plastic wrap, place weight on top (use a heavy pot lid or can), and marinate in refrigerator for 3 days. To serve, carefully brush off some of the spices and seasonings. Starting at tail, slice fish crosswise into paper-thin but uniform pieces. Arrange on pumpernickel bread and serve with Mustard Dill Sauce.

MUSTARD DILL SAUCE

1 cup Dijon mustard
1/2 cup sugar
1 cup chopped fresh dill

1/2 cup white wine vinegar
2 cups salad oil

Combine mustard with sugar and blend with fresh dill. Stir in vinegar and oil and mix thoroughly. Refrigerate.

MARINATED HERRING

SERVES 4–6

2 1-pound jars of herring fillets in wine (usually packed with onions)
3/4 onion, thinly sliced
1 small tart apple, peeled, cored, and sliced

paper-thin
Juice from 1 lemon
Sour Cream Mixture

Place herring in sieve over bowl and drain, reserving juice. Set aside.

In a large, flat-bottomed casserole, place a layer of herring, then a layer of onions, then a layer of tart apples. Sprinkle lemon juice over all. Cover with a layer of Sour Cream Mixture and repeat the process until you run out of herring, ending with onions and then Sour Cream Mixture. Marinate for an hour or so. Serve with rye toast or fresh rye bread.

SOUR CREAM MIXTURE

3/4 cup of reserved juice from herring fillets, or more if needed
3 cups sour cream
1 teaspoon Worcestershire sauce
1/4 teaspoon salt
1/8 teaspoon pepper
Dash of Tabasco sauce
1/4 teaspoon celery seed
Bay leaf, optional

Mix all ingredients until well blended. Remove bay leaf before serving.

SHRIMP AND CABBAGE WITH CAVIAR

SERVES 4–6

Shrimp sautéed with cabbage and topped with caviar is a creation that is unusual and interesting; the flavors work well together. Although the caviar gives a special excitement to the dish, it can be omitted.

20 fresh large shrimp (10–15 to the pound), peeled and deveined
Salt and freshly ground white pepper to taste
8 tablespoons butter
6 cups shredded white cabbage
3 cups heavy cream
1 teaspoon caviar (optional)

Sprinkle shrimp with salt and pepper. Melt 4 tablespoons of the butter in a large skillet. When hot, add shrimp. Sauté over high heat 50–60 seconds. With a slotted spoon, transfer to plate.

Add cabbage to juices in pan and sauté about 10 seconds. Add cream and bring to a boil. Reduce cabbage-cream mixture over high heat for a few minutes, or until cream coats spoon. Add salt and pepper to taste.

With slotted spoon remove cabbage to serving dish. Mix some of the sauce with cabbage.

Stir remaining 4 tablespoons butter, in small pieces, into sauce remaining in skillet.

Arrange shrimp on top of cabbage. Pour rest of sauce over dish and sprinkle with caviar. Serve immediately.

GLAZED PORKLETS

This is superb as an hors d'oeuvre—better than spareribs. It happened as a mistake. I bought some large spareribs and then asked the butcher to cut them into 1-inch chunks. Instead of cutting through the rib bones, he just cut the meat off. I'm so glad he did—no messy bones or sticky fingers.

1 pound lean pork (the closer to the ribs the better), cut into 1-inch cubes
4 tops of scallions, cut into 1-inch lengths
1/4 cup flour
3 tablespoons dark soy sauce

1 egg
2–4 cups oil for deep frying
1/4 cup sugar
1/4 cup vinegar

Place pork in boiling water to cover. Add scallions and boil for 10 minutes. Drain, remove scallions and pork. When pork is cool, cut off extra fat.

Mix together flour, 1 tablespoon of the dark soy sauce, and egg. Add pork and stir well to coat. Let marinate 2 hours or overnight.

Heat oil in wok to 375°F. Deep-fry pork until brown, about 3 to 5 minutes.

In saucepan add remaining soy sauce, sugar, and vinegar. Heat and stir until thick. Add pork and mix until thoroughly glazed.

ESCARGOTS

I guess if I were more adventurous, I would use snails from my garden before they use me—but I'm not, so I buy the canned sure-thing snails. You can buy canned snails with a package of shells attached. The shells are reusable, so this is a one-time-only purchase. Most people feel they've leaped the barrier of hamburgers, fries, steaks, and baked potatoes when they've tried escargots. They're right—it's a leap in the right direction. My son, whose idea of a gourmet dinner was fried chicken and mashed potatoes, fell in love with escargots and actually ordered seconds at a restaurant when a friendly date offered to take him along for dinner with us. (I've never seen that guy since.) It's easier to handle your snail shells with a gadget made for this purpose called snail tongs and a small-tined fish fork to remove meat from shells. Crusty hot French or Italian bread for dipping in the sauce can be served with the snails. Parmesan garlic toast applicable here in spades.

1/4 cup butter, softened
1 tablespoon minced garlic
2–3 tablespoons chopped parsley

1 teaspoon chopped shallots
16 canned snails

Preheat oven to 500°F.

Mix butter, garlic, parsley, and shallots together. Place about 1/2 teaspoon of butter mixture into each snail shell.

Then place a snail in each shell, leaving a tiny edge visible.

Cover each snail well with 1/2 teaspoon butter mixture on top. For best results place in shell dish and bake about 5 to 7 minutes. When butter is nice and brown they are ready. Serve *hot.*

SHRIMP RÉMOULADE

SERVES 12–14 AS AN APPETIZER

This looks like a big batch of sauce and a lot of ingredients, but it keeps beautifully and you can serve it with crab, lobster, or any shellfish, as I'm sure they do at Commander's Palace, who sent us this from New Orleans. You will find many other recipes from chef Gerhard Brill in this book, for which we are extremely grateful.

RÉMOULADE SAUCE

1/2 cup prepared mustard
1/2 cup Dijon mustard
1/2 cup catsup
1/4 cup white vinegar
1/4 cup horseradish
1/4 cup Worcestershire sauce
3 tablespoons paprika
8 ribs of celery, minced
6 green onions, minced

1 bunch fresh parsley, chopped
4 bay leaves
1 tablespoon salt
3 medium eggs, slightly beaten
5 tablespoons Tabasco sauce
2 cloves garlic, minced
1/3 cup vegetable oil
2 medium-sized lemons

Combine mustards, catsup, white vinegar, horseradish, Worcestershire sauce, and paprika. Blend well.

Puree celery, onions, parsley, and bay leaves and add to mustard-catsup mixture. Stir well.

Add salt, eggs, Tabasco, garlic, and oil.

Puree 1 whole lemon and add to sauce mixture with juice of other lemon. Mix well and chill for 24 hours before serving.

FINAL ASSEMBLY

3 pounds shrimp, boiled and peeled
Shredded lettuce

Lemon wedges for garnish

Mix shrimp with Rémoulade Sauce and serve on a bed of shredded lettuce. Garnish with lemon wedges.

NOTE One quart of Rémoulade Sauce is sufficient for up to three pounds of cooked and peeled shrimp.

COMMANDER'S PALACE, NEW ORLEANS

GUAYMAS SHRIMP AND CHILIES IN SHERRY SAUCE

SERVES 6 AS AN APPETIZER

A really different way of serving shrimp as a first course or as an hors d'oeuvre. I first tasted this in Guaymas in Mexico with those enormous shrimp they pull right out of the water and serve. It was unforgettable.

2/3 cup flour
Salt and pepper
1 tablespoon butter
1 tablespoon olive oil
1 clove garlic, finely chopped
1 pound fresh large shrimp, shelled, cleaned

and deveined, leaving tail intact
1/2 cup dry sherry
1 jalapeño pepper, seeds and membrane removed, thinly sliced
4 tablespoons half and half

Season flour with salt and pepper. Coat shrimp evenly on both sides.

Heat butter and olive oil in large skillet. Add garlic and sauté until lightly browned. Add shrimp and brown on both sides. Turn off heat and remove shrimp.

Drain excess butter mixture and garlic from pan. Add sherry and jalapeños. Reduce liquid to one half.

Add half and half. Return shrimp to pan and simmer until shrimp turn pink and are done.

SCALLOPS SORREL

SERVES 6–8 AS A FIRST COURSE

I'm looking forward to visiting Boston because I want to go to Apley's Restaurant and taste Bob Brody's cuisine, which I have simplified slightly so that those of us who are not quite as professional as he obviously is will be able to use it in our kitchens.

1/2 cup carrots, julienned
1/2 cup turnips, julienned
1/2 cup white leeks, julienned
1/2 cup butter
3/4 pound small scallops (if large, cut in

halves or thirds)
Salt and freshly ground black pepper to taste
4 sorrel leaves, cut lengthwise in 1/2-inch strips
4 tablespoons avocado, cut into 1-inch cubes

Blanch carrots, turnips, and leeks in rapidly boiling salted water about 30 seconds. Remove with slotted spoon and keep warm.

Melt butter over high heat in sauté pan. Add scallops and quick-cook on one side for 1 1/2 to 2 minutes. *Do not sauté.* Lower heat, turn scallops over and *poach* 1 1/2 to 2 minutes until they lose their translucence and become opaque, or until they are done. The scallops should not cook longer than 4 minutes. Season with salt and pepper. Remove scallops immediately to a very warm platter.

To remaining butter in pan, add sorrel and avocado briefly to warm them. Remove with slotted spoon and place over scallops.

Heat vegetables briefly in sauté pan. Season with salt and pepper. Place around scallops on platter. Pour butter residue over scallops.

NOTE It is important that scallops be poached rather than sautéed because the liquid that is emitted from the scallops while cooking mixed with the butter gives a sweet flavor to the whole dish.

SCALLOPS WITH IRISH MIST   SERVES 6 AS A FIRST COURSE

I've given you a few alternatives here. I tested the dish with all of them but the Irish Mist is really the best. Of course, if it's the first time your friends have tasted it, they'll only know there's something subtly marvelous, not having had the comparison test in their experience. It's a beauty!

3/4 pound scallops
Flour
4 tablespoons butter
1/4 pint heavy cream
2 tablespoons Irish Mist liqueur (*or* Drambuie)

1 shallot, minced
1/4 cup chopped parsley
Salt and white pepper to taste
2 egg yolks, beaten

Roll scallops in flour and sauté in 2 tablespoons of the butter 3 minutes. Add cream, liqueur, shallots, and parsley. Season with salt and pepper. Allow to cook 2 to 3 minutes more. Remove scallops from saucepan and place in warm heatproof serving bowl or individual heatproof serving dishes.

Reduce sauce to half by boiling. Add remaining butter and egg yolks. Whisk over gentle heat until thickened but do not let boil. Pour sauce over scallops. Place under broiler to glaze, and serve immediately.

SHRIMP AND GARLIC APPETIZER
SERVES 6–8 AS A FIRST COURSE

You'll like this one and so will your guests. It comes from the Al-Roubaie Restaurant in Kansas City, Missouri. Here's proof of my contention that great Kansas City beef is as appreciated and treated as beautifully in Nantucket as Nantucket shrimp is appreciated and treated with delicacy and understanding in Kansas City.

1 1/2 sticks butter, softened
3 cloves garlic, peeled
1/2 medium onion
1/2 cup parsley
2 fillets anchovies
1 ounce cognac
1 ounce sweet sherry

1/4 teaspoon thyme
1/4 teaspoon salt
1/4 teaspoon white pepper
1 1/2 pounds large shrimp, shelled and deveined
1/4 cup freshly grated Parmesan cheese

In food processor or blender mix and chop fine all ingredients except shrimp and Parmesan cheese, 2–3 minutes.

Sauté shrimp in resulting butter mixture until pink and firm, about 4–5 minutes. Sprinkle with Parmesan cheese and serve with thinly sliced rounds of sourdough bread and parsley sprigs or watercress for color.

MINCED SQUAB IN LETTUCE LEAVES

Many fine Chinese restaurants serve this dish. My particular favorite is the Mandarin in Beverly Hills. They were kind enough to send it over for all of us.

It's hard to say how many this recipe will serve. Two of us have polished off a whole serving with no trouble at all as a main dish. It will serve 4 to 6 people and even 8 if one doesn't have too heavy a hand with the fillings. Boning the squab is really misleading here. One simply cuts every morsel of meat and skin off the bones of the squab. It's not like leaving the skin intact for stuffing and reshaping.

If you want to substitute dark meat of chicken or even breast of duckling, it will work very well. I say dark meat because it's a little more moist than breast of chicken. Two thighs and 2 legs of fryers are roughly the equivalent of the squab meat. Use an extra thigh if you're worried. Cut away the excess fat if there is any.

4 to 6 cups peanut oil

1/4 pound uncooked rice noodles

2 large squabs, including skin, boned and minced (by hand)

3 scallions, chopped (white part mostly)

1 cup minced water chestnuts

12 dried Chinese mushrooms, soaked in hot water 20 minutes to soften; remove stem and cut into thin strips

3 tablespoons finely chopped Virginia or Tennessee ham

Ginger root, about size of a quarter, peeled and finely minced

SAUCE

1 tablespoon dry sherry or Chinese rice wine

1/4 teaspoon white pepper

1 tablespoon oyster sauce

1 tablespoon soy sauce

1/2 teaspoon sugar

1 1/2 teaspoons cornstarch

1 tablespoon water

1/2 teaspoon sesame seed oil

Perfect, crisp outer leaves from 2 firm heads iceburg lettuce (about 12)

All the mincing and chopping of the meat and vegetables can be done in the morning and the ingredients placed in small bowls in refrigerator.

In a small bowl combine sauce ingredients: sherry, white pepper, oyster sauce, soy sauce, and sugar. Set aside.

Cut lettuce leaves into large triangular pieces to hold minced squab and place in bowl in refrigerator.

FINAL ASSEMBLY

Heat oil in wok to very hot (400°F.) or until scallion top turns brown within 30 seconds after being dropped into hot oil. Drop in half of rice noodles. As soon as they puff up (should happen immediately), lift out with tongs and drain on paper towels. Remove to warmed platter and set aside. Repeat procedure for other half of rice noodles.

Turn heat off under wok. Remove all oil except 3 tablespoons. Turn heat to medium (350°–375°F.) and reheat oil. Add squab and quickly stir-fry until it loses

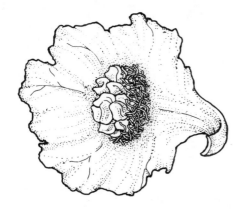

Place 2 or 3 spoonfuls of rice noodles and meat mixture onto center of triangular-shaped lettuce leaf. Roll up like a tortilla.

pink color and is cooked. Add scallions and stir-fry briefly. Add water chestnuts, mushrooms, ham and ginger root and stir-fry to blend well. Add sauce and stir-fry briefly until blended.

Mix cornstarch and water and add to wok. Add sesame seed oil and stir-fry briefly.

Place meat mixture over rice noodles on platter. Then place outer lettuce leaves on a chilled platter.

To serve, bring right to table and place 2 or 3 spoonfuls of the rice noodles—meat mixture onto center of lettuce leaf. Roll up like a tortilla. No forks—this is real finger food. Use plenty of napkins. The lettuce holds all the goodies. Superb!

CEVICHE

SERVES 4

We had fun finding this one. We practically did the blindfold test one day at lunch here on seven different recipes. This is a combination of three of them and really the best.

1/2 pound lean white fish fillet
1/8 cup lime juice
1/2 medium tomato, chopped
1/4 medium green pepper, chopped
1 tablespoon pimiento, chopped
1/4 medium onion, chopped
1/2 garlic clove, minced

1 teaspoon minced parsley
1/4 teaspoon salt
1/2 dried chili pepper, crushed
1/4 teaspoon sugar
1 tablespoon white vinegar
Fresh cilantro, coarsely chopped

Clean fish with damp paper towels and cut into small cubes. Place fish in glass bowl. Add lime juice and stir carefully with wooden spoon. Cover and marinate in refrigerator 24 hours. Turn fish occasionally during marinating process.

Mix together remaining ingredients, reserving some cilantro for garnish. Add to fish mixture. Marinate an additional 3–5 hours to blend flavors. Serve in a large bowl over ice. Garnish with reserved cilantro.

Chapter 3
SOUPS

A great soup served with a lovely salad, crusty bread, and a beautiful cheese might even give Kahlil Gibran pause.

I find good soup irresistible—the thin ones, the thick ones—especially on cold evenings when, instead of an hors d'oeuvre, I bring a big tureen filled with my soup of the day, set out a tray of warmed soup bowls, and ladle it right out in the living room as our first course. Why did I specify cool evenings? I also do this on warm, summery nights out on the patio with a chilled soup and condiments or a light, hot soup like Egg Flower or Avgolemono (Egg Lemon Soup).

Since many great soups begin with a great stock, it's lucky that I can't bear to throw any food away—the outer leaves of lettuce, the last celery stalk, tops and all, a beat-up carrot or two, onions, chicken-wing tips, beef bones, bits of leftover tomatoes (careful with potatoes as they sometimes sour a soup). When we're doing continuous cooking around here, I keep the soup pot going. I save the water from steamed, boiled, or blanched vegetables, label them in a jar, and put them in the refrigerator if the pot is in recess, and add them later to the soup kettle. All these sad-looking little bits and pieces give rich body to a stock or broth for cooking, deglazing, and for a meal in itself—pureed or clear.

In the Basics chapter you will find traditional recipes for stocks (chicken, beef, fish, and vegetable). These work nicely, but I must admit to adding whatever else is handily available. One problem is that your leftovers and extra bits of this and that may be different from mine, so it's hard to pin down a recipe and you may not be able to repeat your last effort exactly, but by the time it bubbles and blends for hours, you'll have developed something equally as appetizing.

In fact, I sometimes let my leftovers determine what soup I'll make: a ham bone leads to bean or lentil soups, lamb bones go well with barley, and beef bones enhance vegetables of all kinds. It almost goes without saying that a turkey or chicken carcass never leaves this house before making its contribution to a perfect soup base.

Since stock-based soups take some time and effort, I always try to make an extra amount which can be frozen and later defrosted for a second meal or first course. If you do this, be sure to leave a little air space—at least an inch—at the top of the container for expansion. One of the many wonderful things about soups is that they can be reheated into practically their original goodness.

You may see that I favor hot rather than chilled soups, though there are a few notable exceptions among the recipes—for example, the Cold Curried Cream of Eggplant Soup, one of the most unique and satisfying summer dishes I've ever tasted. Should you decide to transform any of my hot soups into cold variations, be sure to adjust the seasonings accordingly since chilling tends to diminish the effect of herbs and spices.

The variety of soups is infinite, and we have some here that are certainly unusual—ranging from a combination of fresh spinach and coconut to a Chinese Hot and Sour Soup that is as exotic and delicious as any soup you might taste in the People's Republic. Incidentally, the Chinese have a custom of serving their soups in the middle of the meal. I think it's a great idea, but I can't seem to get my beachnik friends to go along with this.

MEAL IN A MEAT BALL SOUP

It was a cold, foggy morning when I planned this definite stomach warmer for lunch after tennis. As happens in California, the fog melted away and the day turned torrid so I didn't think anybody would go for it. Go for it! They went back for seconds and thirds until I ran out. It's a great Sunday night supper dish or a Monday Night Football special.

1 pound ground beef
1/2 cup uncooked rice
4 teaspoons salt
1 1/2 teaspoons pepper
1 teaspoon paprika
1 teaspoon savory
Flour
2 quarts water
1 bunch scallions, sliced (white part only)
1 green pepper, chopped
2 small carrots, peeled and sliced

3 to 4 tomatoes, peeled and chopped, or 2 cups canned tomatoes
2 small yellow chilies, seeded and cut into small strips (If unavailable, add 3/4 teaspoon Tabasco or your favorite hot pepper sauce.)
1/2 bunch parsley, minced
2 eggs
Juice of 1 lemon
Red pepper flakes
Freshly grated Parmesan cheese

Combine meat, rice, 2 teaspoons salt, 1/2 teaspoon pepper, paprika, and savory. Mix lightly but thoroughly. Form into 1-inch meat balls, then roll in flour.

Combine water, scallions, green pepper, carrots, tomatoes, 2 teaspoons salt and 1 teaspoon pepper in large kettle. Cover, bring to a boil, reduce heat and simmer 30 minutes. Add meat balls, cover, and bring to boil again. Reduce heat and simmer 20 minutes. Add chilies, cover, and simmer 40 minutes or until rice in meat balls is cooked. Add more water if needed to keep it soupy. Add parsley during last 5 minutes of cooking. Taste and adjust seasonings.

Beat eggs with lemon juice. Add a little hot liquid to egg mixture, then slowly stir into soup. Heat and stir until soup thickens slightly and becomes creamy throughout.

Serve immediately in warmed soup bowls with red pepper flakes and Parmesan cheese on the side, and with chunks of French bread and salad.

CUBAN BLACK BEAN SOUP

I may have mentioned from time to time this thing I have about beans in any form. They're especially good in this recipe, the ne plus ultra *(I think that means "there is none better") in black bean soups. Maybe the Cubans have a better title for this soup since it originated there, but I didn't know anybody on the island offhand I could call to check. You can serve it individually or in the tureen with lemon slices and grated hard-boiled eggs.*

4 cups dried black beans
5 quarts water
3 stalks celery, chopped
3 large onions, finely chopped
8 tablespoons butter
Ham bone with some ham left on
1 pound lean beef with bones (what they used to call soup meat)
1 leek, thinly sliced (optional)
1 cup finely chopped scallions

2 cloves garlic, cut in half
1 large tomato, chopped
4 bay leaves
2 teaspoons salt, or to taste
1/2 teaspoon coarsely ground black pepper
1 cup dry Madeira or dry sherry
1/2 cup parsley, finely chopped
3 hard-cooked eggs, finely chopped
Lemon, thinly sliced

Pick over and wash black beans. Soak overnight in cold water to cover. Drain and cook in 5 quarts water over low heat for 1 1/2 hours.

In soup kettle, sauté slowly celery and onions in butter 8 minutes or until tender. Gradually stir in beans and their liquid. Add ham bone, beef bones, leeks, scallions, garlic, tomatoes, bay leaves, salt, and pepper. Simmer soup over very low heat for 4 hours. Adjust seasonings.

Remove and discard ham bone, beef bones, garlic halves, and bay leaves. Strain liquid part of soup through a coarse sieve.

Reserve 1 cup of whole beans and set aside. Puree remaining beans in food processor fitted with metal blade. Then combine broth, pureed beans, whole beans, Madeira or sherry, and parsley in soup kettle and bring to a boil. Remove from heat and stir in hard-cooked eggs, reserving one for garnish. Float thin slice of lemon on each serving and garnish with sieved hard boiled egg.

HOT AND SOUR SOUP

SERVES 4–6

This pungent, superb blend of flavors and exotic (for us) ingredients is just an everyday ordinary experience for Dan Lee, the jovial host and owner of Tai Ping Restaurant in Palm Desert, California. I went in with friends for dinner after one less than successful day of battle between the golf course and my game. Not knowing his menu or cuisine, I asked him to please select our dinner. He did—it was perfect. Afterward, he and his charming wife sat and chatted with us, and we learned a lot about one another. It's purely a Mom and Pop operation with a devoted and extraordinarily talented staff, all trained at home, which was Stockton, California, and at his first and tremendously successful restaurant in Palo Alto. He's a sports fanatic, which certainly gave us lots in common, and spends eleven to twelve hours a day making certain his restaurants maintain the high standards set from their inception. The Hot and Sour Soup requires a few special ingredients. If your specialty store doesn't happen to have them on hand, order a few packages of each from many of the Oriental shops accustomed to shipping these dried enhancers all over the country. They keep indefinitely and can be used in many Chinese dishes. As Dan does such enormous quantities daily, he laboriously broke this down for home use along with his Chinese Hot Chicken Salad (later).

5 cups chicken stock
1/2 teaspoon salt
1 tablespoon soy sauce
1/3 cup shredded bamboo shoots
3 ounces lean pork, shredded, or 1 chicken breast (see Note below)
3 pieces black fungus (cloud ears), soaked in water to soften for 20 minutes and shredded
3 large dried black Chinese mushrooms, soaked in water to soften for 20 minutes and shredded
4 to 5 strands dried lily root, soaked in water to soften for 20 minutes (optional)

1 piece (4 × 4 × 1 1/2 inches) tofu (bean curd), shredded
1 1/2 teaspoons white vinegar mixed with 1 1/2 teaspoons cider vinegar
1 teaspoon sugar
1/2 teaspoon black pepper
1 egg, beaten
1 tablespoon cornstarch mixed with 3 tablespoons water or broth
1 teaspoon sesame seed oil
3 scallions, diced, including tops
Optional for hotter soup:
1 dried red chili with seeds, finely chopped

In large saucepan, combine chicken stock, salt, soy sauce, bamboo shoots, pork, black fungus, mushrooms, and lily root. Bring to boil over high heat, reduce heat to low, and simmer 3–4 minutes. If using chicken breast, prepare as directed in Note below and add with bean curd, vinegars, sugar, and pepper and bring to boil again. Taste for seasoning. You may want to add 1/2 teaspoon more of white vinegar and 1/2 teaspoon more of cider vinegar. And for a hotter soup, add the chopped chili pepper.

Add beaten egg to boiling soup without stirring for a second or two; when set, then stir. Add cornstarch mixture to thicken. Add sesame seed oil. Top with diced scallions before serving.

NOTE If using chicken breast, marinate in 1 teaspoon oil, 1 teaspoon sherry, and 1 tablespoon soy sauce for 15 minutes. Heat 1 cup oil in wok to 375°F. Dust chicken with cornstarch and deep-fry in wok until crisp and brown, 2–3 minutes. Cool and then shred by hand into strips.

WONTONS IN SOUP

SERVES 6–8

40 wonton skins
3 scallions, finely chopped, including green part

1 tablespoon sesame oil
4 ounces (1/2 cup) watercress leaves, blanched in boiling water 10–12 seconds

FILLING

1/2 pound ground pork (ask butcher to grind it only once)
6 ounces (10–12 medium) fresh shrimp, shelled, deveined, and rinsed in running cold water, finely chopped
2 scallions, finely chopped, including green part

1 beaten egg
1/2 tablespoon sesame seed oil
1/4 teaspoon sugar
2 teaspoons pale dry sherry
1 tablespoon thin soy sauce
1 big pinch ground pepper

Mix filling ingredients and refrigerate until ready to use.

BROTH MIXTURE

4 cups clear chicken broth (not condensed)
1/4 teaspoon sugar

3/4 teaspoon salt

Mix in 3-quart pot.

SOY SESAME DIP

1/4 cup black soy sauce

1 tablespoon sesame oil

Put soy sauce in small serving dish and whisk in oil.

Cover wonton skins with a damp tea towel to keep them moist. Have a small bowl of water handy for sealing wontons. Put about 1 tablespoon of filling in the middle of wonton skin. Pull edges together and pinch firmly to seal, using a little water if necessary.

Bring broth mixture to a boil, cover, and simmer over very low heat.

Put chopped scallions and sesame seed oil in a big serving bowl.

Bring a pot of water to a rapid boil. Drop wontons in water and boil over medium high heat for about 7 minutes. Remove wontons with skimmer or slotted spoon and place in serving bowl with scallions and sesame oil.

Pour piping hot broth over wontons. Add watercress. Stir. Serve in hot, individual bowls, with dip in smaller bowls on the side. For added flavor, dip wontons as you eat them.

NOTE You may double the quantity of shrimp and omit the pork. This soup may be prepared ahead of time. Reheat over medium-low heat until wontons are piping hot. *Be sure not to overcook them, otherwise the skins will come apart and the filling will be tough.*

EGG LEMON SOUP

SERVES 6

Telly Savalas guested on our TV show several times. He's a graceful and gracious man, and has that knack of looking at you and talking to you as if you're the only person he ever really wanted to see. Naturally, a jewel of a gent like that brings out the best in one. So one dug out from several Greek cookbooks and drew on one's trip to Greece the best possible Greek Egg Lemon Soup—Avgolemono. One even learned how to say it (spelling doesn't count). He said it was authentic and superbly delicious. He was right! (One modestly avers.)

8 cups chicken broth
Salt to taste
1 cup uncooked rice *or* 1 3/4 cups cooked rice
4 eggs, separated

Juice of 2 lemons
1/2 cup cooked chicken breast, cut into slivers
Lemon slices
Parsley

Bring chicken broth to a boil; salt to taste. Add rice and simmer uncovered for 20 minutes. (If using cooked rice, add to broth when boiling and heat through.) Remove from heat.

In bowl, beat egg whites until stiff; add yolks and beat well.

Slowly add lemon juice to eggs, beating constantly. Add 2 cups of hot broth. *Do not stop beating—constant beating will prevent curdling.*

When eggs and broth are well mixed, add cooked chicken and pour mixture back into remaining broth and rice. Stir well over heat. Do not let boil. Serve immediately in warmed bowls with thinly sliced lemons and parsley for garnish.

CHINESE NOODLE SOUP   SERVES 4–6

This is a homey, comfortable, eye- and stomach-filling Sunday night special. It is the Chinese version of "Jewish penicillin"—good for whatever ails you.

4 dried black Chinese mushrooms, 1–1 1/2 inches in diameter

1/2 cup cooked chicken, sliced 1/8 inch thick and cut into 1-inch squares

1/2 cup cooked pork roast, sliced 1/8 inch thick and cut into 1-inch squares

1/2 cup cooked ham, sliced 1/8 inch thick and cut into 1-inch squares

1/4 cup canned bamboo shoots, thinly sliced

1/2 cup loosely packed watercress leaves

1/2 pound fresh Chinese egg noodles, *or* narrow Italian egg noodles such as taglierini

4 cups chicken stock

1 teaspoon salt

Soak mushrooms in 1/2 cup warm water for 30 minutes. Cut out and discard tough stems. Cut caps in half.

Place meat, bamboo shoots, and watercress in small bowls, cover, and refrigerate until you are ready to use.

Bring 2 quarts of water to a boil over high heat in heavy 3- or 4-quart pot. Drop in noodles and boil vigorously, uncovered, 2 minutes or until almost but not quite done, stirring occasionally. Drain noodles and run cold water over them to stop cooking.

Bring chicken stock to a boil in same pot. Add mushrooms, bamboo shoots, watercress, salt and noodles, and reduce heat to low. Simmer uncovered about 2 minutes.

To serve, lift noodles and vegetables out of simmering soup with bamboo strainer or slotted spoon and transfer to a large tureen or individual soup bowls. Arrange chicken, pork, and ham on top. Pour soup stock down one side of tureen or bowls so as not to disturb arrangement. Serve at once. It's beautiful—it's delicious.

EGG FLOWER SOUP

This is light, fulfilling, and still as delicate as a flower. Maybe that's the reason the Chinese call it that.

5 cups clear chicken broth
1/2 teaspoon sugar
3/4 teaspoons salt
1 tablespoon cornstarch mixed with 1/4 cup cold water

2 eggs, beaten until slightly foamy
2 scallions, coarsely chopped including green part
2 teaspoons sesame seed oil

Put broth in 3-quart saucepan and add sugar and salt. Bring to rapid boil and stir in cornstarch water. Stir and cook until broth is no longer cloudy.

Slowly swirl in beaten eggs—*do not stir!* Turn off heat at once. Drop in scallions and sesame seed oil. Stir gently. Serve hot.

CREAM OF LOBSTER SOUP

SERVES 6

Christian Millau, of the Gault Millau Guides, is not only a fine writer and highly respected restaurant and food critic, but a great and inventive chef. One evening we cooked a dinner for the members of the working and dining press. It took as much organization and advance planning as the assault on the Axis forces during World War II. With the help of Pauline, Bernard Jacoupy of Bernard's Restaurant in the Biltmore Hotel in L.A., and his assistant Roland Gilbert, Liliana, Christian, and I pulled it off. The dishes we served include the superb Chocolate Mousse and Honey Ice Cream that Arlette Millau contributed in her quiet, self-effacing way. It was hard to decide "The Winnah," but on a scale of 1 to 10, 10 being too good for mere mortals, this soup was definitely a 9.

2 tablespoons butter
3 tablespoons flour
2 cups clam juice
1 cup white wine
2 cups heavy cream
Salt and pepper to taste

Pinch 4-Spice powder (available in French gourmet markets)
1 pound raw lobster, cut into bite-sized pieces (shrimp may be substituted)
1/4 cup sherry
1 lime, zest and juice

Melt butter in saucepan, add flour, and stir until golden brown. Stirring continuously, add clam juice and wine and bring to a boil. When mixture has thickened, add cream, salt, pepper, and spices. Simmer 8 minutes.

Add lobster to sauce. Simmer 3 minutes. Add sherry and lime, let simmer 2 minutes more, then serve in warmed bowls.

RED SNAPPER SOUP

SERVES 4

This is a full meal—a real dinner stretcher when guests drop in and stay for supper. I have even added 1 sliced cucumber and have parboiled string beans and put them in the last half hour.

1 medium onion, finely chopped
2 tablespoons oil
1 stalk celery, thinly sliced
1/2 green pepper, thinly sliced
1 carrot, thinly sliced
2 tomatoes, chopped
2 cups water
1 cup clam juice, fish stock, or chicken stock
(if you have it. Just plain water with all
the vegetables makes such a lovely and
flavorful broth that you really wouldn't
miss the juice or broth.)

1 pound red snapper, cut into chunks
Salt, pepper, cumin, thyme, and rosemary to
taste
2 tablespoons parsley, finely chopped
1 potato, peeled, thinly sliced, and placed in
cold water
1 zucchini, thinly sliced
Pinch of saffron (optional)
2 slices french bread, toasted and cut in half
Fresh whole small spinach leaves for garnish
Red pepper flakes for garnish

Sauté onions in oil until transparent. Add celery, green pepper, and carrots.

Add tomatoes, water, and clam juice or fish or chicken broth and a few pieces of red snapper. Let simmer 30 minutes.

Add salt, pepper, cumin, thyme, rosemary, and parsley. Add drained potato and zucchini. Adjust seasonings. Add saffron.

Five minutes before serving, add remaining red snapper chunks.

Just before serving, place 1/2 slice of toast on bottom of each warmed soup bowl; then add 1/4 teaspoon red pepper flakes to each bowl. Pour in hot soup and garnish with spinach leaves. They'll just wilt and be beautiful! Serve a small bowl of red pepper flakes on the side.

DINAH'S TURKEY LEG SOUP   SERVES 6

You will appreciate this soup if you are from a family like mine where more than two people always vie for a leg each time turkey is served. I've sacrificed occasionally—not always too graciously.

I had never seen a turkey leg soup, so I concocted this one for our TV show one day. It feeds six easily, and it's surely as economical as it is tasty. Almost any convivial vegetable can be substituted for the squash and string beans, such as corn or limas, one or both.

1 onion, finely chopped
1 garlic clove, finely chopped
2 tablespoons oil
1 carrot, chopped
3 stalks celery, coarsely chopped
1 small green pepper, cut into slivers
1 turkey leg
2 quarts water, or to cover 2 inches over
meat and vegetables
16-ounce can tomatoes
4 peppercorns
4 small potatoes, peeled, cut into quarters

1/2 pound cut-up string beans
3 small crookneck squash, cut into bite-sized
pieces
Salt and pepper
1/4 teaspoon thyme
1 tablespoon fresh basil *or* 1 teaspoon dried
1 tablespoon fresh tarragon *or* 1 teaspoon
dried
3 tablespoons fresh parsley, chopped
1 bunch escarole or spinach, washed and
drained
Parmesan or Romano cheese

In deep kettle, sauté onions and garlic in oil until translucent. Add carrots, celery, green peppers, turkey leg and water.

Bring to boil; add tomatoes and peppercorns. Cover, reduce heat, and let simmer for about 20 minutes, or until leg begins to get tender. Add potatoes and more water, if needed. Bring to boil and boil for 10 minutes. Add string beans, squash, salt and pepper, thyme, basil, tarragon, and parsley and cook for 10 more minutes.

Remove turkey leg and discard skin. Cut meat into bite-sized pieces and return to kettle. Taste and correct seasoning before adding escarole or spinach.

Blanch escarole by plunging into boiling salted water for 30 seconds or until limp. Lift out and drain. If using spinach, wilt into boiling salted water for barely 3 seconds and drain.

When soup is blended and flavor is just right, add escarole or spinach and serve immediately in hot soup bowls. Sprinkle with Parmesan or Romano cheese or serve cheese in a side dish.

ESCAROLE AND NECK BONES

SERVES 6

This is a delicious, homey Italian recipe. Try it—it's worth the trouble.

3 pounds lamb or beef neck bones	1 large onion, chopped
Water	4 bunches escarole
1 tablespoon salt	3 eggs
1/2 teaspoon pepper	3/4 cups freshly grated Parmesan cheese

Put neck bones in large pot with cold water to cover. Add salt, pepper, and onions. Bring to boil. Reduce heat and simmer for 2 hours.

Wash escarole thoroughly and cook about 5 minutes in same pot with neck bones until limp but still bright green.

Beat eggs and add to pot, stirring constantly. Cook 2–3 minutes. The eggs will cook and form dumpling-like bits. Sprinkle in cheese and stir until melted. Serve immediately.

CHEDDAR CHEESE SOUP

SERVES 4

The Redcoat Return in Elka Park, New York, serves this spicy, hearty wonder.

1/4 cup chopped onions	1 pound Cheddar cheese, grated
1/4 cup chopped celery	1/4 teaspoon Tabasco sauce
1 tablespoon butter	1 teaspoon salt
1 tablespoon flour	Dash of pepper
1 teaspoon paprika	1 teaspoon dry mustard
1 1/2 cups chicken stock	1/4 cup boiled potatoes, peeled and finely
1 1/2 cups milk	diced (optional)

Sauté onions and celery with butter until onions are transparent.

Stirring constantly, add flour and paprika and cook just 5 minutes, then add chicken stock and milk and cook over a low flame until soup begins to thicken, about 12–15 minutes. Add grated cheese, Tabasco, salt, pepper, and dry mustard.

Stir until cheese is melted and strain. Correct seasoning and consistency. You may want to add a little more Tabasco. Add boiled potatoes if you like a thicker soup.

CREAM OF ASPARAGUS SOUP   SERVES 4 TO 6

6 cups chicken stock	chopped
1 teaspoon salt	2 egg yolks
2 pounds fresh asparagus, stalks peeled*	3/4 cup heavy cream
7 tablespoons butter	2 tablespoons butter, softened
6 tablespoons flour	Salt
2 tablespoons shallots or scallions, finely	White pepper

In 3- to 4-quart pot, bring chicken stock and salt to a boil over moderate heat. Drop in asparagus tips and boil slowly 5 to 8 minutes, or until just tender.

Strain stock into a bowl and set tips aside in another.

In the same pot, make a roux by melting 5 tablespoons of butter over moderate heat, then stirring in flour. Cook over low heat, stirring constantly, for 1 to 2 minutes. Do not let mixture brown. Remove pot from heat, letting it cool for a few seconds. Then gradually pour in stock, beating constantly with a wire whisk to blend stock and roux. Return pot to moderate heat and stir until this cream soup base comes to a boil, thickens, and is perfectly smooth. Reduce heat and let simmer very gently.

Melt remaining 2 tablespoons butter in an 8- to 10-inch enamel or stainless-steel skillet. When foam subsides, stir in cut-up asparagus stalks and shallots or scallions and toss gently for 3 minutes over moderate heat. Add to soup base and cook over low heat, stirring occasionally, 15 minutes or until asparagus is tender.

Puree soup in a blender or food processor fitted with metal blade, then strain through a fine sieve back into pot.

With wire whisk, blend egg yolks and cream together in a medium-sized mixing bowl. Whisk in 1/2 cup of pureed soup, 2 tablespoons at a time, then slowly whisk mixture into soup. Stirring constantly, bring to a boil and cook for 30 seconds.

Remove from heat and stir in 2 tablespoons of softened butter, 1 tablespoon at a time. Season soup with salt and white pepper to taste. Add reserved asparagus tips. Ladle soup into a tureen or individual soup bowls to serve.

With a small sharp knife (not a vegetable peeler), peel each washed asparagus stalk of its skin and tough outer flesh. At the butt end the peeling may be as thick as 1/16 inch, but it should gradually become paper thin as the knife cuts and slides toward the tip. Cut off the tips where the scales end and trim away any oversized scales. Trim off and discard about 1/4 inch from the butt ends and cut the rest of the stalks into 1/2-inch lengths.

MEXICAN SOUP

You've heard about pen pals. Ann Perez is my phone friend. We've never had that cook-in we've talked about spoon to spoon, but we've talked endlessly and with great gusto about our mutually favorite subject, food. She's a friend of my friend Betty Rule, who suggested that first call. There was some special info I wanted about a South of the Border dish. I feel I know her well and I think she feels the same way. This is her soup for a wintry day, given over the phone. Tested, tasted, then devoured by all my tastees that day and now straight to you—you'll love it!

1 pound pinto beans, washed and cleaned
2 pounds oxtails, cut into 1 1/2-inch pieces, with fat removed
2 1/2 quarts water
1 whole onion
2 whole cloves garlic, peeled

2 sprigs cilantro
1 tomato, cut into quarters
1 long green poblano chili, cut into strips
15-ounce can hominy, undrained
8-ounce can tomato sauce
Salt and pepper

Combine pinto beans, oxtails, and water in large kettle.

Bring to boil, skim, and add onion, garlic, cilantro, and tomato. Let simmer 2 1/2–3 hours, or until beans begin to get soft.

Add poblano chili, hominy (including liquid), and tomato sauce. Add salt and pepper to taste and simmer for an additional 30 minutes. Remove onion and garlic cloves before serving.

CONDIMENTS

5 medium-sized scallions, chopped (white and green part)
6 radishes, finely chopped

5 serrano chilies, finely chopped
1/2 head lettuce, shredded
6 tablespoons cilantro, finely chopped

Serve soup in tureen surrounded by condiments in individual small bowls.

CREAM OF BROCCOLI SOUP

SERVES 4

I've been making this soup for years and often—nobody's complained so far. I believe in small soup cups and this will serve six nicely, but I do feel a little chintzy when I see the bowl bottom scrapers in action. It is pretty and it is truly delicious. A lot of recipes call for garlic. Much as I love those little nuggets for other dishes, no matter how small the amount it seems to rob this soup of its true essence.

2 medium-sized bunches of broccoli, cut up, including stalks
2 medium-sized potatoes, peeled and thinly sliced
4 tablespoons butter or margarine
1 medium onion, coarsely chopped

4 tablespoons flour
2 cups warm chicken broth
2 cups warm milk
1/2 cup warm heavy cream
Salt and freshly ground black pepper to taste
2 teaspoons dried basil

Cook broccoli and potatoes in salted water until tender. Set aside 8 flowerets of broccoli for garnish.

Heat butter in large saucepan and add onions. Cook, stirring, until onions are transparent but not brown.

Add flour and stir until blended. Cook 3–4 minutes, then stir in chicken broth and milk and cook, stirring, until smooth.

Place broccoli and potatoes in blender or food processor fitted with metal blade and puree. Gradually add half of broth-milk mixture and puree until smooth. Return soup to saucepan. Add remaining broth-milk mixture, and stir well with wire whisk. Add cream gradually, stirring, until soup is right consistency. Add salt, pepper, and dried basil and reheat. Adjust seasonings.

Serve with 2 broccoli flowerets in each warmed bowl of soup.

VARIATIONS Substitute zucchini or summer squash for broccoli. Add a little parsley for color when pureeing vegetables.

CELERY-APPLE SOUP

SERVES 4

1 cup chopped onions (reserve skins)
4 tablespoons butter
1 1/4 cups tomatoes, peeled and chopped
1 1/4 cups tart apples, peeled and chopped

1 1/4 cups chopped celery (reserve leaves)
1/2 cup dry sherry
3 cups chicken stock

Sauté onions in skillet with butter. Add tomatoes, apples, celery, and sherry. Cover and simmer 1 hour.

Meanwhile, heat chicken broth and add onion skins and celery leaves and let simmer 10 to 15 minutes. Strain. Add chicken stock mixture to vegetable and apple mixture.

Put entire mixture in blender or food processor. Blend and serve hot.

CELERY AND TOMATO ESSENCE

SERVES 8

Try this lovely, light soup. It defies the adage that if it's good, it must be fattening.

10 cups chicken stock
1 bunch celery, trimmed and diced (reserving
   2 stalks of celery, cut into fine julienne
   strips)
4 tomatoes, peeled, seeded, and diced *or* 1

cup canned tomatoes, drained and diced
1 tablespoon butter
1/2 teaspoon salt, or to taste
1/4 teaspoon thyme
1/2 teaspoon pepper, or to taste

In large kettle combine chicken stock and diced celery, reserving julienne strips. Bring stock to boil and simmer 30 minutes.

In a skillet toss diced tomatoes in butter. Add salt, thyme, and pepper and simmer tomatoes, covered, over moderately low heat for 10 minutes or until most of liquid has evaporated.

Puree tomatoes in food processor or force through fine sieve into large saucepan. Then strain celery broth into tomato mixture, discarding celery. Add reserved julienne strips of celery to broth.

Heat soup to boiling point, reduce heat, and cook about 10 minutes or until celery is slightly tender. Season with salt and pepper to taste. Serve in warmed bowls.

COLD CURRIED CREAM OF EGGPLANT SOUP

SERVES 4

I tested this soup on some doubting Thomases and Susans who weren't all that sure they liked eggplant. I didn't tell them what it was until after they'd finished the whoooole thing. It's another warm evening cooler to be served before a simple summery dinner menu.

1/2 cup chopped onions
4 tablespoons butter
1 tablespoon plus 2 teaspoons curry powder, or to taste
1/4 teaspoon coriander
1/4 teaspoon cumin
1/4 teaspoon turmeric

1 1/4 pounds eggplant, peeled and cut into 1/2-inch cubes
4 cups chicken stock
3/4 cup heavy cream or half-and-half
Salt and white pepper to taste
Cayenne pepper to taste
Chutney

In saucepan sauté onion in butter until translucent. Stir in curry powder, coriander, cumin, and turmeric. Cook over moderately low heat, stirring, for 2 minutes.

Add eggplant and chicken stock and bring to a boil over moderately high heat. Reduce heat to low and simmer, covered, for 45 minutes or until eggplant is very soft.

Transfer mixture to a blender in batches and puree. Strain puree through a fine sieve into a bowl.

Add heavy cream or half-and-half, salt, white pepper and cayenne pepper to taste, and let the soup cool. Chill soup, covered, for at least 3 hours.

Divide the soup among four chilled bowls. Serve with a little chopped chutney on top.

MUSHROOM BISQUE

SERVES 4–6

I had a lovely time just outside Cleveland, Ohio, in this restaurant with the fresh-sounding, willowy name, Earth By April. It's semi-vegetarian and everyone involved, from the chefs to the young people serving and showing you to your table, is proud and enthusiastic about his or her fresh vegetables, breads, ideas, great salads—and whoever first cooked this one sure knew his/her bisque.

4 tablespoons butter
2 onions, chopped
1 stalk celery, chopped
3 potatoes, peeled and cut into cubes
1 1/2 pounds fresh mushrooms, sliced
3 tablespoons flour
1 1/2 cups Vegetable Stock
3 cups hot milk

1/2 pint heavy cream
2 tablespoons dry sherry
2 tablespoons mild soy sauce
1/4 teaspoon thyme
1 tablespoon freshly ground black pepper, or
   to taste
1/2 teaspoon salt

In saucepan melt butter and sauté vegetables until tender.

Add flour gradually, stirring constantly, and cook 5 to 7 minutes letting mixture brown slightly.

Add vegetable stock and mix until smooth.

Add milk, cream, sherry, soy sauce, and seasonings. Adjust seasonings to taste.

VEGETABLE STOCK

3 stalks celery, coarsely chopped
1 tomato, coarsely chopped
1 whole onion
1 zucchini, coarsely chopped
1/2 cup green beans
1 potato, peeled and coarsely chopped

3 okra, coarsely chopped
2 carrots, coarsely chopped, and
Anything else you may have in the refrigerator
3 cups water

Place all vegetables in large pot. Add water, bring to a boil. Cover and simmer for 10 to 15 minutes. Strain for stock.

ONION SOUP

SERVES 6

4 large onions, thinly sliced
1/4 cup butter
1 tablespoon flour
6 cups hot beef consommé

1 cup grated Gruyère cheese
1/2 cup grated Parmesan cheese
12 slices sourdough bread, twice toasted

Sauté onions in butter until lightly browned. Add flour and stir until well blended. Gradually add hot consommé, stirring vigorously until well blended with flour-butter mixture. Bring to boil and simmer 5 minutes.

Preheat broiler.

Pour soup into 6 individual soup bowls. Float slice of sourdough on top of each bowl and sprinkle generously with cheeses. Place bowls under preheated broiler until cheese melts and bubbles. Serve remaining slices of sourdough on side.

VARIATION

Preheat oven to 425°F.

Eliminate sourdough bread. Add 1 pound puff pastry dough and 2 eggs, slightly beaten. Substitute 1/2 cup Swiss cheese for Parmesan cheese.

Roll out puff pastry dough and cut 6 circles about 1/4 inch larger than tops of soup bowls.

Mix Gruyère and Swiss cheese together. Divide half of cheese among 6 individual soup bowls. Fill with onion soup.

Brush outside of each bowl with egg, place dough on top and seal around bowl. Brush dough with remaining egg and sprinkle remaining cheese over top. Bake for 5 to 6 minutes, or until dough puffs up and is golden brown.

FRESH SPINACH AND COCONUT SOUP

SERVES 6–8

I waited awhile to test this one. The fresh coconut scared me a little until I found this great way to crack it. I almost didn't have enough for the soup because I kept picking at it. That's the only hard part of this elegant soup with its elusive texture. I really feel the flavor is enhanced by serving it hot with a bowl of sour cream or yogurt on the side.

1 pound fresh spinach leaves
2 medium onions (8 ounces total), finely sliced
2 tablespoons unsalted butter
3 1-inch squares *fresh* coconut (2 ounces total), shelled and peeled*

4 cups chicken broth
1/2 teaspoon freshly grated nutmeg
Salt and freshly ground black pepper
Yogurt (optional)
1 medium firm lemon

Wash spinach thoroughly; do not dry. In 3-quart saucepan over high heat, cook spinach in water clinging to its leaves. As soon as it wilts, put in a colander and rinse with cold running water until completely cold. Press out liquid and set aside. Wring out in towel, then roll up like a jelly roll.

In saucepan over moderate heat, cook onions in butter about 10 minutes, until soft but not brown.

With shredding disc of food processor, shred the coconut using firm pressure. Add it along with broth to onions. Add nutmeg, salt, and freshly ground black pepper. Simmer gently, covered, for 20 minutes.

Strain out onions and coconut, reserving the liquid. Fit processor with metal blade and add onions and coconut. Process about 10 seconds. Add spinach and 1/2 cup of liquid.

Transfer this mixture to remaining liquid. Heat thoroughly and season to taste.

If you serve it cold, stir in 3 tablespoons yogurt for every cup of soup. Garnish with lemon slices.

*In a preheated 400°F. oven, bake whole coconut until shell cracks, about 15 minutes. Let cool until easy to handle. Place coconut inside two plastic bags and seal them closed with a wire twist. Place on sturdy work surface. With a hammer hit coconut solidly once or twice where the shell is cracked to split it open. Discard the liquid and separate meat from shell. With a swivel-blade vegetable peeler, remove brown skin from coconut meat.

TOMATO AND ORANGE SOUP

SERVES 4–6

Going into Wimbledon for the tennis matches is a great experience all around. On my visit, unfortunately, it rained during most of the first- and second-round matches so we took a little trip into the Cotswold area and on the recommendation of our concierge at the Berkley Hotel stopped at Brotherton's Wine Bar in the Oxfordshire area. If I hadn't missed those matches, I would have missed Brotherton's! See how these things work out?

The chef is a young lady of about 26 who greeted us after our marvelous luncheon wearing a T-shirt that simply said, "Choosy." I'm sure she could afford to be. When you look like that and you can cook like that, you've got a lot going for you.

You'll find three of her recipes she was gracious enough to share in this book. This one was a smashing first course, and can be served either hot or cold. I prefer it hot. I add 1/4 cup of cream at the last moment and let it warm through just before serving the soup. Float twice-toasted bread cut into small triangles and just a sprinkle of parsley on the top in each warmed bowl of soup. If you have clear glass or crystal soup bowls, wonderful! I used my pure white ones and this tomato red soup looked beautiful.

1 large onion, finely chopped
4 tablespoons butter
2 12-ounce cans of tomatoes or 2 pounds
   fresh tomatoes, peeled
Zest of 2 oranges, finely chopped

2 cups chicken stock
Salt and white pepper
1/4 cup cream (optional)
Twice Toasted Bread (page 13)
Parsley, finely chopped

In saucepan, sauté onion in butter until soft and translucent. Add tomatoes and orange zest and simmer 5 minutes. If fresh tomatoes are used, cook until tomatoes burst open. Add chicken stock and simmer 15–20 minutes.

Puree soup in blender or food processor fitted with metal blade.

Return to saucepan and reheat. Season to taste with salt and pepper and add cream, if desired. Sprinkle with a little parsley and serve.

I find that good amounts of white pepper and salt enhance the flavor of this unusual soup. One word of caution: use only the zest—cut away the bitter white part of the orange peel.

CREAM OF FRESH TOMATO SOUP

SERVES 4

One great summer day when I was visiting Big Burt, Fern, and what's-his-name on the ranch in Florida, a friend, Kathy, and I went tomato picking in one of those marvelous acre-after-acre areas of ripe tomatoes that are picked and packed there. You bring your own baskets, bags, cartons, suitcases, crates—whatever—and pick all you want or can carry. We could carry a lot. They'd sold all the rest to the packers and like sensible, good neighbor farmers couldn't bear to see that beautiful fruit (or is it a vegetable?) go to waste before plowing under for the next crop. We ate them raw and stewed for days and had enough tomato sauces and relishes to give us all a rash. The winner of the bunch was this recipe. If I had my druthers, and if I can be at the right place with the right basket, I'd have this at least once a week.

5 medium-sized fresh tomatoes, peeled and
sliced*

3 medium-sized potatoes, peeled and thinly
sliced

1 small onion, finely chopped

Salt and freshly ground black pepper to taste

1 bay leaf

1 teaspoon dried basil

2 tablespoons butter

2 tablespoons flour

1 cup milk, approximately

1 tablespoon sugar, or to taste

Place tomatoes, potatoes, onions, salt and pepper, bay leaf and basil in saucepan. Cook over medium heat until potatoes are soft. Remove bay leaf. Press the tomato-potato mixture through a sieve or puree in blender until smooth.

Meanwhile melt butter in a saucepan and add flour, stirring. Slowly add half the milk, stirring. When smooth, add pureed tomato-potato mixture. Cook, stirring over low heat until well blended. Add remaining milk. If soup is too thick, add more milk or a little chicken broth. Add sugar to taste. Adjust seasonings. Serve very hot.

*Bring water to boil in a medium saucepan. Plunge tomatoes into boiling water for 30 seconds, then run cold water over them. Skins will slip off easily. Slice tomatoes.

LIGHTEST CREAM OF VEGETABLE SOUP

SERVES 6

1 medium onion, thinly sliced

2 tablespoons butter

1/2 teaspoon sugar

1 green pepper, chopped

4 carrots, peeled and sliced 1/4 inch thick

4 parsnips, peeled and sliced 1/4 inch thick

2 white turnips, peeled and sliced 1/4 inch
thick

1/2 pound green beans, cut in half

2 medium tomatoes, peeled and cut into
chunks

1 stalk celery, thinly sliced

2 medium potatoes, peeled and sliced 1/4
inch thick

2 1/2 cups chicken broth or water

1 teaspoon fresh tarragon or 1/2 teaspoon
dried

1 1/2 teaspoons fresh basil or 1/2 teaspoon
dried

1 teaspoon fresh rosemary or 1/2 teaspoon
dried

1 bay leaf

1/2 teaspoon summer savory

1/4 teaspoon chervil

Freshly ground white pepper

Salt to taste

1/2 cup half-and-half or milk

In large saucepan lightly brown onions in butter. Sprinkle with sugar. Add vegetables, chicken broth or water, herbs and a generous grinding of white pepper. Cook until vegetables are just soft, about 20–25 minutes. Season to taste with salt and white pepper.

Puree in batches in food processor or blender. With motor running, add half-and-half or milk and blend until smooth. Taste for seasoning.

PUREED VEGETABLE AND CELERY ROOT SOUP

SERVES 6–8

This is one of those rare occasions where the stems of the broccoli are the important parts and the flowerets are "reserved for another use." It's combined with that homely knob in the vegetable section, the celery root. Celery root is like that poor-looking relative with a fortune stashed in the bank. Once you get it home, peel and grate it and use it in soup or salad. You will sing its praises.

3 fresh celery roots, cleaned (make sure you get the grainy part out), peeled, and sliced
1 carrot, cut into pieces
1 bunch broccoli, stems only, chopped (save flowerets for another meal)
2 potatoes, cut into small pieces
1/2 onion, chopped
1 cup chicken broth
2 cups water
1/2 cup half-and-half
Salt and freshly ground white pepper
Chopped parsley

Cook vegetables in chicken broth and water until tender. Place in blender or food processor fitted with metal blade and blend for a couple of seconds, then thoroughly strain.

Soup should be consistency of pureed potato soup. Add half-and-half to thin it a little. Add salt and white pepper to taste. Serve hot with a bit of chopped parsley sprinkled over the top.

ROOT VEGETABLE SOUP

SERVES 4–6

5 potatoes, peeled and cubed
2 white turnips, peeled and cubed
1 large onion, coarsely chopped
2 stalks celery, coarsely chopped
2 carrots, coarsely chopped
6 cups water
6 tablespoons butter
Salt and pepper to taste
1 pound spinach, washed and trimmed, *or* 1/2 head of lettuce
Cream (optional)

In soup kettle combine potatoes, turnips, onions, celery, and carrots in water barely covering vegetables. Add butter and salt and pepper to taste. Bring to a boil and simmer, covered, 40 minutes or until vegetables are very tender.

Add spinach or lettuce and simmer mixture 1–2 minutes or until greens are wilted.

Puree mixture in batches in blender or food processor fitted with metal blade and transfer to pot. Taste and add salt and pepper and thin soup with cream if necessary. Heat soup to boiling point and serve in warmed bowls.

WILD RICE SOUP

I've always had a great time in Minneapolis. I love singing there. The people are enthusiastic and hospitable, and it's about as beautiful as any area in our country. I went to several lovely homes on Lake Minnetonka. I kept expecting to run into Hiawatha and Minnehaha by those shiny, big lake waters. No such luck, but of course I dined well. The food is varied and superb and wild rice is cheaper there. They grow it proudly, but harvesting it is no cinch. It's tough for them, but a treat for us. The Marquette Hotel's Orion Room does a beautiful job using only 1/4 cup of this precious grain for a superb soup.

STOCK

2 duck or chicken carcasses
1 smoked ham bone
1 medium onion, sliced
1 tablespoon Kitchen Bouquet
1 teaspoon Worcestershire sauce

Salt and white pepper to taste
1 bay leaf
1/4 celery stalk, chopped
1 1/4 quarts water
2 carrots, chopped

Combine above ingredients and bring to a boil. Simmer approximately 1 1/2 hours. Strain and reserve for soup.

SOUP

1/4 cup butter
1/4 cup raw *or* 2 cups cooked wild rice
2 tablespoons sliced blanched almonds
1/2 cup finely diced onions

1/2 cup finely diced celery
1/2 cup finely diced carrots
1 pint heavy cream
2 teaspoons cornstarch (optional)

Melt butter in heavy pot and sauté above ingredients. Add soup stock and simmer approximately 1 1/4 hours. Then, if necessary, thicken with 2 teaspoons cornstarch dissolved in small amount of the cream. Stir in rest of cream just before serving.

Chapter 4

EGGS, BRUNCH, AND LUNCH

Talk about your basics—trying to cook without eggs in the refrigerator is like putting on your makeup without a mirror. I'm sorry about the dedicated cholesterol counters, but the whites have protein food value and are a leavening agent. So if that's your problem, at least use the whites.

When all else in your larder disappears or refuses to combine with anything else, you have the beginning of an omelet or a crêpe filled with some or any combination for lunch, breakfast, main course, dessert, a midnight snack. Eggs can save the day, and have done so far more times than I can recall. I feel the same way about cheese, the basic kinds that keep: Cheddar, Monterey Jack, Jarlsberg, Swiss or Gruyère, and mozzarella, Parmesan, or Romano for fresh grating. Protect the freshness of your cheese after opening the original package by putting it in a fresh plastic bag with a seal or by wrapping in plastic wrap.

Eggs and cheese should be cooked at a low to moderate, even heat. Too high a heat toughens the protein in eggs and cheese and causes them to become leathery and curdled. The one exception is the omelet, which uses a never-washed special pan—so some say.

Make a perfect omelet in a heavy, much-used, round-bottomed skillet. The trick is to have the pan very hot, the butter very hot, and the omelet beaten lightly with a fork and turned into this heat and stirred briskly until almost set; then turn down the heat, add your filling, shake pan and, using a spatula, lift side nearest you and cover half of filling, tip pan and with the aid of that spatula gently roll it over onto your warm plate. That Wild Rice–Spinach Omelet Roll-Up in this chapter is terrific, as is Omelet Grand-Mère in Chapter 1. A nice finishing touch with an omelet is that grating of fresh Gruyère and/or Parmesan cheese on the omelet. Place omelet and all under the broiler to melt until you've finished at least two or three of your masterpieces.

People have omelet parties. Maybe they do this all the time where you live, but I first saw it in action in New York after a late theater evening. Our host had three omelet pans going, his eggs all beaten in a large bowl, and our choice of fillings he'd done earlier—seven or eight great combinations. We'd point and he'd stir and tip. I don't know if he had as much fun as we did, but I loved it—even after I was drafted into service so he could "eat a little something."

By the way, there's hardly a dish better for Sunday breakfast or brunch than the Sunday Omelet Crêpes, and since we're on what is good for a day starter, do try my French Toast. It's definitely different, I promise you that—but then, so is everything in here.

This chapter also gives you suggestions for lunches and brunches. For instance, those Chinese chicken salads—all of which are in here because each is so different from the others. If I could have thought of another name for any one of them, I would have. The Oriental Noodle and Chicken Salad is not a typical Chinese salad—it is really Indonesian. Just as the Salade de Poulet is not your conventional French chicken salad—it's from our friends at Ma Maison in Los Angeles.

Try Cauliflower Cheese Pie, contributed by my daughter Melissa, for lunch or brunch. Almost every recipe in this chapter can serve as brunch, breakfast or even supper—the late kind so there will be no hole-in-the-stomach hunger pains before bedtime.

Omigosh, did I forget to mention that this chapter also has the Crispy Cornmeal Pancakes and that unusual Italian Chicken Salad? Well, my advice is don't skip any of them.

EGG CROQUETTES

SERVES 4–5

This was one of the first egg recipes I dared to try when I was a bride that wasn't fried or scrambled. I loved it and I may have overdone it—I seem to remember George asking me tactfully one day if there wasn't something else I could do with eggs, just every once in a while. I could, and did, but you must try these.

ONE NICE VARIATION—a couple of tablespoons of crisply fried bacon or ham added to the Béchamel that holds it together.

1 small onion, peeled and quartered
7 hard-boiled eggs
4 sprigs parsley
3 tablespoons butter
4 tablespoons flour
1 cup milk

1/2 teaspoon salt
1 egg, lightly beaten
1 cup fine bread crumbs
Oil for deep frying
Béchamel Sauce (page 2)
Parsley for garnish

Chop onion in food processor fitted with the metal blade. Add eggs and parsley. Chop quickly with 2 or 3 quick on and off turns.

In saucepan melt butter and add flour, stirring constantly. When well blended add milk and salt, continuing to stir. Sauce this thick is hard to handle and must be beaten until smooth. Add ground eggs, onions, and parsley to hot cream sauce. Let cool and chill in refrigerator for 2 hours.

Mold mixture into croquettes (about 10). Place croquettes on cookie sheet lined with waxed paper and return to refrigerator to chill again.

When ready to fry, dip in lightly beaten egg, then roll in bread crumbs. The croquettes are soft and hard to handle, but there will be no damage done if you handle quickly.

Fry in basket in deep hot oil until rich brown. Do not crowd croquettes in basket, as contact makes them burst open.

Place Béchamel sauce on warm platter. Add croquettes. Garnish with parsley.

CAULIFLOWER AND EGG SCRAMBLE

SERVES 4–6

1/2 pound bacon, chopped
2 onions, chopped
4 cups coarsely chopped cooked cauliflower
  (about 1 3/4 pounds), reserving 4 or 5

flowerets for garnish
8 eggs
Salt and pepper

In large skillet cook bacon over moderately high heat until brown and crisp. Drain on paper towels.

Pour off all but 1/2 cup of fat and sauté onions over moderately high heat until lightly browned. Add cauliflower and sauté until mixture is heated through.

Stir in eggs, lightly beaten with salt and pepper and half the bacon. Cook mixture, stirring, until eggs are set. Do not overcook.

Transfer mixture to heated platter and sprinkle with remaining bacon and reserved cauliflower flowerets.

SUNDAY OMELET CREPES

SERVES 4

A good friend came home from location in Vienna for a movie. He described this dish in such great detail, practically salivating over just the description, that I couldn't wait to try and duplicate it. I guess I did a fairly good job. It became a Sunday substitute for Sunday Fried Steak and Biscuits.

CRÊPES

YIELDS ABOUT 15 CREPES

2 eggs
1 cup milk

1/2 cup flour
1/8 teaspoon salt

Beat eggs well. Add milk, flour, and salt, beating thoroughly until mixture is smooth.

Heat a 5-inch skillet. Pour in 1 tablespoon of batter and tip quickly to coat bottom of skillet. Cook over medium heat until small bubbles appear. Shake out onto clean dish towel to cool.

When you've made a few and they have cooled, they can be stacked without sticking together to store. Wrap six in aluminum foil and freeze. They thaw out quickly.

8 crêpes
Raspberry jam or some kind of tart jelly
4 tablespoons butter

8 eggs
2 tablespoons cream
Salt and pepper

In the center of each crêpe, put a scant teaspoon of either jam or jelly. Roll up crêpe and set aside.

Heat omelet pan. Add 1/3 of butter. While butter is melting, beat eggs and cream lightly with fork. Add salt and pepper. Pour 1/8 cup of egg mixture into hot omelet pan. Stir quickly with fork until edges begin to cook.

When omelet is almost set, place rolled crêpe in center and with spatula quickly roll omelet around crêpe and slide onto a warm platter. Follow same steps with the remaining egg mixture. Allow two crêpes per person.

WILD RICE–SPINACH OMELET ROLL-UPS

SERVES 6

This is a luncheon or brunch dish. It's delicious and definitely a good party dish. I allocated one to a customer, but I was wrong. Everyone wanted seconds or half a second! I recommend doubling the recipe for company—you'll need it and they'll love it.

Betty Rule helped me test this one. It was one of those days when we tried at least 10 nominees for the book on her husband, Elton, and several willing guinea pig neighbors out at the beach. I think all the recipes passed that day—this one got a 9 3/4 on a scale of 1 to 10.

RICE FILLING

2 tablespoons butter or margarine
1 small onion, minced
1 clove garlic, minced
1 1/2 cups cooked wild rice
10-ounce package frozen chopped spinach,
  thawed and drained well

1 cup small-curd cottage cheese, drained
1 teaspoon Worcestershire sauce
Salt and pepper to taste
Cheese Sauce
Mushroom Omelet Rounds

Melt butter in skillet. Sauté onion and garlic until tender, about 5 minutes.

Stir in rice. Cook 5 minutes. Add spinach and continue to cook about 2 minutes. Add cottage cheese, Worcestershire, salt, and pepper. Set aside until full recipe is assembled.

CHEESE SAUCE

1/4 cup butter or margarine
1/4 cup flour
1 3/4 cups milk
Salt and pepper to taste

Dash of cayenne pepper
Dash of Worcestershire sauce
1 cup shredded sharp Cheddar cheese

Melt butter in small saucepan. Blend in flour; cook 1 minute. Slowly stir in milk; cook until thickened and smooth. Remove from heat and season to taste with salt, pepper, cayenne, and Worcestershire.

Stir in shredded cheese (cheese does not need to melt). Set aside at room temperature until final assembly.

MUSHROOM OMELET ROUNDS

1/4 cup finely chopped onions
1/2 cup finely chopped mushrooms
Butter or margarine

7 eggs, lightly beaten
Salt and pepper to taste

Sauté onions and mushrooms in 2 tablespoons butter in small skillet. Remove and stir into eggs in bowl. Season *lightly* with salt and pepper.

Heat 2 teaspoons butter in omelet pan or small skillet over medium heat. Pour about 1/4 cup egg-mushroom mixture into skillet. Stir with fork while tilting pan to spread mixture toward edges of pan. Cook until done but moist.

Remove to plate and repeat until 6 omelet rounds are made.

FINAL ASSEMBLY

Preheat oven to 350°F.

Fill each mushroom omelet round with 1/6 of rice filling, then roll up crêpe-style.

Arrange in ovenproof shallow casserole and spoon Cheese Sauce over each roll-up. Cook 15–20 minutes.

GREEN CHILI AND CHEESE OMELET   SERVES 2–3

Omelets are the easiest, most attractive luncheon, diet, supper, breakfast, brunch dish possible. Stretch and use your imagination. You can use canned or frozen goodies, a variety of cheeses and, most definitely, your leftovers—hot, cold, or a combination.

SAUCE

1 tablespoon butter
1 large fresh tomato, peeled and chopped*

1 tablespoon minced onion

Melt butter; add remaining ingredients and simmer about 5 minutes.

*To peel tomato, bring water to boil in medium-sized saucepan. Plunge tomato into boiling water for 30 seconds, then run cold water over it. Skin will slip off easily.

1 tablespoon butter
4 eggs
1/4 cup milk or cream
Salt and pepper to taste

7-ounce can peeled green chilies
1/4 pound Monterey Jack or sharp Cheddar cheese, cut into strips to equal number of chilies.

Melt butter in heavy skillet. Beat together eggs, milk or cream, salt and pepper. Follow basic omelet cooking instructions (page 16), keeping it moist. Do not fold over.

Wrap a chili around each cheese strip and place on one half of omelet. Fold over and serve on heated platter. Pour sauce over all just before serving.

NOTE One slice of cold ripe avocado inside omelet does wonders.

SPANISH OMELET OLE!   SERVES 3–4

Everybody thinks they've had a Spanish omelet. They haven't until they've tasted this version. Peter Viertel, a fine writer, tennis player, skier, bullfighting aficionado, and husband of a dear friend of mine, Deborah Kerr, cooked this one on our TV show—you'll love it!

3 tablespoons olive oil	1/2 teaspoon minced garlic
1 raw potato, peeled and diced	6 to 8 eggs
1 green pepper, chopped	Salt and pepper to taste
1/2 onion, minced	2 medium tomatoes, sliced

Heat oil in skillet and sauté potatoes until almost done, stirring frequently. Add green peppers, onions, and garlic. Continue cooking, stirring frequently, until vegetables are done but still crisp. Add more oil if needed.

Beat eggs with salt and pepper. Pour over vegetables; stir to keep eggs from sticking.

When omelet is almost set, place tomato slices in a single layer over top; cook a moment longer.

Place cover over pan. Invert pan, turning omelet onto cover, and slide omelet back into pan upside down. Cook a moment longer. To serve, invert omelet onto cover again (tomato side up) and slide onto serving plate.

NOTE Be sure to use a skillet with a cover that fits tightly. This is important when you invert the pan. This should be done over the sink, with a towel wrapped around wrist of hand holding cover, to keep from burning yourself.

CRISPY CORNMEAL PANCAKES

YIELDS 25–30 4-INCH PANCAKES

I have this thing about cornmeal anything. Bread, coatings, mush—mushy or fried. It's almost always better served piping hot. These pancakes are exactly what I mean. Heat the serving platter, plates, syrup, and butter for your hot cornmeal pancakes.

3 cups buttermilk	2 teaspoons salt
3 eggs	1 teaspoon soda
1/2 cup oil	1/2 cup white flour
2 2/3 cups yellow cornmeal	

Beat together buttermilk, eggs, and oil. Add cornmeal, salt, soda, and flour. Mix only until smooth.

Heat griddle, oil lightly, and drop batter from large spoon or pour from a measuring cup. Cook until batter rises and surface is dotted with holes. Turn and cook on other side until lightly browned.

SWEDISH POPOVER PANCAKES

SERVES 4–6

This is a variation on the popular popover. A nice breakfast or luncheon surprise. I love the combination of hot pancake syrup and melted butter with a dollop of cold sour cream.

4 eggs, beaten
2/3 cup milk
1/2 teaspoon salt
1/2 teaspoon baking powder
2/3 cup flour

6 tablespoons butter, melted
1–2 teaspoons sugar
Pinch of nutmeg
Juice from 1 lime

Preheat oven to 450°F.

Add milk, salt, and baking powder to beaten eggs. Gradually add flour and beat vigorously. Add 2 tablespoons melted butter, sugar, and nutmeg.

Heat individual pie tins 3 1/2 inches in diameter in oven. Tins should be really hot. Remove and brush generously with remaining melted butter. Ladle batter scantily into pie tins. Bake for 8 minutes. Sprinkle with lime juice and serve immediately with sour cream, melted butter, and hot syrup.

LIGHTEST POTATO PANCAKES

YIELDS 20–25 3-INCH PANCAKES

These are definitely not your everyday mashed-potato pancakes. They are quite different from any other pancakes and definitely worth a company or just family breakfast treat. A valuable plus is that they can be done well ahead except, of course, for the egg white addition.

1 cup cooked mashed potatoes
1 cup flour
4 egg yolks, beaten
1/4 teaspoon salt

2 cups potato water *or* 1 cup potato water
and 1 cup milk
4 tablespoons melted butter
4 egg whites, stiffly beaten

Mix all ingredients except egg whites. Just before you are ready to grill the pancakes, add 2 or 3 tablespoons of egg whites to batter. Stir well to loosen batter and then fold in remaining egg whites.

Heat griddle, oil lightly, and drop batter from large spoon or pour from a measuring cup. Bake until batter rises and surface is dotted with holes. Turn and bake other side until lightly browned. Serve hot with melted butter and hot syrup, cold apple sauce, or a tart jam.

MUSHROOM SOUFFLÉ

SERVES 2 AS A FIRST COURSE
4 AS AN APPETIZER

It's easy, it's low-cal, it's delicious, it's nutritious, it's beautiful! Serve with green salad for a light lunch or as a first course.

8 large mushrooms, stems removed and reserved
Salt and freshly ground white pepper
1 scallion, finely chopped
1 tablespoon butter
1 small tomato, chopped
1 tablespoon flour

2/3 cup non-fat milk *or* half milk and half chicken broth
Cayenne pepper (optional)
2 eggs, separated
1/2 cup Cheddar or Monterey Jack cheese, grated

Wash and quickly wipe mushrooms dry. Sprinkle lightly with salt and pepper. Set mushroom caps aside. Chop stems medium fine.

In medium-sized saucepan sauté scallions in butter, then add mushroom stems. Sauté stems 2 or 3 minutes. Add tomatoes, sauté a minute or two, and season to taste.

Sprinkle flour over vegetable mixture and stir until flour coats all. Add milk or milk and broth, stirring constantly over medium heat until mixture begins to thicken. Taste for seasoning as it may need a little cayenne pepper.

Beat egg yolks lightly and add a little of the hot mixture to the egg yolks. Then add egg yolk mixture slowly to the vegetable mixture, stirring constantly. Add grated cheese. Remove from heat.

Beat egg whites until stiff but not dry. Add 2 tablespoons egg white to vegetable mixture and stir. Fold in remaining egg whites.

Preheat oven to 400°F.

Place seasoned mushroom caps in an eight-inch pie plate. Spoon soufflé mixture over mushrooms. Bake for 5 minutes at 400°, then lower heat to 375° and bake 15 minutes longer or until puffy and golden brown.

PAULINE'S CHEESE SOUFFLÉ   SERVES 4

This recipe appeared in Someone's in the Kitchen with Dinah, *but since then we've adapted it, using Abby Mandel's method of beating egg whites in the Cuisinart. Don't be nervous if it's a little runnier than usual as you're pouring it into the soufflé dish. It rises and rises, almost over the collar.*

4 tablespoons butter
4 tablespoons flour
1 teaspoon salt
Paprika
Cayenne pepper or Tabasco sauce
1 cup milk
1 cup sharp Cheddar cheese, finely grated

1/3 cup freshly grated Parmesan cheese (reserve 2 tablespoons)
4 egg yolks
1 tablespoon white vinegar
1 tablespoon water
6 egg whites

Preheat oven to 475°F.

Melt butter in saucepan. Add flour, seasonings and blend well. Add milk and cook, stirring, until thick. Add cheeses and stir until melted. Cook to room temperature, about 15 minutes. Then add well-beaten egg yolks.

Combine vinegar and water in small bowl. Set aside.

Place egg white in very clean processor bowl fitted with the steel blade and process about 8 seconds. Turn processor on again and add vinegar-water mixture through feed tube. Continue to process 1 minute or until egg whites are very stiff. With rubber spatula, carefully transfer beaten egg whites to clean mixing bowl.

Return work bowl to processor (don't bother washing it) and add cheese-egg yolk mixture. Then spoon egg whites into work bowl. Turn processor on and off quickly 2 to 3 times until whites are combined. (Some streaks of egg white will still show—don't worry about it.) Do not overprocess.

With rubber spatula, gently transfer mixture to well-buttered 5-cup soufflé dish dusted with remaining freshly grated Parmesan cheese and wrapped with a collar. Make a collar by doubling heavy-duty aluminum foil into a strip long enough to go around your dish and 2–3 inches wide. Wrap around outside rim of soufflé dish and tie securely in place with string. Bake for 10 minutes, then reduce heat to 400° and continue baking about 25 minutes longer. Serve at once or sooner.

FRENCH TOAST

SERVES 6

Some people insist upon serving this with maple syrup, but this lily needs no gilding.

1 1/2 cups half-and-half
1 egg
1/4 teaspoon vanilla
2 tablespoons powdered sugar

6 1-inch slices day-old egg bread sliced diagonally
6 tablespoons butter, melted

Beat half-and-half, egg, vanilla, and one tablespoon powdered sugar together and strain through fine sieve into a bowl.

Soak bread in liquid and place in preheated skillet containing melted butter. (Should be about 1 inch of butter in pan.) Cook slowly and turn often. Before serving, sprinkle with remaining powdered sugar.

BLUEBERRY COTTAGE CHEESE PANCAKES

SERVES 6

I think Pauline would rather cook these than anything in our repertoire. I think it's because of my son Jody (short for John David). From the time he was old enough to call the shots on his favorite menus, specifically birthdays, when it was always, "Name it, it's yours," and that went for breakfast lunch and dinner, Jody would have had them for all three without some gentle dissuasion.

One important thing to remember—unlike most dishes, it doesn't work nearly as well with fresh or frozen blueberries. It just has to be the canned, as we tell you in the recipe.

PANCAKES

2 cups low-fat cottage cheese
2 large eggs
1/4 cup sugar
1 tablespoon lemon juice
Pinch of salt

1 cup flour
3 tablespoons butter, melted
3 tablespoons oil
Blueberry Sauce
Sour cream

Whip cottage cheese in medium bowl until creamy. Add eggs, sugar, lemon juice, and salt. Mix well.

Add flour until batter becomes thick. Refrigerate until ready to cook. (Batter may be prepared a day or two in advance.)

When ready to cook, brush hot griddle or large skillet well with melted butter and oil. Drop batter by tablespoonfuls to make pancakes about 3 inches in diameter. When bottom is lightly browned and bubbles have formed on surface, turn over and brown other side.

Place two pancakes for each person on warmed dessert plates, pour hot Blueberry Sauce over them, and put a generous dab of sour cream on top.

BLUEBERRY SAUCE

MAKES ABOUT 2 CUPS

16-ounce can blueberries
2 teaspoons cornstarch

1 tablespoon sugar

Remove 2 tablespoons blueberry juice to small bowl. Add cornstarch and dissolve.

Place blueberries in medium saucepan and add cornstarch and sugar mixture. Bring to boil and cook just until thickened, about 3 minutes. Serve hot.

MIXED GRILL SAUSAGES

SERVES 6 FOR A LUNCHEON OR 12 AS AN APPETIZER

This is one of our best luncheon and heavy cocktail hour combinations. I've listed some of the sausages I find easily in my market, but you may find others. I've yet to find a holdout. It takes a little time because the sausages have to be grilled slowly. This way they won't burn but will brown nicely and cook through without overcooking, which can dry them out.

2 Polish sausages
2 Italian sweet sausages
2 knockwursts
2 Swedish sausages

2 large kosher hot dogs
2 chorizos (hot Spanish sausages)
Dijon mustard and assorted mustards

Cut sausages into 1 1/2 to 2-inch chunks. Place in large skillet and fry until done or grill on griddle. Serve with Dijon mustard and a mild mustard or other assorted mustards that are available in the market.

Serve the mustards in assorted bowls and cocktail toothpicks for the sausages, or if it's for a luncheon—forks. A really good potato salad—hot German or French or a good ol' American cold one—goes great with this.

TOAD IN THE HOLE

Sir Frank and Lady Taylor invited me to be their guests at "The Meadows," a beautiful development of theirs in Sarasota, Florida. I was performing at the Van Wezel Theatre in the evenings and playing golf during the day on the lovely golf course that surrounded our little villa there. It was fun and most certainly the good life. I asked Lady Taylor to tell me about Toad in the Hole. I vowed I'd rather have it than the prized English trifle. She laughed and I guess wondered what one had to do with the other. A few weeks later she sent me this recipe—absolutely authentic, folks—for Toad in the Hole. It's simple and was a big success when I served it for lunch one day at the beach. Thank you, Lady Taylor.

Forgive me, good people of Sarasota, Florida. I promised you I'd never reveal the exact location of your Brigadoon in the middle of so many highly exploited oases. . . . Please invite me back anyway.

3/4 cup all-purpose flour	3/4 cup milk
1/2 teaspoon salt	1/2 cup water
1/4 teaspoon freshly ground white pepper	1 tablespoon oil
2 large eggs	1 pound pork sausage, patty-type

Preheat oven to 425°F.

Make batter by sifting flour, salt, and pepper into bowl. Make a well in the center and drop in eggs. Mix well with a whisk or electric beater. Add milk and water and mix well.

Put oil in the bottom of an 8-inch round cake pan and place it in the oven to heat. When oil is hot, line bottom of pan with sausages. Pour batter over all. Transfer to highest shelf in oven and bake for 40 minutes.

BAKED POTATO WITH CREAMED CHIPPED BEEF ''21''

Everybody has to have one recipe they absolutely love and a lot of people won't touch. This happens to be mine. I was never in the army and never went to boarding school, nor did our summer camp ever serve creamed chipped beef ad nauseam. Somebody else has to like it. They couldn't just run out for a jar of dried chipped beef when they see me come into "21." (Could they?)

4 baking potatoes	packages or jars)
1 1/2 cups Béchamel Sauce "21"	Pepper to taste
1 pound dried beef, chopped (available in	Salt (if needed)

Preheat oven to 400°F.

Bake potatoes 50 minutes or until done. Remove from oven and wrap in dish towel. Pierce top of each baked potato with tines of fork so as to release steam. Open up the baked potato by making a slit down center of each. Then squeeze potato gently to fluff up inside, leaving skin intact.

Add chopped beef to cooked Béchamel sauce. Season to taste with pepper. (Be careful not to add salt unless needed, as the dried beef is salty.) Pour about 1/2 cup of the chipped beef mixture over each baked potato. Serve immediately.

BÉCHAMEL SAUCE ''21''

2 cups milk
2 tablespoons butter
2 tablespoons flour
1/4 teaspoon white pepper

Salt to taste
Dash of Tabasco
Dash of Worcestershire sauce

Preheat oven to 300°F.

Scald milk. Melt butter in a heavy-bottomed saucepan with metal handle. Add flour, stirring with whisk for a couple of minutes. Gradually stir in milk and continue to whisk until mixture is thickened. Season with pepper, salt, Tabasco, and Worcestershire and place saucepan, covered, in preheated oven.

After allowing it to bake for about 1 1/2 hours, strain sauce which should be very thick and fluffy in consistency. Correct seasoning.

COLD SLICED VEAL WITH TUNA SAUCE

SERVES 6–8

The Italians do marvelous things with veal—hot or cold. This is one I fell in love with in a little restaurant just outside of Rome. Be sure to slice the veal as thin and uniformly as possible so that the sauce and the veal blend for the final serving.

2 1/2 pounds lean, boneless top round veal
   roast, firmly tied
1 stalk celery
1 medium carrot
1 medium onion

4 sprigs parsley
1 teaspoon salt
6 bruised or crushed peppercorns
1 bay leaf

In pot large enough to contain veal, put in veal, celery, carrot, onion, parsley, salt, peppercorns, and bay leaf and just enough water to cover. Remove veal and set aside. Bring water to boil, add veal, and when water comes to boil again, cover pot, reduce heat, and keep at a gentle simmer 1 1/2–2 hours. Do not overcook—beautiful veal can dry out if you're not careful. Remove pot from heat and allow meat to cool in its broth.

MAYONNAISE

3 egg yolks
3/4 teaspoon salt
3 tablespoons lemon juice

1/8 teaspoon cayenne pepper
1 1/2 cups fresh olive oil

Place all ingredients except oil in food processor. Process for 30 seconds. The egg mixture should be pale yellow, the consistency of thick cream. Turn off processor and scrape down sides. Then, with motor running, add oil through feed tube, a few drops at a time at the start, and then in thin stream. Blend until thick. Taste for seasoning.

TUNA SAUCE

7-ounce can tuna in oil, drained
6 or 7 flat anchovy fillets, drained
1 1/4 cups olive oil
3 tablespoons lemon juice

3 tablespoons capers
Lemon slices, olive slices, whole capers,
    parsley leaves, and a few anchovy fillets
    for garnish.

In food processor or blender mix tuna, anchovies, olive oil, lemon juice, and capers. Process for a few seconds or until mixture attains a creamy consistency. Remove mixture from food processor or blender and fold it carefully but thoroughly into the mayonnaise. Taste to see if more salt is required. Veal absorbs much of the seasonings.

When veal is cold, transfer it to cutting board, remove strings, and cut into thin and uniform slices. Smear bottom of serving platter with some of tuna sauce. Arrange veal slices over this in single layer, edge to edge. Cover layer well with tuna sauce. Lay more veal over this and cover again with sauce; set aside enough sauce to cover the topmost layer generously. Refrigerate for 24 hours, covered with plastic wrap.

DAN LEE'S CHINESE CHICKEN SALAD

SERVES 4 AS MAIN COURSE
SERVES 8 AS SALAD

Chinese chicken salads are crisp, succulent and definitely different from any chicken salads as we know them. They are also dramatically different from one another. I've tried a dozen. These two are so different and delicious, I had to include them both to give you an idea how good and varied their appeal can be. See page 62 for Dan Lee's Hot and Sour Soup and a little clue to his personality and cuisine. The second is a Ben Moy's Bird Special—see page 191 for his Ginger Beef with Bourbon, and page 111 for his Cucumber Salad with Red Onions and Ginger.

1 cup cornstarch
1 teaspoon salt
1 frying chicken (3–4 pounds), left whole
4 cups oil for deep frying
1 cup rice noodles (Maifun), fried and broken up
1 cup shredded iceberg lettuce

1/2 bunch cilantro, coarsely chopped
3 scallions, tops included, cut into 4 pieces
    and sliced lengthwise
Sauce
1 tablespoon white sesame seeds
1 1/2 tablespoons almonds or cashews (or
    mixture of both), chopped

Mix cornstarch with salt and pat on chicken to coat completely.

Cook chicken in bamboo steamer or vegetable steamer 45–50 minutes. Refrigerate until ready to make salad.

Split chicken in half and deep-fry in hot (375°F.) oil until skin is crisp and golden. Drain on paper towels. Debone chicken by shredding meat by hand *(do not cut)* into strips. Go along the grain and not crosswise.

In large bowl mix together shredded chicken, rice noodles, lettuce, cilantro, and scallions. Pour sauce over all and mix gently but thoroughly, making sure sauce coats all ingredients well. Sprinkle sesame seeds and nuts over salad.

SAUCE

1 heaping tablespoon dry mustard mixed
   with 1 tablespoon water to make a paste
1/3–1/2 cup peanut oil

1/4 teaspoon sesame seed oil
1/2 teaspoon salt
2 teaspoons dark soy sauce

Mix all ingredients in small bowl.

CRISPY CHICKEN SALAD   SERVES 6

*I have no idea in what region or province of China Ben Moy first saw the light of day, but it must
be one of those areas that produces opaline, that delicate hand-painted celadon.*

*The décor of his restaurant—The Bird, in Evanston, Illinois—reflects it, as do the delicacies
that come out of his kitchen. Witness this salad—quite different from any you'll ever experience.
The hardest chore in reproducing this dish is not to eat the chicken directly out of the oven instead
of savoring it to serve in the total combination as one is supposed to. As a matter of fact, after following
the marinade and roasting instructions I wanted to list it as a special dish in the poultry section
on its own.*

1 roasting chicken (3–4 pounds)
Salt
1 cup plus 2 tablespoons white wine
3/4 cup light soy sauce
2 leeks, coarsely chopped
3 scallions, finely chopped including tops
1/2 cup plus 2 sprigs fresh coriander or cilantro
2 cups oil for deep frying
2 cups uncooked rice noodles (Maifun)
1 head romaine, torn into bite-sized pieces

2 heads bibb lettuce, torn into bite-sized
   pieces
1 bunch watercress, stems removed
1/2 cup sweet Chinese cucumbers, sliced, or
   green cucumbers, peeled and salted. Let
   stand for 15 minutes, rinse well, slice and
   sprinkle with sugar. Let stand for up to 2
   hours.
1/4 cup peanut oil
2 tablespoons white vinegar
1/2 teaspoon sesame seed oil

Marinate chicken in salt, 1 cup white wine, and 1/2 cup of the soy sauce, turning
occasionally, for 2 hours.

Preheat oven to 450°F.

Stuff chicken with leeks, scallions, and 2 sprigs of coriander or cilantro.

Roast chicken 1/2 hour and turn oven down to 400°. Bake 45 minutes more,
or until skin of chicken is golden brown or done. Remove chicken from oven and
cool.

Place oil in wok. When oil is 375° to 400°, drop in Chinese rice noodles. When
they pop to surface (in 20 to 30 seconds), remove and drain. Cut meat from chicken
and sliver.

Put meat in large mixing bowl; add romaine, bibb lettuce, watercress, 1/2 cup
coriander or cilantro, cucumbers and toss. Pour in peanut oil, 1/4 cup soy sauce,
white vinegar, 2 tablespoons white wine, and sesame seed oil, and mix lightly. Add
salt to taste. Toss again. If it tastes too flat, add salt and a little extra vinegar and
soy sauce. The greens may need a little extra flavor.

Place mixture on a large serving platter and trim edge with fried rice noodles
before serving.

ITALIAN CHICKEN SALAD

SERVES 5–8

Randy Fuhrman, who is responsible for the Black Pasta (page 247) and the Asparagus Oriental (page 264) brought this equally unusual recipe to our testing party. Again, it's unlike any other chicken salad I've tasted, and I thought I'd been around—food, that is.

DRESSING

1 1/2 cups mayonnaise
1 tablespoon Italian seasoning, crushed
1 tablespoon lemon juice
1/2 teaspoon minced garlic

1/2 teaspoon sugar
1/2 teaspoon salt
1/4 teaspoon red chili pepper flakes

Combine all ingredients and let mellow at room temperature about 1/2 hour. Refrigerate until ready to use.

SALAD

1/4 cup butter
1 teaspoon minced garlic
8 chicken breast halves, cut in 3/4-inch
 chunks
1 red pepper, julienned

1 green pepper, julienned
1 pound asparagus, stems peeled, sliced diagonally 1/8 inch thick
Rediccio for garnish (if unavailable, use inner leaves of red cabbage, shredded)

Melt butter and add garlic. Sauté chicken just until white and cooked through, 4–5 minutes. Toss chicken with peppers, asparagus, and dressing in bowl. Refrigerate several hours before serving.

Arrange individual servings on bed of rediccio. Serve at room temperature.

SALADE DE POULET

SERVES 6

Ma Maison is one of our favorite watering holes in L.A. Patrick Terrial and Pierre Groleau manage it to perfection. Not only this, but the latter is a tiger as a fourth for tennis, provided he's your partner.

You'll see everyone from Orson Welles to Sara Lee Burke from Oklahoma City, who has come to see everyone from TV and the movies. Sara Lee will not only see them, but she'll enjoy marvelously inventive food.

This is one of my favorites—but do serve the optionals with it. It's lovely to look at and delightful to taste. The moutarde de Meaux is found in fine specialty shops. It has wine and herbs and its very own definite flavor. Before giving up on the recipe, blend your own by adding 1 teaspoon red wine, 1/2 teaspoon variety of dried herbs and 1/4 teaspoon crushed green peppercorns to 2 tablespoons Dijon mustard.

1 3-pound chicken, boiled and cooled
1 medium Golden Delicious apple, peeled, cored, and cut into 1/2-inch cubes
1 celery stalk, cut into 1/4-inch cubes
1 tablespoon capers
2 tablespoons moutarde de Meaux
1/2 cup mayonnaise (approximately)

Salt and freshly ground white pepper
Lemon juice
Tomatoes (optional)
Cooked french-cut or sliced green beans (optional)
Hard-cooked egg slices (optional)

Remove skin from chicken. Peel meat from bones and shred. (Do not cut with knife.)

Combine chicken, apple, celery, capers, and mustard. Add enough mayonnaise to coat lightly. Season to taste with salt, pepper, and lemon juice. Add more mustard if desired. Chill until ready to use.

To serve, place salad on large serving plate. Garnish with tomatoes, green beans, and slices of hard-cooked egg.

ORIENTAL NOODLE AND CHICKEN SALAD

SERVES 8

Despite its title this isn't another Chinese chicken salad. I first tasted it in Singapore, which has as many different cuisines as it has nationalities. Each group has held on to its native cooking, as we have here. This recipe comes from Indonesia, I believe. When I was enjoying it (maybe wallowing in it would be more descriptive), I didn't ask questions—except about the ingredients.

3 skinless chicken breasts
2 cups chicken broth
1 small onion, quartered
1/2 stalk celery, thickly sliced

1 bay leaf
3 peppercorns
2 sprigs parsley

In saucepan, combine chicken breasts, chicken broth, onion, celery, bay leaf, peppercorns, and parsley. Bring broth to a boil and simmer chicken over moderately low heat for 5 minutes. Turn off heat and let chicken breasts sit in broth for 20 minutes.

Remove chicken. Strain broth through sieve into another saucepan. Save all but 1/2 cup for some future use. Reduce 1/2 cup of broth to 1/3 cup and reserve it to make Creamy Peanut Sauce. After chicken breasts are cooled, shred by hand.

MARINADE

3 tablespoons soy sauce
1 teaspoon sesame seed oil
1/2 teaspoon finely minced garlic
1/2 teaspoon finely minced ginger root
1 teaspoon salt
1 1/2 teaspoons Chinese chili paste with

garlic (if unavailable use 1/4 teaspoon cayenne pepper to 1/2 small garlic clove, crushed)
1 tablespoon rice wine vinegar
1 teaspoon sugar

Pour marinade over chicken, mix well, and refrigerate.

NOODLES

3 quarts water
1 tablespoon peanut oil
1 teaspoon salt

6 ounces (approximately) thin Chinese egg noodles or spaghettini

In 4-quart pot, bring water, peanut oil, and salt to a boil. Add noodles and cook until they are *al dente.* Drain noodles in colander, rinse with cold running water, and drain well.

Transfer noodles to large platter or bowl and toss with chicken. Taste for seasoning. You may have to add a little salt or light soy sauce.

VEGETABLES

1 1/2 cups bean sprouts
1 whole cucumber, peeled, shredded, salted, and drained well

2 medium-sized carrots, shredded
1/2 cup thinly sliced scallions including some of green portion

Blanch bean sprouts for 30 seconds in boiling salted water. Drain quickly in colander and rinse with cold running water.

Place on top of chicken-noodle mixture. Add cucumbers, carrots, and scallions.

CREAMY PEANUT SAUCE

1/2 cup peanut butter (I like crunchy style)
1/3 cup reserved chicken broth
1/4 cup soy sauce
3 tablespoons sesame seed oil
1 tablespoon finely minced garlic
1 tablespoon minced peeled ginger root

1 tablespoon sugar
2 tablespoons red wine vinegar
2 teaspoons chili paste with garlic or hot pepper oil
1/4 cup heavy cream

In food processor using metal blade, blend peanut butter, chicken broth, soy sauce, sesame seed oil, minced garlic, ginger root, sugar, vinegar, and chili paste until mixture is blended. With motor running, add cream in a stream and blend mixture until smooth.

Early in the day or just before assembling salad, prepare rice sticks.

RICE STICKS

1 package uncooked rice noodles (Maifun)
3 cups oil

Place oil in wok for deep-frying. When oil is very hot (375°F.), drop half the rice sticks into wok. When rice sticks separate and rise to the surface, remove immediately with tongs and drain on paper towels. Repeat with remaining rice sticks.

Add 1/2 cup of Creamy Peanut Sauce to chicken-vegetable mixture. Fold half of the rice sticks into chicken-vegetable mixture. Use remaining rice sticks as bed for salad.

Serve salad with Creamy Peanut Sauce in bowl on side or place a healthy tablespoonful on each portion. If it's a buffet, insist that each guest use a glob of sauce on each salad serving.

HOT SEAFOOD SALAD

This is another recipe from Peggy Greenbaum of Palm Springs—originally Louisiana. She has a tennis tournament every year along with the Kirk Douglases. Peggy's Saturday luncheons are the high points for me. I may not always come in numero uno in the tournament, but I always win first place in the buffet line. She served this one with the Mandarin Orange Salad on page 118. They were cooling complements.

1/2 pound cooked crab meat
1/2 pound cooked shrimp
2 tablespoons finely chopped scallions
1/4 cup finely chopped green pepper
1 cup finely chopped celery
4-ounce can water chestnuts, finely chopped
10-ounce package frozen peas, cooked
1 cup cooked rice

1 teaspoon Worcestershire sauce
1 cup mayonnaise
1/2 teaspoon salt
1/2 teaspoon pepper
Dash of cayenne pepper
1 1/2 cups fresh fried croutons or dry roasted cashews, finely crumbled

Preheat oven to 325°F.

Mix all ingredients together except croutons or cashews. Place in casserole and top with croutons or cashews. Bake for 30 minutes.

SALMON MOUSSE ON MOLDED CUCUMBER SALAD

1 tablespoon vegetable oil
6 scallions, white part only
3/4 cup ricotta cheese *or* 3/4 cup low-fat cottage cheese
6 1/2-ounce can red salmon, drained, with skin and bones removed, plus 8 ounces fresh red salmon, cooked (If fresh salmon is not available, use a 15 1/2-ounce can red salmon.)
3/4 cup mayonnaise
3/4 teaspoon salt
2 teaspoons Dijon mustard
2 tablespoons lemon juice
1/2 teaspoon Tabasco sauce
Dash of Worcestershire sauce

4 packages unflavored gelatin, plus 1 1/2 teaspoons
1 1/2 cups cold water
1/2 cup fish stock or clam juice
1 cup fresh dill sprigs *or* watercress, stems removed
1 large cucumber, peeled
1 zucchini, peeled
1 green pepper
1 cup sour cream
2 tablespoons white wine vinegar
Lemon or lime slices, dill or watercress sprigs, and tomato or radish roses for garnish

Pour vegetable oil into 5 1/2 to 6-cup fish mold and coat entire surface with oil.

In food processor fitted with the steel blade, mince 4 scallions. Through feed tube, add ricotta cheese or cottage cheese and process until smooth. Add salmon, 1/4 cup mayonnaise, 1/4 teaspoon salt, mustard, lemon juice, Tabasco, and Worcestershire. Process until smooth and well mixed, scraping sides as necessary. Add 1 package unflavored gelatin dissolved in 1/2 cup water. Taste and correct seasonings if necessary.

Spoon salmon mixture into fish mold; tap mold gently on counter top to settle contents. Cover with plastic wrap and refrigerate while preparing dill or watercress mixture.

Place fish stock or clam juice in measuring cup and add 1 1/2 teaspoons gelatin. Put cup in pan of hot water and stir until gelatin is completely dissolved. After salmon layer has thickened, spread layer of dill sprigs or watercress over and around it, out to edges, so it will be visible when unmolded. Spoon gelatin mixture over dill or watercress and chill thoroughly before adding vegetable layer.

With medium shredding disk, shred cucumber, zucchini, and green pepper; you should have about 4 cups. Drain vegetables, pat dry with paper towels or wring out gently in tea towel, and set aside.

Mince 2 scallions in processor fitted with metal blade. Add sour cream, 1/2 teaspoon salt, 1/2 cup mayonnaise, and vinegar; process until well mixed.

Add 3 packages gelatin to 1 cup cold water in small saucepan. Place over low heat and stir until gelatin is completely dissolved.

Add dissolved gelatin to food processor and let machine run for 5 seconds. Add vegetable mixture; turn machine off and on twice to blend. Spoon mixture into fish mold over dill or watercress layer. Cover with plastic wrap and refrigerate for at least 5 hours or overnight.

To unmold, carefully run a flexible knife around inside edge of fish mold. Place serving platter on top of mold and quickly invert it. If salad is not immediately released, rinse towel in hot water, place it over entire surface of mold, and tap lightly to release. Garnish with lemon or lime slices, dill or watercress sprigs, and tomato or radish roses.

MOLDED CHICKEN AND HAM   SERVES 8 TO 10

2 cups cooked chicken, chopped
1 cup cooked ham, chopped
2/3 cup each chopped celery, green pepper, and scallions
1/4 cup pimiento, chopped
1 tablespoon parsley, minced
1 tablespoon lemon juice
1 teaspoon salt
1/8 teaspoon freshly ground white pepper
1/8 teaspoon cayenne pepper

2 tablespoons unflavored gelatin
1/2 cup cold water
1 cup milk
1 cup chicken stock
2 tablespoons Madeira *or* sweet sherry *or* white wine
2 teaspoons Dijon mustard
2 egg yolks, beaten
1/2 cup heavy cream
4 deviled eggs

Combine chicken, ham, celery, green pepper, scallions, pimiento, parsley, lemon juice, salt, white pepper, and cayenne. Set aside.

Soften gelatin in 1/4 cup cold water in top of double boiler. Add remaining water, milk, chicken stock, and wine and cook until gelatin is completely dissolved. Add mustard and egg yolks. Cook and stir over boiling water until mixture coats spoon.

Combine gelatin-mustard-milk mixture with meat-vegetable mixture and chill until the consistency of egg whites. Whip cream until stiff and fold in.

Pour 3 tablespoons of mixture into bottom of well-oiled 9-inch ring mold and refrigerate.

When almost set, lay deviled eggs, stuffed side down, in aspic. Pour remaining mixture into mold. Chill three hours. Unmold by dipping mold into pan of warm (not hot) water for about 30 seconds. The water should come almost to the top of the mold. Then cover with serving plate, invert, and aspic should slide out easily.

Garnished with olives, pimientos, tiny fresh mushrooms, or whatever strikes your fancy—or, as I did, remaining two deviled eggs with pimiento strips in between.

DEVILED EGGS

6 hard-boiled eggs
1 teaspoon Dijon mustard
1 teaspoon mayonnaise

Dash Worcestershire sauce
Salt and pepper to taste

Cut eggs in half lengthwise and remove yolks. Mash yolks and mix with remaining ingredients. Stuff whites with yolk mixture, but don't pile it too high.

LOBSTER BEIGNETS
YIELDS ABOUT 2 DOZEN

This can be served alone or with my favorite Seafood Cocktail Sauce.

1 cup flour
1 tablespoon baking powder
2 scallions, finely sliced
2 ounces pimiento, minced
1 clove garlic, finely minced
1 cup water

1 tablespoon olive oil
1/2 pound lobster tail, cooked, peeled, and
   chopped
Salt to taste
Tabasco sauce to taste

Mix ingredients in order listed. Cover bowl with wet towel and set aside in warm place for about 30 minutes.

Mix again, and drop spoonfuls into hot oil (about 325°F.) until lightly browned. Drain on paper towels and serve alone or with Seafood Cocktail Sauce.

SEAFOOD COCKTAIL SAUCE

1 cup chili sauce
2 tablespoons pickle relish
1–2 tablespoons horseradish

1 teaspoon Worchestershire sauce
Dash of Tabasco sauce

Combine and allow to mellow at least 1 hour before serving.

PIROSHKI PIE

This is wonderful as a luncheon dish or for a very hungry cocktail crowd. It can also be baked in a very shallow oblong baking dish, cut into squares, and served very hot. It is the combination of textures and temperatures that makes this a real treat. Just in case there is anybody who thinks he or she doesn't like liver, just tell them it's a Russian meat pie.

FILLING

1 medium onion
2 tablespoons oil
1 pound calves' liver, *or* 1/2 pound each
   lean ground beef and calves' liver, cut into

large chunks
2 hard-boiled eggs, finely chopped
Salt and freshly ground black pepper
3/4 teaspoon sugar

Chop onion in food processor using metal blade. Sauté onions in skillet in oil until transparent.

While onions are sautéing, without cleaning blade or bowl of food processor, chop liver or liver and beef in processor. When onions are transparent, add meat and eggs. Sauté mixture until liver is just done—it should be only slightly pink. Beef can be cooked a minute or two longer than liver. Add salt, a generous amount of pepper, and sugar. Taste for seasoning. This may be made in the morning and placed in refrigerator until you are ready to make pastry. Bring to room temperature before baking.

PASTRY DOUGH

2 cups flour
1 teaspoon salt
1 egg
1 tablespoon chilled sour cream

1/2 cup (1 stick) butter, chilled and cut into
   chunks
1 egg, beaten with 1 tablespoon water (egg
   wash)

Blend all ingredients except egg wash in food processor fitted with the metal or plastic blade, turning off and on until dough forms ball around blade.

Roll dough into waxed paper and chill for 30 minutes if you have time. If not, cut in half, roll each half in waxed paper, and place in freezer for about 10 minutes. It really should be well chilled before it is rolled out.

Preheat oven to 400°F.

On lightly floured surface, roll out dough to fit 9-inch pie tin or glass pie dish. Line pie tin with bottom crust. Add filling. Roll out top crust and place on top of filling, crimping edges. Make a few slits on top crust. Brush top with egg wash. Bake on center rack of oven 10–12 minutes or until crust is golden brown. Serve very hot with gobs of cold sour cream for dipping.

FLÄSKPANNKAKA

There is a Swedish home-style restaurant in Rockford, Illinois. I thought it would be a great surprise for John Rodby, our talented Swede who functions as arranger-conductor-pianist and presides over all new orchestras we encounter on our concert tours. Dinner at the Stockholm Inn is promptly at 6:00 P.M. It is just truly down-home-genuine Swedish food. The rest of our traveling troupe loved it but John wanted a cheeseburger! How was I to know he'd had enough down-home-genuine Swedish cooking to last him a lifetime in his truly genuine down-home Swedish family? At any rate this was the one I gave a few stars to. They serve it as an entrée; I love it for breakfast. Fläskpannkaka is traditionally served with lingonberries on top. I can't imagine it with anything else.

1 pound salt pork
1 cup flour
1/3 cup sugar

5 1/3 cups milk
9 eggs, slightly beaten
2 16-ounce cans or jars lingonberries

Preheat oven to 350°F.

Dice and brown salt pork. Drain on paper towels.

Mix flour and sugar together and add enough of milk to make a paste. Then add eggs and remaining milk.

Place salt pork in the bottom of a 10 × 14-inch ovenproof pan. Pour milk-egg mixture over salt pork. Bake 1 1/2 hours or until set. Serve with lingonberries on the side or on the top.

TOMATO PARMESAN PIE

Pastry for single 9-inch pie crust, unbaked
3/4 cup freshly grated Parmesan cheese
6 scallions, thinly sliced including tops
2–3 ripe tomatoes, cut into 1/2-inch slices
Flour
1/2 cup mushrooms, sliced

2 eggs
1 cup heavy cream
1/4 teaspoon nutmeg
1/4 teaspoon thyme
Salt and pepper

Preheat oven to 400°F.

Line a 9-inch Pyrex pie plate with pastry. Flute edges. Sprinkle bottom of crust with 2 tablespoons cheese and half of onions. Dredge tomato slices with flour. Place in pastry in single layer. Sprinkle tomatoes with half the cheese, remaining onions, and the mushrooms.

Combine eggs, cream, nutmeg, thyme, salt, and pepper. Beat well. Pour over tomatoes, tilting pan to settle cream to bottom. Sprinkle with remaining cheese.

Bake 45–50 minutes, or until pie filling is set and crust is browned. Let pie set for 15 minutes before cutting.

CAULIFLOWER CHEESE PIE

Melissa is my B.D.—Beautiful Daughter—She called one day with this unusual contribution to "the book." It's special—and, of course, so is she!

CRUST

2 cups peeled and grated raw potatoes,
  firmly packed
1/2 teaspoon salt

1 egg, beaten
1/4 cup grated onion
Oil

Preheat oven to 400°F.

    Set freshly grated potato in colander over bowl, salt, and let drain for 10 minutes. Squeeze out excess water and refrigerate (can be used for soup stock). Transfer potatoes to bowl and add remaining ingredients. Pat mixture into well-oiled 9-inch pie pan, building sides of crust up with lightly floured fingers. Bake 40 to 45 minutes or until browned. After first thirty minutes brush crust with a little oil to crisp it. Carefully remove from oven and reduce heat to 375°F.

CUSTARD

1/2 teaspoon salt
2 eggs
1/4 cup milk

Freshly ground black pepper
Paprika

Beat together all ingredients except paprika. Set aside.

FILLING

3 tablespoons butter
1 cup chopped onions
1 medium clove garlic, crushed
Salt
Dash of thyme

1/2 teaspoon basil
2 tablespoons chopped fresh parsley
1 medium cauliflower, broken into small
  flowerets
1 3/4 cups grated Cheddar cheese

Melt butter in skillet and sauté onions and garlic, lightly salted, for 5 minutes.

    Add herbs and cauliflower and cook, covered, for 10 minutes, stirring occasionally.

    Layer baked crust with half of cheese, then herbs and cauliflower, then remaining cheese. Pour custard over and dust with paprika. Bake 35–40 minutes or until set.

MELISSA

Chapter 5

SALADS AND SALAD DRESSINGS

Salads are so important in California, we serve them first. Many other areas of the country have adopted this custom, I know, because with pencil and order pad in hand, the waiter recites the familiar singsong, "Soup or salad?" But in most parts of the country it's served with dinner—a little break in the main course and a bite of crisp and cold between warm meat and potatoes. At formal dinner parties, it's served right after the entree with possibly a wedge of some marvelous runny cheese—Brie or Camembert—and some crusty French bread. That cheese may be dessert if you've had a heavy meal. Serve it with the best fresh fruits in season—plums, pears, apples, peaches, whatever is in—a choice for your well-fed friends.

If it's one of those meals-unto-itself salads you want, this chapter is for you. Try the Bleu Cheese and Bacon Potato Salad or the Beverly Hills Tennis Club Salad. Certainly the Weaver Whatever-you-have-on-hand Salad is a meal and a half, and the light Mandarin Orange Salad takes care of sweet salad lovers.

The greens available are varied, and just buying a firm head of lettuce doesn't satisfy us any longer. A mixed green salad should be more than that. It can be a variety of green, crisp lettuces from iceberg to arugula (I only discovered it recently too; *rugula* in Italian, it's a dark-green, strong—almost bitter—green that bites back), bibb to butter, red-leaf to spinach. When you can find them, bring them home and tenderly wash, remove wilted or brown outer leaves (save for soup), drain on paper towels, and place in plastic bag with some of the paper towels if you're not sure it's moisture-free. Tear into bite-sized pieces and serve with a small amount of a light, well-flavored dressing. Don't drown it, and please don't throw a gob of dressing on top of your greens and let it dribble where it may. Just toss gently and lovingly until every leaf is thoroughly coated. (Of course if your greens are still wet, the dressing won't hold and you'll have a bland bunch of green stuff.)

A word about the dressing. If it's your French-style vinaigrette, make a large batch well ahead; it will keep in a jar for weeks. Place a garlic clove in the jar and shake well before using. Some say you should never wash the jar—just keep adding ingredients in that same, now well-seasoned jar.

If you're using cucumbers or some vegetable that needs marinating, place them on the bottom of your salad bowl, pour the dressing over them, then place your other greens on top and set the salad bowl in the refrigerator until you're ready to serve. Always toss from the bottom to coat the whole works. This is last-minute stuff, you understand—greens wilt quickly.

For a light meal, consider a heavier salad. For instance, simple broiled fish or a chicken will be enhanced with a mixed salad and one of the creamier dressings. Conversely, a heavier meal needs a light touch—a salad with French or Italian dressing. If you have glass or crystal bowls, stack those in the refrigerator for a little while, and serve your chilled jewel of a salad in a frosty setting.

FRIED BRIE GREEN SALAD

SERVES 6

2 heads bibb or limestone, red-leaf, or butter
   lettuce
1 heart of romaine, outer leaves removed
1 Belgian endive
1 bunch watercress, stems removed
1 1/2 pound round good brie, cut into

1/2-inch wedges
1 egg beaten with 2 tablespoons water
1/2 cup fresh fried bread crumbs
1/4 cup light vegetable oil
1/4 cup clarified butter
1/2 cup Basic French Dressing (page 11)

Wash lettuces thoroughly, rinse, and pat dry. Wrap lightly in tea towel and place in refrigerator until ready to serve.

Dip brie wedges in egg mixture and roll in bread crumbs, being sure to coat thoroughly. Chill.

Heat oil and butter in skillet just prior to serving and while it is heating, mix greens thoroughly in large bowl and set aside. When oil is hot, drop in chilled brie wedges two or three at a time (no more—they should not touch while browning). Brown lightly and quickly so cheese doesn't get runny and ruin the nice crust in which they've been rolled.

Pour dressing over greens in salad bowl. Toss lightly until greens are well coated. Place on 6 individual salad plates. Place fried brie on top of each salad and serve immediately.

GREEN SALAD WITH FRESH HERB DRESSING

SERVES 4–6

A fresh, light, and typically California salad. Of course, the ingredients are variable. The lovely thing about salads and dressings is that they are to your taste and use what you have on hand. A small amount of leftover cooked string beans, an artichoke heart or two, broccoli flowerets, jicama, fresh spinach leaves and, for color, sweet red pepper strips and a couple of black olives sliced—just be sure you only use three or four things instead of eight or ten.

Wrap salad greens in a tea towel to absorb all moisture after they have been washed. Place greens in salad bowl in the refrigerator. Bowl will be frosty and greens will be crisp, chilled, and dry to absorb your dressing.

1 small head Boston lettuce, chilled and torn
   into bite-sized pieces
2 Belgian endive, chilled and torn into
   bite-sized pieces or cut into matchstick slivers

2 tablespoons chopped parsley
1/2 cup Fresh Herb Dressing (page 11)
6 sprigs watercress for garnish

Shake dressing vigorously; pour 1/2 cup over salad and toss lightly until greens are well coated. Add more if you need it, but use only as much as greens need—don't drench them. Garnish with watercress. Serve immediately.

SALAD GREENS WITH GOAT CHEESE AND GARLIC CROUTONS

SERVES 6–8

I met a marvelous and very attractive gentleman when I did a little cooking seminar in Napa Valley, California. Everybody in Napa Valley cooks and dines and wines, and Jeremiah Tower is one of the best cooking, wining, and dining instructors there. This is a sample of his creative cuisine.

Salad greens: bitter greens and lettuces like curly endive, Belgian endive, romaine, watercress, young spinach leaves, arugula (Italian greens that are superb!), etc.
6–8 small rounds of goat cheese
1/2 cup olive oil

1/2 cup fresh white bread crumbs
2 tablespoons vinegar or lemon juice
1/2 teaspoon salt
1/4 teaspoon freshly ground black pepper
3/4–1 cup crouton rounds

Wash and trim various greens. Dry and store in towels in refrigerator or, to use right away, do not refrigerate as greens should be at room temperature when used.

Dip rounds of goat cheese in 3 tablespoons olive oil and then in bread crumbs. Refrigerate at least 30 minutes.

Heat 2 tablespoons olive oil in sauté pan; sauté cheese until light golden crust forms on cheese. Reserve oil for frying croutons.

Mix vinegar or lemon juice with salt and pepper in bowl. Whisk in 3 tablespoons olive oil.

Place greens in bowl, pour dressing over all, mix and toss well. Place salad on warm plate, the cheese in center of greens (one round for each person).

Quickly fry croutons in reserved olive oil and place 4 or 5 croutons around edge of each salad plate.

ROMAINE AND STRAWBERRY SALAD GIOVANNI

SERVES 4

During strawberry season I'd fly to Cleveland for this one.

1 large head romaine *or* 2 bunches watercress *or* 1 pound baby leaf spinach
1 pint fresh strawberries, washed, hulled, and sliced in half
1/2 red onion, peeled and thinly sliced
6 tablespoons imported olive oil

2 tablespoons wine vinegar
1/2 tablespoon dry mustard
1/2 tablespoon sugar
Juice from 1/2 lemon
Salt and freshly ground black pepper

Separate leaves of romaine, watercress, or spinach, discarding any bruised or brown parts. Wash thoroughly under cold water. Drain in colander to remove as much water as possible. Wrap in tea towel to ensure that greens will be dry and crisp.

Tear leaves into bite-sized pieces and place in salad bowl with strawberries and onion slices.

In small mixing bowl, whisk together olive oil, vinegar, dry mustard, sugar, and lemon juice. (This can be done ahead of time.)

Just before serving, add remaining salad dressing. Toss carefully and thoroughly, trying not to bruise strawberries. Add salt and freshly ground pepper to taste.

NOTE If your onions are strong, put half of dressing in bottom of salad bowl and marinate sliced onions until ready to use.

GREEN SALAD WITH BELGIAN ENDIVE, VINAIGRETTE
SERVES 6

I never met Miss Dannenbaum but I feel I know her well. She was gracious enough to send me several very special, very simple to prepare, perfectly seasoned recipes at my request after I heard about her special culinary talents.

She lives in Philadelphia and teaches there. Her pupils must learn the finer points of this art without a lot of unnecessary flourishes.

4 heads bibb lettuce
6 heads Belgian endive
8 tablespoons olive oil
2 to 3 tablespoons sherry vinegar

2 tablespoons finely chopped shallots
1 teaspoon salt
1/2 teaspoon freshly cracked white pepper

Wash and dry lettuce and endives. Trim root of endives and remove any discolored leaves. Cut heads lengthwise into matchsticks. Dry thoroughly.

Toss lettuce and endives in chilled salad bowl with vinaigrette dressing made by mixing together olive oil, vinegar, shallots, salt, and pepper. Serve immediately and proudly.

MUSHROOM SALAD
SERVES 4

I don't use lettuce with this one. It's delicate, low-cal, and delightful as is.

12 medium-large mushrooms
2 tablespoons finely chopped scallions
2 tablespoons finely chopped parsley
2 tablespoons white vinegar

2 teaspoons Dijon mustard
1 scant teaspoon salt
White pepper
4 tablespoons light salad oil

Clean mushrooms with damp paper towels. Cut off any woody bottoms. Slice mushrooms, including stems, very thin. Set aside.

In small bowl place scallions, parsley, vinegar, mustard, salt, and pepper. Gradually, in a thin stream, dribble in oil, whisking constantly with a wire whisk. Or place ingredients in food processor bowl and blend for 1 1/2 minutes, adding oil very gradually in thin stream. It will have a creamy consistency. Pour over mushrooms. Mix lightly but thoroughly.

ISABELLE SALAD   SERVES 4

Le Dome is very special. It's on the Sunset Strip in West Hollywood and is very popular, yet quiet. I'll bet more great show business deals are made there per table than in anybody's studio office.

It's elegant yet homey—and the food!!! It takes great talent and originality to make unusual dishes with an economy of ingredients and effort. See page 250 for Le Dome's Cold Pasta Salad.

3/4 cup thinly sliced mushrooms (approximately 4 medium mushrooms)
3/4 cup thinly sliced tart apple (approximately 1/2 apple)
3/4 cup thinly sliced celery hearts (approximately 3 stalks)
3/4 cup artichoke hearts (approximately 1

7-ounce can), cut into quarters or thinly sliced
Salad Dressing
1 teaspoon fresh chervil or 1/2 teaspoon dried
1 teaspoon finely minced fresh parsley

Gently mix mushrooms, apples, celery, and artichoke hearts in salad bowl. Chill in refrigerator.

Pour dressing over chilled salad and mix gently but thoroughly. Top with chervil and parsley.

SALAD DRESSING

1 tablespoon lemon juice
2 tablespoons salad oil

1/2 teaspoon salt
1/4 teaspoon pepper

Mix all ingredients and blend well.

BLACK-EYED PEA SALAD   SERVES 8

1/2 pound dried black-eyed peas, soaked overnight in enough cold water to cover them by 2 inches
1/3 cup red wine vinegar
1 teaspoon salt

Pepper to taste
1 cup olive or vegetable oil
1 onion, thinly sliced
3/4 cup garlic cloves
1/4 cup minced parsley

Drain peas, transfer to large saucepan with water to cover, and bring water to a boil. Simmer peas, adding boiling water as needed to keep them covered, for 30 minutes or until they are tender.

Drain peas in colander and transfer them to a ceramic or glass bowl.

In a small bowl combine vinegar, salt, and pepper. Add olive or vegetable oil in a stream, whisking, and pour dressing over peas while they are still warm, tossing to coat beans. Add onion, garlic, and parsley, toss salad, and chill it, covered, overnight. Remove garlic before serving. Serve in a chilled bowl on a bed of shredded lettuce surrounded by the prettiest outer leaves.

BLEU CHEESE AND BACON POTATO SALAD
SERVES 8

I haven't found anybody who didn't love this one. It's different from your usual potato salad (which I could eat by the pound too)—the hot bacon makes a crisp difference.

3 pounds new potatoes, steamed and quartered
1/3 cup dry white wine
1/3 cup chicken broth
1/3 cup minced parsley

1/3 cup sliced scallions
8 ounces bleu cheese
3/4 cup Basic French Dressing (page 11)
1/4 pound bacon, cut into 1/2-inch pieces

In a large bowl combine potatoes, while they are still warm, with white wine, chicken broth, parsley and scallions, tossing mixture gently with rubber spatulas. Let cool.

Crumble bleu cheese over mixture, add French dressing, and toss gently with same spatulas. Chill salad, covered, for at least 4 hours.

Cook bacon over moderately high heat until crisp, and drain on paper towels.

Transfer salad to salad bowl, sprinkle with bacon, and serve at room temperature.

AVOCADO, CARROT, AND ORANGE JUICE SALAD
SERVES 4

This is pretty to see, and smooth, sweet, and hot to taste.

2 tablespoons seedless raisins
1/4 cup warm water
1 cup fresh orange juice
1/2 teaspoon salt
1/8 teaspoon crushed red pepper

1/8 teaspoon finely grated fresh ginger root
2 cups coarsely grated carrots
1 large, ripe avocado, chilled
3 tablespoons fresh lemon juice

Place raisins in small bowl, cover with warm water, and soak for 20 minutes. Drain.

Combine orange juice, salt, red pepper, and ginger in a deep bowl. Add carrots and turn them about with spoon to moisten thoroughly. Refrigerate at least 1 hour.

Just before serving, cut avocado in half. With tip of small knife, loosen seed and lift it out. Remove any tissuelike fibers clinging to flesh. Strip off skin with your fingers, starting at narrow stem end. (The dark-skinned variety does not peel easily; if necessary, use a small sharp knife to pull skin away.)

Cut avocado halves lengthwise into 2 sections, place each quarter on a chilled individual serving plate, and sprinkle with lemon juice. With a slotted spoon, mound carrot mixture in cavities of avocado quarters. Scatter raisins on top. Moisten each filled avocado with a little of remaining orange marinade and serve at once.

WEAVER WHATEVER-YOU-HAVE-ON-HAND SALAD SERVES 8 TO 10 TO 12

Dennis Weaver and his wife, Gerry, are very much into health foods and natural ingredients. He whipped up this combination on our TV show one day. You can use some or all of the ingredients. We blew the vegetable budget for the week and used them all. I might add there wasn't enough left over to feed a midget mouse.

Use all or any of the following:

Mixed lettuce—romaine, bibb, butter, iceberg, red-leaf, leaf, etc.
1 bunch watercress
1 head cabbage, grated
3 zucchini, grated
3 tomatoes, chopped
1 cucumber, grated or sliced
2 cups diced Cheddar cheese
2 cups cottage cheese
3 hard-boiled eggs, sliced

2 apples, thinly sliced
1 green pepper, chopped
1 bunch scallions, chopped including tops
1 carrot, grated
1 cup alfalfa sprouts
1 cup bean sprouts
2 avocados, chopped
3/4 cup raw peas
3/4 cup mixed walnuts, sunflower seeds,
   sesame seeds, almonds

I put the whole thing in an enormous bowl, slightly smaller than a washtub. Actually, your industrial-size mixing bowl will hold it nicely, or put it in 2 separate mixing bowls and mix well with your favorite dressing. Mine is on page 11 (the Fresh Herb Dressing); just triple the amount.

SPINACH SALAD FOR TWO SERVES 2

John Forsythe (sigh) visited my show one day and brought the chef from the great San Francisco restaurant The Blue Fox with him. I don't remember too much else about the show. I think they cooked, John poured the wine, and I stared—instead of asking questions.

3 bunches fresh spinach, thoroughly cleaned (for salad, use the heart only—the "baby" leaves)
2 tablespoons bacon, chopped and cooked crisp
Juice of 1/2 lemon
2 teaspoons Worcestershire sauce
Salt and pepper to taste
1/2 cup olive oil (approximately)
1/2 teaspoon dry English mustard
2 1/2–3 tablespoons wine vinegar

Place spinach in bowl.

Lightly sauté together bacon, lemon juice, Worcestershire sauce, salt and pepper, olive oil, and mustard. After a minute, add wine vinegar and heat for a few seconds.

Flip pan over top of bowl containing spinach; hold pan over bowl *for at least 30 seconds,* so steam from pan wilts spinach.

Toss and serve immediately on plates that are room temperature or slightly warmed.

CUCUMBER SALAD WITH RED ONIONS AND GINGER
SERVES 6–8

This tangy, unusual cucumber salad is another Ben Moy creation. It all happens in Evanston, Illinois, just outside of Chicago. If you can't get to Evanston this week, you can still sample a few of his wonders: page 93 for the Crispy Chicken Salad and page 191 for the Ginger Beef with Bourbon.

Salt
6 young cucumbers, peeled
2 tablespoons sugar
2 large red onions, peeled and thinly sliced
1/2 cup sliced peeled ginger root
2 tablespoons chopped fresh cilantro
Dressing
1 teaspoon sesame seed oil

Rub salt on cucumbers lightly. Set aside for 15 minutes. Rinse in cold water; remove seeds and slice. Sprinkle sugar over cucumbers and mix well. Marinate approximately 2 hours.

Add onions, ginger root, and cilantro to cucumbers. Mix well and pour half of dressing over mixture. Add salt to taste. Add more dressing, if needed, keep remaining dressing for use at another time.

Cover and let chill 10 minutes to 1/2 hour before serving. Add sesame seed oil just before serving.

DRESSING

1 cup less 2 tablespoons cider vinegar
3/4 cup light soy sauce
1/2 cup chopped scallions (white part only)
2 tablespoons white wine
1 tablespoon finely chopped fresh ginger root
1/4 teaspoon ground white pepper

In a bowl, mix all ingredients until well blended.

CUCUMBER SALAD

SERVES 4

Sutter's Restaurant is one of the most famous and popular in Cleveland. They have very special ways of preparing meats and vegetables—here's the simple cucumber dressed à la Sutter. The little shrimp and crab claw garnishes don't hurt.

2 cucumbers, thinly sliced
1/2 onion, thinly sliced
1 teaspoon tarragon vinegar
2 tablespoons sour cream

Salt and pepper to taste
1/2 teaspoon paprika
Crab claws, shrimp, and black olives for garnish

Combine cucumbers, onions, vinegar, sour cream, salt, and pepper; mix well and chill.

Sprinkle with paprika just before serving. Garnish with crab claws, shrimp and black olives.

ENGLISH EGG SALAD

SERVES 8

This salad is best served with cold meats, such as leftover lamb, pork, beef, or poultry. It can also be served as a luncheon dish. Spoon onto toast points or into deep-fried bread cups and quickly heat under broiler until it starts to bubble. Lightly buttered brussels sprouts, broccoli, or asparagus spears are a fine complement.

1/4 cup Dijon mustard
1 teaspoon English mustard (it's hotter than the Dijon)
1/2 cup mayonnaise (your own—it's fresh, fun, and easy to make)
1 tablespoon Worcestershire sauce
Dash of Tabasco sauce
7 large hard-boiled eggs, peeled and coarsely

chopped
3 stalks celery (1 cup), peeled and coarsely chopped
2 large cucumbers (1 cup), peeled, seeded, and coarsely chopped
1 tablespoon capers, minced
1 tablespoon chopped fresh parsley, *or* 1 teaspoon dried parsley flakes

Gently fold together mustards, mayonnaise, Worcestershire, and Tabasco. Combine eggs, celery, cucumber, and capers and gently fold them into mayonnaise mixture. Sprinkle with parsley and chill.

BEAN SPROUT AND RED PEPPER POTATO SALAD

SERVES 8

3 pounds boiling potatoes
1 cup mayonnaise
Scant 1/4 cup light soy sauce
Scant 1/4 cup cider vinegar

Pepper to taste
6 ounces fresh bean sprouts, drained
2 large red peppers, cut into 1/4-inch pieces
1/3 cup snipped chives

Steam potatoes and let cool slightly before cutting into 3/4-inch cubes.

In bowl, combine potatoes while still warm with mixture of mayonnaise, soy sauce, vinegar, and pepper to taste; toss gently with rubber spatulas. Taste for seasoning; you may want to add salt or a little extra soy sauce. Fold in bean sprouts and red peppers.

Chill salad, covered, for at least 2 hours. Transfer to serving bowl and sprinkle with snipped chives.

CELERY ROOT AND PEPPER SALAD
WITH MUSTARD MAYONNAISE   SERVES 4–6

I never could figure out what to do with those big, dark-brown lumps of stuff the greengrocer had amongst the beautiful fresh greens, reds, yellow-orange profusion of the real vegetables until I tasted Celery Root Salad. I know now and I seek out those big lumpy roots to make one of the most delightful salads. You don't need the green peppers, really—for color a tomato or pimiento will do—but try it!

1 pound celery root (3–3 1/2 cups when julienned)
1 1/2 teaspoons salt
1 1/2 teaspoons lemon juice
1 green pepper, seeded

1 sweet red pepper, seeded
Mustard Mayonnaise
1 tablespoon mixed green herbs: basil, tarragon, oregano, rosemary (if dried, use a little less; if fresh, you can heap them on)

Peel celery root and cut into julienne strips. Toss in bowl with salt and lemon juice and set aside for 30 minutes. Rinse strips in cold water, drain, and dry with paper towels.

Cut peppers into julienne strips.

Fold celery root and peppers into mustard mayonnaise and let marinate for 2 to 3 hours.

Garnish with herbs.

MUSTARD MAYONNAISE

5 tablespoons Dijon mustard
3 tablespoons boiling water
1/3 cup olive oil or salad oil
2 tablespoons wine vinegar
Salt and pepper to taste

1/4 cup mayonnaise
2 tablespoons mixed green herbs: basil, tarragon, oregano and a little rosemary, (if dried, use a little less; if fresh, heap them on)

Place mustard in mixing bowl. Add boiling water in thin stream, beating with wire whisk. Beat in oil in thin stream and then beat in vinegar in thin stream and season to taste.

Add mayonnaise (more if necessary) to make a thick, creamy sauce. Add herbs and mix well.

ERNESTO'S GREEK SALAD

SERVES 4–6

I sang in Phoenix—dined at Ernesto's. Both were eminently satisfying. The applause is a lovely memory and I have instant recall on Ernesto's salad and Pasta Mista on page 244. Here's proof.

2 cucumbers, peeled and sliced crosswise
1/2 red onion, thinly sliced
1 large head romaine, torn into bite-sized pieces
4–6 fillets of anchovy, cut into thirds
2 tomatoes, sliced in half and then into

thirds
6 ounces imported feta cheese, coarsely crumbled
12 Greek olives
1 1/2 cups Ernesto's House Dressing

Mix all ingredients except dressing in a large salad bowl; add enough dressing to coat salad. Toss lightly but thoroughly. Reserve leftover dressing in jar in refrigerator for another salad.

ERNESTO'S HOUSE DRESSING

MAKES ABOUT 1 1/2 CUPS

3/4 tablespoon garlic powder
3/4 tablespoon black pepper
1/4 cup Dijon mustard
3/4 tablespoon ground basil
2 eggs
2 tablespoons soy sauce

1/4 cup red wine vinegar
3 teaspoons fresh tarragon
Dash of Tabasco sauce
1/8 teaspoon salt
3/4 cup vegetable oil

Place all ingredients except oil in large mixing bowl or bowl of processor. Using electric mixer or metal blade of processor, blend until all ingredients have become well mixed. (You can also make this in a blender.)

Add oil in very thin stream, mixing or processing constantly. When oil is totally blended, a creamy, delicious, well-seasoned dressing will be the result.

ROASTED PEPPER AND MUSHROOM SALAD

SERVES 5–6

The dressing for this salad can be made well ahead. As a matter of fact, double or triple the recipe and after you've used the 1/2 cup or so you need for the salad, keep the rest on hand for all simple green salads. It keeps and keeps.

5 green bell peppers
Juice of 1/2 lemon
1/2 teaspoon salt

1 pound mushrooms, washed, stems removed
Salt and freshly ground pepper to taste

Preheat oven to 450°F.

Roast peppers 15–20 minutes, or until skins blister and brown. Cool; remove skins by wrapping peppers in a tea towel and gently rubbing until skins slip off. Remove stems and seeds, slice into 1/4-inch-thick strips. Sprinkle with lemon juice and salt. Mix well.

Slice mushroom caps. Combine peppers and mushrooms. Season with salt and pepper as needed. Chill.

SALAD DRESSING

6 tablespoons oil
3 tablespoons apple cider vinegar
1 teaspoon salt
1 teaspoon pepper

1/2 teaspoon Dijon mustard
1/2 teaspoon sugar
1 small clove garlic, cut in half

Mix well. Allow flavors to blend at least 1 hour. Just before serving, toss peppers and mushrooms with dressing. Remove garlic. Serve in chilled bowls.

CHET ATKINS' COLE SLAW
SERVES 6

Chet is a genius of a guitar player. He plays lots of notes and speaks few words. His verbal economy is reflected in his directions for his favorite cole slaw.

Scant 1/2 cup white vinegar
1/4 cup vegetable oil
1/4 cup sugar
1 teaspoon dry mustard

1/2 teaspoon hot sauce
1 teaspoon salt
1 head cabbage, very thinly shredded

Combine all ingredients and chill.

BEVERLY HILLS TENNIS CLUB SALAD
SERVES 4

Who can say when legends start? I have a feeling that the legend of the Beverly Hills Tennis Club started from day one at the first membership meeting. Some of the more staid, conservative establishments wouldn't allow actors, writers, directors, producers, or anyone connected with the town's principal industry into their hallowed enclosures to play tennis. So they started their own club—good athletes, irrepressible, fun-loving, and hard-working. There was hardly a day when you wouldn't see the likes of Clark Gable, Carole Lombard, John Garfield, Charlie Chaplin, Robert Taylor, Gilbert Roland, or any one of the Marx brothers tearing around the court in a hot tennis match. There were other reasons for the fame and legend of the club than just the members. The food was always fine, and the fun and funny matches gave it a sparkle and excitement definitely missing in its sister establishments.

    One story—and please keep in mind the cast of players:
—The chef, Johnny, a Chinese gentleman who, in addition to serving some of the finest Chinese food in L.A., was in charge of keeping the courts spic and span.
—The teaching pro, Jack Cushingham, a handsome, fun-loving over-6-footer, who set up matches, ran tournaments, played with members, and took a lot of guff.
—Charlie Lederer, a sweet, funny fellow and a most prolific screenwriter; not one of your greater tennis players, but definitely one of your fiercer competitors.

Charlie had a running bet with Jack that he could beat him in singles, given crucial conces-
sions—if Jack would play him left-handed, and with one tennis shoe untied. Finally one day, Jack
said, "Charlie, I could beat you tied to an elephant." The next day Charlie showed up, racquet and
new balls in hand—and an elephant in tow. He manacled Jack's ankle to the elephant's and they
played center court. The crowd cheered, the elephant trumpeted, Jack screamed, Charlie won, and
Johnny quit; and the Beverly Hills Tennis Club gained another notch in its rich historic lore and
lost the best pork-fried rice in the city of L.A.

I don't think there have been any similar legend-makers like that in our recent history at the
BHTC, but the tennis is good, the company is fun—and when he can be enticed away from his
beloved bridge game, Amigo Gilbert Roland might come out and play: slim, lean, 26-inch waist,
jaw line clean and square—and the food is terrific. This salad dressing is one of the reasons people
come from miles and oceans and countries away to have a bite at the Club and play a couple of sets.

Thank you, Chef Karl Johannson.

1 1/2-pound head crisp iceberg lettuce, cut
   into small pieces
1/2 pound medium cooked roast beef, diced
1/2 pound cooked chicken or turkey, diced
1/2 pound white mushrooms, sliced
1/2 pound cucumbers, peeled, cored, and

   diced
1/4 pound carrots, peeled and diced
4 tablespoons freshly grated Parmesan
   cheese
1/2 cup garlic croutons
1/4 pound crisp cooked bacon, crumbled

Toss with dressing and serve cold.

DRESSING

MAKES 1 QUART

3 whole eggs
1/4 teaspoon freshly ground black pepper
1/4 teaspoon sugar
1/4 teaspoon salt
1 teaspoon dry mustard

1/2 cup red wine vinegar
1 cup Wishbone Italian dressing
2 cups soybean salad oil
1 cup cold water

Place eggs, pepper, sugar, salt, and dry mustard in food processor. Blend well for
2 minutes. Add vinegar and Italian dressing and mix for another minute. Slowly
add oil, drop by drop from tablespoon, and then add water to thin down dressing.

CAULIFLOWER SALAD WITH
YOGURT DRESSING

SERVES 6

2 1/2 pounds cauliflower
6 cups boiling salted water
3 tablespoons white vinegar
3 hard-cooked eggs
2 cups plain yogurt
1/3 cup olive oil

1/4 cup minced capers
2 tablespoons minced scallions
2 tablespoons lemon juice
4 teaspoons Dijon mustard
Salt and pepper

Trim and separate cauliflower into flowerets. Bring salted water with vinegar to
boil in saucepan, add cauliflower and simmer, covered, 5 minutes. Drain cauliflower in colander, refresh under cold running water, and drain well. Transfer to
salad bowl and let cool.

Remove yolks from hard-cooked eggs. Chop and reserve whites. Force egg yolks through sieve into bowl. Stir in yogurt, a little at a time, and beat in olive oil drop by drop. Stir in capers, scallions, lemon juice, mustard, and salt and pepper to taste.

Pour half of dressing over cauliflower, toss salad carefully, cover and chill 2–4 hours.

Chill remaining dressing and serve on or alongside salad. Garnish with reserved egg whites.

CAULIFLOWER SALAD · SERVES 4–6

For more about Ben Moy and his lovely restaurant, see Crispy Chicken Salad (page 93) and Cucumber Salad with Red Onions and Ginger (page 111). And try this little something he serves to keep you happy before the big meal starts.

1 large head of cauliflower, cored, cut into flowerets
2 tablespoons sugar
1 large red onion, sliced
1/2 cup finely sliced shallots
1/2 cup fresh sorrel (if not available, use 1 tablespoon fresh cilantro)
1/2 cup chopped green onions
1/2 cup sliced radishes
1/4 cup cider vinegar (or to taste)
1/4 tablespoon salt
1 teaspoon sesame seed oil

Blanch cauliflowerets in boiling water for 2 minutes. Submerge in cold water, then drain.

Place cauliflowerets in salad bowl. Add sugar and mix carefully. Set aside for 1 hour.

Add remaining ingredients except sesame seed oil, mix well, and cover. Set aside at room temperature for 1 hour, then refrigerate for 1 hour or until ready to serve. Add sesame seed oil just before serving.

PICKLED VEGETABLE SALAD · SERVES 4 AS LUNCHEON DISH
SERVES 6 AS SIDE DISH

2 medium carrots, peeled
1 small cucumber, peeled and seeded
1/4 pound green beans
1/2 sweet red pepper, seeded
1/2 green pepper, seeded
1/2 cup sliced bamboo shoots
3 macadamia nuts, crushed
1 clove garlic, peeled and finely minced
1 slice fresh ginger root, peeled and finely minced
3 tablespoons water
1/4 cup white or cider vinegar
1 tablespoon sugar
1 teaspoon salt
1/4 teaspoon turmeric
Dash of cayenne pepper
Scant tablespoon peanut or corn oil

Cut carrots, cucumber, green beans, red and green peppers, and bamboo shoots into julienne strips 2 inches long and 1/4 inch thick.

In small bowl, mix together nuts, garlic, ginger, water, vinegar, sugar, salt, turmeric, and cayenne for sauce.

Heat oil in wok or heavy 10 to 12-inch skillet and add sauce. Cook over moderate heat for 3 minutes to blend flavors.

Add vegetables, raise heat to high, and stir-fry for 3 minutes or until vegetables are partially cooked but still crunchy. There will be very little liquid. This salad can be eaten warm or chilled.

CRANBERRY AND APPLE MOLDED SALAD

SERVES 8

This pretty thing can be done the day before, or even two days before. Sometimes our whole family gathers in San Francisco to have Thanksgiving or Christmas dinner with my favorite niece Linda, and I've carried this one all the way from L.A. in my favorite mold, along with the pecan pies (pages 335 and 337) with no trouble at all—providing I can balance the luggage and my carryall purse on the opposite shoulder.

1 pound cranberries	1 tablespoon unflavored gelatin
1 whole orange (including rind), seeded	3 tablespoons cold water
1/2 cup orange juice	3 1/4-ounce package raspberry gelatin
3 1/2 tablespoons lemon juice	1 cup boiling water
1 1/2 cups sugar	2 tart apples, peeled and chopped

Place cranberries and orange in food processor. Chop with metal blade. Add orange juice, lemon juice, and sugar. Let this mixture stand about 1 hour.

Meanwhile soak unflavored gelatin in cold water. Dissolve raspberry gelatin in boiling water. Add soaked gelatin, stir until dissolved.

Combine these ingredients with cranberry mixture. Add apples. Place mixture in well-greased mold. When firm, unmold and serve on bed of watercress or lettuce leaves.

A nice accompaniment is 1 cup mayonnaise mixed with 1/4 cup fresh orange juice. With or without the mayonnaise, this is perfect for your Thanksgiving or Christmas turkey and trimmings.

MANDARIN ORANGE SALAD

SERVES 6

1 6-ounce package orange gelatin	1/2 of 6-ounce can undiluted frozen orange juice
1 cup hot water	1 pint orange sherbet
Pinch of salt	11-ounce can mandarin oranges, drained
1/2 envelope unflavored gelatin	Sour cream for garnish
1/4 cup cold water	

Dissolve orange gelatin in hot water. Add salt. Soften unflavored gelatin in cold water. Add to orange gelatin and stir to dissolve. Add orange juice.

Whip sherbet with electric mixer. Add gelatin mixture. Blend thoroughly and refrigerate until slightly thick.

Stir once and add mandarin orange slices. Pour into well-greased mold. Chill until firm. Good with dollop of sour cream on top.

BASIL FRENCH DRESSING
MAKES AROUND 1 2/3 CUPS

1/4 cup tomato sauce
1/3 cup red wine vinegar
1 tablespoon sugar
1 teaspoon salt
1 teaspoon dried basil or 1 tablespoon fresh
1 teaspoon Worcestershire sauce

1/4 teaspoon dry mustard
1/4 teaspoon pepper
1/8 teaspoon Tabasco sauce
1 clove garlic, minced
1 cup salad oil

Combine all ingredients except oil in food processor. With machine running, add oil through feed tube in thin stream. Process until smooth. Store in covered container in refrigerator.

VARIATIONS Eliminate tomato sauce and substitute white champagne vinegar for red wine vinegar; or substitute tarragon wine vinegar for red wine vinegar and add fresh or dried tarragon instead of basil.

AVOCADO SALAD DRESSING
MAKES ABOUT 2 1/2 CUPS DRESSING

You're going to love this one. It's truly colorful, tangy, and smooth—all the things an avocado is and isn't!

1/2 cup white vinegar
1/2 tablespoon mixed pickling spices
2 tablespoons lime juice
2 teaspoons Dijon mustard
2 whole eggs
1/2 clove garlic, finely chopped

1 teaspoon sugar
1 teaspoon salt
1/4 teaspoon ground white pepper
1/4 teaspoon Worcestershire sauce
1 1/3 cups salad oil
1 ripe avocado, peeled and cut into chunks

Bring vinegar and pickling spices to boil. Cool and strain.

Put vinegar, lime juice, mustard, eggs, garlic, sugar, salt, pepper and Worcestershire in bowl of food processor fitted with steel blade. Blend well about 1 minute. With machine running, add oil through feed tube in a thin stream. Add avocado and blend well.

ROQUEFORT-SHERRY DRESSING   MAKES 1 1/2 CUPS

This little number needs very little assistance, only the most crispy lettuce. The old standby, hearts of iceberg cut in quarters, works just fine. No radishes, celery, watercress. It's creamy and flavorful.

4 1/2 ounces Roquefort cheese, softened
3 ounces cream cheese, softened
1/4 cup sherry
1 cup thick sour cream

1 tablespoon grated onion
1/2 teaspoon salt
1/4 teaspoon paprika
1 or 2 drops Tabasco sauce

Mix together Roquefort and cream cheese. Add sherry and sour cream and blend until creamy. Then add onions, salt, paprika, and Tabasco sauce. Store dressing, covered, in refrigerator. Serve with different varieties of lettuce.

JODY'S FAVORITE RUSSIAN DRESSING
MAKES ABOUT 2 CUPS

1 cup mayonnaise
1/4 cup chili sauce
1 teaspoon sugar
1 teaspoon Worcestershire sauce
Salt and pepper to taste

Dash of Tabasco sauce
3 celery stalks, finely chopped
1 cucumber, peeled and finely chopped
  (place on paper towel to drain)
1/2 green pepper, finely chopped

Combine mayonnaise, chili sauce, sugar, and seasonings.
    Stir in vegetables. Allow to blend several hours before serving. Serve over wedges of iceberg lettuce.

HONEY DIJON DRESSING   MAKES ABOUT 1 1/2 CUPS

2 egg yolks
1 teaspoon salt
1 generous tablespoon honey
1/4 cup Dijon mustard

1/4 teaspoon cayenne pepper
3 generous tablespoons vinegar or lemon
  juice
2/3 to 3/4 cup light oil

Place all ingredients except oil in bowl of food processor fitted with steel blade. Blend well.
    With machine running, add oil through feed tube in thinnest possible stream. Blend well. It comes out creamy and mayonnaisey.
    Use for seafood salad. Arrange 2 sliced hard-boiled eggs over top and sprinkle with sunflower seeds.

YOGURT CUCUMBER DRESSING

MAKES 1 QUART

3 1/2 cups yogurt
1/4 cup plus 2 tablespoons vinegar
3 tablespoons honey
1 1/2 teaspoons basil

1/4 teaspoon finely minced garlic
1/2 teaspoon salt
1/4 teaspoon pepper
1 cucumber, peeled, seeded, and diced

Place all ingredients in blender or food processor fitted with steel blade and mix until smooth.

BUTTERMILK DRESSING

MAKES 1 QUART

1 1/2 cups cottage cheese
1/4 cup mayonnaise
1/4 cup plus 2 tablespoons buttermilk
1 1/2 cups plus 2 tablespoons tomato puree
1/4 cup tomato juice

1/4 cup plus 2 tablespoons soy sauce
3/4 teaspoon oregano
3/4 teaspoon thyme
1/4 teaspoon garlic

Place all ingredients in blender and mix until smooth.

Chapter 6

POULTRY

Chicken is one of the most used, abused, and taken-for-granted foods available to us. No fair. It's also one of the most accommodating. It freezes well, absorbs flavors readily and gratefully, is healthful and low in calories and cholesterol. So treat it well. Don't, above all, overcook it. I know that down home our chickens used to have to scratch around the ground for the feed that was thrown to them, so they became tougher and stringier—wouldn't you? They had to be cooked for ages, and seasoned highly to have the flavor we have come to expect today.

White meat will cook in a much shorter time than the dark meat—twenty minutes maximum for a whole poached chicken breast. It's done when the juices run clear yellow with no trace of pink. Even that Thanksgiving turkey should be treated this way. Since your bird is brown and crispy, proudly show it around whole, if you like; then slip back into the kitchen and while the white meat is resting—some 15 to 20 minutes before carving—slice off the thighs and legs and either return them to the oven to roast a little longer in another pan (so you can be making your all-important gravy in the original roasting pan) or place them in the microwave oven for 5 to 10 minutes until the joints are no longer red.

If you have to use frozen poultry instead of fresh, defrost your fowl by allowing it to remain in the wrapper in the refrigerator and thaw naturally—if you have the time. If not, unwrap it and defrost at room temperature. Or two more options—if you're really pressed for time, wrap fowl loosely in plastic wrap and microwave; or better yet, poach or steam over well-seasoned water or broth before frying, baking, roasting, or barbecuing.

It's really not all that hard to cut up a chicken yourself with that good sharp knife (mandatory!). And you get so much more for your money. Instead of simply buying those parts of the chicken you need at the moment, buy whole chickens and you'll have wings, backs, necks for broths and stocks, livers for hors d'oeuvres and snacks, gizzards for frying, and the extra fat to render slowly in a skillet—all day, if necessary—for piecrusts or sautéing. It's the purest animal fat available to you. Stored in the refrigerator, it keeps for at least two weeks.

I imagine you've gathered by now that "a chicken is a chicken" is not part of my thinking. If you want to join me, try the Basted Roasted Florida Chicken or the Chicken Curry Cutlets for a real treat. The Molded Iranian Baked Chicken with Rice is so beautiful and so special, and really not all that hard to do, and the Hot-Hot Chicken is a Chinese wonder. If you have people who won't eat duck, they'll eat this one, Le Bistro Roast Duckling, eagerly—not a smidgin of fat left in or on it.

BASTED ROASTED FLORIDA CHICKEN   SERVES 6

This is one of my all-time favorite recipes. I first tasted something like it in a marvelous Florida hotel restaurant called Chalet Suzanne. They wouldn't part with the recipe and I don't blame them. I went back to this quaint, unique place several times and I always ordered the same buttery, melting dish. On one trip I visited the kitchen and watched the young chef carefully, consistently baste the chicken, and I guess that is why it was never allowed to dry out. So make plenty of your basting sauce. Don't worry about the six whole cloves or more of garlic, peeled or unpeeled. They blend with the sauce so gently and exquisitely you'll never taste (or exude) it. Garlic is one of those remarkable vegetables—it loses its strength and undesirability the longer it cooks, particularly if left whole. If by any remote chance after the long cooking the cloves have not dissolved completely, simply remove the little dickenses and keep basting.

3 small broiling chickens, quartered
Our Seasoned Salt (page 11) (optional)
Red pepper flakes
Juice of 1/2 lime
1/2 cup sweet butter
3 heaping tablespoons flour

6 garlic cloves, peeled
3–4 cups chicken broth (medium thin)
2 tablespoons Brown Sauce (page 6) (not essential)
Freshly ground pepper

Preheat oven to 450°F.

Sprinkle salt over top and underside of chicken. Lay chicken skin side up in single layer in shallow roasting pan. Sprinkle very lightly with red pepper flakes and juice of 1/2 lime and set aside.

In large saucepan melt butter and add flour slowly, stirring constantly. Allow to brown, slowly, slowly; don't let it burn. Add whole peeled garlic cloves as roux begins to turn creamy golden. Continue until roux is light brown in color. If any of the garlic cloves show overbrowned edges, remove them. You will have had the value of the flavor anyway and most people do not recognize that there is garlic in this dish. Check seasoning, add salt and freshly ground white or black pepper. (This may be done ahead and set aside until you are ready to prepare chicken; then carefully and slowly reheat before resuming cooking.)

Add chicken broth to roux slowly, stirring constantly with wire whisk until blended and the consistency of cream soup. Add a little Brown Sauce for extra richness. Check seasoning carefully to avoid oversalting.

Spoon sauce over chicken, completely covering edges. Put chicken legs in oven first—they take a little longer to cook. Five minutes later add breasts. Baste with sauce in pan every 5 or 10 minutes. Chicken must be kept moist with sauce. Bake 45–60 minutes. Since you will be using both racks of oven, switch the racks after 20 minutes to ensure even cooking.

CHICKEN CURRY CUTLETS

SERVES 6

1 whole chicken (2 1/2–3 pounds)
2 1/4 cups soft white bread crumbs
1 cup finely chopped onions
1/2 cup fresh tomatoes
1/4 cup finely chopped fresh coriander (cilantro)
1 tablespoon plus 2 teaspoons finely chopped fresh ginger root
1/2 teaspoon cinnamon
1/2 teaspoon finely chopped garlic

3 heaping teaspoons curry powder
1 1/4 teaspoons ground cumin
Scant 1/2 teaspoon ground hot red pepper
1 tablespoon salt
1/4 teaspoon black pepper
1/2 cup apple, finely chopped
1/2 cup raw unsalted cashew nuts, chopped
1 egg
1/4 cup clarified butter

Skin and bone chicken, then grind it in food processor by turning off and on a few times. Don't overgrind, as it will be too mushy.

In a large bowl, combine ground chicken, 1 cup of bread crumbs, and all other ingredients except clarified butter. Knead vigorously with both hands or beat with a wooden spoon until mixture is smooth. Divide into 12 equal portions and shape them into flattened rounds about 2 1/2 inches in diameter and 3/4 inch thick. Dip both sides of each round into the remaining 1 1/4 cups of bread crumbs and arrange them side by side on long piece of waxed paper.

In heavy 10 to 12-inch skillet, heat clarified butter over moderate heat until a drop of water flicked into it splatters instantly. Reduce heat to low, add chicken cutlets and fry them 7–8 minutes on each side, turning them gently with a wide spatula. The cutlets are done when outside surfaces are crisp and brown. As furthur indication of their doneness, insert a small knife in center of one of the cutlets and spread it apart gently to make sure meat shows no sign of pink.

Serve at once from heated platter with yogurt and your own peach and plum chutney. (See page 14.)

MOROCCAN CHICKEN PIE

SERVES 6–8

This too is one of my favorite recipes. I know you get the feeling I keep saying that, but this dish is stunning to see, to serve, and to taste. It looks complicated and difficult. It isn't. Many of the herbs and spices are cooked right with the hens, so there goes half your formidable array of ingredients. Also, as the recipe indicates, much of the preparation can be done in the morning. If you haven't had much experience with phyllo dough, keep in mind that you need a flat pastry brush, a flat surface, and a bowl or cup to hold your melted butter.

I serve this with Special Bulgur Pilaf (page 260). Most Moroccans serve it with couscous, which is the North African equivalent of grits or cornmeal mush.

3 Rock Cornish game hens
4 cloves garlic, minced
1 tablespoon salt
1 teaspoon finely minced ginger root
1 teaspoon fresh coriander or cilantro
1/2 teaspoon ground black pepper
1/4 teaspoon turmeric
Pinch saffron
1 cup hot water
3 cinnamon sticks, broken
1/4 cup butter (1/2 stick), cut into pieces

1 large onion, chopped
1 cup minced fresh parsley
3 tablespoons butter
1 1/2 cups slivered blanched almonds
1/4 cup powdered sugar
2 teaspoons ground cinnamon
3 tablespoons lemon juice
6 eggs, beaten until frothy
4 plain phyllo sheets
8 buttered phyllo sheets

Wash hens well and pat dry inside and out. Rub well inside and out with garlic and salt. Place hens in heavy pan to fit snugly. Combine ginger, coriander, pepper, turmeric, saffron, and hot water and pour over hens. Add enough water to cover hens. Sprinkle cinnamon stick pieces on top along with butter, onions, and parsley. Simmer over low heat 1 hour or until tender. Cool in stock. Remove hens, reserving stock, and shred meat.

In skillet, brown meat and almonds in 3 tablespoons butter. Remove meat and almonds with a slotted spoon and cool. Combine with powdered sugar and cinnamon and set aside.

Strain stock and cook over medium high heat until reduced to 1 1/2 cups. Lower heat and add lemon juice. This much of recipe may be done ahead.

Gently warm 1 1/2 cups stock; bring to a simmer and gradually beat in eggs. Cook, stirring constantly, 10 minutes or until eggs are cooked to custard consistency. Do not allow to scramble.

Preheat oven to 400°F. "Fluff" 4 plain phyllo sheets on cookie sheet, as if they were clouds. Bake at 400° for 1 minute or until they are very lightly browned. Set aside.

ASSEMBLY

Keep phyllo dough wrapped in damp—not wet—tea towel until ready to use. Arrange 6 buttered phyllo sheets in 12-inch iron skillet, letting edges hang over sides. Sprinkle with meat and almond mixture. Cover with half of egg mixture. Top with 2 "fluffy" phyllo sheets. Cover with rest of meat mixture. Top with other 2 "fluffy" phyllo sheets, and then with remaining egg mixture. Fold edges of buttered phyllo sheets over pie and brush with additional melted butter. Arrange 2 remaining buttered phyllo sheets on top, tucking edges under pie to enclose it completely. Brush with more melted butter and bake at 425°F. for 20 minutes or until golden brown. Shake pan lightly to loosen edges of pie and invert on a cookie sheet or ovenproof platter. Bake 10 minutes more or until golden brown. Sprinkle lavishly with additional powdered sugar and ground cinnamon. Serve immediately.

Brush phyllo dough with melted butter.

ROAST CHICKEN

A perfect way to roast a chicken. It's flavorful, self-basting, golden, delicious. Because it is so basic, your accompaniments can be more complicated, such as Red Cabbage with Apples (page 270) or Broccoli alla Ziti (page 239).

1 roasting chicken (3–3 1/2 pounds)
Coarse salt and freshly ground black pepper
1 garlic clove, peeled and end of clove cut off
3 sprigs fresh parsley
3 sprigs fresh basil

3 sprigs fresh rosemary (not essential, but gives a lovely flavor)
Juice of 1 lemon
1/4 cup chicken broth
2 teaspoons chopped shallots (optional)

Preheat oven to 400°F.

Wipe chicken inside and out with clean damp cloth or paper towel. Rub inside with garlic clove and sprinkle generously with coarse salt and freshly ground pepper. Place parsley, basil, and rosemary in cavity of chicken. Dust outside with salt and repeat garlic rubbing, being careful to cover entire surface of chicken.

Truss or fold wing tips under body and tie legs securely. Squeeze lemon and pour half of juice inside and other half over breast, spreading it evenly with your fingers. Dust once again with salt and freshly ground pepper.

Place chicken on rack in roasting pan and pour a little water in pan to prevent juices from burning. Add shallots. Put bird in oven, close door and cook 1 hour. Basting is not needed. Once out of oven, allow chicken to rest in warm spot 5–10 minutes.

Remove chicken from roasting pan. Place roasting pan with juices over high heat, add 1/4 cup chicken broth if necessary, and deglaze pan. Be sure to get all the little goodies in the pan juices. Pour pan juices over bird before carving.

ROAST CHICKEN PIMIENTO

Some night when you're serving Italian—having an antipasto of pimientos (the ones that come in a large can in small Italian grocery stores) and anchovies with thin slices of mozzarella cheese in between and a little fresh basil—save out a couple of pimientos for this dish. It's worth it.

1 chicken (3–3 1/2 pounds)
Salt and pepper
1 tablespoon fresh olive oil
2 scallions, white part only, thinly sliced
1 shallot, chopped
2 small carrots, thinly sliced
1 stalk celery, chopped
1/4 green pepper, cut into strips
1/4 cup chopped parsley

2 cups toasted bread crumbs (I prefer corn-bread)
Salt and freshly ground black pepper to taste
2 large pimientos, sliced, or a small can of pimiento strips
2 tablespoons butter, softened
1/2 cup tomato sauce
3/4 cup chicken broth

Preheat oven to 350°F.

Salt and pepper inside and outside of chicken generously.

Sauté scallions, shallots, carrots, celery, and green pepper in oil until softened but not brown. Add parsley, bread crumbs, and salt and pepper. Stuff loosely in chicken.

Lay pimiento strips inside chicken right under breast for full flavor.

Rub softened butter all over chicken. Place chicken in a small roasting pan and pour over it the tomato sauce mixed with the chicken broth. Cover tightly with foil or lid of roaster and bake 35 minutes, basting occasionally. Remove foil, turn oven to 450°, and bake 15 minutes, basting frequently, until chicken is tender and brown.

CHICKEN NIÇOISE
SERVES 4–6

1 chicken (3 1/2–4 pounds)
Salt and pepper
10 sprigs parsley
2 stalks celery, including tops
2 scallions
Fresh thyme (optional)
1/4 cup olive oil or less
12 small white onions, peeled
2 large green peppers, cut into thin strips
2 cloves garlic, minced
3 tomatoes, peeled, seeded, and coarsely
   chopped

1 teaspoon tomato paste
1/2 cup chicken broth
Bouquet Garni
   6 sprigs parsley
   3 sprigs thyme
   1 bay leaf
1/2 cup dry white wine
1 cup chicken stock or broth
1/2 cup small black olives
Minced parsley or fresh basil
Cooked rice
Lemon wedges

Preheat oven to 325°F.

Generously sprinkle chicken inside and out with salt and pepper. After seasoning fill cavity with parsley, celery, scallions, and thyme. Truss it.

In heavy flameproof casserole brown chicken on all sides in olive oil over moderate heat. Transfer to dish.

Add onions to casserole and brown on all sides. Add green peppers and garlic and cook, stirring, 3 minutes. Add tomatoes, tomato paste mixed with chicken broth, and bouquet garni. Salt and pepper to taste. Add white wine and simmer mixture over moderately high heat, stirring occasionally, 3–5 minutes.

Return chicken to casserole breast side up, add chicken stock, and bring liquid to a simmer. Braise chicken, covered, for 1 hour.

Transfer chicken to warmed platter. Skim fat. Discard bouquet garni. Place casserole on burner and reduce liquid over high heat for 6 minutes. Return chicken to casserole, add black olives, and sprinkle with parsley or basil. Serve chicken with seasoned steamed rice and lemon wedges for each person—a little squeeze adds a nice flavor.

ZUCCHINI-STUFFED CHICKEN

Suzanne Somers is not just another pretty face and figure. She is a bright lady who writes beautiful poetry, sings, and can cook. She and Alan Hamel, her husband, went to the Cordon Bleu school of cooking in Paris. I'm not sure she got this recipe there, but it's a prize.

1 chicken (3 pounds), split up back and flattened (you may bone it if desired)
Olive oil

Herbs de Provence—oregano, basil, and rosemary

Place fingers between skin and meat of chicken and gently separate skin from breast, legs, and all parts of chicken, making room for your stuffing.

Rub both sides of chicken with olive oil and sprinkle with Herbs de Provence.

STUFFING

1 1/4 pounds zucchini, grated
1/2 bunch chives, chopped
2 tablespoons soft butter
1 1/4 cups soft bread crumbs
4 ounces ricotta cheese
2 tablespoons freshly grated Parmesan

cheese
1 egg
Freshly ground pepper
Pinch crushed tarragon
Pinch herbs de Provence

Preheat oven to 450°F.

Salt zucchini well, grate on kitchen towel, and let stand for 10 minutes. Squeeze well in towel to remove most of the moisture.

Sauté zucchini and chives in butter and let cool, then add remaining ingredients.

Stuff chicken under skin. Bake at 450°F. for 10 minutes and then reduce heat to 375° and bake 50 minutes. Baste frequently with pan juices.

SESAME FRIED CHICKEN

Just to prove great women golfers do more than practice their chipping and putting, Marlene Hagge cooked this on my TV show one day. It's high flavor from a low scorer.

1 1/4 cups flour
1/4 cup sesame seeds
1 1/2 teaspoons salt
1 teaspoon poultry seasoning
1/2 teaspoon paprika

Freshly ground black pepper
2 (2 1/2–3-pound) frying chickens, quartered
2/3 cup evaporated milk
1/2 cup butter
1/2 cup oil

Combine flour, sesame seeds, salt, poultry seasoning, paprika, and pepper. Dip chicken quarters in milk, then roll them in sesame seed mixture.

Sauté chicken in combined butter and oil for 30 minutes or until golden brown and tender, turning frequently.

ANDALUSIAN CHICKEN

I suppose because of the title this is a Spanish chicken dish. It's terrific and great for a party. Remember, it's only 1/2 cup cream for all that chicken and sauce so it's not fattening, especially if you serve it with steamed rice. If you aren't having six people, make the same amount of sauce and save the extra for a later date—a later chicken. It will really serve more than six people unless they're actors or tennis players, who are generally hungrier than most people.

2 or 3 small broiling chickens, cut into quarters
Salt and pepper
1/2 cup flour
1 tablespoon light olive oil or salad oil
1/4 cup butter
1/3 cup cognac
1 tablespoon minced shallots or scallions

1 1/2 cups fresh tomato pulp (5 or 6 tomatoes peeled, seeded, and cut into 1/2-inch pieces)
2 teaspoons tarragon
1/2 cup dry white wine or vermouth
1/2 cup chicken stock
1/2 cup heavy cream
2 to 3 tablespoons chopped fresh parsley

Season chicken lightly on each side with salt and pepper, dredge with flour, and shake off excess.

Heat oil and 2 tablespoons butter in large skillet. Add thighs and legs first (they take longer to cook). After legs have been browning almost 5 minutes, add chicken breasts and sauté until lightly browned. Turn and sauté on other side only until meat is light and springy when you press it with your finger as opposed to raw state. Continue until all chicken pieces are lightly browned, adding more oil and butter to keep pan filmed.

Flame chicken.* Remove chicken pieces from pan. Add another tablespoon or so of butter, stir in shallots or scallions, and cook for a moment or two; then add tomatoes and tarragon and cook over high heat 2–3 minutes more.

Pour in wine and stock. Add cream and boil for several minutes until liquids have reduced and sauce has thickened slightly. Taste and correct seasoning.

Return chicken pieces to pan and baste with sauce. Cover and reheat 2–3 minutes at below simmer, to warm meat through without overcooking it. Arrange chicken pieces on hot platter, swish parsley into sauce and spoon it over meat. Serve immediately.

*Return pieces to pan and pour in cognac. When bubbling, avert your face and ignite liquid with a long match; shake pan for several seconds.

HONEY BAKED CHICKEN

There's hardly anybody that spends any time around me who isn't into food, recipes, and cooking. This is one of Shirley Secretary's many contributions to this book. She cooked this one for her children and I've cooked it for mine and if your kids like anything outside of McDonald's, you can be sure it's a winner.

2 (1 1/2–2-pound) frying chickens, cut up
1/2 cup butter or margarine, melted
1/2 cup honey
1/4 cup Dijon mustard

1 teaspoon salt
1 teaspoon curry powder
1 tablespoon chutney

Preheat oven to 350°F.

Place chicken pieces in shallow baking pan, skin side up.

Combine butter, honey, mustard, salt, curry powder, and chutney and mix. Pour over chicken and bake 1 1/4 hours, basting every 15 minutes, until chicken is tender and nicely browned.

COQ AU VIN

SERVES 6–8

Coq au Vin *always looks so gorgeous and sounds so—so French, but I have always found it a little on the heavy and greasy side for my taste. I almost guarantee that this one isn't. Don't be afraid to use your second-best red wine in the preparation of this dish. It won't be wasted. I would save the first-best for the first round at dinner with your* Coq au Vin *and if I hadn't used all the second-best for this dish, I'd serve it for the next round or use it for a wonderful* boeuf *or something other.*

3 tablespoons oil (or oil and butter mixed)
3 large onions, sliced medium thick
5 cloves garlic, finely chopped
1/4 cup salt pork, rendered in boiling water, then diced
2 shallots, finely chopped
1 tablespoon tomato paste
6–8 mushrooms, sliced

3 cups red wine
3 cups chicken broth
8 tablespoons Brown Sauce (page 6)
2 (2 1/2–3-pound) frying chickens, cut up (thighs disjointed and breasts cut in 2 pieces)
Salt and pepper to taste
Juice of 1/2 lime

In a large, heavy saucepan heat 1 tablespoon oil. Add onions, garlic, and salt pork. Sauté until salt pork is soft. Add shallots and sauté. Drain off any oil that is left. Add tomato paste. When onions are pink, add mushrooms and 1/2 cup red wine. Let come to a boil and add 1 cup broth and 1 tablespoon Brown Sauce.

Increase heat and let liquid reduce, then add another cup of broth and 2 table-spoons Brown Sauce. Reduce liquid again. Add remaining broth and remaining 5 tablespoons Brown Sauce. Reduce heat, as vegetables will be tender by now.

Season chicken with salt and pepper. In large heavy skillet, heat remaining 2 tablespoons oil and arrange chicken skin side down in single layer in oil. Press down. Fry until skin is crisp and brown. Turn chicken frequently and carefully so that it does not fall apart.

When chicken pieces are browned, pour off excess oil. Pour remaining 2 1/2 cups red wine over chicken. Cover and cook 20 minutes or longer, until wine has almost cooked away and chicken is done. Test with fork on thigh as you may have to cook it longer.

Squeeze lime juice over chicken. Keep chicken warm while you reheat sauce and pour over chicken. Serve hot. It reheats beautifully.

CHICKEN IN GREEN TOMATO AND NUT SAUCE

SERVES 4–6

This is a most unusual Mexican recipe—it's piquant and crunchy and easy to do. Those little green Mexican tomatoes or tomatillos are the clincher. I hope you have them in your market. If not, make a big pitch for a small shelf section for Mexican peppers, sauces, and tomatoes. Also some of the Chinese spices, rices, sauces, and vegetables. We're living in a wonderful international world in our kitchens today, and it's up to the grocer to roll with it.

1 chicken (2 1/2–3 pounds), cut into serving pieces

2 cups water with 1 teaspoon salt

SAUCE

1/2 cup pumpkin seeds
1/4 cup walnuts
1/4 cup blanched almonds
1 cup chicken stock
2 fresh poblano chilies *or* 2 fresh green peppers about 3 1/2 inches in diameter
10-ounce can Mexican green tomatoes, drained

1/2 cup coarsely chopped onions
1/4 cup coarsely chopped cilantro
1 canned serrano chili, drained and rinsed in cold water
1/4 teaspoon finely chopped garlic
1/2 teaspoon salt
1/8 teaspoon freshly ground white pepper
1 tablespoon lard or oil

In heavy 4 to 5-quart flameproof casserole, combine chicken and salted cold water. Bring to boil over high heat, then reduce heat to low, cover, and simmer 25–30 minutes, or until chicken is tender but not falling apart. Let chicken cool in broth.

Place pumpkin seeds in blender or food processor fitted with the metal blade and blend at high speed for 15 seconds or until finely ground. With back of spoon, force ground pumpkin seeds through coarse sieve set over bowl. Grind walnuts and blanched almonds separately in same fashion. Return pumpkin seeds, walnuts, and almonds to blender. Pour in chicken stock and puree at high speed for about 15 seconds.

Roast poblano chilies or green peppers one at a time on the tines of a long-handled fork, turning them over a gas flame until skin blisters and darkens on all sides. Or place chilies or peppers on broiler pan and broil about 3 inches from heat for about 5 minutes, turning so they color on all sides. Be careful not to let them burn. Wrap chilies in damp towel and let them rest for a few minutes, then gently rub with towel until skins slip off. With small sharp knife, cut out and discard stems, thick white membranes, and seeds.

Cut chilies into chunks and place in blender or food processor. Blend at high speed for 10 seconds. Add green tomatoes, onions, cilantro, serrano chili, chicken stock-nut mixture, garlic, salt, and pepper and blend for 30 seconds or until mixture is reduced to smooth puree.

In heavy 8 to 10-inch skillet, melt 1 tablespoon lard or oil over moderate heat, pour in chili-nut puree and cook 5 minutes, stirring frequently. Remove skillet from heat.

Drain chicken of cooking liquid and in its place pour sauce into casserole.

Gently stir chicken around in sauce to coat it thoroughly, then simmer over low heat, covered, about 10 minutes or until chicken is hot and well flavored with sauce.

Serve either directly from casserole or arrange chicken attractively on very warm serving platter and pour sauce over it. Garnish with coarsely chopped walnuts, almonds, and pumpkin seeds.

BUFFET CHICKEN CACCIATORE   SERVES 16

Olive oil
2 large onions, coarsely chopped
3 garlic cloves, coarsely chopped
5 frying chickens, cut up
Salt and pepper
2 28-ounce cans Italian plum tomatoes
1 teaspoon sugar
1/2 teaspoon red pepper flakes

1/2 teaspoon salt
1/4 teaspoon pepper
1/2 teaspoon oregano
1/2 teaspoon basil
1/4 teaspoon thyme
1 bay leaf
3 green peppers, cut into strips

Preheat oven to 350°F.

Cover bottom of large roasting pan with olive oil. Add onions and garlic and brown lightly. Salt and pepper chicken parts and lightly brown.

Place tomatoes with juice in blender or food processor and blend briefly to break up. Add sugar, red pepper flakes, salt, pepper, oregano, basil, thyme, and bay leaf. Mix well. Add green peppers, pour over chicken, and let come to a boil. Turn off heat.

Remove chicken pieces to large shallow baking dishes. Layer dark meat in one and white meat in another. Pour sauce over all. Cover with foil and bake 1 hour or less.

Remove foil, increase heat to 450°, and bake until chicken is delicately brown. Baste with sauce a few times. It will have cooked down a bit. Serve hot.

CHICKEN AND RED PEPPERS   SERVES 4–6

2 sweet red peppers, cut into 1/2-inch strips
    (If red peppers are not available, use green
    peppers. It is not as pretty but tastes the
    same.)
2 tablespoons oil
2 tablespoons butter
2 chicken breasts, skinned, boned, and cut
    into 1/2-inch strips
1/4 cup red wine
1/2 cup chicken broth

1 tomato, peeled, seeded, and chopped
1/4 cup half-and-half
Pinch of thyme
Pinch of rosemary
Pinch of fresh basil
Salt and white pepper
1/4 cup mushroom duxelles (Chop and sauté
    mushrooms with chopped shallots, pars-
    ley, salt, and pepper until water cooks
    out.)

Sauté peppers in hot oil and butter. Remove to colander to drain.

Add chicken to skillet (add more butter if necessary) and sauté quickly until chicken turns white, about 5 minutes. Do not overcook.

Deglaze pan with wine and broth. Cook mixture down until syrupy.

Add tomatoes and half-and-half; let the mixture cook down. Add herbs, salt, and white pepper. Add peppers and chicken and warm through. Sprinkle with mushroom duxelles.

FRESH CORN AND CHICKEN TAMALE PIE

SERVES 4

1/2 cup yellow cornmeal
1 cup boiling water
3 tablespoons oil
1 frying chicken (2 1/2–3 pounds), cut up
2 cloves garlic, finely minced
2 medium onions, coarsely chopped
2 medium tomatoes, peeled and chopped,

or 1 1/2 cups canned tomatoes, drained
8-ounce can peeled green chilies, diced
1/2 teaspoon oregano, crushed
1/2 teaspoon cumin
1 1/2–2 tablespoons salsa jalapeño, or your favorite chili relish
Salt

TOPPING

3 ears fresh corn *or* 1 10-ounce package frozen corn
2 tablespoons butter or margarine, melted

2 egg yolks, lightly beaten
2 egg whites
Salt

Soak cornmeal in boiling water for 30 minutes. Fry chicken in oil in large skillet, but do not brown. Add garlic, onions, tomatoes, chilies, oregano, cumin, salsa, and salt. Cover and cook slowly for 15 minutes. Add cornmeal mixture and mix gently.

Meanwhile slightly grate corn, just to break skin of each grain. Then, with table knife, scrape all the pulp from cob. If using frozen corn, let thaw a little, then place in processor and turn on and off 3 times to break up large kernels.

Combine butter and egg yolks, add corn and salt.

Beat egg whites until stiff but not dry, and fold into corn mixture.

Preheat oven to 350°F. Place chicken and vegetable-cornmeal mixture into a buttered 2-quart casserole; pour corn mixture over top and bake 1 hour and 15 minutes.

PARMESAN BAKED CHICKEN LEGS

SERVES 12

2 cups bread crumbs
3/4 cup Parmesan cheese
1/4 cup chopped parsley
1 clove garlic, minced
2 teaspoons salt

1/2 teaspoon black pepper (if you like it hotter, add a few red pepper flakes or a dash of cayenne pepper)
24 chicken legs
1 cup butter, melted (more if necessary)

Preheat oven to 350°F.

Mix bread crumbs with Parmesan cheese. Add parsley, garlic, salt, and pepper. Dip each chicken leg into melted butter and then into crumb mixture. Be sure each piece is well coated. Lay pieces in shallow open roasting pan.

Pour remaining butter over chicken legs and bake about 40 minutes or until fork-tender. Do not turn chicken, but baste frequently with drippings in pan or additional melted butter. Pile high on warmed platter to serve.

CHICKEN WITH SOUR CREAM SERVES 4

Seasoned flour (salt, pepper, paprika)
1 chicken (2 1/2–3 pounds), cut into serving
  pieces
1/4 cup oil
6 tablespoons butter
1/4 cup chicken broth

1 small onion, chopped
1 clove garlic, cut in half
1/2 pound fresh mushrooms, sliced
1/2 cup sour cream
1/2 cup heavy cream
Salt and pepper

Preheat oven to 350°F.

Roll chicken pieces in seasoned flour. Heat oil in large skillet and brown chicken, turning to color all sides.

Arrange chicken pieces in roasting pan. Dot with 4 tablespoons butter. Pour broth over it and bake until chicken is tender. Do not overcook.

In small skillet heat 2 tablespoons butter and sauté onion, garlic, and mushrooms until just softened (don't brown). Discard garlic and add mixed sour and sweet cream and salt and pepper to taste. Heat gently but *do not* boil. Arrange chicken on hot platter, pour sauce over it, and serve with pride or noodles.

GREEK CHICKEN SERVES 6

You never know where you'll find a good recipe. Alex Karras is a football lineman turned actor, an all-around nice guy who loves to eat and loves good food. His mother sent this recipe along when he came on the show one time and I cooked it for him. It's fun and delicious!

2 (2 1/2–3-pound) chickens, cut into serving
  pieces
Salt and pepper
1/4 cup butter
2 onions, finely chopped
1 clove garlic, minced
28-ounce can whole tomatoes

8-ounce can tomato sauce
1 teaspoon sugar
Dash cinnamon
1/2 cup sherry
2 cups chicken broth
2 cups uncooked rice

Wipe chicken dry and sprinkle with salt and pepper. Melt butter in Dutch oven and brown chicken pieces on all sides. Remove and set aside. Add onions and garlic and sauté until onions are soft. Add tomatoes, tomato sauce, sugar, and cinnamon. Stir in sherry. Return chicken to Dutch oven. Correct seasoning with salt and pepper. Add hot water as needed, and simmer for 25 minutes or until chicken is tender. Remove from heat.

In another pot combine chicken broth with 1 cup water and 1 cup of the tomato sauce in which chicken was cooked. Bring to boil, add rice, salt lightly, stir, cover, lower heat, and simmer for 20 minutes (do not uncover during cooking). Remove from heat, stir gently with fork, cover, and let stand a few more minutes.

Pack rice into demitasse cups or teacups. Unmold just before serving on warm plates with chicken, and pour sauce over rice and chicken. Serve remaining rice on platter with rest of chicken.

CHICKEN BREASTS WITH MUSHROOMS AND CREAM
SERVES 4

4 chicken breasts, skinned and boned
1 teaspoon lemon juice
1/3 teaspoon salt
Pinch of white pepper
1 lobster tail, cooked and shelled (optional)
6 tablespoons butter
1 tablespoon minced shallots

1/4 pound fresh mushrooms, sliced thick
1/2 teaspoon salt
1/4 cup chicken stock
1/4 cup Madeira wine
1 cup whipping cream
1 teaspoon lemon juice
Parsley for garnish

Preheat oven to 400°F. Place chicken breasts between 2 pieces of waxed paper and lightly flatten with meat pounder. Remove to platter, rub with lemon juice, and sprinkle with salt and pepper. Let stand for 10 minutes.

Cut lobster meat into 1-inch chunks.

Heat butter in heavy ovenproof casserole just large enough to hold chicken breasts one layer deep. Add shallots and mushrooms. Sauté 3 minutes without browning. Sprinkle with salt.

Roll chicken breasts (coating both sides) in butter mixture. Arrange in casserole. Roll lobster chunks in butter mixture and set aside. Cover casserole with piece of waxed paper cut to fit. (Butter paper on side touching chicken breasts.) Place in oven. After 6 minutes remove and test for doneness.*

When chicken breasts are almost done, place lobster chunks in oven to warm through. Remove chicken breasts and lobster to warm platter, leaving mushroom mixture in casserole. (Cover chicken breasts and lobster to keep warm while making sauce.)

Add chicken stock and Madeira to casserole and boil over high heat until liquid is reduced and syrupy. Add whipping cream and boil down again until cream has thickened slightly. Taste for seasoning. Add lemon juice. Pour sauce over chicken breasts and lobster chunks. Sprinkle with parsley and serve.

*Chicken is perfectly cooked when its juices run clear yellow if pricked with a fork.

PECAN-BREADED CHICKEN BREASTS WITH MUSTARD SAUCE

SERVES 2–4

2 whole chicken breasts, skinned, boned, and cut in quarters
Salt and freshly ground pepper
10 tablespoons butter
3 tablespoons Dijon mustard

5–6 ounces pecans, ground
2 tablespoons safflower or other light oil
3/4 cup chicken broth
2/3 cup sour cream

Lightly flatten chicken breasts between 2 pieces of waxed paper with meat pounder. Season with salt and pepper.

Melt 6 tablespoons butter in small saucepan over medium heat. Remove from heat and whisk in mustard. Dip each piece of chicken into butter and mustard mixture and heavily coat each with ground pecans by patting them on with your hands.

Melt remaining butter in 12 to 14-inch skillet. Stir in oil. When hot, sauté as many pieces of chicken at a time as you can without crowding them. Sauté about 3 minutes on each side. Remove to baking dish and place in a 200°F. oven to keep warm. Continue cooking chicken pieces until all are done.

Discard all butter and oil and any burned pecans. Spoon loose nuts over chicken.

To deglaze skillet, place it over heat and add chicken broth, scraping all little bits of chicken, skin, and unburnt pecans from skillet. Add sour cream. Heat through but do not boil. Pour sauce over chicken and serve.

CHICKEN MARCO POLO

SERVES 4

There is a school of thought that I've never been a pupil of which says, "A chicken is a chicken." Not so. For instance, the two recipes that follow depend on chicken and a beautiful green complement. In one case, broccoli, and in the other, spinach. I don't understand why the one with broccoli is called Marco Polo, but then for some obscure reason which I have never bothered to research, anything Marco Polo is broccoli and anything Florentine is spinach. I give you this bit of wisdom and hope it will serve you well, but I don't think you need it.

2 whole chicken breasts, boned and cut into 4 fillets
3 tablespoons butter or margarine
1 1/2 pounds broccoli
4 thin slices cooked ham
2 tablespoons butter
Dash cayenne pepper
Dash Tabasco sauce

Dash Worcestershire sauce
2 tablespoons grated Parmesan cheese
2 tablespoons shredded Swiss cheese
2 cups hot white sauce (see Béchamel Sauce, page 2)
Salt and pepper to taste
2 tablespoons whipped cream
4 tablespoons Parmesan cheese, grated

Pound chicken fillets to flatten slightly. Sauté until lightly browned and tender. Set aside.

Cook broccoli until barely tender in salted water, drain thoroughly and divide among four individual shallow flameproof baking dishes. Dot broccoli with butter. Place a chicken fillet on broccoli, then a slice of ham on each portion.

Add 2 tablespoons butter, cayenne, Tabasco, Worcestershire, and Parmesan and Swiss cheeses to white sauce and stir until cheese is melted. Taste for seasoning; add more salt and pepper if needed. Slowly stir in whipped cream. Spoon sauce over ham and sprinkle grated Parmesan cheese on top. Broil until glazed and bubbly, about 5 minutes.

CHICKEN FLORENTINE

SERVES 4

2 pounds fresh spinach, cleaned thoroughly
Salt and pepper
4 chicken breasts, skinned and boned
1/3 cup seasoned flour (salt, pepper, and paprika)
2 eggs, beaten
3–4 tablespoons vegetable oil

1/3 grated Parmesan cheese
4 slices (4 ounces) mozzarella cheese
1 tablespoon butter
1/3 cup dry white wine
Juice of 1/2 lemon
1/2 cup chicken broth

Preheat oven to 350°F.

Cook spinach in boiling water. Drain, chop, and season with salt and pepper.

Season chicken breasts with salt and pepper and let sit awhile. Then dredge chicken breasts with seasoned flour and dip into eggs. In heavy flameproof pan, sauté chicken breasts in oil over low heat about 10 minutes on each side.

In same pan, place tablespoon of spinach on each chicken breast, sprinkle with Parmesan cheese, and cover each with a slice of mozzarella cheese. Bake 10–12 minutes. Remove from oven and transfer chicken to heated platter.

Place same pan over low heat. Add butter, wine, and lemon juice, stir until sauce reduces in volume. Stir in chicken broth.

To serve, place chicken breasts on bed of chopped spinach and pour lemon sauce over each piece of chicken. Serve with green salad and fettucine.

CHICKEN AND MUSHROOMS WITH BASIL GARLIC SAUCE

SERVES 6

It may seem to you that I've given all the secrets of this recipe in the title. Not so. You have to taste it to test it, and it passes the test every time. It's really chicken with a pesto sauce, so, if fresh basil isn't available, wait until summer. I've got a million other recipes.

3 whole boneless chicken breasts
Salt and pepper to taste
Flour for dredging
2 tablespoons butter
1 tablespoon olive oil
3 tablespoons fresh basil, minced, *or* 1 tablespoon dried, soaked in 2 tablespoons dry
white wine and drained well
4 garlic cloves, mashed

5 tablespoons olive oil
5 tablespoons tomato paste
1/4 cup freshly grated Parmesan cheese
Salt and pepper to taste
12 slices french bread, 1/2 inch thick
1/4 cup clarified butter or oil
1/2 pound small mushrooms, wiped with
dampened paper towels and trimmed
2 tablespoons olive oil

Quarter chicken breasts, place between sheets of waxed paper, and flatten with a mallet until they are 1/4 inch thick. Sprinkle chicken with salt and pepper and dredge with flour, shaking off any excess.

In heavy skillet sauté chicken in butter and olive oil over moderately high heat 2–3 minutes on each side, or until golden. Transfer to flameproof casserole.

In a bowl, combine basil with garlic cloves mashed to a smooth paste, and add olive oil in a stream, stirring. Whisk in tomato paste, Parmesan cheese, and salt and pepper to taste. Blend sauce until smooth.

In skillet over moderately high heat, sauté french bread slices in clarified butter or oil, turning them until they are golden. With a slotted spatula, transfer to paper towels to drain.

In another skillet sauté mushrooms in olive oil over moderately high heat. Stir 3–4 minutes until they are golden. Add sauce and simmer mixture, stirring, for 3 minutes. Pour mushroom mixture over chicken and place over moderate heat until chicken is warmed through. Transfer mixture to heated serving dish and surround with sautéed bread slices.

MOLDED IRANIAN BAKED CHICKEN WITH RICE
SERVES 6–8

The first time I made this my friend Marianne said, "Please pass me some more of the Trousdale special." I tried not to look wounded at the Blue Plate sound of it. Then she explained that after our new cookbook came out she was sure she'd be served this one at every buffet in Beverly Hills and Trousdale for months on end. I hope so.

1/4 cup softened butter, plus 2 tablespoons
butter cut into 1/4-inch pieces
3 cups uncooked Italian or oriental rice
2 (2–2 1/2-pound) chickens, skinned and
boned and cut into bite-sized pieces

Salt and freshly ground pepper to taste
1 1/2 cups milk
1 cup heavy cream
4 cups chicken stock

Preheat oven to 400°F.

Using pastry brush, heavily coat bottom and sides of 8-cup soufflé dish with 1/4 cup softened butter. Don't miss corners and crevices.

Rinse rice in sieve under running water until water runs clear. Spread 1 1/2 cups of rice evenly in dish, arrange pieces of chicken on top, and sprinkle liberally with salt and pepper.

In saucepan bring milk, cream, and 2 cups of stock to a boil over high heat. Pour over chicken. Spread rest of rice on top and dot evenly with cut-up butter.

Bake uncovered 15 minutes on lowest shelf of oven.

Meanwhile bring remaining 2 cups of stock to simmer in small saucepan and keep it barely simmering over low heat. Pour 1 cup of simmering stock into casserole and bake 15 minutes longer.

Pour in remaining stock and transfer casserole to upper third of oven. Continue baking another 45–50 minutes until golden brown. Remove casserole from oven, cover tightly with lid or foil, and let rest at room temperature about 20 minutes or until you're ready to serve—it won't cool off too quickly.

To unmold and serve, run sharp knife around inside edges of casserole to loosen rice and let it rest 10 minutes longer. Place heated serving platter upside down over top and, grasping casserole and platter together firmly, quickly invert them. The molded golden rice should slide out easily and perfectly. Serve at once.

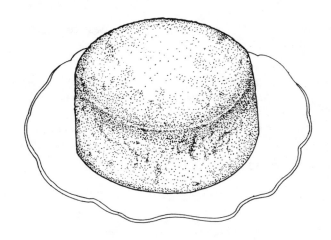

Serve Iranian baked chicken unmolded. Golden brown in color, this dish will slip easily from mold when turned upside down onto serving platter.

CHICKEN WITH ALMONDS

SERVES 4

When I was about ten years old our family took its first trip across the United States—to California from Tennessee. It was memorable for many reasons. In Los Angeles I saw fourteen genuine movie stars, got autographs from twenty-seven possibles, and almost saw Greta Garbo walking around the corner of a movie set. It was awesome.

We drove up to San Francisco and it was memorable for two reasons. My father, ordinarily a very taciturn man, kept exclaiming, "Look how this car is taking these hills!" (We had a Studebak-

er.) And to my mother, "That Buick you wanted would never have made it." I don't exactly remember her rebuttal, but she was never known as one for not having her say.

My other vivid memory was my first encounter with Chinese food. I had not the foggiest notion of what it was, but I was not going to leave San Francisco without having at least tasted the national world-famous obligatory dish of China—Chop Suey. The family wouldn't touch it. I remember them standing around watching me doggedly plow through the whole bowl. It was not the best thing I ever tasted, but it was the newest and I pronounced it deeeelicious. Even then I knew a new city was its food as well as its history. If I had only known what to order. My next encounter was luckier. Someone ordered sweet and sour pork or chicken with almonds. It was also deeelicious and I have been in love with it ever since.

1 cup oil

1/3 cup uncooked skinless almonds, rinsed and dried on paper towels

CHICKEN OR PORK MIXTURE

1 1/2 chicken breasts, boned, skinned, and cut into 1/2-inch cubes (to make 1 cup) *or* 1 cup pork cut into 1/2-inch cubes
1/4 teaspoon salt

1 egg white
Pinch white pepper
1/8 teaspoon sugar
1 teaspoon cornstarch

Mix well together to coat chicken or pork and let sit at least 15 minutes before deep-frying. Place in separate container:

2 slices fresh ginger root, each as big and thick as a quarter
1 clove garlic, peeled and crushed
4 dried Chinese mushrooms, soaked in hot water 20 minutes; discard stems, cut caps into 1/2-inch squares
1/2 cup green or red peppers in 1/3-inch

pieces
1/2 cups pineapple in 1/3-inch cubes
1/2 cup quartered water chestnuts
1/3 cup bamboo shoots in 1/3-inch cubes
1 scallion cut into pea-sized pieces, including green part

SAUCE

4 tablespoons thin soy sauce
2 tablespoons black soy sauce
1 teaspoon sugar

2 tablespoons pale dry sherry
1 tablespoon sesame seed oil

Mix all ingredients in small bowl.

1 teaspoon cornstarch

2 teaspoons water

Heat oil in wok over high heat to deep-fry temperature (300°–380°F.). Deep-fry almonds until golden brown. Drain on paper towels.

Reheat oil in wok. Add chicken mixture and stir to separate pieces. Stir-fry chicken quickly just until it turns white. Remove with slotted spoon. Place in bowl. If using pork, stir-fry until pork is very crisp. Remove with slotted spoon and drain on paper towels.

Remove all but 1 tablespoon of oil from wok. Heat oil, add ginger and garlic. Brown them slightly and discard.

Add mushrooms, peppers, pineapple, water chestnuts, and bamboo shoots. Stir-fry about 1 minute. If using pork, return pork to wok and stir-fry 30 seconds. If using chicken, return chicken to wok. To chicken or pork mixture, add scallions and stir-fry 30 seconds. Add sauce mixture and cornstarch mixed with 2 teaspoons water, stir-fry another 30 seconds. It will thicken slightly and glaze. Place on serving platter. Top with almonds. Serve hot.

HOT-HOT CHICKEN

SERVES 4–6

SAUCE

2 teaspoons chili paste with garlic
1/4 cup dark soy sauce
2 tablespoons dry sherry
2 teaspoons red wine vinegar

2 teaspoons sugar
1/2 cup chicken stock
2 teaspoons cornstarch
2 teaspoons sesame seed oil

Blend sauce ingredients and set aside.

4 chicken breasts, skinned, boned, and cut
    into 1/2-inch cubes
1 teaspoon salt

1 egg white (or 2 if eggs are small)
2 tablespoons cornstarch

Combine chicken, salt, egg white, and cornstarch. Mix well and set aside.

To simplify wok cooking, prepare and measure all ingredients several hours before serving. Refrigerate if necessary. Just before cooking, place on tray near wok in order of use.

2 to 3 cups peanut oil
1 cup roasted peanuts
15–20 whole dried red chili peppers

4 scallions, cut into 1/2-inch lengths
4 cloves garlic, minced

Heat oil in wok to 375°F. Use enough oil for deep-frying. Deep-fry chicken pieces until they separate and are almost cooked. Remove with strainer. Set aside and keep warm.

Reheat oil. Deep-fry peanuts over moderate heat until golden brown. Remove with strainer. (Be careful here—they brown quickly.) Remove all but 2 tablespoons oil in wok. Reheat oil in wok until very hot—smoking.

Stir-fry chili peppers until dark red. Lower heat and add scallions and garlic. Stir-fry 30 seconds. Return heat to high and cook chicken in wok about 1 minute. Add sauce and stir until heated through and chicken pieces are glazed. Add peanuts and serve immediately with steamed rice.

LE BISTRO ROAST DUCKLING—WITH MY ORANGE SAUCE
SERVES 6–8

I love duckling—but it has to be just right. One of the few places you can count on consistently having it "just right" is our little Beverly Hills hangout, Le Bistro. Kurt Niklas, owner and managing director, persuaded their fine chef to part with his secret. It's so simple that really there was no secret at all.

Meanwhile, here's their duckling with my Orange Sauce, which some ducks have been known to fly all the way from Long Island just to be accompanied by.

2 5-pound Long Island ducklings
Salt and pepper

2 tablespoons oil or butter, or enough to barely cover bottom of roasting pan

Preheat oven to 475°F.

Wash ducklings inside and out and dry well. Season with salt and pepper inside and out. Pierce skin of ducks all over. Roast uncovered for 25 minutes on each side or up to 1 hour and 15 minutes total. Pierce duck skins again from time to time to allow grease to run out. When three fourths done, pour grease out of roasting pan. Return to oven and finish roasting.

When ducks are done, cut into quarters and remove backbone. Place quarters skin side down on preheated griddle. Weight by placing a large roasting pan filled with unopened heavy cans of vegetables, fruits, etc. (you may use other weights such as bricks) on top of duck. Grill 8–10 minutes, or until skin is very crisp.

ORANGE SAUCE

2/3 cup brown sugar, tightly packed
2/3 cup granulated sugar
Scant 2 tablespoons cornstarch
2 tablespoons grated orange rind
1 1/2 cups orange juice

1/2 cup Cointreau or Grand Marnier or any orange-flavored liqueur
1/2 teaspoon salt
Skin of 1/2 orange, cut into very thin strips

Combine sugars in saucepan. Add cornstarch, orange rind, orange juice, liqueur, salt, and orange strips. Simmer 3–4 minutes, until transparent and slightly thickened. The Orange Sauce is an accompaniment and not a disguise for this duck, so I let people sprinkle a little on top and a little on the side.

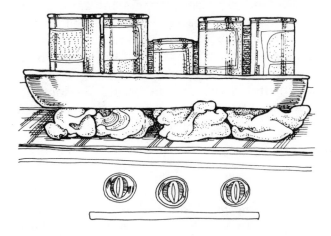

Place duck quarters on griddle and weight with shallow roasting pan filled with heavy cans.

TURKEY AND RED PEPPERS IN TOMATO CREAM SAUCE

SERVES 4

Carl Sontheimer is a good friend who is interested in food to the nth degree. He brought the Cuisinart into my life and many recipes along with it. He has a monthly magazine, called Pleasures of Cooking. *This was in it. The dish ends up so beautiful and delicious I asked his permission to pass it along to you. It's an inexpensive winner!*

2-pound turkey breast
2 medium red bell peppers
1 medium tomato, peeled, seeded, and diced
1 tablespoon butter
1 tablespoon olive oil
Salt and freshly ground pepper to taste
1/4 cup Madeira wine
1/2 cup chicken stock

1 teaspoon fresh minced thyme or 2/3 teaspoon dried, crumbled
1 teaspoon fresh minced marjoram or 2/3 teaspoon dried, crumbled
1/2 cup heavy cream
Juice of 1/2 lemon
1 tablespoon minced chives
1 tablespoon butter, cut into 2 pieces

Skin and bone turkey breast and remove tendons. Cut meat into 1 1/2 × 3/4-inch strips.

Remove stems and seeds from peppers. Cut peppers into strips same size as turkey strips.

Bring small pot of water to boil. Place diced tomato in sieve and immerse in boiling water for 1 minute. Drain on paper towels.

Heat butter and oil in large heavy skillet. Add peppers and stir-fry over high heat about 3 minutes, until crisp and tender. With slotted spoon remove peppers to colander. Drain over bowl and reserve juice.

Place turkey in hot skillet, adding more oil if necessary, and stir-fry over high heat about 3 minutes, until turkey is white and firm to the touch. With slotted spoon, add turkey to colander. Season peppers and turkey with salt and pepper.

Add Madeira, chicken stock, reserved juice, thyme, and marjoram to skillet and boil over high heat until reduced to thick syrup, using wooden spoon to scrape up any particles clinging to bottom of pan. Add heavy cream and continue to boil until reduced and thickened.

Lower heat and stir in lemon juice and chives. Season with salt and pepper. Whisk in butter, a piece at a time. Add turkey, peppers, and tomato and cook over low heat until just heated through. Serve immediately.

TURKEY EDEN   SERVES 4–6

Graham Kerr, the galloping Australian gourmet, made several visits to the show. On one occasion he cooked something that is very similar to this. It could have come right from the Garden of Eden before Weight Watchers.

2-pound turkey breast, uncooked   2 medium onions, finely chopped
4–6 tablespoons clarified butter

SAUCE

6 ounces (3/4 cup) tarragon vinegar   6 egg yolks, lightly beaten
3 teaspoons dried tarragon   1 cup butter
Salt and freshly ground white pepper to
   taste

Green spinach noodles
Fresh parsley, chopped

Slice meat away from breastbone, remove skin and tendons, and cut each breast into long thin strips. Heat serving dish in warming oven.

Pour clarified butter into heated skillet to just cover bottom, and add turkey strips. When turkey is white, remove from skillet with slotted spoon. Add onions to butter remaining in skillet, sauté slightly, add turkey and juices, and salt and freshly ground pepper to taste. Turn over lightly to get onion seasoning over all.

In another smaller skillet mix tarragon vinegar and dried tarragon and season with salt and white pepper. Bring to boil and watch carefully until liquid has almost completely reduced. (You need only 2 tablespoons.) Put 2 tablespoons of tarragon mixture in top of double boiler over simmering water, add egg yolks, and stir gently. Whisk in butter gradually. Season with salt and white pepper and whisk briskly so all ingredients are blended well together and texture is light and creamy.

Lower heat under skillet with turkey and stir in sauce. The pan must not be too hot or else sauce will curdle. If pan heat is too high and sauce curdles, all you have to do is add 1 ice cube and whisk it around in sauce. Ice has the effect of making butter harden, allowing sauce to smooth out once more. Place green spinach noodles on heated platter. Top with turkey mixture. Garnish with parsley.

Chapter 7

FISH

I hope we don't run out of fish. I was a long time discovering it as the great, delectable treat it is. We had crisp-fried fish, salmon croquettes, tuna in salads, fresh oysters in cartons, and crab meat from cans. Tennessee is not exactly a coastal state and we hardly ever traveled to one. But now that I've learned, there's never a week that passes that I don't have some marvelous sea-bred delicacy. You'll find a large number in this book, and many ways of preparing them. Today they're shipped, almost immediately after they're caught, to all parts of the country in the water in which they lived or in ice.

Freshness is vitally important. Look for clear, bulging eyes, elastic, firm flesh, and reddish-pink gills—and remember, it shouldn't smell fishy.

Frozen fish is almost as good these days as the fresh, as it is flash-frozen before it has a chance to deteriorate in any way. This is especially true of shrimp. Unless you pulled it out of the water yourself or watched someone do it, odds are it was flash-frozen. When a recipe calls for fresh, raw, or green shrimp, it generally means fish that was caught, flash-frozen, and allowed to defrost under ideal circumstance and in small batches for sale at your fish counter, so don't buy it for refreezing. Only after you've cooked it may it be refrozen.

Fish that is a day or so old—an extra fillet or so in your refrigerator—can be refreshed by soaking in milk (especially true with scallops, fresh or not). Or, better still, slip the fish into a shallow bowl with a few ice cubes floating in it for 15 to 30 minutes and it will think it's been swimming upstream and will taste delicious.

Be careful not to overcook fish or shellfish. They're delicate in flavor and texture and are done when the shrimp turn pink, the lobster red, the scallops white and opaque and lose that translucent look. Fish is done when it's whitish and opaque and flakes when pricked delicately with a fork. When buying fish, figure on 1/2 pound per serving; or if you're cooking Chinese-style, as with meats, allow 1/4 pound per person.

Fish is a great diet dish. It has enormous nutritional value, is low in cholesterol (except for shellfish—shrimp and lobster in particular), and (again with some exceptions) is economical. If you *are* buying the expensive varieties, serve small portions accompanied by lots of other goodies.

Did I tell you about the first time I baked a fish? We had very thorough and well-conducted home economics classes once a week in grammar school—cooking alternating with sewing, housekeeping, art, and penmanship. (Well, two out of five ain't bad.)

One day I arrived late for my favorite class of the whole curriculum (something to do with a discussion about a missing math paper, I think), but I missed the first part where they had already studied, scaled, and cleaned the fresh fish inside and out, and were on to the stuffing and baking part. It was terrific! I couldn't wait to cook it for Daddy for dinner. My tolerant family let me. I washed it outside—sort of—and prepared the good part, the stuffing. It didn't taste or smell like the one we had done in class that morning, but Daddy plowed right through his generous portion, shaking his head from time to time, which I took for "Good—really good." I've forgiven him many times over for the times we had strong disagreements over boys, clothes, singing career, and my grades for this sweet generous moment when he ate that fish despite the fact that I hadn't scaled the outside nor removed the entrails before stuffing the thing!

You probably won't be faced with this problem today. They always scale and clean the fish they sell you and bone them if you ask. If they don't, it's not all that hard to do. Just keep the knife sharp and *voilà!*—you're an expert. Try the Stuffed Red Snapper with Shrimp Sauce and the Baked Red Snapper Mexico City Style. They're different and go a long way in serving a good-sized crowd. The Chinese Scallops is a piquant wonder, as is the Crispy Sweet and Sour Fish. When I say, "Shrimpers and Rice (Are Very Nice)" I'm understating. Just to get to salmon or any other thin fish scallops for a moment, those Fish Scallops with Spinach Sauce are "mmmmwah"! Not to mention the crispy Goujonnettes of Sole. Need I go on? You're dealing with a relative novice to the fish field, all the more devoted an experimenter to make up for lost time!

BROILED SEA BASS OR RED SNAPPER WITH VERA CRUZ SAUCE   SERVES 4

Here's that antidote to that rich creamed-and-sauced dinner you gorged on the night before—delicious, virtuous, and no deprivation here.

1 1/2 pounds fresh sea bass or red snapper	Juice of 1/2 lemon or lime
Salt and pepper	Vera Cruz Sauce

Season fish with salt, pepper, and lemon or lime juice.

Broil about 2 minutes on each side on rack closest to heat. Test with fork. When fish flakes, it is done. Do not overcook.

Add juice from broiler pan to sauce. Pour over broiled sea bass or red snapper and serve hot with steamed green buttered vegetables in season, such as broccoli, spinach, or asparagus.

VERA CRUZ SAUCE

1 teaspoon oil or butter	1 tablespoon finely chopped green pepper
1 tablespoon chopped scallions	3 mushrooms, finely chopped
1 large shallot, chopped, *or* 1 teaspoon finely minced garlic	1 tomato, peeled and chopped
1 tablespoon finely chopped celery	1 teaspoon red salsa, or to taste
	1/2 teaspoon salt, or to taste

Sauté all sauce ingredients in oil or butter. Simmer, covered, until flavors are blended.

STUFFED RED SNAPPER WITH SHRIMP SAUCE

One beautiful day I was strolling out to the end of the Malibu pier through the singles and pairs of people—washed in that California sunshine, chatting, fishing off the sides of the pier, reading or knitting—comfortable, calm, rare peaceful images that for no reason become indelibly stamped in your mind. You've been there dozens of times. I walked into the fish market at the end of the pier to the fish tanks with live crabs swimming around, along with crawfish, California lobster, shrimp, bass, etc. I wanted to take them all home, knowing they would stay as fresh as the day I was enjoying.

Suddenly an enthusiastic fellow with a beaming smile and an irresistible Italian accent burst through the door with a fish dangling from his line. "Anybody want a red snapper?" he asked. "Just caught him and I already have mine for dinner. No point in wasting it." He didn't need any sales pitch for me. "I do! What will I do with him? He looks pretty big." "Stuff him," he said, "with some of these beautiful shrimp over here, some bread crumbs, a little parsley and onions and call in all your friends." I did and a recipe was born. I've seen, read, tasted stuffed red snapper a variety of ways, but none have been better than this—my Malibu bit of California Dreaming.

1 (4–5-pound) whole red snapper or sea bass, head and tail intact	Juice of 1 lemon or lime
Salt and freshly ground black pepper	Unsalted butter, softened

Clean fish thoroughly. Bone it, disturbing shape of fish as little as possible. (Your fish man will do this for you at no extra charge.) Place fish in shallow oblong roasting pan. (It may have to be placed in pan diagonally to accommodate length.)

Sprinkle inside cavity with salt, pepper, and lemon or lime juice. Spread with softened butter.

STUFFING

2 tablespoons butter	1 teaspoon dried basil
2 tablespoons finely chopped or grated onion	1 tablespoon chopped parsley
1 tablespoon finely chopped green pepper	6 medium-sized raw shrimp, shelled, deveined, and cut into small chunks
1 tablespoon finely chopped celery	
1/2 cup fresh bread crumbs	1/4 cup toasted chopped or slivered almonds
Salt and freshly ground black pepper	2 tablespoons fish stock (page 8) or clam juice
1/2 teaspoon dried tarragon	

Preheat oven to 400°F.

Heat butter in 10-inch skillet and sauté onions until just transparent. Add green peppers, celery, bread crumbs, salt, pepper, tarragon, and basil; then add parsley and uncooked shrimp. Continue cooking and stirring until shrimp barely start to turn pink. Add almonds and fish stock. Stuffing is done when shrimp are all pink.

Stuff fish and secure cavity loosely with toothpicks or skewers. Sprinkle outside of fish with salt, pepper, and a little lemon or lime juice. Dot generously with unsalted butter.

Cover with foil pressed around edges of baking pan. Place fish in oven and bake 20 minutes. Uncover and bake 15 minutes longer or until fish flakes easily. Carefully remove fish to hot platter, using 2 large spatulas so it won't break.

SHRIMP SAUCE

1 tablespoon cornstarch
1/2 cup fish stock or clam juice
Salt and freshly ground black pepper to taste
1/2 teaspoon dried basil
1/2 teaspoon fresh dill, chopped (optional)

1/2 cup dry white wine or vermouth
2 medium-sized raw shrimp, shelled, deveined, and cut into small chunks
1/4 cup heavy cream

Place roasting pan from which fish has been removed over medium heat on top of stove. Add cornstarch to drippings in dish. Stirring with wire whisk, pour in fish stock or clam juice. Add salt, pepper, basil, and dill. Add white wine or vermouth.

Raise heat to reduce sauce slightly, cook about 3 minutes. Add shrimp and when shrimp are pink blend in cream, stirring constantly with wooden spoon to keep from sticking to pan. Taste for seasoning. Pour a little sauce over fish, reserving the remainder to be served on the side. Garnish with parsley.

BAKED RED SNAPPER MEXICO CITY STYLE

SERVES 6

You may feel that this section has an inordinate number of recipes for red snapper. There is a reason. It's available year round, is wonderfully accommodating, and tastes totally different each time depending upon your extra added dimensions. Plain broiled fish with a squeeze of lemon or lime is just fine, but it could get a little boring. I guarantee that nobody will give you the "not again" look with the variety that I have gathered, garnered, and culled here.

The Stuffed Red Snapper with Shrimp Sauce is another baked red snapper. Baked Red Snapper Mexico City Style looks similar but is entirely different in form and flavor. One day Clara, our accommodating butcher at Trancas Market in Malibu, had not one left of the whole red snapper or sea bass she usually keeps in quantity. She found four beautiful fillets, sewed two together on one side with kitchen twine (easily removed after cooking) and voilà! The fish had no bones, no skin—it was perfectly whole and ready for stuffing.

1 large whole fresh red snapper or 4 fillets
Salt and pepper
4 tablespoons butter
1 tablespoon green chile salsa (picante style)
3 scallions, chopped medium fine
1/2 green pepper, finely chopped
1/2 sweet red pepper, finely chopped
1/2 pound large shrimp, peeled, deveined, and cut into thirds
1/2 cup fresh bread crumbs
2 tablespoons plus 2 teaspoons fresh lemon juice
2 tablespoons plus 2 teaspoons fresh orange juice
2 tablespoons finely chopped cilantro
Salt and pepper to taste
1/2 cup plus 3 tablespoons chicken broth
1/2 green pepper, cut into strips
1/2 sweet red pepper, cut into strips
Lemon slice or wedges for garnish
Iceberg lettuce, shredded for garnish

Remove center bones from fish, trying not to tear one side of fish, so that you have a pocket the full length of fish. (If you are unable to get a whole red snapper, sew two fillets together with kitchen string, leaving one side open for a pocket. Repeat procedure with remaining 2 fillets.)

Sprinkle salt and pepper inside and out. Rub lightly with 2 tablespoons butter, inside and out. Rub green chile salsa inside fish.

Preheat oven to 375°F.

In skillet heat 2 tablespoons butter, add scallions, and cook until pale and translucent but not brown. Add chopped red and green peppers and half of shrimp, and sauté until shrimp are just pink. Add bread crumbs, 1 teaspoon lemon juice, 1 teaspoon orange juice, and 1 tablespoon cilantro. Taste for seasoning and add salt and pepper and 3 tablespoons chicken broth. Mix lightly but thoroughly.

Pack mixture lightly in pocket of fish. Place fish in well-greased baking pan. Sprinkle with remaining shrimp, green and red pepper strips, and 1 tablespoon cilantro.

Mix 1/4 cup chicken broth, 1 tablespoon lemon juice, and 1 tablespoon orange juice. Pour mixture over fish. Cover with foil. Bake 30 minutes or until fish flakes easily when tested with fork. Remove foil 5 minutes before fish is done so it will brown. Place fish on bed of shredded lettuce on warmed platter.

Deglaze pan with remaining chicken broth and lemon and orange juices. Reduce sauce until it is slightly thickened. Pour over fish and garnish with lemon slices or wedges.

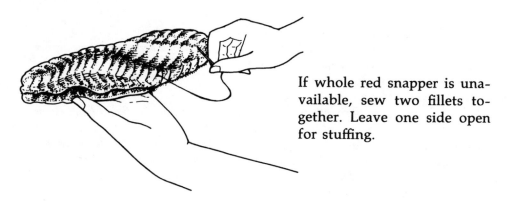

If whole red snapper is unavailable, sew two fillets together. Leave one side open for stuffing.

BROILED FISH PIMIENTO

SERVES 6

Low-calorie cooking at its simplest, purest, and most beautiful, courtesy of Pleasures of Cooking.

1 (2 to 3-pound) whole red snapper, trout, or sea bass, boned with head and tail attached, *or* 2 large red snapper or sea bass fillets

2 tablespoons vegetable oil

Coarse salt

Freshly ground black pepper

4 tablespoons (1/2 stick) unsalted butter

4 shallots, peeled and minced

2 4-ounce jars pimientos

1/4 cup vegetable stock (page 8)

1/2 teaspoon salt

1 small green pepper (about 3 ounces), diced

1 tablespoon green peppercorns, crushed (optional)

3 tablespoons minced fresh chives or parsley

Wash fish and pat dry with paper towels. Oil entire surface. Sprinkle one side with coarse salt and pepper. Set aside.

Line broiler pan with heavy-duty aluminum foil or double thickness of regular foil. Place pan 6 inches from heat and preheat broiler. When pan is hot, remove and oil foil generously, using pastry brush. Sprinkle with coarse salt. Place fish seasoned side down on foil. Sprinkle top with coarse salt and pepper. Broil for 5–10 minutes, depending on thickness of fish, until top side is firm but not hard.

Turn fish gently by rolling it over with aid of foil and spatula. Broil 3 to 5 minutes longer, until second side is firm but not hard. Transfer to warm serving platter and cover with aluminum foil while you prepare sauce.

Melt 2 tablespoons butter in 7-inch skillet over moderately high heat. Add shallots and cook, stirring, for 2 minutes until soft but not brown.

Place pimientos with liquid in processor bowl and process until smooth, about 30 seconds. Add vegetable stock and process for 5 seconds. Add pimiento mixture to skillet with shallots and heat through. Season with salt and pepper. Lower heat to keep mixture warm.

In another small skillet, melt remaining 2 tablespoons butter over moderately high heat. Add diced green pepper and crushed green peppercorns. Cook, stirring, 2–3 minutes, just until warm. Sprinkle green peppers and peppercorns over fish. Spoon warm pimiento sauce around fish. Sprinkle with chives or parsley.

BROILED FILLET OF RED FISH WITH OYSTER AND ARTICHOKE SAUCE SERVES 8–10

Red fish is red snapper. It's as popular in New Orleans with Madame Pichon, who sent us this, as it is with us out here. This is an unusually simple combination that makes broiled fish a party. Just be sure to make the sauce first—the fish can't wait.

4 pounds red snapper fillets
Salt and pepper to taste
Juice of 1–2 lemons

2 tablespoons (1/4 stick) margarine, melted
Paprika
Oyster and Artichoke Sauce

Rinse fish fillets in cold water and pat dry. Season with salt and pepper. Pour lemon juice and margarine over fish and sprinkle lightly with paprika.

Broil under direct heat on top rack about 8 minutes. Do not turn fish. When fish is done, set aside and keep warm. When ready to serve, pour sauce over broiled fish in large heated casserole.

OYSTER AND ARTICHOKE SAUCE

1/4 cup finely chopped shallots
1/2 teaspoon minced fresh garlic
1/2 cup (1 stick) margarine
1/2 pint oysters, cut into bite-sized pieces
    (reserve liquor)

16-ounce can artichoke hearts
1/2 cup chicken broth
1 bay leaf
1/8 cup finely chopped fresh parsley
2 teaspoons cornstarch

Sauté shallots and garlic in margarine in small skillet.

Scald oysters in their liquor about 2 to 3 minutes until puffy and edges begin to curl. Drain well and set aside, reserving liquid.

Remove outer leaves of artichoke hearts and cut into less than bite-sized pieces, reserving liquid.

In small saucepan, add liquid from oysters and artichokes to chicken broth to make at least 1 cup. Add bay leaf and parsley to liquid and combine with shallot and garlic mixture. Simmer until liquid is reduced and slightly thickened, about 5 minutes. Add artichokes and simmer 5 minutes more. Remove bay leaf.

Mix cornstarch with 2 or 3 tablespoons of sauce and add to sauce for thickening.

Just prior to serving, add oysters to sauce and mix well. Sauce should be made before broiling fish.

FILLET OF SOLE–SALSA FRESCA   SERVES 4–6

This is another marvelous dish I first tasted in Mexico, where they have a wonderful way with fish fillets. This is equally good with red snapper fillets.

SALSA FRESCA

2 red, ripe tomatoes, peeled and finely chopped
1/2 cup finely chopped fresh onion
1 teaspoon fresh garlic, mashed with 1/2 teaspoon salt

1 tablespoon chopped fresh cilantro
3 fresh yellow chilies, seeded and finely chopped
1/4 teaspoon sugar (optional)

Mix all together well; add a little tomato juice if you wish.

SEASONED SOUR CREAM

1 tablespoon butter
4 tablespoons tiny shrimp
1 cup sour cream
2 tablespoons finely sliced green scallion

tops
1/2 fresh garlic clove, crushed in salt
Salt

Heat shrimp in butter. Mix well with sour cream, scallion tops, garlic, and salt.

6 sole fillets (about 2 pounds)
1/2 cup milk
1 cup seasoned fresh bread crumbs (salt and pepper to taste)

1/4 cup butter
Apples, carrots, and zucchini, julienned and briefly sautéed in butter, for garnish
Toasted sunflower seeds for garnish

Soak fish fillets in milk for 1/2 hour or more. Remove and pat dry.

Dip in seasoned bread crumbs.

Melt butter in a large heavy skillet over moderately high heat and sauté fillets 3 or 4 minutes on each side. They'll be light golden brown and thoroughly cooked.

Place slightly heated Salsa Fresca on each plate. Place cooked fillet in sauce and spoon it over center of fillet. Top with a dollop of Seasoned Sour Cream in center. Garnish with sautéed apples, carrots, and zucchini and sprinkle with toasted sunflower seeds.

RED SNAPPER PERNOD

SERVES 4–6

1/2 pound mushrooms, thinly sliced
1 tablespoon minced shallots
3 tablespoons butter
2 cups white fish stock (page 8) or 1 cup each clam juice and dry white wine

6 red snapper fillets, 8-ounces each
1 cup half-and-half
1/4 cup Pernod
1/2 stick cold butter, cut into bits
Salt and white pepper to taste

In large heavy skillet cook mushrooms and shallots in butter over moderate heat, stirring, for 5 minutes.

Add fish stock or clam juice and white wine and bring liquid to simmer.

Add fish fillets and poach 3 minutes on each side, until they just flake when tested with fork. Transfer fish and mushrooms with slotted spatula to heated platter.

Over high heat, reduce poaching liquid by two thirds, add half-and-half, and again reduce by half.

Add Pernod and bits of cold butter, 1 piece at a time, whisking well after each addition and adding next piece before preceding one is completely melted. Season sauce with salt and white pepper and pour over fish.

STEAMED FILLET OF SOLE WITH GREEN PEPPERCORN SAUCE

SERVES 4–6

QUICK FISH STOCK

Fishbones or 1/4 pound mild fish (red snapper or fillet of sole)
1 small onion
2 stalks celery, cut into halves

1 carrot, cut in half
2 sprigs parsley
Salt and pepper
2 cups water

2 pounds fillet of sole, or any mild, firm fish
2 bunches fresh spinach (if not available use outer leaves of lettuce)
2 tablespoons butter
Scant 2 tablespoons flour

2 tablespoons green peppercorns, drained, rinsed, and lightly crushed
1/4 cup white wine
2 tablespoons cream (optional)

Make fish broth in bottom of vegetable or fish steamer with fishbones or mild fish, onion, celery, carrot, parsley, salt, pepper, and water. Bring to boil and let simmer 10 minutes. (You may substitute 2 cups chicken stock or clam juice for this fish broth.)

Salt and pepper sole fillets lightly and set aside.

Thoroughly wash fresh spinach and remove stems. Blanch in boiling water 10 seconds until just limp. Drain well.

Wrap fish fillets with spinach leaves to cover completely. Tie with string to hold together. Set remaining spinach leaves aside and keep warm. Place spinach-wrapped fish fillets gently in single layer in tray of steamer. Be sure broth is at least 1 inch below steamer tray. Cover tightly and let steam 6–7 minutes while you make sauce.

In skillet melt butter, stir in flour and cook slowly; don't brown it, just cook long enough to remove raw flour taste. Add green peppercorns and stir well. Add up to 1 cup fish broth from steamer by small ladlefuls, whisking constantly to make smooth sauce. Add white wine. Raise heat and reduce sauce by one third. Taste for seasoning; you may or may not need salt. A couple of tablespoons of cream are nice if you're not dieting.

Place spinach-wrapped fillets on a warm platter. Carefully cut string and remove. Arrange reserved spinach as a garnish around fish. Spoon sauce over fish. Serve immediately.

MEXICO CITY SOLE

SERVES 4–6

Sole fillets usually appear in our markets about one-fourth to one-third inch thick. If it doesn't, ask your butcher or fish man to slice it for you. His knives may be sharper than yours. Serve immediately when done—don't wait; the combination of hot and cold temperature is irresistible.

2 pounds thinly sliced sole fillets (about 8 slices)	3 cups oil for deep frying
Salt and pepper	1/2 cup Pancake Batter
16-ounce can whole green chilies	1/4 cup melted butter
1/4 pound medium shrimp	1/4 cup Monterey Jack cheese, grated
	Guacamole

Lay fillets flat. Salt and pepper lightly. Place a whole green chilie and half a shrimp on each fillet, roll up, and seal with toothpicks.

Heat oil in deep, heavy frying pan or wok to 375°F. or until a scallion top browns in oil in 30 seconds.

Dip rolled sole in pancake batter and fry in hot oil for 1 1/2 minutes.

Remove with slotted spoon, place in shallow baking pan, and bake at 375°F. for 5 minutes.

Drizzle with melted butter and sprinkle generously with grated cheese. Place under broiler until cheese is melted. Serve with a generous tablespoon of cold Guacamole on top.

PANCAKE BATTER

1 1/2 cups flour	1 egg
1/4 teaspoon salt	2 tablespoons melted butter or oil
1/2 teaspoon baking powder	1 cup low-fat milk or water
1 teaspoon sugar	

Mix all ingredients to make a thin pancake batter. If too thick, add more milk or cheat a little. Use your favorite packaged pancake mix and add a little more liquid than called for.

GUACAMOLE

1 avocado
1/2 clove garlic, crushed
1 small tomato, peeled, seeded, and chopped

Salt
Tabasco sauce to taste
1 teaspoon lemon juice

Mash avocado with fork. Whip in other ingredients until smooth. Taste for seasoning.

FISH SCALLOPS WITH SPINACH SAUCE

SERVES 8

Le Français, just outside Chicago in Wheeling, Illinois, is known all over the world for its elegance and adherence to the early precepts of fine, no-holds-barred French cuisine. With so many choices, I decided I needed a week of intensive selective *dining to get the feel of it. Unfortunately, we were on the road, but I did get a couple of good goes at it before our troupe had to move on. Monsieur Banchet was kind enough to part with this light, delicate recipe, and also the Gâteau au Chocolat (page 326), which is so rich that one thin slice will carry you through your chocoholics for a week.*

2 pounds sole fillets
1 pound fresh spinach
1 tablespoon chopped shallots
2 tablespoons dry vermouth
2 tablespoons dry white wine
1 cup fish stock or clam juice

1 cup half-and-half
Salt and freshly ground pepper to taste
1 teaspoon lemon juice
1 egg yolk, lightly beaten
Flour for dredging
3/4 cup clarified butter

Place fish fillets on flat surface and, holding knife at an angle, slice fish on the bias, as you would smoked salmon. There should be about 16 slices, each slightly less than 1/2 inch thick.

Remove tough stems from spinach and discard any blemished leaves. Rinse leaves well and drain. Place leaves on flat surface and cut into very fine slivers.

In saucepan combine shallots, vermouth, white wine, and fish stock or clam juice. Cook until almost all the liquid has evaporated. Add half-and-half and cook over high heat about 5 minutes. Add salt and pepper to taste, then lemon juice. Stir in finely shredded spinach. Remove from heat and add 1 egg yolk.

Sprinkle fish slices with salt and pepper and dredge lightly in flour.

Heat about 1/2 cup clarified butter in a 12-inch skillet. Cook fish pieces, first on one side and then the other, about 1 or 2 minutes to each side. Do not overcook or the fish will become dry. Transfer to heated platter.

Swirl remaining butter into spinach sauce, and when it is melted and blended, pour hot sauce over fish. Serve immediately.

TROUT WITH ROASTED PECANS, CREOLE MEUNIÈRE SAUCE

I made the mistake of serving this first one evening at dinner. I say mistake—it was like opening the show with Sinatra or Pavarotti: nobody—nothing—could follow it. It is from Commander's Palace in New Orleans.

2 medium eggs, beaten
1 cup milk
1/2 teaspoon garlic powder
1/2 teaspoon salt
1/2 teaspoon black pepper
1/2 teaspoon cayenne pepper
1/2 teaspoon thyme

2 cups flour
6 6-ounce trout fillets
1/2 cup butter
1/2 cup roasted pecans, chopped for garnish
Fresh parsley for garnish
Lemon wedges for garnish

Beat together eggs and milk until well blended. Set aside.

Mix garlic powder, salt, peppers, thyme, and flour in large mixing bowl. Dredge trout fillets with seasoned flour, dip in egg-milk mixture, and dredge again with flour.

Melt butter in large skillet over medium high heat. Add trout and sauté quickly. Turn trout only once. Set aside in warm place.

PECAN BUTTER

1/2 cup chopped roasted pecans
1/4 cup butter
Juice of 1/2 medium lemon (approximately 3

tablespoons)
1 teaspoon Worcestershire sauce

Puree roasted pecans in blender or food processor. Add butter, lemon juice, and Worcestershire and blend well.

CREOLE MEUNIÈRE SAUCE

1 cup Brown Sauce (page 6)
1 cup butter, softened and cut into chunks
2 tablespoons Worcestershire sauce

Juice of 1 medium lemon
1/4 cup chopped fresh parsley

In 2-quart saucepan quickly bring Brown Sauce to a simmer.

Whip butter and Worcestershire into Brown Sauce, using wire whisk, until butter is completely absorbed.

Add lemon juice and parsley. Whip again. Remove from heat.

NOTE Sauce must be used within 45 minutes of preparation.

To Serve: Place one trout fillet on each individual plate. Top with heaping tablespoon of pecan butter to cover entire fillet. Sprinkle with heaping tablespoon of chopped roasted pecans. Cover trout and toppings with Creole Meunière Sauce. Garnish with fresh parsley and lemon.

CHINESE SCALLOPS

Instead of the pale, fragile manner in which scallops are treated in most recipes, this is one with a rich, pungent, dark sauce. Very satisfying and a great addition to a complete Chinese dinner. As with most Chinese dishes, a great deal of the preparation can be done ahead and assembled at that last lovely moment before serving. Tangerines are not always in season, of course, so when they are I peel a few and keep the peelings in a jar in the refrigerator. They keep for months and are used in several Chinese dishes, so they won't be wasted.

2 cups oil
1 pound fresh scallops (If big, slice each crosswise into 1/4-inch pieces)
1 tablespoon cornstarch

Mix cornstarch and scallops in bowl. Refrigerate before use.

SEASONINGS

1 piece dried tangerine peel, soaked in hot water for 15 minutes or until soft, and minced to make about 1 tablespoon
2–3 dried chili peppers with seeds, torn into small pieces
1 tablespoon minced garlic
1 teaspoon finely minced fresh ginger root
3 scallions, cut into pea-sized pieces including green part
1/4 cup green or red pepper, cut into 1/2-inch pieces (optional)

Place all ingredients on plate and set aside.

SAUCE

3 tablespoons tomato catsup
5 tablespoons dark soy sauce
1 tablespoon sugar
1 teaspoon white vinegar
2 teaspoons pale dry sherry
1 tablespoon water

Blend all ingredients in small bowl.

Heat oil in wok to 375°F.

Add scallops. Stir to separate them, and deep-fry in oil for 30 seconds or until they are almost done, no more. Remove with strainer to bowl.

Remove all but 2 tablespoons oil from wok. Heat oil over medium heat, then drop in plateful of seasonings. When garlic and ginger turn golden, swirl in sauce mixture.

Return scallops to wok. Mix well. Cook and stir gently until sauce begins to bubble. Put on serving platter. Serve at once.

MY SPECIAL SCALLOPS

Scallops go a long way and so don't seem inordinately expensive. This was a substitute for a shrimp dish I had wanted to serve one day, but there weren't any raw shrimp around so I bought the scallops and raced home, beating the guests by thirty minutes. Scallops cook quickly—sometimes the simpler done the better.

2 pounds scallops, washed and cut in half
1 cup milk
Salt and pepper to taste
1/4 cup flour for dredging
2 tablespoons butter
2 teaspoons chopped shallots

2 teaspoons very fine quick-mixing flour
1/4 cup chicken or fish broth
1/4 cup white wine
2 tablespoons cream
Lemon wedges for garnish
Parsley for garnish

Soak scallops in milk for 30 minutes, longer if you have time. Pat dry with paper towels. Sprinkle generously with salt and pepper and dredge lightly in flour, brushing off excess.

Heat large skillet and add butter. When very hot, add shallots and then scallops. Shake skillet and turn scallops with spatula to brown on all sides. (Cook 2 minutes maximum.) Remove to warm platter.

Add 2 teaspoons flour and stir into residue remaining in skillet. Add chicken or fish broth, stirring constantly. Raise heat to high and reduce liquid by half.

Remove pan from heat and add cream. Bring to boil over high heat. Taste for seasoning. Place scallops in sauce for a few seconds, just to heat through. Serve immediately, garnished with lemon wedges and parsley.

SCALLOPS VITTORIO

SERVES 2–4

Mrs. Irene C. Montague at the Cucina della Campania in Chelmsford, Massachusetts, has a wonderful way with scallops. She sent me this one. Vittorio is the lucky guy who sampled her first effort and approved.

1 pound medium scallops
1/2 cup dry white wine
2 tablespoons butter
2 shallots, finely minced (green or yellow onions may be substituted)
1 small garlic clove, finely minced
2 teaspoons flour

Salt and freshly ground pepper
1 tablespoon flat-leafed (Italian) parsley, chopped
2 thin slices prosciutto, diced, *or* 2 slices crumbled crisp bacon
Freshly grated Parmesan cheese

Rinse scallops in cold water and drain. Place on paper towels to absorb excess moisture. Cut into 1/2-inch slices.

Place scallops in 1 1/2-quart saucepan, add white wine, bring to full boil. Separate scallop slices with wooden spoon and boil for 1 full minute, *no more*. Drain. Reserve cooking liquid.

Reduce cooking liquid to about 1/2 cup (it will be almost 3/4 cup due to liquid from scallops).

Melt butter in skillet and sauté shallots and garlic for 2 minutes. Blend in flour and gradually add cooking liquid from scallops, stirring constantly until well blended and thickened. Sprinkle with salt and freshly ground pepper to taste (not too much salt as prosciutto or bacon and cheese are also salty).

Add chopped parsley, scallops, and prosciutto or bacon, blending well with wooden spoon. Place in greased individual ramekins, sprinkle with grated cheese, and broil until bubbly and cheese has melted. Serve *immediately*.

SHRIMPS AND SCALLOPS BENGALESE

A light, delicately flavored curry from The Pear Tree in Rumson, New Jersey. Another of their lovely recipes is on page 232.

1/4 cup butter, softened
2 tablespoons finely chopped shallots
2 tablespoons curry powder
2 teaspoons ground ginger
2 dashes Tabasco sauce
2 dashes Worcestershire sauce
2 tablespoons chutney, cut into 1/4-inch chunks (I use Major Grey's)

1/8 teaspoon cayenne pepper
1 cup heavy cream
1/2 cup Brown Sauce (page 6)
4 large raw shrimp, shelled, deveined, and cut into halves
1/2 pound scallops, cut into halves
Salt and white pepper to taste

CONDIMENTS

Toasted coconut
Mandarin oranges (optional)
Chutney

Peanuts, chopped
Raisins

Heat butter in large skillet, add shallots, and sauté until golden brown.

Add curry, ginger, Tabasco, Worcestershire, chutney, cayenne, cream, and Brown Sauce. Simmer over medium heat. Reduce sauce until it becomes smooth.

Add shrimp and cook until pink, then add scallops (they don't take quite as long to cook). Cook 3–5 minutes or until shrimp are cooked and scallops are white and opaque. Season to taste with salt and pepper and a little more curry and cayenne if you like it more piquant.

Serve in a large casserole surrounded with little individual bowls of condiments and hot boiled rice sprinkled with coconut.

SCALLOP BALLS

One of those light, crispy, puffed-up Chinese dishes that make you a legend in your own home. This recipe looks long, but only because I want you to see clearly the simple steps which, if followed, will make the dish a cinch.

1 pound fresh scallops, chilled
2 teaspoons minced peeled fresh ginger root
2 teaspoons Chinese rice wine or pale dry sherry
1 1/2 teaspoons coarse (kosher) salt
1/2 teaspoon white pepper

4 teaspoons cornstarch
2 egg whites, chilled
1 cup untoasted white sesame seeds (approximate)
3 cups oil for deep frying

SAUCE

3 tablespoons white vinegar
4 tablespoons sugar
2 teaspoons thin soy sauce
2 tablespoons catsup
1/2 cup hot water

2 tablespoons vegetable oil
1 teaspoon finely chopped garlic
1/2 teaspoon minced fresh ginger root
2 teaspoons cornstarch dissolved in two tablespoons cold water

Place scallops and ginger in bowl of food processor fitted with metal blade. Process until scallops are coarsely minced. Add wine, salt, white pepper, cornstarch, and egg whites and process until scallop mixture is smooth. Remove to a small bowl.

Spread sesame seeds on flat surface or plate. Put a piece of waxed paper about a foot long on a large platter or cookie sheet, and clear a place in your refrigerator for cookie sheet holding finished scallop balls.

Place in this order on counter in front of you: a tablespoon measure, small bowl of ice water, scallop mixture, sesame seeds, and waxed-paper-lined cookie sheet. Dip spoon in ice water and scoop up 1 heaping tablespoon of scallop mixture. Dip your fingers and palms in water next. Form the tablespoon of scallop mixture into a small ball, rolling it between your palms and smoothing surface with your fingers. Roll scallop ball in sesame seeds until it is fully coated. Put coated ball on waxed paper on cookie sheet. Repeat this process until all scallop mixture has been used. Place cookie sheet with coated scallop balls in refrigerator. Up to this point, Scallop Balls can be prepared in the morning.

Put wok or deep pan over high heat and add enough oil to deep-fry scallop balls. While oil is heating, prepare sauce by combining vinegar, sugar, soy sauce, catsup, and hot water. Set aside. Heat a small saucepan over high heat for 10 seconds and add 2 tablespoons oil to pan. Reduce heat to medium, wait 10 seconds, and add garlic and ginger. Allow garlic and ginger to sizzle in oil for 1 minute and then add combined liquids to pan. Stir until mixture is heated through. Turn off heat and cover pan tightly.

Have a flat pan lined with paper towels near wok on which to drain fried scallop balls. By this time oil should have a slight haze over its surface. Wait a bit if it does not. When top of scallion dropped in oil turns brown in 30 seconds, oil is ready.

Remove scallop balls from refrigerator and try deep-frying one. The oil should be hot enough so that scallop ball rises to surface within 7 seconds, but not so hot that the sesame seeds will pop.

Deep-fry scallop balls about 5 at a time until they are light brown, about 3–5 minutes. Remove them to prepared pan to drain. When all scallop balls have been fried, allow oil to heat another 5 minutes and then drop in all of scallop balls at once to fry a second time. This time fry only for 1–2 minutes, or until seeds brown and balls swell. Remove with large, long-handled slotted spoon to fresh paper towels to drain. Arrange them on a serving plate.

Quickly raise heat under sauce to high. Stir sauce once, stir cornstarch mixture to recombine it and add it to sauce. Stir for minute or so until sauce thickens slightly and clears. Pour half into small bowl for use by those with an extra-sweet tooth. Pour remaining half over scallop balls. Serve immediately.

SALMON SCALLOPS WITH SORREL   SERVES 8–10

Sorrel has a short, happy season each year. When it's in, I use it in every possible way (see page 54). It's delightful with thin slices of salmon and you can use it as an hors d'oeuvre, but I really prefer it as a first course for a dinner party—a special one!

1/4 pound sorrel (if not available, you may use spinach with 1 tablespoon lemon juice)
1 cup vermouth
1 cup dry white wine or champagne
1 cup Fish Stock (page 8)
1/8 cup finely minced shallots

2 cups half-and-half
Salt and pepper
3 1/3 pounds fresh salmon, sliced into thin scallops
Butter
10 baked Pâte Brisée I half-moons (see page 19)

Devein sorrel and blanch in boiling salted water until just soft. If using spinach, blanch until just soft in boiling salted water to which you have added 1 tablespoon lemon juice. Drain well and set aside.

In saucepan combine vermouth, wine or champagne, fish stock, and shallots. Reduce to 1/2 cup. When it becomes thick and syrupy, remove from heat and cool.

Add half-and-half and reduce sauce again to bind liquids. Add salt and pepper to taste and then add sorrel or spinach. Set aside and keep warm.

Salt and pepper the salmon scallops. Sauté them in butter in a large skillet for a few seconds on both sides. Do not permit them to dry out.

To serve, place sorrel or spinach sauce on warmed plate and gently position scallops on top of sauce. Garnish with puff pastry half-moon.

POACHED SALMON   SERVES 4–6

2 stalks celery
1 tablespoon salt
Freshly ground pepper
2 scallions, including tops
Fresh dill, chopped
1/2 bay leaf

2 tablespoons chopped parsley
Juice of 1 lemon
2 cups white wine
Water to cover halfway up fish
2 1/2-pound whole piece of fresh salmon, boned

Pierce salmon gently here and there on sides and underneath to absorb flavorings. Rub a little salt into the cuts.

In large roasting pan, place all ingredients except salmon. Bring to boil and simmer 5 minutes.

Wrap salmon in cheesecloth and place in boiling liquid. Lower heat, cover (use heavy-duty aluminum foil if pan has no cover), and simmer gently 18–20 minutes or until salmon just begins to flake and has turned light pink.

Remove salmon carefully. Unwrap and serve hot or cold with Dill Mayonnaise (page 9), Mustard Mayonnaise (page 9), Cucumber Sour Cream (page 10), or Sauce Verte (page 10).

SOUTHERN FRIED CATFISH WITH HUSH PUPPIES

Catfish—!

One of the most succulent, juiciest, and ugliest-looking fish in existence (well, maybe not to another catfish). They used to scavenge the river bottoms for sustenance, but no more. They are now commercially grown—pure, still juicy, but not any prettier.

The story I always heard about the funny name of their constant companion is that after the hunt, while somebody was cooking up the catch of the day from the nearby river, the dogs would bay and yelp around the campfire so loudly that nobody could have a civilized conversation without shouting over the din. Then whoever was the cook that day dropped these delicate, light cornmeal dumplings in the frying fat and tossed them to the hounds, saying, "Hush, puppies." They did.

Some of my friends don't feel these are complete without a little syrup or honey drizzled over the hush puppies. I don't mind. To my notion, there's hardly anything that can hurt them.

HUSH PUPPIES

1/4 cup flour	3/4 cup buttermilk
2 teaspoons baking powder	1/4 cup vegetable oil
1/2 teaspoon salt	1/2 teaspoon baking soda
1 1/2 cups cornmeal	1 tablespoon finely chopped onion
1 egg, beaten	Oil

Combine flour, baking powder, and salt. Sift together into a deep bowl. Stir in unsifted cornmeal, then add egg and beat vigorously with wooden spoon until mixture is smooth.

Mix buttermilk and oil with soda, add it to flour mixture, and stir until completely absorbed. Batter should hold its shape in a spoon: if it seems too thick, add more buttermilk; if too thin, add more cornmeal. Beat in chopped onion.

Preheat oven to 200°F. Line large shallow baking dish with double thickness of paper towels and place dish in middle of oven.

In deep fryer or large heavy saucepan, place enough oil to fill pan to a depth of 2–3 inches. Heat oil until it reaches temperature of 375° on thermometer (or until a small bread cube turns brown in 1 minute).

For each Hush Puppy, push a rounded tablespoon of batter into hot oil with another spoon. Deep-fry 4 or 5 at a time, turning frequently with slotted spoon, about 3 minutes or until they are golden brown. Transfer them to lined baking dish to drain and keep warm in oven while you deep-fry the rest. Serve hot with butter.

1 3-pound catfish, filleted with skin left on	1 cup cornmeal, seasoned with salt and pepper
Salt and pepper	
1 egg, lightly beaten with 1 teaspoon water	Oil

Wash fish and dry completely with paper towels. To keep fish from curling up while frying, score flesh and skin sides of each fillet with small sharp knife, making 3 diagonal slashes about 2 inches long and 1/8 inch deep, spaced about 1 inch apart.

Season fillets on both sides with salt and pepper. Dip them into egg, then into cornmeal, coating evenly. Gently shake off excess meal.

In heavy 12-inch skillet at least 2 inches deep, pour oil to a depth of about 1/2 inch. Heat oil to 375°F., very hot but not smoking. Add fillets and fry 4 minutes. Turn them with slotted spatula and fry 3–4 minutes longer or until they are richly and evenly browned. Arrange fillets attractively on heated platter and serve at once.

PUFFY FISH

SERVES 4–6

Another variation of the puffy shrimp. Marvelously succulent as a main dish, first course, or one of many. It would be the third course in a whole Chinese dinner.

The puffy, crispy look and texture you want for this favorite of mine is accomplished through some strange wonder of chemistry, by making certain that the batter is made by adding oil to flour first and then adding cold water.

2 pounds sole fillets, cut into 2-inch diagonal strips	1/2 teaspoon pepper
1/2 teaspoon salt	1/2 teaspoon sesame seed oil
	A little water

Sprinkle sole with mixture of above ingredients and let stand 15 minutes.

PUFFY BATTER

1 cup flour	green part
1 tablespoon baking powder	5 tablespoons oil
1/4 teaspoon salt	2/3 cup cold water
4 teaspoons sesame seeds	4 cups oil for deep-frying
3 tablespoons minced scallions, including	

Mix all ingredients together. It is very important to add all of oil to flour before adding cold water.

Dip each piece of fish in batter and coat thoroughly. (Batter coats and clings without being too thick.)

Heat oil in wok to 375°F. or when a scallion tip browns in 30 seconds.

Fry fish strips 2 or 3 at a time until they puff up and are light golden brown. Remove with strainer and drain on paper towels on a warm platter. (Don't try to fry a lot of fish at one time, as oil will get cold. If oil gets too hot, fish will brown too quickly without cooking through.)

Serve hot with warm sauce in separate bowl for dipping. Scrumptious!

SAUCE

3 cups white vinegar	1 1/4 cups sugar
2/3 cup catsup	2 teaspoons salt
3 tablespoons Worcestershire sauce	

Mix all ingredients and cook over medium heat until well blended.

CRISPY SWEET AND SOUR FISH

This is that sweet and sour fish so crisp that you can almost eat the bones (don't). It's one of the better delicacies in fine Chinese restaurants. The sauce can be made well ahead, scallions and ginger chopped, catsup and vegetables placed in separate little bowls, and fish gashed and seasoned an hour or so before cooking. All you have to do is be the genius who remembers the order in which you put these goodies together in your hot wok.

SAUCE

3 cups water

3/4 cup sugar

3/4 cup red wine vinegar

2 teaspoons chili paste with garlic

Mix all ingredients in bowl and set aside.

1 whole fish, 1 1/2–2 pounds, cleaned and scaled (sea bass, red snapper, or 2 or 3 small trout)

2 tablespoons sherry

2 teaspoons salt

1/2 cup flour

4 cups oil

4 scallions, shredded

4 slices ginger root, shredded

1/2 cup catsup

2 tablespoons plus 1 1/2 teaspoons cornstarch dissolved in 4 tablespoons water

1 cup preserved mixed vegetables (sold in cans in Oriental markets)

Cut three gashes on each side of fish. Wipe until dry. Rub inside with sherry. Rub inside and out (gashes too) with salt. Sprinkle flour generously over all.

Heat oil in wok to 375°F. Deep-fry fish, turning every 5 minutes, until fish is crisp and brown, about 15 minutes (less for trout—they're smaller). Remove with strainer and drain on paper towels. Place on warmed platter.

Remove all but 1 tablespoon of oil in wok. Stir-fry scallions and ginger root 30 seconds. Remove from wok and set aside.

Reheat oil in wok and pour in catsup. Stir-fry 1 minute.

Pour sauce ingredients into wok and bring to a boil. Add cornstarch mixture. Add ginger, scallions, and mixed vegetables. Bring to a boil over high heat. Pour over fried fish. Serve with simple boiled rice and a couple of other great Chinese dishes such as Shrimp Cantonese (page 173), or Chinese Jade Broccoli (page 267). Different flavors combine to create a perfect Chinese menu.

SALMON PIE

Jackie Desmarais and her husband, Paul, are friends of mine who live in Canada and are the absolute perfect hosts—love their guests and show it. Jackie and Madame Lapoint serve three full-fledged, irresistible, unrivaled meals a day in addition to snacks, tea, and cocktails. I don't know when I've had more fun, food, and good company. The following salmon pie is an example of some of their delicious food.

Before I brushed the crust with the egg yolk mixture, I rolled out some leftover crust and with the sharp tip of a knife cut a few (6 or 8) fat fish, bubbles and all, and laid them over the top. It was beautiful but I hated to cut into it until everybody had oohed and aahed.

1 large onion, finely chopped
3 tablespoons butter
5 cups hot boiled potatoes (5–6 medium)
1 cup milk or half-and-half
2 1/2-pound poached fresh salmon (page 163), broken into bite-sized chunks
16-ounce can salmon, broken into bite-sized chunks
Salt and pepper to taste
Pastry (Pâte Brisée I, page 19) for a double-crust 12 × 8 × 2-inch rectangular casserole (or you can use only top crust)
1 egg yolk beaten with 2 tablespoons water

Sauté onions in butter until they are just translucent but not brown. Force butter and onions through fine sieve, pressing to extract all juice.

Mash potatoes while still hot, making sure you don't leave any lumps. Add butter-onion juice to potatoes. Add 1/2 cup heated milk, or more if necessary, a little at a time, stirring until potatoes are well mixed but not too creamy.

Add a few pieces of salmon and then stir in remaining milk, a little at a time. Add salt and pepper to taste. Add remaining salmon and gently fold into potatoes. Do not beat potato mixture again. Recipe up to this point can be done ahead the day before or in the morning and placed in refrigerator.

Preheat oven to 350°F.

Roll pastry to one-eighth-inch thickness. Line bottom and sides of casserole with pastry and fill with potato-salmon mixture. Moisten rim of lower crust, place top piecrust on filled casserole. Tuck rim of top under edge of undercrust and flute with fingers, making a tight seal. Cut slits in top for escape of steam. Brush crust with egg yolk-water mixture.

Bake 35–40 minutes or until brown and heated through. Cut into squares and serve with Salmon Sauce on the side.

SALMON SAUCE

2 tablespoons butter
2 tablespoons flour
2 cups hot milk
2 egg yolks, beaten
Salt and pepper to taste
(A sprinkle of fresh dill on top of sauce is lovely if you have it.)

Melt butter over moderate heat without letting it brown. Add flour and stir with wire whisk until it is well blended. Gradually add milk, whisking constantly. Whisk a little of white sauce into beaten egg yolks. Then add egg yolks gradually, whisking constantly. When mixture comes to boil, it will thicken automatically. Simmer for 5 minutes, whisking constantly. Season to taste with salt and pepper. Sprinkle fresh dill on top.

INDIVIDUAL LOBSTER PIE

This delicacy may sound formidable simply because its main ingredient is lobster, and for those of us who don't live near seacoasts, they're neither plentiful nor inexpensive. However, if you can't get live lobster, consider one large lobster tail as the pound needed here to serve four and possibly six people, depending on the size of your serving dishes. I use small 1-cup individual soufflé dishes (onion soup bowls). Maybe Buddy Adler, innkeeper at the Publick House in Sturbridge, Massachusetts (lobster country), uses larger portions. I'll ask him.

4 tablespoons melted butter
4 tablespoons flour
1 pint hot milk
1/4 cup butter
1 pound lobster meat, cut into bite-sized
   pieces

1/2 teaspoon paprika
1/3 cup dry sherry wine
Pinch cayenne pepper
1 teaspoon salt
4 egg yolks, beaten
1 pint light cream

Preheat oven to 400°F.

In saucepan combine melted butter with flour. Cook, stirring, over low heat but do not brown. Add hot milk and cook 15 minutes, stirring often. Strain.

In a skillet, heat butter and gently sauté lobster meat. Sprinkle with paprika, add 1/4 cup of the sherry, and cook another 2–3 minutes. Remove from heat.

Add cayenne pepper and salt to thin cream sauce. Blend 4 tablespoons of sauce into egg yolks, then stir this back into whole mixture. Add cream. Stir over medium heat until sauce bubbles and thickens. Add lobster mixture, remove from heat, and stir in remaining sherry.

Spoon into individual 1-cup casseroles, making sure to distribute lobster meat evenly. Sprinkle with topping and brown in upper part of oven 5 minutes, or until warmed through and topping is crisp and brown.

TOPPING

3/4 cup grated fresh bread crumbs
3/4 teaspoon paprika
3 tablespoons crushed potato chips

1 tablespoon grated Parmesan cheese
5 tablespoons melted butter

Mix together in small bowl.

SEAFOOD PAN ROAST

Charlie's Crab is a very special after-hours oyster bar at the Hilton Hotel in Troy, Michigan.

This looks, tastes, and is rich, but such a creamy bubbly delight. I felt I owed it to myself after a heavy singing engagement. Yes!—I was heavier the next day, but not unhappier.

This is neither panned nor roasted, but it's called Pan Roast so I won't argue. I just follow the recipe as they gave it to me at Charlie's Crab. Make your Pan Roast sauce first and while it is simmering and blending do your fish.

1 tablespoon butter
8 medium scallops, cut in half
3 oysters
2 ounces (1/4 cup) king crab meat
1 cup Pan Roast Sauce

1 medium tomato, peeled, lightly salted, peppered, and broiled until soft but not mushy
Pinch of paprika

Heat butter in a heavy sauté pan. Add all shellfish meat and pour Pan Roast Sauce over it. Allow to come to boil to cook meat. When oysters begin to curl, the fish is cooked.

Place broiled tomato in center of your serving bowl. Pour pan roast and sauce around tomato. Sprinkle with pinch of paprika for color.

PAN ROAST SAUCE

1/2 cup clam juice
1/4 teaspoon cayenne pepper

2 level teaspoons paprika
2 quarts half-and-half

Place 1 quart half-and-half in blender. Add clam juice, cayenne pepper, and paprika. Blend 5–6 minutes. Pour into bowl and add remaining half-and-half. Mix well.

SHRIMP CREOLE AND RICE
SERVES 6

There are two ways I prepare this fabulous traditional dish. There are as many versions of Shrimp Creole as there are shrimp in the Gulf, I'm sure—but of course this one is the best. I pile the rice high in the center of the Shrimp Creole and is it ever pretty and tasty!

1/4 cup pure rendered chicken or bacon fat
1/4 cup flour
1 medium-sized leek, thinly sliced, *or* 4 scallions (white and part of green), thinly sliced, *or* 1 small yellow onion, thinly sliced
2 small green peppers *or* 1 large green pepper, chopped
1 stalk celery, chopped (no leaves)
3 cloves garlic, slivered
3 large fresh tomatoes, peeled and coarsely chopped, or 1 16-ounce can whole tomatoes and juice
2 1/2 cups chicken broth (more if necessary)
8-ounce can tomato sauce

1 small bay leaf
1/2 teaspoon red pepper flakes, or to taste
1/2 teaspoon dried basil
1/2 teaspoon dried rosemary
1/2 teaspoon cumin
1/2 teaspoon thyme
Salt to taste
6 medium mushrooms, sliced
3 tablespoons butter
1 cup rice
3/4 teaspoon brown sugar
1/4 cup chopped parsley
2 pounds fresh shrimp, shelled, deveined, and cut in half

In large heavy saucepan melt chicken or bacon fat, add flour. Stir over low heat with wooden spoon until it becomes a dark golden brown. This is your roux; don't let it burn. It can take 20–30 minutes.

Add leeks or onions, green peppers, celery, and garlic. Sauté until leeks or onions are transparent and soft. Green peppers will not be as soft.

Place tomatoes in processor and process 1–2 seconds. Add tomatoes to other vegetables in saucepan. Rinse out processor bowl with 1/2 cup chicken broth and add to vegetables. Add tomato sauce, cover, and let come to a boil. Reduce heat and simmer 20–30 minutes.

Add bay leaf, red pepper flakes, dried basil, rosemary, cumin, thyme, and salt. (Sauce can be done well ahead and set aside until ready to assemble.)

About 1/2 hour before serving, slowly reheat your sauce while you sauté mushrooms in heavy-bottomed skillet until lightly browned. Remove with slotted spoon and add to sauce.

In same skillet, melt 1 tablespoon butter. Add rice and sauté quickly until lightly browned and separated. Add 2 cups chicken broth. Cover and cook slowly for 20 minutes. Add 1 tablespoon butter and brown sugar to sauce; let come to boil. Cover and simmer approximately 15 minutes. Add parsley.

In another skillet, melt 1 tablespoon butter and over high heat sauté shrimp until they are just pink.

Raise heat on sauce. Add shrimp and cook about 5 minutes. You may have to add more chicken broth, if it is too dry. If it is still too dry, add some tomato juice as this dish should be slightly soupy. Serve in warmed deep platter with green salad.

MR. WHIPPLE'S SEAFOOD FILÉ GUMBO

SERVES 6–8

Mr. Whipple sent me this from his bar and restaurant in South Louisiana. I couldn't resist the name of the dish. It is true gumbo as I remember it on the rare occasions when somebody in Tennessee would cook it up. It is not one of our indigenous dishes, obviously, but is it ever good! I hope Mr. Whipple doesn't mind that I cut down on the proportions of lard and bacon fat he recommended. Something about today's diet consciousness made me do it. It didn't seem to hurt it.

2 tablespoons bacon fat
1 tablespoon shortening
1 tablespoon butter
1/2 cup flour
1/4 cup chopped celery
1/2 cup chopped yellow onions
1/2 cup chopped leeks
1/2 cup chopped red onions
1/2 cup chopped green peppers
1 cup young okra, cut crosswise into 1-inch pieces
5 garlic cloves, minced

1 1/2 quarts hot chicken or fish broth
1 1/2 pounds fresh shrimp, peeled, deveined, and washed (reserve shells)
1/2 pound fresh crab meat or lobster
1 pint fresh oysters (save liquor)
Salt, black pepper, 1/2 teaspoon cayenne pepper, 1/2 teaspoon crushed red pepper, and Tabasco sauce to taste
1/4 cup chopped parsley
1/2 cup chopped scallions
Filé powder (1/2 teaspoon dusted on the bottom of each bowl)

Put bacon fat, shortening, and butter in heavy-bottomed pot over medium heat. When oil is very hot, stir in flour gradually, stirring constantly until golden brown: this is your roux.

When roux is golden brown, add celery. Cook until soft, then add yellow onions, leeks, red onions, green peppers, okra, and garlic. Let simmer 1 hour, covered.

Bring chicken or fish broth to a boil; add reserved shrimp shells and simmer 15 minutes. Strain.

After vegetable roux has simmered 1 hour, add shrimp, cover, and simmer 10–15 minutes. Add hot chicken or fish broth and the oyster liquor. Bring to boil and add crab meat or lobster, and then oysters. Cover and simmer 5 minutes.

Add salt, black pepper, cayenne pepper, crushed red pepper and Tabasco sauce to taste (some like it hot—I'm one of them).

When ready to serve add parsley and scallions and dust each bowl with filé powder. Pour gumbo over filé and place a dollop (2 tablespoons to you) of boiled rice in center of bowl.

NOTE By the way, okra has a short season, but the frozen okra is quite good and works almost as well as the fresh. Just add it at the end, with seasonings, instead of earlier as described above. The canned doesn't work at all. It seems to have been prepared in too salty a solution for the subtle okra flavor.

CRISPY SHRIMP WITH MUSTARD CHUTNEY SAUCE

SERVES 4–6

This is an approximation of one of the many superb, special dishes served at the Four Seasons Restaurant in New York. It's really, really close. I make trips to New York just to check it out for you (and me).

COURT BOUILLON

2 slices lemon
1/2 teaspoon salt
4 peppercorns

1 stalk celery with leaves
1/2 onion
2 cups water

Combine all ingredients in large saucepan. Bring to boil, reduce heat, and simmer 10 minutes.

2 1/2 pounds large raw shrimp
2 cups Court Bouillon
1 cup fruit chutney, minced
1 cup flour
2 eggs, beaten with a little water

1 cup very fine fresh bread crumbs
Oil for deep-frying
2 cups Mustard Chutney Sauce (prepare before deep-frying)

Poach unshelled shrimp in Court Bouillon, adding more water to cover shrimp. Bring to boil and poach shrimp until they turn pink. Strain and reserve fish stock.

Shell and devein shrimp, leaving tails intact.

Slit shrimp halfway through on back side and stuff with chutney. (This can be done ahead of time and shrimp placed in refrigerator until ready to deep-fry.)

Roll stuffed shrimp gently in flour, dip in egg, and roll in bread crumbs. Heat oil to 400°F. and deep-fry stuffed shrimp until golden brown. Drain and place on warm platter.

MUSTARD CHUTNEY SAUCE

2 tablespoons butter	1/2 cup milk
3 tablespoons flour	Salt and pepper
1 cup reserved fish stock	1 1/2 tablespoons dry mustard
1/2 cup chicken broth	6 tablespoons chutney, coarsely chopped

In saucepan melt butter over low heat. Blend in flour and cook slowly, stirring, until butter and flour froth together for 2 minutes without coloring. (This is now a roux.) Remove roux from heat.

Heat reserved fish stock, chicken broth, and milk to boiling point. Pour hot liquid gradually into roux, stirring with wire whisk to blend and gathering in all bits of roux from inside edges of pan.

Set saucepan over moderately high heat and stir with wire whisk until sauce comes to boil. Boil 1 minute, stirring constantly. Remove from heat and add salt and pepper to taste. (This can be made ahead of time and set aside. To prevent skin from forming on surface, drizzle melted butter on top.)

Just prior to serving, reheat and slowly add dry mustard and chutney. If sauce is too thick, bring to simmer. Thin with milk, chicken broth, or fish stock, beating in a tablespoon at a time.

To serve: Pour 2 tablespoons of sauce in center of warm plate. Place shrimp around sauce, tails on plate edge and fleshy part lying in edge of sauce. Serve rest of Mustard Chutney Sauce in a separate dish for dipping.

SHRIMPERS AND RICE (ARE VERY NICE)

SERVES 6–8

Once, many years ago when the world and geography and crises were different, I spent a very glamorous evening in Washington at the Iranian Embassy. One of the many, many dishes served in the course of the dinner was the one following. I never forgot it and asked for the recipe. (I have no shame, even in embassies.)

Thinking that the Ambassador's lady, born and reared in servant-surrounded luxury far from kitchens, wouldn't know a cream sauce from a cookie cutter, I asked if she would have her chef send it to me. My eyebrows and respect went up to here *when the lovely lady took notepad and pen in hand and wrote it out for me in great detail. You have it here and it's a delight.*

If you want it just as delightful and less voluptuous-making, use half-and-half instead of the cream, and two tablespoons of butter in sautéing the onions, celery, and green pepper.

Great for a luncheon with a little escarole, arugula (Italian lettuce), Belgian endive, and watercress salad with a light vinegar and oil dressing.

1/2 cup wild rice
1/2 cup white rice
1/2 pound butter
1 onion, finely chopped
1/2 cup finely chopped celery
1 small green pepper, chopped medium fine
1/2 pound fresh mushrooms, rinsed lightly and patted dry, stems removed and caps cut into 8 pieces
1/2 pound freshly cooked shrimp, shelled and split in two
1/2 pound cooked crab meat
Salt and coarsely ground black pepper
3–4 drops Tabasco sauce
2 cups heavy cream
1/2 cup toasted bread crumbs
1/3 cup slivered almonds
2 tablespoons flour
1 cup hot milk
Salt and white pepper
2 tablespoons chopped parsley

Wash wild rice and place in heavy saucepan. Cover with 2 cups cold salted water, place on low heat and cook gently without stirring until all water has been absorbed, about 45 minutes. Watch carefully and shake occasionally to avoid scorching.

Wash white rice and cook in boiling salted water 18 minutes. Drain, run cold water over it, drain and set aside.

Melt 6 tablespoons butter in large skillet and sauté onions, celery, and green peppers until soft and just beginning to brown. Then add mushrooms and cook about 5 minutes.

Preheat oven to 400°F.

Remove vegetable mixture from heat, add wild rice and white rice, and stir lightly with fork. Add shrimp and crab meat and mix together gently. Season with salt, coarsely ground black pepper, and Tabasco sauce. (Don't wash skillet yet.)

Transfer to well-buttered 2-quart casserole and pour 1 cup heavy cream over all.

Melt 2 tablespoons butter in same skillet, add bread crumbs and stir over low heat until crumbs are well buttered. Sprinkle them lightly over mixture in casserole. Dot casserole with 4 tablespoons butter. Cover and bake 30 minutes. Remove cover last 10 minutes to allow bread crumbs to brown on top.

Meanwhile sauté slivered almonds in 2 tablespoons butter until lightly browned.

Make medium-thick cream sauce by melting 2 tablespoons butter in saucepan to which you add 2 tablespoons flour and 1 cup hot milk gradually. Cook and stir constantly until slightly thickened. Season lightly to taste with salt and white pepper and then stir in 1 cup heavy cream. Keep hot over boiling water.

When casserole is done, remove from oven and sprinkle lightly with chopped parsley. Serve accompanied by cream sauce and toasted almonds.

SHRIMP CANTONESE

SERVES 6–8

This is one of my favorites. Though some friends maintain I have this addiction thing to hot, spicy Hunan and Szechwan flavors, I don't have. I just happen to love variety and flavor. This is typical. It's mild and not tricky and can be done well ahead. Have your ingredients assembled and ready for final cooking and assembly. It says three eggs. I sometimes use four or five, depending upon the size of the eggs and the guests. It may take a little longer than the two minutes mentioned for the eggs to set, but don't let them overcook. Remember, they continue to cook when the heat is off just from contact with the hot shrimp and pork.

6 tablespoons oil

SHRIMP MIXTURE

1 pound fresh shrimp, shelled, deveined, and washed under cold running water. Drain and pat dry.
1/2 teaspoon pale dry sherry
1 egg white

1/4 teaspoon salt
1/2 teaspoon baking soda
1/2 teaspoon sesame seed oil
1/8 teaspoon ground pepper

Mix in bowl. Refrigerate for at least an hour.

SEASONINGS

2 scallions, cut into pea-sized pieces including green part
1 teaspoon finely minced ginger root
2 teaspoons minced garlic

1 tablespoon salted black beans, placed in small sieve under running hot water to remove excess salt, and mashed with back of teaspoon into paste.

Mix in bowl and set aside.

SAUCE

1/4 teaspoon sugar
2 teaspoons cornstarch
1 tablespoon black soy sauce
2 teaspoons thin soy sauce

1/2 teaspoon sesame seed oil
1/2 cup clear chicken broth or water
2 tablespoons Chinese rice wine or pale dry sherry

Mix in bowl and set aside.

4 ounces (1/2 cup) pork, minced
1/2 green or red pepper, cut into 1-inch

squares
3 eggs, slightly beaten until foamy

Heat wok over high heat. Swirl in 4 tablespoons oil. When hot add shrimp mixture. Stir-fry until shrimp just turn white-pink (less than a minute). Remove with strainer or slotted spoon to bowl. Turn off heat. Clean and dry wok with paper towels.

Return wok to high heat until it smokes a little. Swirl in remaining 2 tablespoons oil. When oil is hot, add seasonings. Stir-fry over high heat until garlic turns golden (about 1 minute).

Add pork. When pork loses its pink color, add peppers. Mix well. Add sauce mixture, stirring constantly. When sauce begins to bubble, return shrimp to wok.

Pour eggs evenly over shrimp. Do not stir. Cover and cook over medium heat 2 minutes or until eggs are slightly set around edge. Stir well to mix. Put on serving platter. Serve hot.

SHRIMP WITH EGG FOO-YONG

Dining with Cecilia and Joseph Chung in their lovely San Francisco restaurant, The China House, is a unique and personal experience. In a town noted for its varied and mostly superb cuisine, were I a writer-grader for Gault Millau, The China House would be somewhere in the stratosphere of the top ten. Each dish is lovingly and delicately balanced and prepared. For instance, this Shrimp with Egg Foo-Yong.

When I first asked for the recipe, Cecilia and Joseph wrote it out in great detail. Then Joseph called with a couple of suggestions for its preparation to ensure my understanding of the technique, which is definitely different from any Foo-Yong I've cooked before and you either. It bears no resemblance to the delicious hot-sauced egg pancake most often tendered as Shrimp, Egg, Pork, or Bean-sprout Foo-Yong.

Cecilia called with a couple of additional constructive suggestions—insurance. This conscientiousness runs through the whole presentation of each dish on the menu. For instance, don't stir-fry the egg whites—roll them around the wok; clean wok between steps; and most importantly, serve it directly and hot—and stop the conversation until after the first one or two bites. Then you can talk to your heart's content.

The last suggestion is mine. I learned it from Danny Kaye who we know is a superb chef and tolerates no extraneous conversation—baseball scores, bypass surgery techniques, Dow Jones averages or National Enquirer *gossip—until the dish has been passed, served, tasted, and commented upon; it's a great idea. It plays havoc with punch lines, but to paraphrase the great Harry Kurnitz, "We're here for dining, not joking."*

4–5 ounces of spinach, washed and drained

9 tablespoons cottonseed oil (I had to use light vegetable oil. I couldn't find cottonseed oil.)

1/4 teaspoon salt, or salt to taste

1/8 teaspoon sugar

10 large fresh shrimp, shelled and deveined

5 egg whites, beaten *very* lightly with a little salt

SAUCE

6 tablespoons chicken stock

1 teaspoon Chinese rice wine

1/4 teaspoon salt

1 1/2 teaspoons cornstarch

1 1/2 teaspoons water

Use only young and tender leaves of spinach. Heat wok over high heat for 30 seconds, then pour in 3 tablespoons of oil and heat for 30 seconds until very hot. Put spinach into wok and stir-fry it for 3 minutes. To stir-fry, use Chinese metal cooking shovel or large spoon to scoop spinach from sides of wok to center; then use cooking shovel to turn spinach over in center of wok. Repeat this process until spinach turns dark green. Add salt and sugar. Remove spinach from wok to warm platter.

Clean wok and add 3 tablespoons fresh oil. Heat oil to high temperature (30 seconds). Add shrimp and stir-fry 2 minutes or until they turn pink. Remove shrimp to separate warm platter.

Clean wok again. Heat wok without oil until it is very hot (1 minute); then add 3 tablespoons of fresh oil. Heat oil for 30 seconds. (The technique of heating oil in wok is to lift wok about an inch from range but still touching flame and roll it in a circular motion so that oil will cover entire inner surface of wok.) Pour in egg whites. Lift and swirl wok to prevent egg whites from gluing together and to wok. *(Do not stir-fry).* As soon as egg whites turn white and form into a shape, turn off heat immediately and lift wok from range while removing egg whites.

Clean wok in order to make sauce. Pour in chicken stock and let it heat until boiling. Add Chinese rice wine, salt, and cornstarch mixed with water and thoroughly mix with chicken stock. Then pour in shrimp and egg whites and cook a few seconds only. *(Do not stir).* Pour it carefully, so as not to break egg whites, over spinach and serve immediately. The taste of this delicate dish is at its best when eaten hot—that is, immediately on removing from wok.

PRAWN CUTLETS
SERVES 4

6 large prawns (approximately 1 pound)	2 tablespoons flour
1 teaspoon Chinese rice wine or dry sherry	2 teaspoons cornstarch
1 teaspoon sesame seed oil	3/4 cup bread crumbs
1/2 teaspoon salt	4 cups oil
8 egg whites	

Peel prawns, leaving tails intact. Split down center back to divide in half.

Blend wine, sesame seed oil, and salt. Sprinkle over prawns and let stand 5 minutes.

Beat egg whites to soft peaks and mix to a smooth batter with flour and cornstarch. Beat again until egg white mixture stands in stiff peaks.

Dip each prawn half in batter to coat thickly; then sprinkle with bread crumbs.

Heat wok and add oil; when very hot (375°F.), reduce heat slightly. Deep-fry prawns, 2 at a time, until deep golden color and cooked through, about 3 minutes. Drain on paper towels and serve.

GINGER SHRIMP
SERVES 4–6

1 pound fresh shrimp, shelled, deveined, and cut in half lengthwise	1/4 cup catsup
1/2 teaspoon salt	1/4 cup chicken stock
1 1/2 teaspoons cornstarch	1 tablespoon sugar
1 tablespoon sherry	1 tablespoon dry sherry
1/4 cup finely chopped onions	2 tablespoons chili paste
2 scallions, finely chopped	1 clove garlic, crushed
2 tablespoons finely chopped fresh ginger root	3 cups peanut oil
	2 teaspoons cornstarch mixed with 4 teaspoons water

In a large bowl combine shrimp, salt, cornstarch, and sherry and mix well by hand. Set aside for at least 15 minutes.

In a small bowl mix onions, scallions, and ginger and set aside. In a medium bowl mix catsup, chicken stock, and sugar and set aside. In a small bowl mix sherry, chili paste, and garlic and set aside.

FINAL ASSEMBLY

Add oil to wok for deep-frying. Heat to 375°F. Add shrimp and deep-fry 1 minute. Remove and drain shrimp and place on warm platter.

Remove all but 2 tablespoons oil from wok. Stir-fry onions, scallions and ginger 1 minute.

Add catsup, chicken stock, and sugar to wok. Bring to boil. Return shrimp to wok. Add sherry, chili paste, and garlic mixture. Stir-fry briskly on high heat for 30 seconds. Add cornstarch mixture and blend. Serve immediately.

PUFFED BUTTERFLY SHRIMP   SERVES 4

Oh, this is pretty and tasty and not tricky if you remember one thing: be sure to add the oil first. The Japanese do this beautifully. In the same batter, dip the vegetables cut in large round or long slender chunks (sweet potatoes or yams, zucchini and parsnips) and serve them along with the shrimp and dipping sauce.

SAUCE

1/4 cup catsup
1/4 cup sugar
1/4 cup white vinegar
1 cup water

2 tablespoons cornstarch, dissolved in 2 tablespoons water
1/2 green pepper cut into 1/2-inch chunks

Place first four ingredients in saucepan. Bring to a boil and thicken with dissolved cornstarch. Add green pepper and bring to a boil again. Remove from heat and set aside. This may be done ahead and reheated.

GINGER JUICE MIXTURE

1/4 teaspoon fresh ginger-root juice (use garlic press)
1 teaspoon very finely minced garlic

1/4 teaspoon salt
1 teaspoon pale dry sherry

Mix all ingredients in bowl and set aside.

1 pound (15–16) medium shrimp
1 cup flour, unsifted
1 tablespoon baking powder
1/4 teaspoon salt
5 tablespoons oil

2/3 cup cold water
5 teaspoons sesame seeds
3 tablespoons minced scallions including green part
4 cups oil for deep-frying

Shell, devein, and butterfly shrimp. (Remove shell, leaving tail portion intact. Split shrimp down back without cutting through. Remove vein and spread open.) Wash in cold water 1 minute, drain, and pat dry.

Using pastry brush, spread Ginger Juice Mixture on split side of shrimp.

Mix flour, baking powder, and salt in bowl. Add oil gradually while stirring. Mix well. The dough should look like pie dough.

Stir in water a little at a time, until mixture becomes thick batter. Add sesame seeds and scallions and mix well. (The big trick to puffy batter is addition of oil before cold water.) To test whether consistency of batter is right, hold a shrimp by tail, dip it into batter, then hold it over bowl. Batter should drip down slowly from shrimp.

Heat oil in wok to deep-fry temperature (375°F.). Take each shrimp by tail and dip into batter, then put directly into hot oil. Shrimp should puff up and swim to top immediately. (If it stays on bottom, oil is not hot enough.) Deep-fry a few at a time; too many cool down oil. Turn shrimp with tongs when batter is set. Fry until light gold. Drain on paper towels. Serve with hot sauce on the side. They should be served immediately, but warm oven will keep them pretty crisp for 1/2 hour or so.

SZECHWAN SPICED SHRIMP SERVES 4

These marvelous Chinese dishes! So much can be prepared ahead. All three steps in this spicy Sze-chwan wonder can be done in the middle of the day, kept in refrigerator in separate little bowls, and moved over to the wok in the order in which they will be used. Cook in the steps described and you'll have a succulent Chinese wonder. Serve with rice, a mild chicken vegetable dish, your Egg Flower Soup (page 66) (served third, not first) and voilà! A full Chinese dinner with less last-minute preparation than broiled steak and baked potato . . . well, almost.

SHRIMP MIXTURE

1 pound fresh shrimp, shelled, deveined and cut in half lengthwise, rinsed in cold running water, drained and patted dry
1/4 teaspoon salt
1 teaspoon Chinese rice wine or pale dry sherry

1 teaspoon light soy sauce
2 tablespoons flour
1 tablespoon cornstarch
1 egg, lightly beaten
1/2 teaspoon baking soda

Mix together and keep refrigerated for at least an hour before use.

SEASONINGS

1 teaspoon finely minced fresh ginger root
2 teaspoons minced garlic
2 scallions, cut into pea-sized pieces including green part

2–3 dried chili peppers, torn into small pieces (do not discard seeds—that's the hot part)

Place in bowl and set aside.

SAUCE MIXTURE

3 tablespoons sugar

5 teaspoons black soy sauce

3 tablespoons catsup

2 teaspoons pale dry sherry

1 teaspoon white vinegar

1 tablespoon water

Mix in bowl and set aside.

3 cups peanut oil for deep-frying

1 teaspoon sesame seed oil

Heat oil in wok to deep-fry temperature. Test by dropping 1/2-inch scallion top in oil. When it sizzles noisily and turns brown, oil is ready for deep-frying.

Add shrimp mixture, half at a time, and stir briskly until shrimp turn whitish pink (about 12–15 seconds). Remove with strainer to bowl.

Remove all but 2 tablespoons oil from wok. Heat oil, add seasoning mixture and brown, stirring constantly until aroma floats around you. Be careful not to burn it.

Stir in sauce mixture. Stir and cook until it begins to bubble. Return shrimp to wok. Stir-fry for several seconds (shrimp will be bright pink). Swirl in sesame seed oil. Put on serving platter and serve hot.

GOUJONNETTES OF SOLE WITH TARTAR SAUCE
SERVES 4

1 cup milk

1 egg yolk

Pinch of salt and pepper

6 fillets of sole, cut into diagonal strips about 1/2 inch wide

3 cups fine fresh bread crumbs

2–3 cups oil for deep-frying

Parsley

Tartar Sauce

In a shallow dish mix together milk, egg yolk, salt, and pepper. Place strips of fish in milk mixture and let stand for several minutes.

Lift out fish strips and coat completely with bread crumbs.

Fry fish strips in deep hot oil (375°F.) and drain them on paper towels. Serve with fried parsley and Tartar Sauce.

TARTAR SAUCE

1 teaspoon Dijon mustard
1/8 teaspoon pepper
1 teaspoon powdered sugar
1/4 teaspoon salt
2 teaspoons grated onion
2 egg yolks

1/2 cup olive oil
3 tablespoons vinegar
1 tablespoon chopped olives
1 tablespoon capers
1 tablespoon chopped dill pickle
1 tablespoon chopped parsley

In small bowl combine mustard, pepper, sugar, salt, grated onion, and egg yolks. Beat well.

Drop by drop, add olive oil and vinegar as you would in making mayonnaise. This may be done in your blender or food processor.

When mixture is thick, add olives, capers, pickle, and parsley. If parsley is omitted, the sauce will keep for weeks in your refrigerator.

Chapter 8

MEATS

I suppose we're not the meat eaters we used to be, but you couldn't prove it by me. There are so many varieties of cuts and ways of preparing beef, lamb, pork, and veal that even if you have meat daily there never has to be a sameness to your meals and you don't have to fall into the cliché of serving that old familiar standby. That's probably in here too, as well as the Swedish Pot Roast, Pork Minho Style, Curried Cashew Lamb, Chinese Pork Shreds, Black Beans, and Green Peppers, and on and on.

You may want a new light ground meat instead of the simple meat loaf. Well, on second thought, why not the meat loaf? Try the Mushroom-Stuffed Meat Loaf and those Russian Meat Cakes with Sour Cream. That lump of cold butter placed in the center and inside of each meat cake does wonderful things. Then there's Wiener Schnitzel, like no other. A delicate happy home-keeper is Veal Stew with Mushrooms (Blanquette de Veau), served with Spaetzle. And if you want a dark, lusty stew, try the Beef Carbonnade. Of course, we don't eat nearly the large portions we used to, but that's true all the way down the line.

On roasts and opaque cuts of meat, I've been told, you ruin them, render them juiceless and tasteless (horror of horrors) if you season them before searing the outside. I don't agree. I poke deep holes in the thicker cuts of meat before searing and rub my favorite seasoning salts and peppers, herbs, whatever, all over and into the crevices and holes so that the meat is flavored all the way through. The meat has been cut off of somewhere, unless you're roasting a whole steer or pig, so how is it going to know it's been cut again and lose its flavor?

If you have extra cuts or chops left over, wrap in plastic wrap and then in foil and label them what they are, along with weight and dates of purchase. No point in having a freezer full of well-wrapped, intriguing little anonymous packages that you don't have the foggiest idea how to use.

Tender cuts should be roasted uncovered at a medium-low temperature (325°F.) or broiled or grilled, or sautéed quickly over high heat. Don't overcook thin slices of anything. They dry out, and don't forget that they continue to cook after removal to your warm platter. When you sauté, be sure to deglaze the pan with a good broth to release all the pan juices and those extra bits and pieces clinging to the pan, for flavoring your sauce. Tougher, heavier cuts of meat can be browned all over and cooked covered in a slow oven or on top of the stove, unless otherwise specified, like Roast Lamb with Green Peppercorn Sauce, and Gloria's Mexican Pork Roast.

One of the best medium-sized beef roasts I've cooked was in a preheated 500°F. oven. After meat is placed in oven, turn heat off completely and never open that oven door for one hour. Perfect crusty outside and tender, juicy, and pink inside. Take your choice—they're all good.

Whatever you do, save those pan juices. Deglaze them and pour over meat, strained, enhanced, thickened or unthickened, according to the recipe. If you have potatoes, serve it over potatoes. If you have rice, serve it over rice. Noodles? Serve it over noodles. Dip your biscuits, bread or cornbread in it. Maybe there is something way back inside that makes me vaguely mistrustful of anybody who doesn't understand the beauty of gravies and sauces. That's the essence of what you've been cooking the whole time!

STEAK MADRID

Madrid, Spain, is not only paella or tiny grilled lamb chops, it's hearty, family-style dishes like this—which is why everything closes from 12:00 to 2:00, or possibly 3:00, for afternoon siestas. It's also why dinner is not generally served until 10 in the evening. Then you go to watch the flamenco dancers work it off for you. Of course, if you're shooting scenes around the city early in the morning, forget it until your Spanish fellow workers amble over around 10 A.M. or so. It makes sense to me, especially the siesta.

SAUCE

Drippings from 1/2 pound bacon (reserve
  bacon for garnish)
1 medium onion, finely chopped
1 clove garlic, finely chopped
1/2 cup chopped celery
1 green pepper, finely chopped
1 green chili, finely chopped
16-ounce can tomatoes, undrained
8-ounce can tomato sauce
1 cup rich beef gravy or Brown Sauce

(page 6)
6-ounce can tomato paste
3–4 drops Tabasco sauce
1 tablespoon Worcestershire sauce
1/4 teaspoon black pepper
1/2 teaspoon salt
Bay leaf
1/8 teaspoon oregano
1/4 teaspoon thyme
1/2 teaspoon chili powder

Heat bacon fat and sauté onion, garlic, celery, green pepper, and green chili until vegetables are soft but not brown.

Add tomatoes, tomato sauce, gravy or Brown Sauce, tomato paste, Tabasco, and Worcestershire. Stir to blend well.

Lower heat and add pepper, salt, bay leaf, oregano, thyme, and chili powder. Cook sauce until well blended. Set aside.

4 1/2-inch-thick round steaks, with bone in
  center, approximately 1 1/2 pounds each,
  or 4 sirloin steaks, approximately same
  size as round steaks
1 teaspoon salt

1/2 teaspoon pepper
1/2 cup flour
3 tablespoons oil
2 cups mild Cheddar cheese, grated
1/2 cup or 4-ounce can pimientos

Ask your butcher to tenderize the round steak and remove the center bone. Cut steaks in half and cut away rind and edges and some of fat. Have meat almost at room temperature. Work mixture of salt, pepper, and flour into both sides of steaks.

Heat oil in 12-inch heavy skillet until very hot. Brown steaks very quickly on each side and transfer them to a rectangular ovenproof casserole or baking dish that can be well covered.

Preheat oven to 375°F.

Lay 2 half steaks on bottom of casserole. Cover generously with 1/3 of cheese and pimientos. Then cover cheese with another 2 half steaks. Cover generously with another 1/3 of cheese and pimientos. Repeat the process, ending with steak on top. Cover with the sauce (remove bay leaf).

Bake, covered, for 2 hours or until steak is done.

Slice and serve garnished with bacon.

LONDON BROIL

Do you suppose they serve London Broil in London? (Maybe it's like Chinese chop suey which they never saw in China.) If they don't, they should. See if you don't agree after sampling the following.

GREEN PEPPERCORN BUTTER

MAKES ABOUT 1/2 CUP

1/2 cup unsalted butter, softened
1/4 cup finely chopped fresh parsley
1 tablespoon bottled green peppercorns, drained

2 teaspoons fresh lemon juice
1/2 teaspoon Dijon mustard
2 teaspoons Worcestershire sauce

In food processor or blender combine all ingredients and mix until smooth. Transfer mixture to bowl, cover, and chill 1 hour.

MARINADE

1 cup dry red wine
1/2 cup olive oil
1 scallion, minced
3 garlic cloves, minced
1 teaspoon salt, or to taste

1/2 teaspoon black peppercorns
1/2 teaspoon dry mustard
1/2 teaspoon dried thyme
6 parsley sprigs
1 bay leaf

In large glass dish, combine all marinade ingredients.

3 1/2-pound top sirloin steak, about 2 inches thick
2 tablespoons black peppercorns, crushed or

pulverized with a mortar and pestle
Salt to taste
1/2 cup Green Peppercorn Butter

Punch holes in steak with tines of large fork so that marinade will penetrate steak.

Place steak in dish, coating completely with marinade. Cover and chill. Let marinate, turning occasionally, at least 4 hours or overnight.

Drain meat, pat dry, and press crushed black peppercorns into it. Let meat stand 30 minutes to an hour. Season with a little salt and grill over hot coals or under broiler 5–10 minutes on each side for rare, 8–12 minutes for medium.

Transfer to cutting board, brush with half of softened Green Peppercorn Butter, and let stand for 15 minutes. Cut London Broil into thin slices at a 45-degree angle across the grain and dribble remaining half of Green Peppercorn Butter over slices.

HAMBURGER STEAK AU POIVRE

SERVES 4

1 1/2 tablespoons black peppercorns
2 pounds ground sirloin
Salt
4 teaspoons butter

1/4 cup brandy
3 tablespoons lemon juice
1/4 cup butter, sliced (optional)
Parsley springs for garnish

With flat end of cleaver or with meat pounder crush peppercorns between sheets of waxed paper. Shape beef lightly into four patties and press pepper into both sides of patties.

Sprinkle a light layer of salt over bottom of heavy skillet just large enough to hold the hamburger patties. When salt begins to brown, add 4 teaspoons butter and heat until it is very hot. Add hamburgers and cook until well browned on one side. Turn and cook 30 seconds over high heat, then lower heat to medium and cook for 1–2 minutes for rare. Transfer to warmed platter.

Pour fat from skillet. Add brandy and carefully ignite with a long match. Shake skillet until flames go out. Add lemon juice.

Swirl in the sliced butter and pour sauce over hamburgers. Garnish platter with sprigs of parsley.

ASIAN LEMON PEPPER BEEF SERVES 4

This is one of those subtle ways to make a good cut of fillet of beef go a long way. There are two special ingredients, the Japanese horseradish and the star anise. If your specialty shop or gourmet shop does not have them, they'll get it for you with a little notice.

MARINADE

2/3 cup chicken broth	1 tablespoon wasabi (Japanese horseradish)
2/3 cup Japanese soy sauce	1/4 teaspoon pepper
1/3 cup lemon juice	1/4 teaspoon cinnamon
1/4 cup sugar	1/4 teaspoon ground star anise
1 tablespoon salt	Freshly grated nutmeg to taste

In enamel or stainless-steel saucepan combine all marinade ingredients. Bring to boil over moderately high heat, skim froth that rises to surface, and let cool.

1 1/2 pounds fillet of beef, well trimmed	1/2 cup chicken broth
2 teaspoons minced lemon peel	1 tablespoon cornstarch or potato starch
2 teaspoons peppercorns	Snipped chives for garnish

With sharp knife make several small incisions in beef and put lemon peel and peppercorns into incisions. Add meat to marinade and let marinate 30 minutes.

With slotted spatula transfer meat to cutting board, pat dry with paper towels, and cut in half crosswise. Strain marinade into bowl and reserve 1/2 cup of it.

In small saucepan combine reserved marinade, chicken broth, and starch. Bring liquid to boil over moderate heat and cook sauce for 1 to 2 minutes or until slightly thickened. Cover and keep warm.

Broil meat on broiler rack under preheated broiler about 4 inches from heat for 3 minutes on each side for rare meat.

Transfer meat to cutting board, let stand for 2 minutes, and cut into 1/4-inch slices. Divide the meat among 4 plates, nap it with the sauce, and sprinkle with snipped chives.

PEPPER STEAK

SERVES 4

4 3/4-inch boneless strip or shell steaks	1/2 cup heavy cream
3 tablespoons black peppercorns	1 1/2 teaspoons salt
1/4 cup brandy	1/4 cup butter, sliced
1 cup brown stock	Watercress sprigs for garnish

Have butcher trim steaks, reserving a piece of fat.

With flat of cleaver or with meat pounder crush peppercorns between sheets of waxed paper and press pepper into both sides of steaks. Flatten steaks between sheets of waxed paper to 1/2 inch.

Rub heavy skillet just large enough to hold steaks with reserved fat over moderately high heat and heat fat until it is very hot.

Sear steaks for 1 1/2 minutes on each side. Reduce heat to moderate and cook steaks for 1 to 2 minutes more on each side for rare meat. Transfer steaks to heated platter.

Pour fat from skillet, add brandy and ignite it. Shake pan until flames go out. Add brown stock and heavy cream, reduce liquid over high heat by half. Add salt, or to taste, swirl in sliced butter and pour sauce over steaks.

Garnish platter with sprigs of watercress.

STEAK WITH GREEN PEPPERCORNS   SERVES 4–6

A favorite for many reasons. It's economical—your beautiful 1 1/3-inch loin strip steak is cut into 4 thin slices. The green peppercorns give it a sense of piquancy, and the small amount used—only 2 tablespoons—means one jar will last a long time in the refrigerator or freezer. It can be partially prepared ahead—and it's definitely not a "Throw another steak on the fire, dear," number.

4 1/3-inch boneless loin strip steaks (approximately 2 1/2 pounds)	1/2 cup chicken broth
3 tablespoons oil	1/2 cup Brown Sauce (page 6)
2 tablespoons soy sauce	1 tablespoon tomato paste
2 tablespoons green peppercorns, drained and crushed	1 tablespoon Worcestershire sauce
2 tablespoons butter	1/4 cup brandy
	Salt

Spread surface of each steak with 1 teaspoon oil, then 1 1/2 teaspoons soy sauce and 1 teaspoon green peppercorns. Roll steaks up and set aside in refrigerator until ready to cook.

In large skillet melt 1 tablespoon butter and 1 tablespoon oil. Unroll steaks and cook quickly on each side. Roll up again and place on warmed platter.

Add a little more butter to hot skillet, then add chicken broth, Brown Sauce, tomato paste, Worcestershire, brandy, and remaining green peppercorns. Add salt to taste. Let come to boil, lower heat, and reduce sauce by half.

Unroll steaks and return them to sauce with drippings from platter. Warm steaks through and serve immediately with sauce poured over steaks.

MAGIC EYE OF THE ROUND

Don't let the amount of salt called for in this one scare you away. It's just a coating outside the beef to hold in those juices.

1 beef eye of the round roast (4 1/2 pounds)
1 teaspoon black pepper

8-ounce jar brown mustard
3–4 cups kosher salt

Preheat oven to 475°F.

Sprinkle pepper over roast. Cover all sides and ends of roast with brown mustard. Place kosher salt on plate or board. Roll roast in salt, covering completely. (Salt coating should be thick with no meat or mustard visible. Handle roast at all times with tongs. Fork or knife might pierce salt casing.)

Place on rack in roasting pan. Bake 10–12 minutes per pound for rare, 12–15 minutes per pound for medium, and 15–20 minutes per pound for well done. A 4 1/2 -pound roast will take about 50 minutes total time for medium.

When roast is cooked to desired doneness, remove from oven to platter or shallow roasting pan. With knife, crack surface of outer casing of salt and mustard. Discard casing. Add released juices to juices in roasting pan in which meat was cooked, checking first to make sure they and the roasting pan juices are not too salty.

Let stand 10–15 minutes, then carve in thin slices. Garnish with cherry tomatoes and parsley.

BEEF RAGOUT

SERVES 4–6

I was singing at a beautiful outdoor theater in Detroit, and on one of our nights off we drove miles and miles to a restaurant called the Dearborn Inn. A calm, elegant hotel and restaurant steeped in tradition. The menu is large and varied, and of course by the time our group had ordered "some of this—a little of that," we almost covered it.

The chef, Mr. George Riley, serves this ragout nightly to dozens and dozens of eager diners. He sent us the whoooole thing. Here it is reduced in size for four to six healthy appetites.

2 tablespoons butter
1 1/2 pounds beef stew meat, cut into
   bite-sized pieces
3 ounces (1/4 cup plus 2 tablespoons) Bur-
   gundy wine

2 1/2 tablespoons paprika
1 cup diced onions
1 1/2 cups diced mushrooms
Sauce

Melt butter in flameproof stew pot or casserole and when butter is hot, brown beef. Add wine and paprika and simmer 5 minutes; add onions and mushrooms and then add sauce.

Cook, covered, 1 1/2 hours over moderate heat, stirring frequently, or bake in a preheated 350°F. oven 1 1/2 hours or until meat is very tender. Serve over noodles.

SAUCE

1/2 cup chopped carrots
1/2 cup chopped onions
1/2 cup chopped celery
1 clove garlic, chopped
1/2 cup butter or oil
1/2 cup flour

3 cups hot beef stock (page 7)
1 bay leaf
2 tablespoons Maggi seasoning
1/2 tablespoon Worcestershire sauce
1 1/2 teaspoons salt
1/2 teaspoon white pepper

In large saucepan sauté carrots, onions, celery, and garlic in butter or oil. Add flour and let brown. Add hot beef stock, bay leaf, Maggi, Worcestershire sauce, salt, and pepper. Cook until well blended. Correct seasonings. Remove bay leaf before adding sauce to stewpot or casserole.

BEEF CARBONNADE   SERVES 6–8

The Belgians originated this dish, I believe. It's hearty, rich, and quite wonderful for a friendly gathering. It's different (take it from a stew lover) from your ordinary beef stew, and the difference is definitely delicious.

3–3 1/2 pounds boneless chuck, pot roast, or
  lean brisket
Salt and freshly ground black pepper
5 tablespoons butter (more if needed)
1 cup thinly sliced onions
1 tablespoon oil
2 tablespoons sugar
2 tablespoons quick-mix flour or 1 tablespoon quick-mix and 1 tablespoon

all-purpose
1 1/2 cups stout or dark beer (I use Guin-
  ness stout or Foster lager)
1 can (10 1/2 ounces) rich chicken or beef
  broth, or fresh chicken or beef broth
2 tablespoons vinegar
2 cloves garlic, pressed
Pinch of thyme
2 or 3 sprigs parsley

Remove all excess fat from beef. Dry with paper towels. Cut into 1 1/2-inch cubes and sprinkle with black pepper.

In large casserole melt 4 tablespoons butter. Add onions and cook over low heat.

Meanwhile, in large heavy skillet melt 1 tablespoon butter and 1 tablespoon oil. Brown meat evenly on all sides in hot fat, about 12 pieces at a time. (Add butter if needed between batches.) Place browned meat in casserole with onions. Sprinkle sugar over meat and onions. Salt and pepper to taste.

Preheat oven to 350°F.

If needed, add a little butter to skillet in which meat was browned and add flour. Cook roux until golden. Then pour in stout or dark beer and chicken or beef broth. Lower heat and whisk sauce until it begins to bubble. Simmer about 15 minutes until it has reduced and thickened a little.

Add vinegar, garlic, thyme, and parsley. Taste for seasoning. Stir and simmer sauce another minute or two before pouring into casserole. If sauce doesn't come halfway up sides of meat, add more beer or stout.

Cover tightly and cook in oven 1 1/2 hours or until meat is tender when pierced.

Remove parsley and serve immediately with buttered noodles, boiled potatoes, or steamed rice.

POTTED SHORT RIBS OF BEEF

SERVES 6

When our concert tour took us to Detroit, all our unimpeachable sources agreed on Mrs. Morgan's boarding house. So after landing at the airport and loading luggage and instruments in the limos and vans, we began to search out Mrs. Morgan's for dinner. We found it. Granted, it was not too prepossessing from the outside, but once inside the enormous, long, cool dining room, it wasn't what we'd expected—it was a lot more. Crisp, spotless, gleaming white tablecloths on long, family-style dining tables; waiters in black tie and starched white shirts serving the best soul food north of the Mason-Dixon line—barbecued chicken, ribs, chicken and dumplings, corn bread, green beans, peach cobbler, stewed corn, and this Potted Short Ribs of Beef. It was a great way to be introduced to and feel in tune with Detroit.

The show went great (it did rain and almost freeze up one night and drown beautiful Pine Knob) but it didn't matter, the orchestra was superb; the audience never left to take shelter. I sang my little heart out and thanked the Lord it wasn't theater in the round; after a couple of evenings of Detroit dining, the gown stayed slinky as I grew—how should I put it?—I guess "chunky" would do.

6 (10–12-ounce) pieces of short ribs (choice meat)
Salt and pepper to taste
1 cup sliced carrots
1 cup chopped celery
1 cup sliced onions

2 cups water
1/2 cup chicken stock or beef broth
1/2 cup Brown Sauce (page 6)
2 tablespoons flour
4 tablespoons water

Preheat oven to 350°F.

Season ribs with salt and pepper. Lay ribs in roasting pan. Add water and cover with vegetables. Cover and bake 1 1/2 to 2 hours or until tender.

Lift ribs out of liquid. Skim oil from top. Add stock and Brown Sauce to liquid in pan. Bring to boil over moderate heat. Thicken broth with flour mixed with water and simmer a few minutes longer. Serve with buttered noodles.

SWEDISH POT ROAST

SERVES 4–6

When you're planning ahead for one of those long weekends, three days with the extra Monday thrown in, with company dropping in, they can all stay for dinner if you have this treasure juicing along in the oven. The sauce alone is worth the trouble. Serve with little, crispy, hot potato pancakes or red cabbage and apples or crispy potato skins and cold fresh apple sauce.

1 4-pound boneless chuck or rump roast, trimmed and tied with string at 1-inch intervals (Ask butcher to prepare it for you.)

MARINADE

2 cups dry white wine
1/2 cup white wine vinegar
1 large onion, sliced
1 carrot, sliced
4 sprigs parsley
2 garlic cloves, crushed

1 tablespoon tarragon
2 bay leaves
6 peppercorns
1 teaspoon salt
1/2 teaspoon thyme

Combine all marinade ingredients in large glass or ceramic bowl. (Marinade ingredients will sometimes be affected by protracted soaking in metal bowl.) Pierce meat 1 inch deep with tines of large fork or sharp knife tip before placing in marinade. Let roast marinate, covered and refrigerated, turning it once a day for 2 to 4 days.

PREPARING THE ROAST

2 tablespoons vegetable oil
1 cup chopped onions
1 cup chopped carrots
1 cup chopped celery
1/3 cup heavy cream
Salt and pepper to taste
Pinch of sugar

2 tablespoons flour
2 tablespoons butter, softened
3 tablespoons drained prepared horseradish, or to taste
1 tablespoon Dijon mustard
2 tablespoons minced parsley

Preheat oven to 300°F.

Remove roast and strain marinade through fine sieve into bowl.

In deep flameproof enamel or stainless-steel casserole just large enough to hold roast, brown it on all sides in oil over high heat and transfer to plate.

Add onions, carrots, and celery to casserole. Place roast on top of vegetables. Add marinade and bring liquid to boil. Braise roast, covered, in oven for 3 hours or until tender. Let cool in cooking liquid, partially covered.

Transfer roast to plate and keep warm. Strain cooking liquid (reserving vegetables) into saucepan. Skim the fat, if there is any, and reduce liquid over moderately high heat to 2 cups. It should take about 5 minutes.

Puree vegetables in blender. Add cream and whisk in bits of beurre manié, made by kneading together flour and softened butter. Whisk in horseradish, mustard, pureed vegetables, salt and pepper to taste, and sugar. Keep sauce warm.

Remove and discard string from roast, slice meat thin and arrange on heated platter. Pour some sauce over sliced roast, sprinkle with minced parsley, and serve remaining sauce in a gravy boat.

ORANGE BEEF

Beef is a great dinner dish. I have a hard time with big chunks of rare beef, but this is a crispy, tangy delight for beef lovers like me.

1 pound flank steak
1 tablespoon dark soy sauce
1 teaspoon sugar
6 tablespoons flour

1 egg, slightly beaten
2 cups oil for deep-frying
20 dried red chili peppers
1/4 cup orange peels*

SAUCE

2 tablespoons orange juice
2 tablespoons dark soy sauce

4 tablespoons sugar
1 tablespoon catsup

Mix together in medium-sized bowl and set aside.

4 tablespoons water

1 tablespoon cornstarch dissolved in 1 table-spoon water

Cut beef into 1/2-inch-thick slices and pound 3/8 inch thick. Marinate in soy sauce and sugar for 15 minutes to 2 hours.

Add flour and egg to beef. Mix well by hand. Recipe up to this point can be prepared in advance.

Heat oil for deep-frying. Slip beef in piece by piece to prevent sticking together. Fry until crisp. Drain on paper towels.

Remove all but 2 tablespoons oil from wok. Stir-fry chilies until black; remove.

Add orange peels and sauce mixture. Add 4 tablespoons water and thicken with dissolved cornstarch. Add beef and toss.

Serve with Chinese boiled rice (page 254).

*Peel oranges and remove as much of white part as possible. Leave to dry overnight in the oven with the pilot light on or for a couple of days at room temperature.

GINGER BEEF WITH BOURBON

This delectable dish is another Ben Moy specialty.

SAUCE

1/2 cup beef or chicken stock
1 tablespoon oyster sauce

1 tablespoon light soy sauce

Mix ingredients in small bowl and set aside.

FINAL ASSEMBLY

1/4 cup peanut oil
1 medium red onion, sliced
1 teaspoon sugar
1/2 cup fresh ginger root, sliced very thin
1 pound sirloin steak, cut into bite-sized
   pieces
2 1/2 tablespoons good bourbon
1/2 pound snow peas, strung and blanched

1/2 teaspoon dried basil *or* 1 teaspoon fresh
   basil, chopped
1/2 teaspoon salt
1 teaspoon cornstarch mixed with 2 tablespoons juice from wok or 2 tablespoons
   water
1/2 teaspoon sesame seed oil

Heat wok with oil to high temperature. Stir-fry onions sprinkled with sugar about 3 minutes until thoroughly softened. Add ginger and stir-fry until aroma is released.

Add beef, stir-fry until it loses its pink color and begins to brown and seal. (Don't overcook it or it will become watery.)

Add bourbon, snow peas, basil, salt, and continue to stir-fry. Add sauce, stir-fry to mix well, and add cornstarch mixed with juice from wok or water. It will thicken almost immediately. Sprinkle with sesame seed oil and serve hot.

RUSSIAN MEAT CAKES WITH SOUR CREAM
SERVES 8–10

This is a Ukrainian specialty. It's cold a lot of the time there. Perhaps that is one of the reasons they have large families and even in a medium-sized family they have large appetites. However, for smaller families and eaters, freeze half of the patties before coating. Wrap separately in aluminum foil or freezer paper with directions on top for coating, cooking, and serving.

1/2 cup minced onion
2 tablespoons butter
2/3 cup oatmeal
2/3 cup milk
1 pound twice-ground beef
1 pound twice-ground pork
2 eggs, lightly beaten
2 teaspoons salt

1 teaspoon basil
1 teaspoon thyme
1/2 teaspoon pepper
10 teaspoons chilled butter
2 cups sour cream
1 cup fresh bread crumbs
6–8 tablespoons clarified butter
Snipped dill for garnish

Sauté onions in butter.

Soak oatmeal in bowl of milk for 5 minutes.

Combine beef and pork in another bowl; add eggs, oatmeal mixture, sautéed onions, salt, basil, thyme, and pepper; blend well. Divide mixture into 10 parts. Flatten each into a 1/2-inch-thick round. Press 1 teaspoon chilled butter in center of each round and push meat up around butter to enclose it. Flatten rounds into patties 1/2 inch thick; coat each patty with about 1 teaspoon sour cream, spread thinly all over, and roll in fresh bread crumbs.

In large skillet cook patties in clarified butter for 4 minutes on each side, or until golden brown. Top each patty with 2 tablespoons sour cream, cover, and continue cooking for 5 minutes more.

Garnish patties with snipped dill and place on warmed serving platter. Serve with your favorite potato dish.

LO-CHOLES-CAL MEAT BALLS MAKES 10 LARGE MEAT BALLS
5 SERVINGS

Jack Cassidy was a remarkably talented, handsome actor and singer with a volatile personality and a wonderfully crazy, offbeat sense of humor. He was married to Shirley Jones. They occasionally visited on our TV show together, and many times separately. Jack was a great cook but tried, I think, to hide it because it didn't jibe with the other aspects of his image. This is his recipe for low-cholesterol, low-calorie meat balls. It's de"light"ful as a main dish and, with smaller-sized meat balls, as an appetizer. Incidentally, if your butcher is busy or charges for extras, you can buy the turkey and veal and grind it in your food processor with the metal blade with no trouble at all.

3/4 pound ground turkey
1/4 pound ground veal
1/2 cup chicken broth or consommé
1/4 cup bread crumbs
1 heaping tablespoon chopped parsley
1/4 teaspoon thyme
1/4 teaspoon sweet basil

1/2 teaspoon salt
1/2 teaspoon cumin
1 tablespoon Worcestershire sauce
1/4–1/2 teaspoon cayenne pepper or Tabasco
  sauce
1 egg
Extra bread crumbs

Preheat oven to 400°F.

Combine all meat ball ingredients except extra bread crumbs and shape into large balls (about 1 1/2 inches in diameter). Roll in bread crumbs and place in buttered baking dish. Bake 30 minutes. To make crustier and browner, place under broiler for a few minutes. Place meat balls in shallow heated serving dish, pour 1/3 of heated Barbecue Sauce in bottom. Place meat balls over this and pour rest of hot sauce over all.

BARBECUE SAUCE

1/3 cup catsup
1/3 cup beef broth
1 tablespoon soy sauce

1 tablespoon brown sugar
1 tablespoon vinegar

Combine sauce ingredients and heat slowly 3–4 minutes.

CHILI MIGNON

When you do a good turn you never know the benefit that accrues to you. For instance, I'm on the National Board of an organization called Junior Achievement, which encourages young people to be motivated and enterprising. As a board member, I make occasional trips around the country. One cold wintry evening I was a guest at a small dinner hosted by a fellow board member, Hicks Waldron. Sometimes you worry, when you meet so many new people, whether you'll run out of things to talk about. It never happened in Hartford. Mrs. Hicks Waldron (Evelyn) is an enthusiastic, bottomless source of ideas and recipes, as were many of the wives of the executives present. We exchanged dozens and dozens of ideas and occasionally interrupted our gustatory train of thought with the reason for our being there—Junior Achievement. The whole evening was a great success and you'll find some of Evelyn's specialties throughout this book. Here is one of my favorites.

4 filet mignon steaks, about 1 inch thick
Salt and pepper
1 tablespoon oil
1 small onion, sliced
1 medium clove garlic, minced
6 fresh medium-sized mushrooms, sliced
1/4 cup green chile salsa, or more if desired

4-ounce can chopped green chilies (medium mild)
1/4 cup dry red wine
1 teaspoon chili powder
1 avocado, thinly sliced for garnish
1 teaspoon sour cream for garnish

Sprinkle filets with salt and pepper. In large skillet, sauté steaks in oil until cooked as desired. Remove to platter and keep warm.

In same skillet, cook onion and garlic until onion is translucent. Stir in remaining ingredients except avocado and sour cream. Cook, stirring, until sauce is reduced and thickened. Spoon sauce over steak. Top with avocado and sour cream.

FRIKADELLER—DANISH MEAT PATTIES

The great Kenneth Hansen owned and ran the Scandia Restaurant in Los Angeles with a velvet glove and total contempt for mediocrity in any area of his kitchen or dining room. It was a home away from home for those of us who spent long days taping shows from early in the morning until late at night. We'd traipse over to Scandia sure of a smiling welcome and a perfect light supper, sometimes prepared at the table by Ken himself who waited to dine with us.

1/2 pound boneless veal shoulder or loin
1/2 pound boneless pork shoulder
1 medium onion, coarsely chopped or grated
3 tablespoons flour
1 1/2 cups club soda

1 egg, well beaten
1 teaspoon salt
1/4 teaspoon pepper
4 tablespoons butter
2 tablespoons vegetable oil

Remove fat and gristle from veal and pork. Place in bowl of food processor fitted with metal blade and grind it finely, or have your butcher grind meats twice. Add onion.

In large mixing bowl, vigorously beat flour into ground meat mixture with a wooden spoon. Gradually beat in club soda, a few tablespoons at a time, and continue to beat until meat is light and fluffy. Now thoroughly beat in egg, salt, and pepper. Cover bowl with aluminum foil or plastic wrap and refrigerate for 1 hour; this will make meat mixture firmer and easier to handle.

Shape mixture into oblongs about 4 inches long, 2 inches wide, and 1 inch thick. Melt butter and oil over high heat in heavy 10 to 12-inch skillet. When foam subsides, lower heat to moderate and add meat patties, 4 or 5 at a time, taking care not to crowd them. Cook 6–8 minutes on each side, turning patties with wide spatula or two wooden spoons. When they are rich mahogany brown, remove from pan and set aside on heated platter. Continue with remaining patties. To be certain they are cooked through, puncture one with tip of small knife. The juices should run clear and show no tinge of pink.

Frikadeller are traditionally accompanied by boiled potatoes and pickled beets, cucumber salad, or red cabbage.

CABBAGE ROLLS (GOLABKI) SERVES 4–6

Carroll O'Conner brought this recipe over to the TV show one day. I cooked it with him and it is delicious. I can't say for sure if it's an old traditional family recipe handed down from generation to generation, unless Golabki is some ancient Gaelic expression for stuffed cabbage.

1 medium head of cabbage	1/2 pound ground pork or veal
1/2 cup rice	1 egg
2 tablespoons butter	Salt and pepper to taste
1 onion, finely chopped	1 cup tomato puree
1 pound ground beef	5 slices bacon

Remove core from cabbage. Blanch leaves in boiling water 2–3 minutes. Drain and remove leaves carefully (don't tear). Set leaves aside to cool.

Stir rice into 2 quarts boiling salted water. Boil vigorously 10 minutes. Strain. Run cold water through rice in strainer.

Sauté onions in butter until transparent. In large bowl, combine meats, rice, egg, onion, and seasoning. Mix well. Place large spoonful of meat mixture on each cabbage leaf. Turn edges of each leaf and roll lengthwise. Secure with toothpick if necessary (if each roll is placed seam side down, they should hold without toothpick).

Place rolls side by side in shallow baking dish. Pour tomato puree over rolls and place bacon over top. Bake, uncovered, 2 hours at 325°F. Serve with sour cream.

MUSHROOM-STUFFED MEAT LOAF

SERVES 8

1 large onion, chopped coarsely
1/2 cup finely chopped celery
2 tablespoons butter or margarine
1 pound medium-sized mushrooms, sliced
3/4 cup tomato juice
1 cup soft fresh bread crumbs
1 1/2 teaspoons salt, or to taste

1/4 teaspoon freshly ground pepper, or to taste
1/2 cup sour cream
2 pounds ground chuck
1/2 teaspoon cumin
2 eggs, lightly beaten

Sauté onions and celery in butter. Add mushrooms and sauté until vegetables are limp. Add 1/2 cup tomato juice and simmer 10 minutes.

Mix in bread crumbs, 1/2 teaspoon salt, and 1/8 teaspoon pepper, or to taste. Add sour cream. Taste for seasoning and set aside.

Mix together lightly ground meat with 1 teaspoon salt, 1/8 teaspoon pepper, cumin, remaining 1/4 cup tomato juice, and eggs. If a little dry, add more tomato juice.

Preheat oven to 450°F.

Shape meat mixture into loaf in greased loaf pan. Scoop out center, fill with mushroom mixture, and pat remaining meat mixture over mushroom stuffing, enclosing completely with ground meat. Bake 20 minutes. Reduce oven to 350° and bake 30 minutes longer.

VARIATION To raw ground meat, add 2 tablespoons chopped jalapeño peppers. It gives a certain piquancy to an ordinary or out of the ordinary meat loaf. Incidentally, meat loaf is almost better the second time around, sliced cold, than the first.

RACK OF LAMB PROVENÇALE

SERVES 6–8

Occasionally there will be a special on racks of lamb at your butcher. It's truly special in any sense of the word. Simply roasted in a hot oven it is a treat, but this recipe makes it even more so.

Have your butcher prepare a rack of lamb, removing excess fat. The smaller the rib chops the better—figuring approximately two to three rib widths per person. Two racks will fit nicely in a roasting pan.

2 racks of lamb with 8 ribs each (3–3 1/2 pounds, untrimmed; 2 pounds each, trimmed)
Salt and pepper
3 1/2 garlic cloves, peeled

1/3 cup dried bread crumbs
1/4 cup parsley
2 tablespoons Romano or Parmesan cheese
1/4 cup Dijon mustard
1/4 cup melted butter

Preheat oven to 425°F.

Cut 1/2-inch slits between ribs at large end of racks. Rub salt, pepper, and 1/2 clove garlic over lamb and into slits.

Place in shallow open roasting pan, using the ribs as a rack, and roast uncovered for 20 minutes. Remove roast from oven and let cool.

Meanwhile mince remaining garlic in food processor. Add bread crumbs, parsley, and cheese; process lightly. Set aside.

Spread mustard over top of lamb. Firmly pat crumb mixture into the mustard and into slits if you can work it in without tearing the meat. Drizzle melted butter over lamb.

Return lamb to oven and roast 25 minutes, or until thermometer inserted in fleshy part of lamb registers 135°–140° (medium rare). Transfer to warmed platter. Garnish with parsley. Let stand about 10 minutes before carving. Serve with our Hot Pepper Jelly (page 15).

ROAST LAMB WITH GREEN PEPPERCORN SAUCE
SERVES 6

Jimmy Murphy is a quiet-spoken, great tennis-playing, semi-long-distance runner who also happens to own and run, with equal discipline and dedication, one of our finest restaurants in Beverly Hills. Along with the constantly new dishes of the day are his old standbys. Here's one that's so in demand he couldn't take it off the menu if he tried: We wouldn't let him.

4 1/2 pounds lamb shoulder, boned (if given a little notice, your butcher will do this for you)
Salt and freshly ground black pepper
Oil

1 cup dry white wine
1/2 cup chicken stock
1 teaspoon cornstarch dissolved in 1 tablespoon water
2 tablespoons green peppercorns

Preheat oven to 350°F.

Season lamb well with salt and pepper.

Heat oil in large roasting pan and sauté lamb, browning on all sides. Roast uncovered in oven for 1 hour or until meat thermometer reaches 150°. The lamb should be medium rare.

Remove lamb from roasting pan, pour off any grease in drippings, and add wine. Reduce sauce by two thirds and add chicken stock. Stir in cornstarch dissolved in water and cook sauce for 5 minutes. Strain and add peppercorns. Arrange lamb on warmed serving plate and serve sauce on the side. Good with pureed potatoes and turnips.

COSCE DI AGNELLO AL PEPE VERDE serves 8–10

I was nervous about the six cloves of garlic called for in this beautiful leg of lamb with the lyric Italian name from the Restaurant DiLullo in Philadelphia, Pennsylvania. I needn't have been. If you truly sliver the garlic cloves and slip the slivers into the slits with all the other niceties it calls for, it melts into a succulent whole that is a memory-maker. Be sure to take advantage of those beautiful pan juices, as they're necessary for the sauce or gravy. I'm a confirmed believer that serving some of those larger roasted specialties like pot roast, turkey, roast lamb, without a little sauce is like doing your whole makeup without the lipstick—or gloss.

5–6-pound leg of lamb, trimmed completely of fat, boned, and butterflied

6 cloves garlic, peeled and cut into thin slivers

1 cup Dijon mustard

1/2 cup quality olive oil

3 sprigs fresh thyme *or* 1 tablespoon dried thyme, crushed

With tip of sharp knife, poke 10–12 holes into flesh of lamb. Insert garlic slivers into holes. Place lamb in large pan.

Combine mustard, 1/4 cup oil. Rub entire surface of lamb with mixture. Place thyme on surface, pressing down on meat to absorb flavor. Cover pan with plastic wrap. Refrigerate at least 24 hours.

Preheat oven to 325°F.

In a large heavy skillet heat remaining oil over high heat. Sear meat 2–3 minutes on each side. Place on rack in roasting pan and then in oven until meat is pink, about 45 minutes (150° on meat thermometer).

Place meat on warm serving platter and keep warm until ready to serve. Slice just before serving.

If desired, serve with Green Peppercorn Sauce.

GREEN PEPPERCORN SAUCE

2 cups white wine
2 cups heavy cream
3 tablespoons green peppercorns
2 tablespoons Dijon mustard

2 tablespoons butter
1 teaspoon white pepper
Sprigs of fresh parsley for garnish

Deglaze roasting pan with wine and cream, stirring constantly with whisk. Transfer to skillet and reduce volume by half.

Reduce heat to low and stir in peppercorns, mustard, butter, and pepper. Stir well. Cook over low heat until butter is melted and sauce is very warm. Pour sauce over lamb and garnish with sprigs of fresh parsley.

tip Do not add salt, for mustard already is salty. Do not boil sauce after butter is added, or sauce will separate.

LAMB IN PUFF PASTRY

A pretty party dish nobody will have served last Wednesday. The first time I ever had it was at Milwaukee's Le Bistro. It's simpler than it sounds at first reading and is well worth the effort. Since your puff pastry is the only problem to be anticipated, line it up ahead of time and put it in your freezer until you're ready to use it. You'll find it in specialty shops or in the freezer section of your supermarket. It's right there along with the phyllo dough.

2-pound boneless loin of lamb, trimmed of
   fat and tendons
Salt and pepper to taste
2 tablespoons vegetable oil or margarine
1 sheet (8 × 14) puff pastry dough

1/2 cup sliced fresh mushrooms
6 slices prosciutto, sliced paper-thin
1 pound fresh spinach leaves, blanched and
   drained on paper towels
1 egg beaten with 1 tablespoon water

Preheat oven to 400°F.

Rub lamb with salt and pepper after piercing top and bottom with tines of fork so it will penetrate well. In 12-inch heavy skillet heat oil or margarine and brown lamb on all sides, using spatula or wooden spoons so as not to pierce meat while browning.

Place in shallow roasting pan and bake for 15–17 minutes, cooking to rare. Set aside.

Lay out puff dough on floured board. Roll out to about 1/8 inch thick and 12–18 inches in size to cover roast. Remove from board and place in a clean shallow roasting pan. Place lamb roast in center. Arrange mushrooms diagonally over top; then layer of ham; then arrange well-drained spinach to cover ham evenly. Pull up side and corners of puff dough to completely surround lamb loin and vegetables. Seal edges with egg wash, brushing and pressing edges, overlapping and completely sealing. This may all be done ahead of time and placed in refrigerator until ready to be baked.

About 1 hour before serving time, brush with remaining egg wash. Place in oven and bake approximately 30 minutes or until golden brown.

Before slicing, let rest at least 10 minutes after cooking. Slice 1/2 inch thick, allowing 2 slices per person. Serve immediately with White Wine Sauce.

WHITE WINE SAUCE

2 cups chicken broth
1 cup white wine
1 cup heavy cream
2 tablespoons sweet butter
2 tablespoons flour

1 tablespoon chopped shallots
1/4 cup sliced fresh mushrooms
1/2 teaspoon salt
1/4 teaspoon white pepper

Combine chicken broth, wine, and cream in heavy saucepan. Reduce by 1/3, cooking slowly.

Combine butter and flour to make a roux and cook 1–2 minutes. Gradually add liquid mixture, stirring constantly until smooth and velvety. Simmer.

In separate pan, sauté shallots and mushrooms in small amount of butter until tender. Add these to sauce. Season to taste with salt and pepper and serve over sliced lamb loin.

ROASTED DOUBLE LAMB CHOPS WITH GLAZED TURNIPS

SERVES 6

The best meal I had in Paris was at the home of Christian and Arlette Millau. During their last Los Angeles trip, we cooked a meal together in my home. We got great reviews, especially from us. After the guests left we sat around and rehashed the whole hectic, hilarious day, particularly the scene in the kitchen with Christian's assistants, me, my Pauline and her sous-chef Liliana, our note takers (we were testing, don't forget), the still cameras and the 20/20 crew covering the disorderly order of things. This was one of Christian's contributions to the menu.

12 large turnips, thinly sliced
1/2 cup clarified butter
6 double rib lamb chops
2 whole cloves garlic, crushed

1/2 cup butter
1 1/2 cups Lamb Broth
Salt and pepper

Preheat oven to 350°F.

In large skillet sauté turnips in clarified butter 5 minutes or until they caramelize. Then bake them in roasting pan 35–40 minutes.

Sauté lamb chops and garlic in butter in large heavy skillet 3 minutes on each side. Seven minutes before turnips are done, place lamb chops on top and continue baking.

To serve, place turnips in an overlapping circle on a heated platter, leaving space to stand your beautiful lamb chops upright in the center of the circle of turnips. Deglaze pan juices with Lamb Broth. Add salt and pepper to taste. Serve sauce on side.

LAMB BROTH

2 pounds lamb bones
1 carrot, diced
1 stalk celery, chopped
1 onion, chopped

3 tomatoes, peeled, seeded, and swirled
   briefly in blender
1 clove garlic, crushed
Bouquet garni

Preheat oven to 350°F.

Bake cut lamb bones 20 minutes. Remove fat from pan and add carrots, celery, and onions. Bake 10 minutes more. Deglaze pan by adding water to cover bones and vegetables. Add crushed tomatoes, garlic, and bouquet garni.

Transfer to pot and cook 20 minutes. Strain broth and reduce slowly to 1 1/2 cups.

LAMB STEW WITH PRUNES AND SWEET POTATOES

SERVES 6

1 1/2 pounds lamb shoulder, cut into chunks
1 onion, minced
2 tablespoons butter or margarine
Salt and pepper

2 sweet potatoes, peeled and sliced
1 cup pitted prunes
1/2 cup lightly toasted blanched almonds for
   garnish

Sauté onion in butter until translucent. Add lamb and brown. Season with salt and pepper to taste and add water to cover.

Bring to boil, reduce heat, cover and simmer 1 hour or until meat is tender.

Add sweet potatoes and cook, covered, 20–25 minutes. Add prunes and cook 10–15 minutes longer or until sweet potatoes and prunes are done. Transfer to warmed serving platter and garnish with almonds.

CURRIED CASHEW LAMB   SERVES 4

Alan Alda is as popular as any man has ever been on TV. He works constantly—acting, writing, producing, directing, and trying to commute between home and family in New Jersey and work in Los Angeles. Arlene, his wife, is an artist in her own right—a flutist and a great photographer. She had to stay most of the time in New Jersey to keep the home humming.

Occasionally between pictures, traveling, and writing Alan would come on our TV show. I kept trying to fatten the poor dear up a little. He loves to eat, but I had the feeling he had spent most of his evenings in Los Angeles over TV dinners. When I learned that one of his favorite dishes was lamb curry, I made this one from scratch. It took practically the whole show so I didn't get to ask many significant questions, but it was worth it—especially when he had already reached for thirds before I could ask, "What do you think of the state of the world?" (little light questions like that got us a whole audience of intellectuals).

1/2 cup plain yogurt
1/4 teaspoon finely minced fresh ginger root
Salt and pepper to taste

1 1/2 pounds lamb, loin or shoulder, fat and tendons removed, and cut into 1 1/2-inch cubes

Mix yogurt, ginger, and salt and pepper. Marinate lamb in mixture at room temperature for about 20 minutes.

MASALA (CURRY PASTE)

1/4 cup raw cashews
3 red chilies, seeded
1 piece (1 inch) fresh ginger
1 cup water
1 stick cinnamon, crushed

1/4 teaspoon cardamom seeds
2 cloves garlic
3 cloves
2 tablespoons poppy seeds
1 teaspoon cumin seeds

In food processor using metal blade, mix cashews, chilies, ginger, and water until well blended and smooth. Add remaining ingredients and blend again. Set aside.

FINAL ASSEMBLY

1/4 cup boiling water
1/2 teaspoon saffron threads
6 tablespoons clarified butter
1 cup chopped onions
1 teaspoon salt
1/4 teaspoon turmeric

1/4 teaspoon powdered coriander
Dash powdered cinnamon
1 scant tablespoon curry powder
2 tablespoons chopped cilantro
1 tablespoon fresh lemon juice

Pour boiling water over saffron. Soak 10 minutes.

Heat butter in large skillet, add onions and cook, stirring constantly, 7–8 minutes.

Stir in salt and Masala. Add marinade and lamb. Cook and stir a few minutes. Add turmeric, coriander, cinnamon, and curry powder.

Mash saffron against sides of bowl and add (with liquid) to meat mixture. Reduce heat; cover and cook 20 minutes. Sprinkle with cilantro and cook 10 minutes more. Serve on rice and sprinkle with lemon juice.

BREAST OF LAMB WITH CURRIED RICE STUFFING

SERVES 4–6

2 2-pound breasts of lamb, boned and
  trimmed of all fat (each should weigh
  about 1 pound when boned)
1 cup thinly sliced onions
4 tablespoons butter
1 small tart apple, peeled, cored, and
  chopped
2 tablespoons raisins
2 teaspoons curry powder
1 large clove garlic, minced
1/2 teaspoon ground cumin
1/4 teaspoon cayenne pepper
Salt and pepper to taste

1/2 cup cooked rice
1 cup plain yogurt
1/4 cup toasted and chopped blanched almonds
Lemon juice
1 carrot, chopped
1 small onion, chopped
1 tablespoon vegetable oil
1/2 cup dry white wine
1/2 cup chicken broth
1 tablespoon flour (optional)
1 tablespoon softened butter (optional)

Spread meat out so that it lies flat. Place between sheets of waxed paper. With meat mallet, pound it to as even a thickness as possible.

Cook onions in 3 tablespoons butter in skillet over moderate heat, stirring, for 5 minutes. Add apples, raisins, curry powder, garlic, cumin, cayenne, and salt to taste. Cook mixture, stirring, 3 minutes.

Stir in rice, 1/4 cup yogurt, and almonds, combining the mixture well; then let mixture cool.

Sprinkle boned surface of lamb with lemon juice and salt and pepper to taste; cover with rice mixture, leaving 1/2-inch border. Roll the lamb jelly-roll fashion, starting with short side, and tie securely at 2-inch intervals with kitchen string. Close ends by continuously wrapping string around lamb.

Preheat oven to 350°F.

In shallow flameproof baking dish, cook chopped carrots and onions in 1 tablespoon butter and vegetable oil over moderate heat, stirring, for 3 minutes. Add lamb. Roast in oven 15 minutes.

Add wine and chicken broth and cook lamb, covered, 20 minutes more or until tender. Transfer lamb to plate, cover and keep warm.

Strain cooking liquid through sieve and mash the vegetables through sieve into saucepan. Skim fat and reduce liquid over moderately high heat to 1/2 cup.

Whisk in remaining yogurt and cook mixture over moderate heat 5 minutes or until thickened slightly. If sauce is too thin, whisk in bits of buerre manié, made by kneading together 1 tablespoon each of flour and softened butter. Add salt, pepper, and lemon juice to taste. Remove and discard string. Then slice lamb 1/2 inch thick. Arrange slices on heated platter and serve the sauce in a gravy boat.

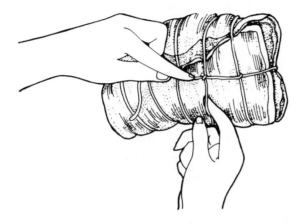

Secure lamb with string by tying at 2- or 3-inch intervals.

Roll lamb, jelly-roll fashion; start with short side and wrap gently.

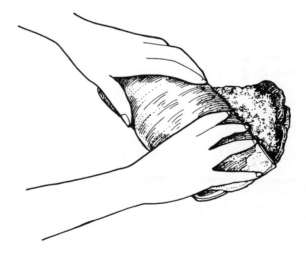

MARINATED ROAST BONELESS PORK LOIN

This recipe came from Shaw's Restaurant in Lancaster, Ohio. We never got there—something to do with two concerts in one day—but their reputation had reached all through the Midwest where we were traveling. This was a dish most often mentioned. I tried it at home. It's all they said it was. The long and short marinade versions work deliciously. Somehow I preferred the overnight version. It seemed to have penetrated more.

1 5-pound boneless pork loin
2 cups dry white wine
1/2 teaspoon powdered thyme
1/2 teaspoon dried rosemary
1/2 teaspoon dried tarragon
2 tablespoons kosher salt
1/4 cup brown sugar
2 tablespoons Dijon mustard

2 large cloves garlic, put through a press
Handful of celery leaves
1 medium onion, coarsely chopped
1 carrot, quartered
2 tablespoons flour kneaded with 2 tablespoons butter
1 1/2 cups chicken stock
2 tablespoons currant jelly

Pierce meat with tines of fork in several places on both sides to let marinade penetrate. Marinate pork in white wine, thyme, rosemary, and tarragon overnight in refrigerator. If you don't have that much time, heat marinade and pour over pork. Let stand at room temperature for a few hours. Pour off marinade and reserve.

Preheat oven to 350°F.

Rub pork with kosher salt, brown sugar, mustard, and garlic. Place in pan and arrange celery leaves, onions, and carrots around it. Pour over about 1/2 cup of marinade and roast pork, uncovered, about 1 1/2 hours.

Remove pork from pan and keep warm. Spoon off as much excess fat from liquid in pan as you can. Discard celery leaves, carrots, and onions.

Place pan on burner on medium heat and add butter and flour mixture; cook until brown. Stir with whisk. Add chicken stock and currant jelly. Taste for seasoning. Place pork on platter and pour sauce over top.

CROWN ROAST PORK

Crown roast pork is an excellent company dish you can serve with pardonable pride. Call your butcher a day or two before your dinner and tell him how many people you want to serve. Usually you count on about two chops per person. Make sure he removes the backbone, and ask him to leave room in the center for your stuffing. Also, ask him the length of cooking time he suggests. They're very well informed in this area. Remind him you would like paper frills for the chops.

P.S. Ask him how to put them on without getting you and them greasy.

12 to 16 chop crown roast of pork (cut from center rib section)
Salt and pepper

1/2 teaspoon thyme
Stuffing
Peach halves and sour cream for garnish

Preheat oven to 400°F. Cover rib ends of chops with foil to avoid excess browning. Sprinkle roast cavity with salt, pepper, and thyme. Bake 20 minutes, then reduce heat to 325° and continue baking 40 minutes more.

Remove pork from oven and fill roast cavity with prepared stuffing. Mound the stuffing in center to form dome. Return meat to oven and roast 1 1/4 hours more at 325°F.

You'll have stuffing left over. Serve on the side in bowl. Warm peach halves through and place a dab of sour cream in center. Remove foil ends from chops and replace with paper frills.

BARLEY PILAF FOR STUFFING

1/4 cup butter
1/3 cup chopped shallots or onions (be generous)
1 1/2 cups pearl barley

3 cups beef or chicken broth
1/2 teaspoon freshly ground black pepper
1/4 cup chopped parsley

Melt butter in a heavy 3-quart saucepan and gently sauté shallots or onions.

Add barley and broth heated to boiling point. Add pepper. Stir well, cover, and bring to boil. Lower heat so broth just simmers, and cook for 50–60 minutes or until barley is tender and liquid is absorbed. Add water if broth cooks away too fast. Taste pilaf and add salt and more pepper, if necessary. (If broth is well seasoned, salt may not be needed.)

Toss with chopped parsley and a little extra butter.

DINAH'S STUFFED PORK CHOPS   SERVES 6

This is from home—Tennessee. I think it was one of the first recipes I remember Mother letting me try on my own. What a triumph!

1/2 green pepper, finely chopped
3 stalks celery, finely chopped
2 tablespoons butter
1 cup bread crumbs (or leftover corn bread)
12 ounces fresh or 1 (8-ounce) package frozen corn (if using fresh corn, cut from 3 ears and blanch in salted water 1 minute)
Salt and pepper

6 pork chops, 1 inch thick
Seasoned flour (salt, pepper, paprika)
4 tablespoons vegetable oil
Sliced onion for garnish
Sliced green pepper for garnish
16-ounce can of tomatoes including juice, put in blender or food processor briefly to break up

Preheat oven to 300°F.

Sauté green peppers and celery in butter. Add bread crumbs, corn and salt and pepper to taste. Mix well.

With sharp knife make horizontal pocket through the center of pork chops almost to the bone. Salt and pepper the inside of pocket. Fill loosely with stuffing.

Dust chops lightly with seasoned flour and brown lightly in hot oil in large skillet. Transfer chops from skillet to ovenproof casserole and garnish each with sliced onion and sliced green pepper. Salt and pepper to taste. Put tomato pulp around sides and in spaces between chops. Bake, covered, 1 1/4 hours. Serve with Homemade Applesauce.

HOMEMADE APPLESAUCE

**12 large green apples, peeled, cored, and
 quartered**

Cook, dry (I really mean no water) in covered saucepan over low heat until mushy, 20–30 minutes. Blend in processor if necessary.

PORK CHOPS WITH ORANGE SLICES   SERVES 2–4

One summer we had an apartment in mid-Manhattan. Unlike California, where your local super-market has it all, in New York you go to the butcher, the baker, the greengrocer, the poultry shop, the fish market, the cheese place, ad infinitum. I learned a lot of respect for New York homemakers and cooks.

This dish was the only thing that looked reasonably close to fitting my slenderly stocked larder. Whoever said "Necessity is the mother of invention" has my vote for president of anything.

4 single pork chops, 1/2 inch thick	**1/3 cup brown sugar**
Salt and pepper	**1 orange, sliced with rind on**
Seasoned flour (salt and pepper)	**1/2 cup fresh orange juice**
1 tablespoon oil	**2 tablespoons orange liqueur (Triple Sec or**
1 tablespoon butter	**Cointreau or Grand Marnier)**

Season pork chops on both sides with salt and pepper. Place seasoned flour in paper bag. Drop chops in bag and gently shake to coat thoroughly.

Put oil and butter in large skillet; when hot, brown chops on both sides. Remove and set aside.

In same skillet add brown sugar, then orange slices. Lower heat and brown orange slices. Add orange juice and orange liqueur and blend carefully.

Remove orange slices and put chops back into pan. Cover and cook over low heat 15–20 minutes until pork chops are done. Place orange slices on top of pork chops for last 5 to 10 minutes of cooking time.

WILD RICE, PORK, AND APPLE SKILLET

SERVES 4

I don't know where I got this one. It sounds like Minnesota, one of my favorite places and one of the few states producing wild rice in quantity, and no one there is shy about telling you ways to use it.

4 pork chops, about 1 inch thick
Salt and pepper
Oil for frying
1 cup wild rice

1 large onion, sliced into rings
2 1/2 cups chicken broth
2 large red apples, cored and sliced

Generously salt and pepper chops on both sides. In heavy-bottomed skillet over moderately high heat, brown chops on both sides, using as little oil as possible. Remove chops and sprinkle rice into pan.

Arrange chops and onion rings over rice and pour chicken broth over all. Bring to boil. Cover and reduce heat to maintain a slow simmer for about 1 hour. Taste for seasoning. Add unpeeled apple slices and simmer, covered, 15 minutes longer or until apples, rice, and chops are tender.

GLORIA'S MEXICAN PORK ROAST SERVES 6–8

Gloria is our friend from Mexico who has worked off and on in our home for years. She has a delightful sense of humor, a little trouble with Ingles, and a great knack of cooking her native dishes. She also has definite ideas about which chilies go in what. I think I brought her seven different varieties before she pointed out that the ordinary one I had in the bottom of the bag was exactly right for this elegant roast. It's the large dark red dried pasilla and can be found in great quantities in almost any specialty market.

5-pound boneless pork loin roast
1 1/2 cups raisins
2/3 cup halved almonds
1 teaspoon salt
1 teaspoon pepper
3 tablespoons vegetable oil
2 sweet pasilla chilies, washed and seeds removed
2 whole tomatoes, cored but unpeeled

2 medium onions, cut in half
1 1/2 cups water
1 bay leaf
1/4 cinnamon stick (about 3/4 inch long)
1/4 teaspoon thyme
1/4 teaspoon oregano
7-ounce can green olives, drained
1 tablespoon brown sugar
1/4 cup red wine

Cut 1-inch slits every 1 1/2 inches lengthwise across fatty part of roast. (You should have about 42 slits in roast.) Place 4 or 5 raisins in each slit and then place halved almond in each slit. (You should use about 1 cup of raisins.) Rub salt and pepper into roast on all sides.

In Dutch oven, brown meat in oil very slowly until thoroughly browned on all sides. While meat is browning, add chilies, tomatoes, and onions to Dutch oven and brown slowly. Do not let chilies burn or get black. Remove chilies when meat is browned.

Add water, bay leaf, cinnamon stick, thyme, oregano, remaining 1/2 cup raisins, olives, brown sugar, and wine. Bring to boil, cover, and simmer 2–2 1/2 hours until pork is done.

About 30 minutes before serving, remove meat and slice on an angle, but not too thick. Return to sauce in Dutch oven and heat through, about 20 minutes.

Carefully remove meat to warmed platter. Remove bay leaf from sauce and cover meat with sauce unstrained.

CRISPY PORK CHOPS

6 very thin pork chops
4 scallions, chopped into 2-inch lengths and
   then mashed with cleaver
1-inch piece of fresh ginger root, cut into
   narrow strips and mashed with cleaver

3 tablespoons soy sauce
1 teaspoon sesame seed oil
1 teaspoon sugar
1 cup peanut oil
1/2 cup cornstarch

Trim most of fat from pork chops. Do not remove bones. Score lightly on each side. Place chops between two pieces of waxed paper and with back of cleaver flatten meat until chops are very thin. Place on large shallow plate or in shallow baking pan.

Sprinkle the scallions and ginger over pork chops. Mix soy sauce, sesame seed oil, and sugar well. Turn pork chops over and over in mixture until they are well coated with the marinade. Set aside until you are ready to use—at least 10 minutes, and longer if you can.

Heat wok over high heat for 15 seconds. Pour in cooking oil. While oil is heating, pour cornstarch onto flat plate or on waxed paper.

Pick scallions and ginger off from pork chops. Dip each pork chop into the cornstarch. Pat cornstarch in to make sure each piece is thoroughly coated. When oil in wok is smoking, add pork chops. Turn after 30 seconds. Fry about a minute on second side. Turn again and fry for a final 15–30 seconds until a deep golden brown. Drain and serve.

CHINESE PORK SHREDS, BLACK BEANS, AND GREEN PEPPERS

Chinese black beans are a special tiny little lentil-like legume, fermented in a sauce that's pretty salty. Before they're used in recipes they're rinsed in a sieve in cold water to remove the salt, and mashed with the back of a spoon in that same sieve to separate and spread the flavor throughout the dish. They come in small cans and can be found in the specialty section of most supermarkets or in your special import grocery stores.

A wise Chinese lady once told me the Chinese never double a recipe as we do for extra guests. They simply add another dish to the menu. One dish per guest is the ratio (rice doesn't count as it's prepared in large quantities for everyone). It's my favorite way to dine—try a little of this, a lot of these, a smidgen more of that, small amounts of large numbers of unusual and complementary flavors.

3/4 cup Chinese dried, salted black beans
3 medium pork chops (for a yield of approximately 3/4 pound of meat)
2 scallions, including tops
1 teaspoon sesame seed oil
2 tablespoons soy sauce
4 hot green peppers, approximately 3 inches long (if you can't find hot green peppers

use 2 green bell peppers, but add 1/2 teaspoon of hot pepper flakes to the dish)
4 cloves garlic, peeled and coarsely chopped
4 tablespoons peanut oil
1/2 teaspoon salt
1 teaspoon granulated sugar
Salt to taste
2 tablespoons water (optional)

Rinse black beans thoroughly under cold water 1 minute. While still in sieve, mash a little with back of spoon and set aside in a small bowl.

Cut fat and bone away from pork chops, then slice meat into shreds about 3 inches long and 1/8 inch wide, the width of a wooden match stick. (It is easier to slice meat very fine if you first put it in freezer for about 10 minutes, until it becomes stiff but not frozen.) Cut scallions into 3-inch lengths. Slice scallions approximately same size as the meat shreds. Place shredded pork and scallions in small shallow bowl. Add sesame seed oil and soy sauce and mix thoroughly. Set aside to marinate.

Slice peppers in half lengthwise and remove seeds, then cut into shreds approximately same size as pork.

Heat wok over hot flame for 15 seconds, then add 1 tablespoon peanut oil. It will be ready when first tiny bubbles form and a few small wisps of smoke appear. Add green peppers. Stir-fry vigorously for 30 seconds, using cooking shovel or spoon in scooping motion to toss pepper shreds around in pan so every piece is exposed to hot oil. Add salt and continue to cook about 2 more minutes, stirring occasionally, until peppers are slightly limp. Remove peppers from wok.

Reheat wok and add remaining peanut oil. When hot, add garlic and stir-fry vigorously for 15 seconds. Quickly add black beans and sugar and stir-fry about 1 minute. Then add meat mixture and peppers. Stir-fry 3 more minutes, until pork has lost its pinkish color and is thoroughly cooked. Just before serving, taste for seasoning. If dish is too salty, add a few tablespoons of water and stir thoroughly. Serve with rice, of course. Chinese Jade Broccoli (page 267) would be lovely with this.

PORK WITH GREEN CHILI SAUCE   SERVES 4–6

I have done this with the little tomatillas and it's truly a green sauce. If you use canned tomatillas, include juice. If fresh, remove protective leaf surrounding tomatilla, but don't peel. Add 1/4 cup water. It changes the flavor from our sweet red tomato. Try them! If they're available, you'll love 'em!

2 pounds lean pork, cut into bite-sized cubes
1/2 cup water
2 cloves garlic, peeled and cut in half
Salt and pepper to taste
1 large onion, finely chopped
1 cup solid-pack tomatoes, drained

2 teaspoons chopped fresh cilantro (coriander)
7-ounce can peeled green chilies, chopped or cut into strips
2 hot jalapeño peppers, seeded and chopped

Put meat into heavy-bottomed stewpot, cover with water, and bring to boil over high heat. Reduce heat, add garlic and salt and pepper. Cook, covered, until all water is absorbed, about 25–30 minutes. Discard garlic. Let meat fry in its own fat until it starts to turn brown, turning occasionally to brown on all sides.

Add onions, cook a few minutes longer to soften. Then add tomatoes, cilantro, chilies, peppers, and additional salt if desired. Cook, covered, 30 minutes longer or until pork is tender. Serve over rice.

PORK MINHO STYLE

This world-traveling friend of mine, Marty Leshner, used to send post cards. He now sends letters—usually with a recipe enclosed, after patiently standing over some native chef and making his proper notations. I don't think he even has his interpreter around all the time, observing and making copious notes. It may have cut down on his sightseeing, but he's become a better, plumper person for it.

    This recipe of Marty's calls for fresh cilantro or fresh coriander. They are the same thing, but unlike all those other marvelous pungent dried herbs we use when the fresh are out of season, the dried coriander seed on your grocer's spice shelf unfortunately bears no resemblance to the fresh. The good news is that like parsley, fresh cilantro or fresh coriander is growing somewhere nearby all year round. Mention it to your vegetable man and he'll get some in for you.

4 pounds lean boned pork, trimmed of fat
  and cut into 1-inch cubes
Salt
1/4 cup flour
1/4 cup bacon fat or solid shortening
1 cup white wine
2 1/2 teaspoons ground cumin
1 teaspoon chopped garlic

1 teaspoon salt
1/8 teaspoon ground black pepper
1/2 cup chicken broth
1 thinly sliced lemon, each slice cut into
  quarters
1 heaping tablespoon chopped fresh cilantro
  or coriander

Lightly salt pork cubes and dust with flour.

    In large skillet brown meat in shortening. Stir in 1/2 cup white wine. Add cumin, garlic, salt, and pepper; increase heat to bring to fast boil. Stir and cover skillet; reduce heat and simmer about 30 minutes or until meat is tender.

    Pour in remaining white wine and chicken broth. Let come to boil, reduce heat. Add quartered lemon slices. Cook slowly until sauce has thickened slightly.

    Taste for seasoning. Add cilantro or coriander, stir, and pour entire pork and sauce mixture into serving bowl.

    Serve with rice or crisply fried or mashed potatoes for the gravy.

WIENER SCHNITZEL

I thought I'd had Wiener Schnitzel. I always liked it a lot, but I never had it quite the way they serve it at Schumacher's New Prague Hotel in New Prague, Minnesota. It's meltingly tender.

1 1/2 pounds veal scallops, cut into thin
  slices (about 1 1/2 ounces per slice)
1/4 loaf fresh white bread
1 tablespoon flour
1 cup flour, seasoned with salt, pepper, and

  paprika
4 eggs beaten with 2 tablespoons water
1/2 cup clarified butter
2 tablespoons lemon juice
12 lemon slices

Preheat oven to 350°F.

Place veal between sheets of waxed paper and pound until very thin.

Cut crusts off bread, place bread in food processor with 1 tablespoon flour, and make crumbs. Dip veal in seasoned flour, then in egg mixture, then in bread crumbs.

Heat clarified butter in a large heavy skillet. When butter starts to bubble, add veal slices so they lie flat in skillet, not overlapping, and brown. Turn over and splash with lemon juice.

When all veal is browned, place in single layer in warmed baking dish. Cover with foil and bake 15–20 minutes.

Place 2 or 3 slices of veal on each warmed dinner plate and cover each with a lemon slice.

VEAL À LA PEYTON
SERVES 6

This is one of the rare meat dishes served at Earth by April in Cleveland Heights, Ohio. I don't know who or what Peyton is, but I like its veal.

6 slices of veal scallops, pounded 1/2 inch
  thick
Flour
1/2 cup sweet butter
Salt and freshly ground pepper
2 teaspoons chopped fresh basil

1 shallot, very finely chopped
1 zucchini, cut into fine julienne strips
1 tomato, cut into 6 slices
1/2 cup Marsala wine
6 slices (1/2 inch thick) mozzarella cheese

Dry veal slices thoroughly and flour lightly. Heat butter in large heavy-bottomed skillet over medium heat. Add veal and brown on each side for 2 minutes; season with salt, pepper, and basil.

Add shallots and zucchini and cook for 2 minutes; add tomato and cook 1 minute more.

Remove veal to a flameproof plate and deglaze pan with wine. Reduce sauce over high heat for 1 minute. Top each veal slice with zucchini, then tomato slice. Then top each with slice of mozzarella. Place under broiler and melt cheese until slightly brown. Serve with noodles or Special Bulgur Pilaf (page 260).

VEAL CARAWAY
SERVES 4

John Schumacher's restaurant in the New Prague Hotel in New Prague, Minnesota, is a lovely experience. John does all the cooking and his wife is the hostess. The atmosphere is homey and romantic and the food is superb. This is one recipe that he shared with us as well as the Wiener Schnitzel on page 210.

His Spaetzle (page 251) is great with this sauce. If you want fewer calories, you can use half-and-half instead of cream and if "they've" never tasted the original version, "they'll" never know the difference.

1 pound veal scallops, sliced thin and
   pounded slightly
1 cup seasoned flour (salt, pepper, and paprika)
1/4 cup clarified butter
2 shallots, finely chopped

2 teaspoons caraway seeds
1/4 cup sweet sherry wine
1/4 cup white wine
1 pint heavy cream
Salt and pepper to taste
1/2 teaspoon chopped parsley for garnish

Dust scallops of veal with seasoned flour.

    Heat heavy skillet. Add clarified butter and heat to bubble. Add shallots and sauté until transparent. Add caraway seeds and veal. Sauté lightly about 20 seconds on each side. Remove to warm platter.

    Combine sherry and white wine. Add to skillet, turn heat to medium high, and reduce sauce by about 1/3. Remove skillet from heat and slowly add heavy cream. Simmer on low heat until sauce thickens. Adjust seasoning with salt and pepper.

    Just before serving, return veal to sauce and heat through. Garnish with chopped parsley.

VEAL KOTTWITZ

SERVES 6

Commander's Palace is worth a trip to New Orleans. Here's one of the reasons.

CREOLE MEAT SEASONING

MAKES 3 3/4 CUPS

1 1/2 cups salt
3/4 cup finely minced garlic
3/4 cup black pepper

1/2 cup cayenne pepper
1/4 cup cumin

Combine all ingredients and mix thoroughly. Pour into large glass jar. Keeps indefinitely.

1 tablespoon Creole Meat Seasoning
6 6-ounce pieces veal scallops

1/2 cup flour
1/4 cup butter

Season veal with Creole Meat Seasoning, then lightly flour. In large skillet melt butter. Sauté veal until nicely browned (3–5 minutes). Set aside, keep warm.

MUSHROOM ARTICHOKE SAUCE

1/2 cup butter
3 tablespoons finely chopped scallions, including tops
1 cup sliced fresh mushrooms
1 can (8 1/2 ounces) artichoke hearts, rinsed

well, drained, and sliced
1 tablespoon flour
1/4 cup lemon juice
1 tablespoon Worcestershire sauce
Creole Meat Seasoning to taste

Melt butter in skillet. Add scallions and sauté until tender, 4–5 minutes. Stir in mushrooms and artichoke hearts, cook 5 minutes.

Stir in flour and blend until creamy. Add lemon juice, Worcestershire, and Creole Meat Seasoning. Adjust meat seasoning to taste.

Place meat on heated dinner plate, spoon 1/3 cup sauce over each piece.

It's wonderfully spicy without singeing your tonsils. Serve with noodles, rice, or boiled potatoes and a bright green vegetable.

VEAL SCALLOPS IN THE STYLE OF FLORENCE

SERVES 4

Florence is not your stylish cousin. In this case, it's in the style of Florence, Italy—Firenze—and our friends at Giovanni in Cleveland have certainly been there.

To make this go farther, use 6 medium shrimp and serve 2 scallops per person. I'm developing a large-portion complex.

8 large shrimp, shelled and deveined, leaving tails intact
1 pound spinach, washed and stems removed
12 2-ounce veal scallops, sliced 1/4 inch thick and pounded thin
Salt and freshly ground pepper

3 tablespoons flour
3 tablespoons unsalted butter
6 ounces clarified margarine
3 tablespoons finely chopped red onions
1/4 cup sherry wine
1 cup heavy cream
3 tablespoons chopped parsley

Wash shrimp thoroughly under cold water and pat dry.

Steam spinach until wilted.

Season veal scallops with salt and pepper and dust them with flour.

Heat 1 tablespoon each of unsalted butter and clarified margarine in large skillet until light haze forms over it. Add 1 tablespoon of red onions and sauté until lightly browned. Add wilted spinach, salt, and pepper and sauté for 1 minute. Remove from heat and keep warm.

Combine 2 tablespoons butter and 1 tablespoon of flour and set aside.

In large skillet heat remaining margarine, add shrimp, veal scallops, salt, and pepper and sauté until brown. Turn them and drain off excess fat from skillet. Add remaining onions and lightly brown over high flame.

Add sherry and deglaze pan. Add heavy cream and heat until cream begins to boil. Add butter and flour mixture and stir until sauce thickens slightly.

Make bed of spinach on each serving plate, top with veal scallops and shrimp, and pour remaining sauce over all. Sprinkle with parsley and serve.

GOLDEN VEAL STEW

SERVES 5–6

Another veal stew—another flavor—another family or company dish that's out of the ordinary. Again, noodles or boiled rice are perfect for the lightly seasoned sauce.

2 pounds veal, cut into 1-inch-square chunks	1 teaspoon salt
1 cup white wine	1/2 teaspoon pepper
4 carrots, sliced	2 tablespoons butter
1 large onion, sliced	2 tablespoons flour
1 bouquet garni (parsley and thyme) tied in a cheesecloth bag for easy removal	1 egg
	Juice of 1 lemon

Place veal in large pot and cover with cold water. Add wine, carrots, onions, bouquet garni, salt, and pepper. Bring to boil, skim, reduce heat, and simmer 2 hours.

Remove meat, strain broth, and reserve. Make a roux by melting butter, adding flour over low heat, and stirring with whisk until flour is golden brown. Gradually add the hot broth, stirring constantly. Simmer for 10 minutes.

Beat egg in bowl; add lemon juice and slowly pour in hot sauce. Pour over the veal and serve with noodles or rice.

VEAL STEW WITH MUSHROOMS

SERVES 8–10

The French call this Blanquette de Veau—a white veal stew. It is, when properly done, about as beautiful and succulent a stew as ever devised. It's as light as its color and it's one of those dishes I've never had quite as much of as I'd like.

4 pounds veal stew meat, cut into 2-inch cubes	Herb bouquet tied in cheesecloth:
5–6 cups chicken broth or veal stock	8 parsley stems, without leaves
1 large onion	1 bay leaf
1 large carrot	1/2 teaspoon thyme
2 celery stalks	2 celery stalks, chopped
	Salt to taste

In 3 to 4-quart flameproof casserole, place veal with water to cover. Bring to boil. Turn low and simmer 2 minutes. Drain veal and wash under cold water to remove scum.

Put veal back into casserole and add chicken broth or veal stock. Bring slowly to simmer, and skim as necessary for several minutes.

Add vegetables and herb bouquet. Taste for seasoning and salt lightly.

Cover partially and simmer very slowly 1 1/4–1 1/2 hours until veal is tender. Do not overcook. When veal is tender, pour contents of casserole into colander set over a bowl, reserving stock for use in sauce.

Return meat to casserole and put casserole in a warm place.

SAUCE WITH MUSHROOMS

6 tablespoons butter
7 tablespoons flour
4 3/4–5 cups reserved veal stock
18–24 medium-sized fresh mushroom caps
   (about 1 inch in diameter)
1 tablespoon lemon juice

Salt and white pepper
2 tablespoons white wine or lemon juice
1 tablespoon cream
4 egg yolks
2/3 cup whipping cream
3 tablespoons minced parsley

In 2-quart saucepan melt butter, add flour, and stir over low heat until it foams for 2 minutes. Remove from heat and add veal stock, beating vigorously with wire whisk. Bring to a boil, stirring. Simmer 10 minutes, frequently skimming off film that rises to surface.

Toss mushroom caps with lemon juice. Fold in mushroom caps and simmer 10 minutes more, skimming film. Taste sauce for seasoning. Add salt, pepper, and white wine or lemon juice to taste.

Pour sauce and mushrooms over veal. Drizzle thinnest layer of butter on top of sauce to prevent film from forming. Set aside, partially covered. About 10 to 15 minutes before serving, reheat slowly to simmer, basting veal with sauce. Cover and simmer 5 minutes. Remove from heat.

Beat egg yolks and whipping cream in bowl with wire whisk. Beat in by spoonfuls 1 cup of hot sauce. Then pour mixture into casserole, tilting it and basting veal and vegetables to blend rest of sauce with egg yolk mixture. Set over moderate heat, gently shaking casserole until sauce has thickened lightly, but do not let it come to simmer. Sprinkle parsley over all.

Serve out of casserole or on warmed platter surrounded by rice, noodles, potatoes, or spaetzle.

If not served at once, film top of sauce with spoonful or two of stock, partially cover casserole, and keep warm over hot but not simmering water for 10–15 minutes.

Chapter 9

CASSEROLES AND ONE-DISH MEALS

Here's where you can really let go—let your imagination fly! It's fun for a "waste-not, want-not," trained from day one like me, to incorporate leftovers with the fresh. If it's fast and fun, almost anything goes.

Well, maybe not carrot cake with broccoli, but logical combinations. The first one in the chapter, One-Dish Dinner for Vegetarians and Civilians, saved a whole Sunday for me as I imagine Keshy Yena on page 223 could do for you. There is no end of invention. A few of those "your own things" are in this chapter and also in the vegetable chapter, but you'll also find some great, orderly, carefully delineated specific combinations that are perfect meals with a simple salad.

There are great advantages to these one-dish meals. Obviously, much of the preparation can be done ahead, and in many cases it can be served in the dish in which it was prepared. This allows you to do whatever else it is you have to do during the day, and then spend more time with your guests.

This is one chapter that really brings out the "down home" no matter where "home" happens to be—that aspect of the book that I keep mentioning from time to time. From Keshy Yena to Picadillo with Rice and Beans to Yugoslavian Meat and Potato Pie to Lentils and Macaroni (Pasta Lendecia). It's all home cooking—nourishing, delicious, and more than filling.

A Feijoada Completa takes about as much time to study as it does to cook, but it's exact and it really needs no help except the lightest salad and fruit dessert, but oh, it is worth it! Then there's Cioppino, with a crusty bread for sauce sopping, and—well, see for yourself.

LAYERED BROCCOLI–WILD RICE CASSEROLE
SERVES 8

This beautiful simple luncheon or dinner dish can be prepared well ahead of the time your guests will arrive, leaving you free to fuss with the flowers, the table setting, or yourself—all of which will be fuel for your glowing, effortless grace at entertaining.

2 tablespoons butter or margarine
2 tablespoons finely chopped onion
2 tablespoons flour
1/2 teaspoon salt
1 cup milk
1/2 cup sour cream

4 cups hot cooked wild rice
6 stalks broccoli, halved lengthwise through flowerets
1 cup shredded Cheddar cheese
6 slices bacon, cooked, drained, and crumbled

Melt butter in skillet. Add onions and sauté, stirring, until onions soften slightly. Sprinkle in flour and salt, stirring constantly over low heat until mixture is smooth. Slowly add milk, cooking and stirring until sauce thickens slightly. Fold in sour cream. Stir mixture into prepared rice.

Steam broccoli until barely tender, about 3 minutes. Drain well.

Layer half of rice mixture in greased 11 × 7-inch casserole. Alternating flowerets toward sides of casserole, place broccoli, cut side down, on top of rice. Spoon remaining rice down center of broccoli. Sprinkle cheese and bacon over rice. Cover and refrigerate until almost ready to serve.

Preheat oven to 350°F. Bake, covered, for 20 minutes, then uncover and bake 10 minutes longer or until cheese is bubbly and casserole is heated through.

ONE-DISH DINNER FOR VEGETARIANS AND CIVILIANS
SERVES 6–8

One cool, foggy day at the beach Murray Manager and his wife, both good friends, dropped by with a business associate of theirs and mine for what I thought was a spot of tea or a 5:00 P.M. toast to the sunset. After the spot of tea and the toast, we decided to take a little walk on the beach into the sunset. As we were walking, the business associate said, "I can hardly wait for dinner. Murray has told me so much about your cooking." I concealed my panic from their eyes—I heard my lips saying, "I'm so glad you reminded me—I forgot to turn off the oven." I ran back to the house and began to search frantically through the refrigerator and cupboards for something that would do justice to this incredible reputation for ingenuity that had preceded me. This is it, folks! It was everything I had left in the refrigerator, but I do happen to keep a good supply of seasonings and dried vegetables for just such emergencies. I was grateful it was a wintry day instead of a summery one.

1/2 cup pinto beans
1 teaspoon salt
3/4 cup rice
2 carrots, sliced
1 1/2 cups chicken broth
1 whole onion, chopped
2 whole cloves garlic, finely chopped
4 stalks celery, chopped
1 green pepper, chopped
2 tablespoons butter
1 large tomato, chopped

5 summer squash, sliced
2 unpeeled zucchini, sliced
2 ears corn, kernels cut from cob
1/2 cup chopped walnuts (optional; be sure they are fresh)
Salt and pepper to taste
1 teaspoon cumin
1/2 teaspoon thyme
2 teaspoons good chili powder, or to taste
(If I'd had jalapeños, I would have added them.)

Cook pinto beans in water to cover without salt until just soft. (The quick method to cook pintos is to wash and drain them and then just cover with fresh water. Let come to boil and then turn off heat, letting beans sit until you are ready to cook them. They will have absorbed most of liquid.)

Add salt, rice, carrots, and chicken broth. Let come to full boil and cover. Lower heat and simmer 30 minutes or until all liquid is absorbed.

In large, heavy kettle sauté onions, garlic, celery, and green pepper in a little butter until just soft.

Add tomatoes, squash, zucchini, corn, walnuts, and seasonings. Add beans, rice, and carrots. Cover and simmer about 10 minutes over low heat. Check for seasoning. This dish should be well seasoned and spicy hot.

P.S. They loved it!

I served it with a very light salad, a heavy wine, and vanilla ice cream balls rolled in moist coconut with hot fudge sauce right off the chocolate box. They waddled out of there never knowing the difference until the next day when I called Murray Manager and threatened mayhem.

ARROZ CHILI CASSEROLE BLANCA

SERVES 6–8

1 cup sour cream
2 7-ounce cans medium-mild chopped chili peppers
4 medium-sized jalapeño peppers, sliced and seeded
4 canned tomatillos (little green Mexican tomatoes), cut into little pieces
3 scallions, sliced including tops

4 mushrooms, diced
1 teaspoon butter
1 teaspoon finely chopped cilantro
Salt and white pepper
2 1/2 cups cooked rice
3/4 pound Monterey Jack cheese, cut into 1/2- or 3/4-inch strips
1/2 cup grated sharp Cheddar cheese

Preheat oven to 350°F.

Butter 2 1/2-quart casserole or soufflé dish. Mix sour cream with chilies, jalapeños, and tomatillos.

Sauté scallions and mushrooms in butter; add cilantro, a little salt, and white pepper.

TO ASSEMBLE Start with a layer of rice, then a layer of sour cream mixture, then a layer of jack cheese. Repeat. On top of second layer of cheese, add scallion-mushroom mixture. Then repeat with rice and Jack cheese, this time ending with sour cream mixture.

Bake 30 minutes. During last 5 minutes of baking, sprinkle Cheddar cheese over top. When hot and bubbly, serve.

CHILES RELLENOS CASSEROLE

SERVES 6–8

We took the whole TV crew to San Diego to tape some shows. The shows turned out great, and while we were there the station manager threw a lovely party catered by The Carriage Trade. The Carriage Trade threw in this recipe—it's a great party dish.

3 4-ounce cans whole green chilies (remove seeds)
1 pound Cheddar cheese, grated
1 pound Monterey Jack cheese, grated
6 eggs

13-ounce can evaporated milk
1 can water (use milk can for measure)
1 1/2 tablespoons flour
Salt and pepper to taste
1 cup green chile salsa

Lightly grease a 9 × 13-inch ovenproof casserole and cover with a layer of chilies so that none of bottom of dish is visible.

Sprinkle 3/4 cup Cheddar and 1/2 cup Jack cheese over chilies.

Add more chilies, using them sparsely and somewhat broken up. (This is to allow egg mixture to penetrate throughout.)

Fill until rounded on top with remaining grated cheese, but do not pack it in; it should be light and fluffy so egg mixture can penetrate. I suggest more Monterey Jack than Cheddar on this layer, as it doesn't turn dark as fast as Cheddar in baking. Place dish in refrigerator while making egg mixture.

EGG MIXTURE

Preheat oven to 350°F.

Separate 6 eggs. Combine yolks, milk, water, flour, salt, and pepper. Whip egg whites until stiff but not dry. Add to yolk mixture. Pour over cheese dish.

HINT This is difficult because the egg mixture is so fluffy. To help it along, pour half of egg mixture into top layer of cheese, being careful not to disturb middle layer of chilies. Then top with remainder of egg mixture.

Place casserole in a larger pan containing hot water to a depth of 1 inch. Bake for 20 minutes, then cover top with heavy-duty aluminum foil, being careful not to have foil touch top. Bake about 1 1/2–2 hours total or until firm enough for knife to cut clean. Remove from oven. With knife, make 1/4-inch cuts across top every two inches. Into these cuts spoon a little green chile salsa.

STEAK STRIPS STONEMASON STYLE   SERVES 5–6

4–5 jalapeño peppers
3 tablespoons oil
1 1/2 pounds boneless round steak trimmed
  and cut into strips 1 inch long, 1/2 inch
  wide, and 1/8 inch thick

2 medium onions, sliced
30 fresh mushrooms, sliced
1 tablespoon Worcestershire sauce
Salt and pepper
Corn tortillas (2–3 per person)

Roast peppers on an ungreased griddle or under broiler until blistered on all sides. Wrap in damp towel. Loosen skins with towel and peel. Seed and cut into thin strips.

Heat oil in Dutch oven. Add meat and brown on all sides. Add onions and cook until they are tender. Add mushrooms, Worcestershire, and salt and pepper to taste.

Cover and simmer very gently, so as to retain juices, for 45 minutes to 1 hour. Add peppers last 5 to 10 minutes of cooking time.

Meanwhile, place tortillas in foil in oven preheated to 350°F. and heat 10–15 minutes. Serve tortillas warm in napkin and basket to be eaten with steak strips.

INDIAN SAFFRON RICE AND LAMB   SERVES 8

This is an Indian dish—not a curry, but lovely and filling. It looks more complicated than it actually is, as there are a lot of ingredients listed. It's a wonderful, inexpensive (except for the saffron—which keeps and keeps) lamb and rice dish with all sorts of hidden, unexpected flavors. It will probably make you a star overnight. It's a tough life, but learn to live with it!

1/2 teaspoon saffron threads
3 tablespoons boiling water
3 cups water
2 teaspoons salt
2 cups long-grain white rice, washed and drained
1–1 1/2 cups clarified butter
2 medium onions, peeled, cut lengthwise in half, then sliced lengthwise into paper-thin slices
1/4 cup unsalted cashews
1/4 cup slivered unsalted blanched almonds
1 cup shelled unsalted pistachios
1/4 cup seedless raisins
1 tablespoon peeled, finely chopped fresh ginger root

1 teaspoon finely chopped garlic
1 teaspoon cumin seeds
1/4 teaspoon ground hot red pepper
2 pounds lean boneless lamb, preferably from the leg, cut into 1-inch cubes
1 4-inch stick of cinnamon
8 whole cloves
6 whole black peppercorns
The seeds of 4 cardamom pods or 1/4 teaspoon cardamom seeds
1/4 teaspoon ground mace
1/4 teaspoon ground nutmeg, preferably freshly grated
1 1/2 cups chicken stock
1/2 cup unflavored yogurt combined with 1/2 cup half-and-half

Drop the saffron threads into small bowl or cup, pour in 3 tablespoons boiling water, and soak for 10 minutes.

Bring 3 cups water and 1 teaspoon salt to boil in 3 to 4-quart saucepan. Stirring constantly, pour in rice in slow, thin stream and cook briskly, uncovered, 10 minutes. If necessary, drain rice in sieve or colander and set aside.

In heavy 4 to 6-quart casserole with tightly fitting lid, heat 1/2 cup of clarified butter over moderate heat. Add onions and sauté 7–8 minutes or until soft and golden brown. Don't let them get too brown or burn. With slotted spoon, transfer onions to paper towels to drain. Set aside.

To same butter add cashews, almonds, pistachios, and raisins, adding a little more butter if needed. Cook nuts and raisins about 1 minute, or until lightly browned. Transfer mixture to a bowl and set aside.

Add ginger, garlic, cumin, and red pepper to casserole and, stirring constantly, cook for a minute or so in same butter (again add a little more butter if needed).

Place meat in casserole, add remaining teaspoon of salt, and stir over high heat until cubes of meat are lightly browned on all sides.

Stirring well after each addition, add cinnamon, cloves, peppercorns, cardamom seeds, mace, nutmeg, 3/4 cup of stock, and yogurt and cream mixture. Reduce heat to low, cover casserole tightly, and cook 15 minutes. Then remove casserole from heat and let it rest covered 3–5 minutes.

With slotted spoon transfer cubes of meat and cinnamon stick to one bowl, then pour cooking liquid and its seasonings to another. Add remaining 3/4 cup of stock to cooking liquid and stir well.

Preheat oven to 375°F. Wash the casserole and dry it thoroughly. Pour 2 tablespoons clarified butter into casserole and tip it from side to side to coat bottom evenly. Pour in half the rice, smoothing it evenly with a spatula. Sprinkle with a tablespoon or so of saffron and its soaking water. Scatter half of meat on top and place cinnamon stick in center.

Add a cup or so of cooking liquid to casserole, pouring it slowly down sides. Add all remaining rice and, over that, rest of lamb cubes. Sprinkle remaining saffron and its water over the top and pour remaining cooking liquid into casserole as before.

Cover casserole with a sheet of heavy-duty foil, crimping the edges to hold it firmly in place, and place lid on top. Bake in middle of oven for 20 minutes, or until lamb and rice are tender and most of liquid has been absorbed.

To serve, mound entire contents of casserole on large heated platter and sprinkle with reserved fried onions, cashews, almonds, pistachios, and raisins.

KESHY YENA

SERVES 6

I wish I knew where I first tasted this intriguing dish. I found the recipe on a piece of paper in an old travel book. It isn't Dutch but it uses Dutch cheeses. It's spicy and the combination of pickle, raisins or prunes, and olives makes me think it might be North African, but I haven't been there. Sorry I can't give you the origin of this strangely titled delicacy, but I can give you the recipe with an enthusiastic recommendation.

1 pound round steak, cut into strips as thin
  as possible
2 tablespoons flour seasoned with salt and
  pepper
1/4 cup vegetable oil
1/4 cup dry red wine
1 green pepper, coarsely chopped
1/4 cup finely chopped onion
1/4 pound fresh mushrooms, sliced
1 medium tomato, peeled, seeded, and

  coarsely chopped
1/8 teaspoon cayenne pepper
1/2 tablespoon finely chopped sour pickles
1 1/2 tablespoons seedless raisins or
  chopped prunes
3 small pimiento-stuffed olives, drained and
  finely chopped
1/2 cup plus 2 tablespoons beef stock (page
  7)
1/2 pound Edam or Gouda cheese

Dredge beef strips in seasoned flour.

Heat 1/8 cup vegetable oil in heavy pan and brown beef strips. Add wine and cook 1–2 minutes. Remove from heat and set aside.

Heat remaining oil and sauté green pepper, onions, and mushrooms until soft but not brown. Add tomatoes and cayenne and cook briskly until most of liquid in pan has evaporated. Remove from heat. Stir in pickles, raisins or prunes, and olives.

Combine vegetable mixture with beef. Blend well and add beef stock.

Preheat oven to 350°F.

Line a well-buttered 1 1/2-quart casserole with round slices of cheese 1/8 inch thick. Reserve some cheese for top. Spoon meat and vegetable mixture into casserole and top with remaining cheese slices. Bake 20–30 minutes, or until cheese is brown and bubbly.

CHICKEN ENCHILADAS ROJAS SERVES 12–15

It helps to have a friend when you first try this one—you can get an assembly line going. This is Arminda LeClerc's recipe and the assembly line that first day consisted of Bee (short for Bernice) Korshak and Arminda and me. One tortilla dipped in sauce, fried and handed over to the counter group for filling with chicken mixture, scallions, black olives, etc. etc. Then placed seam side down in the sauce-covered baking dish. I've done these alone many times since and it's no big deal to make. Just line up the ingredients in little bowls and zip, zip, zip. Incidentally, make a large batch. They freeze beautifully. Simply let sit out awhile to defrost, sprinkle cheese over all, and follow directions for baking.

6 whole chicken breasts, each about 3/4
    pound
Water to cover
1 small onion
1 small garlic clove, minced
1 stalk celery, sliced
1 carrot, sliced
Salt and pepper to taste

1 onion, thinly sliced
1 tablespoon oil, plus oil for frying tortillas
30 corn tortillas
12 scallions, finely chopped
16-ounce can of black olives, finely chopped
4 cups (1 pound) grated cheese, sharp Cheddar and Monterey Jack (mixed)
Enchilada Sauce

Place chicken breasts in heavy saucepan, cover with water; add onion, garlic, celery, carrots, salt, and pepper; bring to boil over high heat. Reduce heat to lowest point, cover pan, and simmer breasts 15–20 minutes until tender but not falling apart.

Transfer chicken to plate and reserve stock. When chicken is cool enough to handle, remove skins, cut meat away from bones, and shred into small pieces.

In large skillet, sauté onion in 1 tablespoon oil until translucent but not brown. Add chicken and 1 cup Enchilada Sauce. Simmer and taste for seasoning.

Preheat over to 350°F.

Dip tortilla in Enchilada Sauce. In skillet, heat oil until hot. Lower heat and fry tortillas lightly, one at a time, turning once, until they are just limp.

As each tortilla is fried, fill center with chicken mixture, scallions, olives, and cheese. Fold one side of the tortilla over filling, then roll tortilla up completely into a thick cylinder. Place it seam side down in a shallow baking dish; nap with Enchilada Sauce.

When all tortillas are arranged in one layer in baking dish, pour Enchilada Sauce over all, completely covering tortillas. Sprinkle with cheese and bake 20 minutes or until sauce bubbles. Serve immediately.

ENCHILADA SAUCE

2 small onions, grated
2 tablespoons oil
16-ounce can whole peeled tomatoes, coarsely chopped
2 cups chicken broth
4 8-ounce cans Mexican hot tomato sauce
4 10-ounce cans enchilada sauce
3 10 3/4-ounce cans tomato soup
Salt and pepper to taste
1/2 teaspoon sugar, or to taste
Dash of Tabasco sauce
Salsa de chile fresco sauce to taste, canned (El Pato) or your own

Sauté onions in oil until golden. Add tomatoes, chicken broth, tomato sauce, enchilada sauce, and tomato soup. Season with salt, pepper, sugar, Tabasco, and Chile salsa to taste. Let simmer 1 hour.

ENCHILADAS VERDES   SERVES 6

2 whole chicken breasts, about 3/4 pound each
1 cup chicken broth
6 ounces (2 3-ounce packages) cream cheese
2 cups heavy cream
3/4 cup finely chopped onion
6 fresh poblano chilies, about 5 inches long, or 6 fresh green peppers, about 3 1/2 inches in diameter
10-ounce can green Mexican tomatoes, drained
2 canned serrano chilies, drained, rinsed in cold water, and finely chopped
5 teaspoons fresh cilantro, coarsely chopped
1 egg
1 1/2 teaspoons salt
1/4 teaspoon freshly ground black pepper
3 tablespoons shortening or bacon fat
12 corn tortillas
1/3 cup freshly grated Parmesan cheese

Place chicken breasts in heavy 2 to 3-quart saucepan, pour in broth and bring to boil over high heat. Reduce heat to its lowest point, cover pan, and simmer breasts 20 minutes, or until tender but not falling apart. Transfer breasts to plate and reserve stock.

When chicken is cool enough to handle, remove skin, cut meat away from bones, and shred.

In large bowl, beat cream cheese with wooden spoon until smooth, then beat into it 1/2 cup cream, 3 tablespoons at a time. Stir in onions and shredded chicken. Mix thoroughly and put aside while you make sauce.

Roast poblano chilies by holding them over flame on tines of a long-handled fork, turning until skin darkens and blisters on all sides. Or place chilies on baking sheet or broiler pan and broil them about 3 inches from heat for 5 minutes or so, turning them so they color on all sides. Be careful not to let them burn. Wrap chilies in damp tea towel and let them rest in towel for a few minutes. Gently rub with towel until skins slip off. Cut out and discard stems, thick white membranes, and seeds.

Chop chilies coarsely and place in blender or food processor. Add green tomatoes, serrano chilies, cilantro, and 1/4 cup of reserved chicken stock. Blend at high speed until mixture is reduced to smooth puree. Pour in remaining 1 1/2 cups cream, egg, salt, and pepper, and blend for 10 seconds longer. Scrape puree into large bowl.

Preheat oven to 350°F.

In heavy 8 to 10-inch skillet, melt shortening or bacon fat over moderate heat until light haze forms over it. One at a time dip tortillas in chili-tomato puree, then drop into skillet and fry for a minute or so on each side, or until limp. Transfer tortilla from pan to plate and place 1/4 cup chicken filling in center. Fold one side of tortilla over filling, then roll tortilla up completely into thick cylinder. Place it seam side down in a shallow 8 × 12-inch baking dish. Fry and fill remaining tortillas in similar fashion, replenishing shortening in skillet when necessary. When all tortillas are arranged in one layer in baking dish, pour remaining chili-tomato sauce over them and sprinkle top evenly with grated cheese. Bake on middle shelf of oven 15 minutes or until cheese melts and enchiladas are lightly browned on top. Serve immediately.

NOTE You may substitute 2 cups of leftover lean roast pork, finely shredded, for chicken.

CIOPPINO

SERVES 10

2 tablespoons olive oil
2 tablespoons butter
3 cups chopped onions
1 leek, trimmed, well washed, and finely chopped
2 to 4 cloves garlic, finely chopped
2 green peppers, cored, seeded, and cut into thin strips
4 cups canned tomatoes (preferably imported), chopped
1 cup tomato sauce
Salt and freshly ground black pepper
1 bay leaf
1 teaspoon dried oregano
1 teaspoon dried thyme
1 tablespoon dried basil

Red pepper flakes
2 cups fish stock (page 8) plus 1 cup bottled clam juice, or 3 cups fresh clam juice
1 cup dry white wine
1 pound firm-fleshed fish such as striped bass, red snapper, rock cod, or sea bass, cut into bite-sized pieces
1 pound shrimp, shelled and deveined
1 dozen well-washed clams in the shell
1/4 cup shucked oysters with their liquor
1/2 pound fresh scallops (preferably bay scallops)
1/2-pound lobster tail, cooked in shell (optional)
1 hard-shell crab, cooked in shell and cracked (optional)

Heat oil and butter in kettle and add onions, leeks, and garlic. Cook, stirring often, until vegetables are lightly browned. Add green peppers and continue cooking, stirring until peppers wilt.

Add tomatoes, tomato sauce, salt and pepper to taste, bay leaf, oregano, thyme, basil and about 1/4 teaspoon red pepper flakes. Add fish stock or clam juice and cook slowly about 2 hours, stirring often to prevent burning. More fish stock may be added if desired.

Add wine and continue cooking about 10 minutes. The soup may be made in advance to this point.

Fifteen minutes or so before serving, remove bay leaf, return soup to boil, and add striped bass or other fish. Cook about 3 minutes and add shrimp. Cook 2 minutes more and add clams. Cover and simmer about 6 minutes. Uncover, add oysters, scallops, lobster tail, and crab. Cook, stirring, about 5 minutes or until clams open. Serve in warmed soup bowls with red pepper flakes on the side.

SEA SANDWICH   SERVES 6

Okay, Barbara Ann, here are your Tuna Boats—renamed, but I didn't think you'd mind as much as you did when we almost had that falling out over their not making the last book. Barbara Ann, for your information, is Barbara Ann Sinatra, good friend and good cook (though she doesn't like to admit it). I have a great idea for your next at-home party menu. Frank can cook up a great pasta, you cook the Tuna Boat/Sea Sandwich and top it off with your Apricot Soufflé (page 363).

6 sourdough french rolls
7-ounce can tuna
1/4 cup chopped green pepper
1/4 cup chopped celery
2 tablespoons grated or finely chopped onion
6 pimiento-stuffed olives, sliced
1/2 cup Cheddar cheese, cut into medium-small cubes

Dash of Worcestershire sauce
Dash of Tabasco sauce
6 water chestnuts, coarsely chopped (optional)
1/4 cup blanched toasted almonds (optional)
Scant 1/2 cup mayonnaise
6 pimiento strips for garnish

Slice off tops of rolls and scoop out centers (you can use leftover bread for crumbs or croutons). Mix tuna, green peppers, celery, onions, olives, cheese, Worcestershire, Tabasco, water chestnuts, and almonds. Fold in mayonnaise.

Preheat oven to 400°F.

Pile mixture high into roll shells. Garnish each with pimiento strip and bake until rolls are crisp.

BRAISED OXTAILS WITH OLIVES   SERVES 4–6

I kept seeing oxtails in the meat counter and kept hearing people rave about oxtail stew, so I finally got around to trying it myself. It's all they said it was. If they'd only call them something else.

6 pounds oxtails, trimmed of all fat
Salt and pepper to taste
1/4 cup oil
1 1/3 cups bourbon
Bouquet garni wrapped in cheesecloth:
    6 sprigs parsley
    4 sprigs thyme

3 strips orange peel
2 cloves garlic
Brown Stock or beef broth (enough to cover oxtails)
1 1/2 cups pitted small black olives
Minced parsley for garnish

Preheat oven to 325°F. Sprinkle oxtails with salt and pepper. In large ovenproof skillet over high heat, brown oxtails in oil about 10–15 minutes.

Remove oxtails from skillet and pour 1/3 cup bourbon into hot pan. Ignite bourbon with a long match, being careful to tilt pan away from you. Shake pan until flame is gone. Add remaining bourbon and reduce over high heat by half; it takes about 10 minutes.

Add bouquet garni and oxtails to skillet with enough Brown Stock or beef broth to cover. Bring liquid to boil.

Transfer to oven, cover, and cook for 3 1/2 hours or until meat is very tender. Cool.

Chill overnight and skim fat off.

Before serving, bring meat and liquid to boiling point over moderate heat. Add olives and simmer until mixture is heated through.

Remove meat to heated serving platter. Discard bouquet garni. Season pan juices with salt and pepper.

Garnish oxtails with parsley. Serve over buttered noodles, rice, or kasha. Pour pan juices over all or serve in gravy boat.

PICADILLO WITH RICE AND BLACK BEANS

SERVES 6

A very popular Southern California al fresco one-dish meal—try it and you'll see why.

BEANS

1 cup dried black beans	1 medium onion, chopped
3 cups water	2 tablespoons chopped green peppers
1/2 pound ham hock	2 large garlic cloves, chopped
1 1/2 teaspoons salt	1 tablespoon oil

Cover beans with water and let stand overnight. Drain. Add water and bring to boil. Skim scum from top. Add ham hock and simmer, covered, until beans are tender, about 2 hours, adding more water if necessary. Add salt.

Remove ham from hock and cut into small chunks. Add to beans.

Brown onions, green peppers, and garlic in oil. Add to beans and serve as sauce for picadillo and rice.

PICADILLO

1 tablespoon oil	1 tablespoon raisins
1 onion, chopped	1 teaspoon capers
1/2 green pepper, chopped	1/2 teaspoon Tabasco sauce (optional)
1 1/2 pounds lean ground beef	Salt and freshly ground pepper to taste
2 cups canned tomatoes, undrained	
3 cups cooked rice	4 bananas, sliced lengthwise and sautéed in
2 hard-cooked eggs, forced through a sieve	butter
4 slices bacon, fried crisp and crumbled	

Sauté onions and green peppers in oil until brown. Add ground beef, tomatoes, raisins, capers, Tabasco, salt, and pepper. Cook, stirring, until mixture is almost dry.

Arrange beans and picadillo over rice on warmed platter. Sprinkle grated egg and crumbled bacon over top. Garnish with bananas.

HUNGARIAN CASSEROLE
SERVES 6

1/2 cup rice
1 cup chicken broth
8 slices bacon
1/2 cup chopped onions
1 pound lean pork, cut into 1/2-inch cubes
1/2 pound Kielbasa (Polish sausage), sliced into 1/3-inch rounds
3 teaspoons paprika, mixed with 1/2 tea-
spoon cayenne pepper
1 1/2 teaspoons minced garlic
1 1/2 teaspoons salt
3 1/2 cups sauerkraut
3 teaspoons caraway seeds
1 cup sour cream
1/3 cup milk
1 egg, lightly beaten

In small saucepan cook rice in chicken broth over moderate heat 10 minutes.

Preheat oven to 375°F.

In skillet cook bacon until crisp; drain on paper towels, crumble, and set aside.

Remove all but 2 tablespoons bacon fat from skillet. Add onions and cook, stirring, for 10 minutes. Add pork cubes, sausage, paprika and cayenne, garlic, and salt and cook 5 minutes.

Drain sauerkraut and squeeze dry. Arrange half of sauerkraut in bottom of a well-buttered 10 × 6-inch baking dish and cover with layers of half meat mixture, remaining sauerkraut, and bacon. Sprinkle caraway seeds over all.

In small bowl combine sour cream, milk, and egg. Top dish with this sauce, spreading it evenly, and bake 50 minutes or until lightly browned.

FRIED NOODLES WITH MIXED MEAT AND VEGETABLES
SERVES 6–8

2 1/2 ounces (1/4 cup plus 1 tablespoon) lean pork, shredded
1 1/2 ounces (3 tablespoons) chicken breast, shredded
1/2 teaspoon cornstarch
Pinch of salt
6 ounces (3/4 cup) thin Shanghai noodles or vermicelli
1/4 cup cooking oil
1 1/2 ounces (3 tablespoons) canned bamboo
shoots, shredded
1 1/2 ounces (3 tablespoons) broccoli flowerets, quartered
1/4 teaspoon salt
1/4 teaspoon Chinese rice wine or dry sherry
3/4 cup chicken stock
2 teaspoons cornstarch mixed with 1 tablespoon water
1/2 ounce fried Tennessee or Virginia ham or prosciutto, shredded

Mix pork and chicken with 1/2 teaspoon cornstarch and salt and marinate 15 minutes.

Drop noodles into pot of boiling salted water and when it begins to boil again, untangle noodle cakes. Remove and drain. Rinse under cold running water until cool. Drain well, then spread on tray to partially dry.

Heat wok. Add 2 tablespoons oil and heat to smoking. Add noodles and stir in hot oil until golden brown. Turn once. Drain away oil and continue to fry noodles on both sides until lightly brown and crisp. Remove, drain on paper towels, and place on serving plate.

Reheat wok, add 2 tablespoons oil. Add chicken, pork, and bamboo shoots. Stir-fry until meat changes color, about 1 minute. Remove from wok and set aside.

Stir-fry broccoli 1 minute, then return meat and bamboo shoots to wok and add salt, wine, and chicken stock. Stir-fry briefly.

Add cornstarch mixed with water, cover, and cook until sauce thickens, stirring occasionally. Pour over noodles and garnish with shredded ham.

YUGOSLAVIAN MEAT AND POTATO PIE

SERVES 6–8

1 small onion, minced
2 tablespoons butter
1 tablespoon olive oil
1/4 pound fresh mushrooms, chopped
3 cups diced cooked meat (ham, chicken, beef, veal, alone or in combination)
1 heaping cup diced cooked potatoes
1 dill pickle, diced

1/2 cup chopped stuffed olives
1/2 teaspoon salt
1/8 teaspoon pepper
1 1/2 cups sour cream
2 hard-cooked eggs, chopped
2 tomatoes, peeled and sliced
1/2 cup grated Cheddar cheese

Sauté onions in butter and oil 2–3 minutes. Add mushrooms and cook 2 minutes longer. Add cooked meat, potatoes, pickles, and olives and mix well. Season with salt and pepper and stir in sour cream. Taste for seasoning.

Preheat oven to 350°F.

Put mixture in shallow 2-quart baking dish and sprinkle with chopped eggs. Place tomato slices around edges and sprinkle cheese over top. Bake 25–30 minutes.

SZEKELY GULYÁS

SERVES 6–8

Who'd ever have thought that beautiful, glamorous Zsa Zsa could or would cook? Well, she does and with a hearty but subtle touch. So much for that old canard that all one could find in her refrigerator were orchids and champagne!

1 onion, diced
1 tablespoon oil
1 tablespoon butter
1 pound pork stew meat, cut into bite-sized
  pieces
1 pound veal stew meat, cut into bite-sized
  pieces
2 tablespoons paprika (more if desired)

2 teaspoons salt
1 tablespoon caraway seeds
1 cup beef or chicken broth, or water
4 pounds sauerkraut
2 pounds Hungarian or Polish sausage, cut
  into 1-inch slices
1 pint sour cream

Sauté onions in oil and butter until soft. Remove onions and set aside.

In same oil and butter brown pork and veal. Replace onions and add paprika, salt, caraway seeds, and broth or water. Cover and cook, stirring occasionally, 1 1/2–2 hours or until meat is tender. Remove lid last half hour of cooking to reduce liquid if necessary.

Rinse sauerkraut thoroughly and drain. Add with sausage to meat mixture and cook 1/2 hour more.

Blend half of sour cream into stew and heat carefully (do not boil). Top with remaining sour cream and serve immediately.

SOUTH OF THE BORDER CHICKEN AND PORK CASSEROLE

SERVES 8–10

1 1/2 pounds lean pork loin, cut into small
  cubes and fat removed
2 tablespoons butter or margarine (more if
  necessary)
2 tablespoons oil (more if necessary)

Flour seasoned with salt, pepper, and paprika
2 2 1/2 to 3-pound frying chickens, cut into
  serving pieces

SAUCE

2 tablespoons blanched almonds
2 teaspoons sesame seeds
2 medium-sized onions, chopped
2 medium-sized green peppers, chopped
2 8-ounce cans tomato sauce
2 cups water, boiling
2 cups chicken broth, boiling
2 tablespoons chili powder
4 tablespoons sugar
1 teaspoon cinnamon

Herb bouquet (tied securely in cheesecloth
  bag):
  6 whole cloves
  2 bay leaves
Salt to taste
1 medium-sized sweet potato, cut into long,
  thick strips
1/2 cup apple, peeled and cubed
1 cup pineapple chunks
Sliced bananas (optional)

Brown pork in skillet in mixture of oil and butter. Remove to large saucepan.

Dredge chicken in seasoned flour and brown in same drippings. Remove from skillet and add to pork.

Lightly sauté almonds and sesame seeds in same oil, add onions and green peppers and sauté a few minutes longer. Add tomato sauce and put entire mixture in blender or food processor. Blend thoroughly. Combine this mixture with water, chicken broth, chili powder, sugar, cinnamon, herb bouquet, and salt. Cook 10–15 minutes to blend flavors. Remove herb bouquet.

Pour half of this sauce over pork and chicken. Let stand until ready for final preparation.

Forty-five minutes before serving, reheat pork and chicken, add remaining sauce, and simmer for 30 minutes. Remove chicken and pork and keep warm.

Add sweet potatoes and simmer another 10–12 minutes until sweet potatoes are barely done. Add apples and pineapple chunks and cook just long enough to blend (about 5 minutes). Replace chicken and pork and simmer long enough to heat through, about 5–7 minutes. Dish into warmed soup bowls and slice bananas right into hot stew.

ALSATIAN MEAT PIE

SERVES 6

For everyone who loves to collect recipes, it helps to do concerts all over the country. This delicious beauty came from The Pear Tree in Rumson, New Jersey. First-rate food, service, and ambiance. The artistry is the work of a dentist, Dr. Burt Kornfeld, who became a restaurateur as a hobby and decided it was more fun than filling teeth, and his partner, a housewife-turned-businesswoman, Mrs. Sidney Hiefetz. They and their great chef, a young man named Keith Eldridge, gave me several recipes, all of which work. *This is one of my favorites.*

P.S. You can use half-and-half for the heavy cream.

1 tablespoon oil
1 medium onion, finely diced
2 bay leaves
2 tablespoons finely diced shallots
1 teaspoon nutmeg
1/4 pound ground beef
1/4 pound ground veal
Salt and white pepper to taste

3/4 quart heavy cream
5 whole eggs
5 egg yolks
Salt and white pepper to taste
10-inch short flaky pie shell (Pâte Brisée I, page 19)
Grated nutmeg

Heat oil in skillet. Add onions and bay leaves; sauté until onions are transparent. Add shallots and nutmeg; sauté. Add beef and veal and cook, stirring constantly, until meats have lost their pink or whitish color. Add salt and white pepper to taste. Put aside to cool.

Preheat oven to 375°F.

In bowl thoroughly mix cream, whole eggs, egg yolks, and salt and white pepper.

Roll out pie dough and put in pie pan. Spread cooled meat over bottom of piecrust, then cover all with egg mixture. Sprinkle grated nutmeg over top. Bake 1 hour until eggs are set and knife inserted in middle comes out clean.

LENTILS AND MACARONI

SERVES 4

This is Pasta Lendecia—one of those satisfying Italian gems like Pasta Fazool (or Pasta e Fagioli, if you want to be technical), that is genuine "cucina di casa" (down-home cooking). Be sure you have crusty french bread, hot pepper flakes, and a salad to follow. You don't even need a dessert with this one—just some soft cheese and whole apples or pears.

1 cup lentils
2 tablespoons olive oil
2 slices salt pork, diced (optional)
2 garlic cloves, pressed
Boiling water
1 leftover ham bone

2 1/2 cups chicken broth
1 cup small elbow macaroni (uncooked)
1/2 teaspoon oregano
2 tablespoons finely chopped parsley
1 peeled tomato, chopped
1/2 teaspoon red pepper flakes (optional)

Soak lentils in water at least 12 hours or overnight.

Combine oil and salt pork in heavy saucepan. Cook gently until salt pork turns light brown. Remove pork and discard. Add pressed garlic and cook gently about 30 seconds, stirring; do not burn. Add drained lentils and ham bone and then boiling water to cover, and cook lentils 20 minutes. Add more liquid if necessary.

Add chicken broth and, when mixture returns to boil, add macaroni and simmer 5–8 minutes until macaroni is just *al dente.*

Add oregano, parsley, tomatoes, and red pepper flakes. Turn off heat, cover, and let stand 10 minutes. Stir and serve.

LILIANA'S GUATEMALAN CHILES RELLENOS

SERVES 6–8

I came home from the market one day with some beautiful long green chilies and asked Liliana, our Guatemalan friend, if she'd make some rellenos for lunch. We were expecting the cheese-filled variety, but this is what we got and they're great.

12 large green chilies
1/2 onion, finely chopped
3 cloves garlic, finely chopped
1 tablespoon oil
1 pound ground pork
1 pound ground beef
1 tomato, peeled and chopped
2 tablespoons chopped parsley
1/8 teaspoon grated nutmeg

2 bay leaves
Salt and pepper to taste
1/2 pound green beans, chopped very small
   and cooked
2 carrots, chopped very thin and cooked
Egg Mixture
Oil for frying
Salsa

Hold each chili on fork over flame to remove skin or place under broiler until skins blister and turn brown. Place on damp tea towel, then gently rub to peel off skin. Make a slit down side of chili to remove seeds. Try not to tear chilies any more than necessary.

Sauté onions and garlic in oil until translucent but not brown. Add ground pork and beef and sauté until lightly browned. Add tomato, parsley, nutmeg, bay leaves, salt, and pepper. Cook until meat is done.

Add cooked green beans and carrots and warm through. Remove bay leaves and discard.

Stuff chilies with meat mixture. Then place stuffed chilies in large dish in which you have put Egg Mixture. Roll chilies in mixture until completely coated. Fry in hot oil until both sides are brown. Serve with Salsa.

EGG MIXTURE

6 egg whites   1 tablespoon flour
6 egg yolks   Pinch of salt

Beat egg whites until stiff. Add flour and salt to egg yolks and beat mixture slightly. Fold egg whites into egg yolk.

SALSA

1 tablespoon finely chopped onions   4 tomatoes, peeled and pureed
1 clove garlic, finely chopped   Salt to taste
1 tablespoon oil

Sauté onions and garlic in hot oil until translucent but not brown. Add tomatoes and salt. Cook over low heat 10 minutes until Salsa is well blended.

FEIJOADA COMPLETA

SERVES 8–10

This is not a recipe—it is a career. It takes a while to assemble the ingredients and cook them, but oh is it worth it! Try it some cold wintry night; you'll make some good friends really happy. It is supposed to serve eight to ten and you will think you are cooking enough for the Brazilian National Guard, but since everybody has to have a tiny bit of everything, it doesn't stretch as far as you think.

ONE SMALL NOTE I have found a few people who, when it is announced there is tongue in the dish, make a small sound resembling "yuck." My advice is—don't announce it, and if they insist on knowing the ingredients mumble something like corned beef, because every time I've served it those very same unadventurous muttonheads are the first ones to plow in and return for seconds of some of that "tenderest meat they ever tasted."

Here is the national dish of Brazil—

1 3-pound smoked beef tongue
1 pound spareribs, cut in half crosswise by
    your butcher
1 pound chorizos or other smoked, spicy
    pork sausage
1 pound fresh breakfast-type pork sausage
1 fresh pig's foot, if available (if not, 1
    1/2-pound pork butt)
Water
4 cups dried black beans, washed
1 pound lean bacon in 1 piece, rind removed
1 pound lean beef chuck in 1 piece
1/2 pound Canadian-style bacon in 1 piece

2 tablespoons lard or shortening
1 1/2 cups coarsely chopped onions
1 tablespoon finely chopped garlic
3 medium tomatoes, peeled, seeded, and
    coarsely chopped or 1 cup canned Italian
    plum tomatoes, drained and chopped
1 8-ounce jar (about 10–12) hot jalapeño
    peppers, drained, seeded, and finely
    chopped
1 teaspoon salt
1/2 teaspoon freshly ground black pepper
5 large oranges, peeled and thinly sliced or
    cut into wedges

Place tongue in large pot, cover with water, and soak overnight. Place spareribs in another pot, cover with water, and soak overnight.

Drain tongue, cover with fresh water, and bring to boil over high heat. Partially cover pan, reduce heat, and simmer 2 1/2 hours. The tongue should be kept covered with water; if it boils away, add more boiling water. Remove tongue from pot and let cool slightly, then skin with sharp knife, cutting away fat, bones, and gristle at its base.

Drain spareribs, add chorizos, fresh sausage, and pig's foot or pork butt, and cover with fresh water. Bring to boil, reduce heat to low, and simmer uncovered 15 minutes. Drain and set meats aside.

In heavy 12-quart casserole or large soup kettle, bring 3 quarts of water to boil over high heat. Drop in beans and boil briskly 2 minutes. Turn off heat and let beans soak 1 hour.

Add peeled tongue, spareribs, pig's foot or pork butt, and lean bacon. Bring to boil, reduce heat to low, cover and simmer 1 hour. Check water in pot occasionally; it should cook away somewhat, leaving beans moist and slightly soupy, but if beans get too dry, add some boiling water.

Preheat oven to 250°F.

Transfer tongue to large heatproof platter, cover it with foil, and place in oven to keep warm.

Add chuck to kettle and continue cooking beans and meat for 1 hour. Finally, add smoked and fresh sausage and Canadian bacon and cook for 30 minutes. When meats are tender, remove from kettle and place in oven on platter with tongue.

Skim fat from surface of beans and remove kettle from heat.

In heavy 10-inch skillet, melt lard or shortening over moderate heat. Add onions and garlic and cook, stirring frequently, 5 minutes until onions are soft and transparent but not brown. Stir in tomatoes, peppers, salt, and black pepper and simmer 5 minutes.

With slotted spoon, remove 2 cups beans from kettle and add to skillet. Mash them thoroughly into onion mixture, moistening them with 2 cups of bean liquid as you mash. Stirring occasionally, simmer sauce over low heat 15 minutes until it becomes thick.

With rubber spatula, scrape sauce into kettle and cook, stirring occasionally, over low heat 20 minutes.

With large sharp knife slice tongue, lean bacon, chuck, Canadian bacon, spareribs, and pig's foot or pork butt into thin serving pieces, and separate smoked and fresh sausages.

Transfer beans to serving bowl. Traditionally, all meats are presented in one large, heated platter, with sliced tongue in center, fresh meat on one side, smoked meats on the other. Garnish with orange slices or wedges.

Serve with Arroz Brasileiro.

ARROZ BRASILEIRO

1/4 cup olive oil
1 large onion, thinly sliced
3 cups long-grain rice
3 cups chicken stock, boiling
3 cups water, boiling

2 medium tomatoes, peeled, seeded, and coarsely chopped *or* 2/3 cup canned Italian plum tomatoes, drained and coarsely chopped
1 teaspoon salt

In heavy 3 to 4-quart saucepan, heat oil over moderate heat for 30 seconds, tipping pan to coat bottom evenly. Add onions and cook, stirring constantly, for 5 minutes or until soft and transparent but not brown.

Pour in rice and stir 2–3 minutes until all grains are coated with oil (do not let rice brown).

Add stock, water, tomatoes, and salt and return to boil, still stirring. Cover pan, reduce heat to its lowest point, and simmer 20 minutes or until all liquid is absorbed. If rice must wait, drape pan loosely with towel and keep warm in preheated 250°F. oven.

Chapter 10

PASTA, RICE, POTATOES, AND BEANS

Potatoes in almost any form and pastas are among the great joys in my life. When we were doing our TV shows, my producer convinced me it wasn't chicken soup or meat loaf that cured the tireds, it was pasta! Fred and Marianne Tatashore and I consumed enough different pastas each week to keep us chipper through 400 shows instead of the 232 we actually taped per season.

If you only knew how painful it was to cull any pasta, rice, potatoes, or bean recipe from this chapter, you'd have a clue as to how firm and unrelenting my editors were. There are many absolutely essential and sensational recipes lying here waiting patiently for the next book.

When you get around to it, make your own pasta. It's fun and the difference is startling, but there are some fine store-bought brands too, like De Cecco. I won't go into making your own pasta here. That's waiting with those sad little regrets mentioned above.

Careful instructions for cooking are given in each recipe, but here are a few general hints:

1. Salted water must be boiling before and during pasta cooking. Stir in pasta so that individual pieces will not stick together. It should always be cooked just until tender (*al dente*—it bites back) to preserve flavor and texture. Remember, it continues to cook even draining in the colander after being removed from the pot. I rarely run cold water over my hot pasta unless I'm fearful of its overcooking. I want it hot for the sauce. I generally mix sauce and pasta in the pot in which it was cooked. The water's been drained and the pot is still warm.
2. A little oil poured into the water for broader and thicker noodles and pasta like lasagna helps keep them separate. Spaghetti cannot be cooked ahead and kept unless, after draining, you return to pot and mix in 1/2 cup of sauce and a little butter and toss.

I will never forget the expression on Gina Lollobrigida's face when she was all set to cook her special pasta, Spaghetti Carbonara for the television audience. Our conscientious home economist, knowing the time limitations on TV, cooked the spaghetti, drained it, and set it on the stage for the big moment. This mass of stuck-together stringy guck fell out of the colander in one big lump into the guest of honor's beautiful sauce bubbling on the range. The Lady and the Latin had a struggle going there. Humor won, but it was all we could do to finish the show, we were laughing so hard.

Pasta has a great flexibility and is that perfect vegetarian dish. If that is what suits somebody's fancy on occasion, there's Broccoli alla Ziti or the heavenly Angel Hair with Fresh Tomatoes and Capers. You say you feel up to something creamy? Have we got something for you! Look at Ernesto's Pasta Mista. These dishes are worth the time they take and, like most pastas and rice, are meals unto themselves.

If you're like me, potatoes have the same heartwarming effect. For instance, Potatoes Grand-Mère. (Those grandmothers in France knew how to get a little meat on those bones.) If you feel you've got enough meat on those bones for a while and still need a potato, try Chile Papa or Steamed Crisp Potatoes.

When I don't use pasta or potatoes I serve rice, either all by itself or as an accompaniment for some of my favorite prize dishes, such as Veal Stew with

Mushrooms or Chicken Breasts with Mushrooms and Cream, and with many of the Chinese dishes rice is a must.

Incidentally, I never think of rice as being a total starch. Maybe it's because I cook it the way the Chinese and Japanese do. It's quite different from our traditional Uncle Ben's, which I grew up with and still use. I buy the Chinese or Japanese rice in large bags in bulk. It's less expensive, shorter, rounder, and stickier.

Here are a few hints for cooking rice:

1. Wash rice many, many times until water runs clear.
2. Add water to cover rice up to the first joint of your index finger.
3. Add salt, about 1/3 teaspoon for each cup of rice. (The Chinese don't use salt, but I do.)
4. Let water come to full boil uncovered. Lower heat and simmer until water appears to disappear and little holes appear on the top of the rice (little "eyes," I read in one book). Cover and remove from heat and let rice sit for 15 to 20 minutes. *Do not peek.* The steam is cooking every grain. It will keep warm this way for over an hour.

Rice and grains are irresistible too! Try the Spanish Rice El Dorado. That will do it for you, as will the Special Bulgur Pilaf or the Kasha Varnishkas.

Now as to beans. You've been spared old favorites like My Red Beans and Rice and Mother's Chili, but I made up for it. Try the Cuban Black Bean Soup and the Lima Pot. Did I forget the Frijoles Rancheros? Well, don't you—they're terrific. And on and on!

BROCCOLI ALLA ZITI   SERVES 4

There is something about broccoli and pasta that is as compatible and satisfying as the sounds of a great vocal quartet who have spent much of their lives together. The combination of the hot ziti—a large, tubular macaroni-type pasta—and the cold tomatoes, the bland pasta and hot pepper and crunchy broccoli, is maybe what they mean by yin and yang. But if a stranger happens into your midst immediately after you've dined on this little number, inhale only or get out the Listermint. If they grow faint, it's from envy—trust me.

3 cloves garlic, chopped	stems left on
1 teaspoon red pepper flakes	8 ounces ziti
1/4 cup olive oil	2 fresh tomatoes, chopped
1 tablespoon butter	Freshly grated Parmesan cheese
1 bunch broccoli flowerets with 1 inch of	

In a large, heavy skillet sauté garlic and red pepper flakes in oil and butter.

Blanch broccoli flowerets by plunging in boiling salted water for 30 seconds.

Cook ziti in boiling salted water until just *al dente.* Drain well.

Pour broccoli over hot ziti. Add chopped cold fresh tomatoes and Parmesan cheese; serve immediately with extra Parmesan cheese on the side, and the red-pepper-flake dispenser handy for the asbestos-lined palates.

EGGPLANT SPAGHETTI

One Sunday afternoon in our mostly eternal summers out here, a lovely couple, visiting Los Angeles while he was making a movie, came by. They wanted to go swimming! Everybody in L.A. has a pool (I think it is in the city by-laws), but hardly anybody uses them except the kids and out-of-towners. We went swimming. I liked it. Then Edmonda volunteered to make her Julio's favorite pasta. It took no time and, as you'll see, was absolutely delicious. This recipe is for a main course. If you want it vegetarian or lighter and perhaps for a side dish, omit the Italian sausage and ground beef. (I really prefer it this way.)

SAUCE

1/2 pound Italian sausage, cut into chunks
1/2 pound ground beef
3 tablespoons olive oil or butter
1/2 onion, finely chopped
1 clove garlic, finely chopped
1 stalk celery, finely chopped
1 carrot, finely chopped
2 cups Italian plum tomatoes, mashed or

placed in blender for 3 seconds
6 sprigs parsley, finely chopped
Salt and freshly ground black pepper to taste
Pinch oregano
Pinch basil
1/2 cup chicken broth (optional)
1/2 cup cream

In skillet, sauté sausage and ground beef in 1 tablespoon oil or butter until lightly browned. Set aside to drain on paper towels.

In large saucepan, sauté onions, garlic, celery, and carrots in oil or butter until onions and celery are soft but not brown and carrots have softened. Add tomatoes, parsley, sausage, and beef. Let sauce come to boil over high heat.

Add salt, pepper, oregano, and basil. Let sauce simmer over low heat, half covered so it won't reduce too quickly, 1 hour or more. If sauce becomes too thick, add chicken broth. Just before serving, add cream.

1/2 eggplant, peeled and sliced 1/2 inch
  thick
1 tablespoon plus 1/4 teaspoon olive oil
1 pound spaghetti

1 1/2 tablespoons salt
3 quarts water
Freshly grated Parmesan cheese

Soak eggplant in salt water, or salt slices and let stand upright in colander 30 minutes. Pat dry and sauté in 1 tablespoon olive oil. Drain on paper towels.

Cook spaghetti in boiling water to which you have added 1/4 teaspoon oil and salt. When spaghetti is just *al dente,* drain immediately in colander and run cold water over it quickly to stop the cooking action.

In pot in which spaghetti was cooked or large mixing bowl, mix half of sauce with spaghetti, turning well to coat. Dish portions onto warmed plate. Place eggplant slice on each portion. Pour remaining sauce on top of eggplant and spaghetti. Sprinkle Parmesan cheese over each portion.

THIN SPAGHETTI WITH FRUITS
OF THE SEA

Giovanni's in Cleveland! Unless you've had an all-day rehearsal—coffee in Styrofoam cups, sand-wiches in plastic wrap, a case of nerves, a concert that evening that really comes together—and finally, "starving," you end with a trip to Giovanni's with gracious Giovanni and his chef staying open a few extra moments to serve you their specialties, you don't know what real hospitality is! It was one of the best moments of a tour that had many wonderful moments—and a good reason to go to Cleveland. For more of Giovanni's, see pages 241, 245.

1/4 cup imported olive oil
1 pound swordfish steak, cut into 2 pieces
12 medium-sized shrimp, shelled, deveined, with tails left intact
2 garlic cloves, finely chopped
12 littleneck clams, thoroughly washed
16 fresh mussels, washed and bearded
1 teaspoon fresh basil, chopped
1 bay leaf
3 ounces (1/4 cup plus 2 tablespoons) cha-

blis wine
2 cups Marinara Sauce (page 4)
3 ounces (1/4 cup plus 2 tablespoons) chicken or fish broth (pages 7, 8)
Salt to taste
Freshly ground pepper to taste
Red pepper flakes
1 pound spaghettini
2 tablespoons unsalted butter
1 teaspoon chopped fresh parsley

In heavy flameproof casserole, heat olive oil until light haze forms over it. Add swordfish and shrimp and sauté until shrimp turn pink and swordfish turns white and slightly opaque. Remove from casserole with slotted spoon and set aside on warmed platter.

To same casserole add garlic, clams, and mussels. When garlic begins to brown, add fresh basil, bay leaf, and chablis and lightly deglaze pan.

Add Marinara Sauce, chicken stock, salt, pepper, and red pepper flakes. Cover casserole and cook until clams open.

Cook pasta in boiling salted water until just *al dente*. Drain, rinse with cold water, and set aside on warmed platter.

Stir butter into sauce. With slotted spoon remove clams and mussels from sauce and keep warm. Remove bay leaf from sauce, add cooked pasta, and toss.

Divide evenly into serving dishes, divide swordfish, clams, mussels, and shrimp, place on top of pasta, and pour remaining sauce over all. Sprinkle with parsley and serve immediately.

ANGEL HAIR WITH FRESH TOMATOES
AND CAPERS

This is also from Giovanni's of Cleveland. I tested it very successfully on a large group of gourmet food experts and critics at a dinner Christian Millau and his wife, Arlette, and I cooked together. Christian is one of the authors of the Gault Millau guides, which tell you in no uncertain terms where to dine and where not to dine, describing ambiance, cuisine, and service with wit and unsparing honesty. He is not only a critic and fine writer, but a great cook. For a sample of his recipes see pages 241, 245. I was a nervous wreck cooking with and for him, but we had a great time and the dinner was a smashing success! Champagne before dinner didn't dim anybody's appreciation of our combined efforts.

2 tablespoons olive oil
1 clove garlic, finely chopped
1 teaspoon fresh basil, chopped
1 tablespoon capers
1 teaspoon caper brine
1/4 cup dry white wine
1 1/2 cups Marinara Sauce
3 tablespoons unsalted butter

1 tablespoon salt
1 pound capelli di angelo (angel hair—thin pasta)
4 tomatoes, peeled, seeded, and thinly sliced
Salt and freshly ground black pepper
Fresh parsley, chopped
Freshly grated Parmesan cheese

Heat olive oil in medium sized skillet until light haze forms over it. Add garlic and stir for 30 seconds. Add basil, capers, caper brine, and white wine and cook for 2 minutes. Add Marinara Sauce, bring to boil, and cook an additional 3 minutes. Remove skillet from heat and keep warm.

In large kettle bring 6 quarts water to rapid boil over high heat, add 2 tablespoons butter and 1 tablespoon salt. Add capelli di angelo, stirring gently for a few seconds with wooden fork to be sure noodles do not stick to one another. Cook until pasta is *al dente,* or somewhat resistant to bite (about 3 minutes). Drain pasta into colander and run cold water over to stop cooking.

Return skillet to heat and add tomatoes. Stew for 3 minutes, add remaining tablespoon of butter, and season with salt and pepper to taste. Put cooked pasta and caper sauce in kettle pasta was cooked in or large mixing bowl and toss until sauce is incorporated with pasta. Divide evenly onto serving plates, sprinkle with Parmesan cheese and parsley, and dot with a few capers.

NOTE Caper sauce can be prepared in the morning. Be careful when reheating; if necessary add a little chicken broth or 1/4 cup red wine to soften sauce so it will be less likely to scorch. Since the angel hair cooks quickly, the sauce must be hot.

MARINARA SAUCE

MAKES ABOUT 2 CUPS

2 tablespoons olive oil
1/2 cup finely chopped onions
6 large tomatoes, peeled, seeded and chopped, *or* 8 canned Italian plum tomatoes, cut into 2 or 3 pieces, plus 1/4 cup of juice
3 tablespoons tomato paste
2 cloves garlic, cut in half and removed be-

fore serving
1 tablespoon finely chopped fresh basil *or* 1 teaspoon dried
3/4 teaspoon sugar
1 teaspoon parsley
1/2 teaspoon salt
Freshly ground black pepper to taste

Using 2 to 3-quart saucepan, heat olive oil until light haze forms over it. Add onions and cook over moderate heat until they are soft but not browned.

Add tomatoes with juice, tomato paste, garlic, basil, sugar, parsley, and pepper. I add salt after almost 20 minutes of cooking.

Reduce heat to medium and simmer, stirring occasionally, 30–40 minutes until tomatoes are soft and shapeless. Taste for seasoning.

PASTA PRIMAVERA

SERVES 6–8

This is one of the most popular pastas served. I first sampled it in a beautiful restaurant in New York called Le Cirque. I thought it was my discovery until I found out that people from Memphis to Montevideo would come to sample the springtime pasta at Le Cirque. This is their recipe, but the vegetables are variable. Serve what is most fresh and beautiful at that time of year.

1 cup sliced zucchini	2 teaspoons minced garlic
1 1/2 cups broccoli flowerets	Salt
1 1/2 cups snow peas	Freshly ground black pepper
1 cup baby peas	1/4 cup chopped Italian parsley
6 stalks asparagus, sliced	1/3 cup pine nuts
1 pound spaghetti (preferably the Italian De Cecco brand)	1/3 cup butter
	1/2 cup freshly grated Parmesan cheese
10 large mushrooms, sliced	1 cup heavy cream
12 cherry tomatoes, cut in half	1/3 cup chopped fresh basil
3 tablespoons olive oil	1/3 cup chicken broth

Blanch zucchini, broccoli, snow peas, baby peas, and asparagus in boiling salted water 1–2 minutes each until just crisp-tender. Drain and refresh under cold water. Set aside. This can be done ahead of time.

Cook pasta in boiling salted water until *al dente,* about 8–11 minutes, no more. Drain and set aside.

In skillet sauté mushrooms and tomatoes in 1 tablespoon oil with 1 teaspoon garlic, salt, pepper, and parsley. Set aside.

In another large skillet sauté pine nuts in remaining oil until brown. Add remaining garlic and vegetables. Simmer a few minutes until hot.

In saucepan large enough to hold pasta and vegetables, melt butter. Add cheese, cream, and basil. Stir to blend and melt cheese. Add pasta and toss to coat with sauce. If sauce gets too thick, thin with a little chicken broth. Add about 1/3 of vegetables, toss again. Taste for seasoning.

Divide pasta among 6 broad soup plates and top with remaining vegetables. Top with cherry tomatoes.

ERNESTO'S PASTA MISTA

SERVES 4

1/4 cup sliced mushrooms
1 tablespoon butter
2 cups Cream Sauce
1/4 cup chopped walnuts

3 tablespoons finely chopped parsley
8 ounces white fettuccine
8 ounces green fettuccine

Sauté mushrooms in butter. Add to Cream Sauce along with walnuts and parsley.

Cook fettuccine in boiling salted water until just *al dente*. Slowly turn fettuccine into sauce with wooden spoon so as not to break noodles. If sauce is too thick, half-and-half or milk may be used to thin it.

SAUCE ALLA CARLO CASTI (CREAM SAUCE)

MAKES 2 CUPS

1/2 cup butter
1/2 cup flour
3 cups half-and-half
1/4 teaspoon salt

1 1/4 teaspoons white pepper
3/4 cup freshly grated Parmesan cheese
1/4 cup chablis wine

In saucepan melt butter and stir in flour, making a paste. Add half-and-half and bring to boil. Add salt, white pepper, Parmesan cheese, and wine.

Simmer and stir until mixture thickens. Keep sauce warm by placing saucepan in larger pan of simmering water, or transferring to top of double boiler.

BEE'S LINGUINE WITH WHITE CLAM SAUCE

SERVES 8

Bee is Bee Korshak, my long time friend and traveling, cooking and tennis-playing companion. We raised our children on new tastes, new foods, and a sprinkling of great junk food like hamburgers, hot dogs, and french fries. As a result they all love to cook and entertain. However, I seem to remember occasionally in France, Italy, or Hawaii some not-too-well-concealed rebellion on their part when the choice was between some exotic French or Oriental bistro we enthusiastically recommended and McDonald's, only four blocks down the street from the hotel.

7 pounds littleneck clams
4 tablespoons butter
4 tablespoons oil

2 whole cloves garlic
3/4 cup chopped parsley
2 pounds linguine

Clean and scrub clams with stiff brush. Rinse in several changes of cold water until all sand is removed.

In large, deep skillet, heat butter and oil, garlic cloves, and 1/2 cup parsley. Add clams and cook over medium heat until clams open.

Remove clams from skillet, reserving sauce they were cooked in. Reserve 24 whole clams in shells, allowing three clams per person to be placed on top of linguine. Remove remaining clams from shells and mince.

Cook linguine in boiling salted water until just *al dente.* Drain well in colander and place in large serving bowl. Add minced clams and reserved sauce (remove garlic cloves). Just before serving, add the remaining 1/4 cup of parsley to linguine and place reserved whole clams in shells on top.

Serve hot with crusty French or Italian bread, a light green salad, a nice Italian white wine, or red if you prefer. I happen to prefer red, because of the temperature and flavor with the deeply scented, simple pasta.

VERMICELLI WITH BROCCOLI AND MUSHROOMS
SERVES 4–6

Another Giovanni jewel. See page 241 for how I came by his specialties. The broccoli and mushrooms will make you feel as if you're on a health food kick. I guess you could use half-and-half instead of the heavy cream. Giovanni didn't, but I didn't ask any questions. I rationalized that I owed it to myself as I hit the high notes that night right on the nose, clear and sure. Maybe it was because I'd skipped breakfast and lunch in anticipation.

1 cup unsalted butter (2 sticks)
1 teaspoon finely chopped shallots
1/2 pound fresh broccoli flowerets, cooked *al dente* and cooled
3 ounces (1/4 cup plus 2 tablespoons) sliced fresh mushrooms
1/4 cup chablis wine
1 cup half-and-half

2 cups heavy cream
1/4 teaspoon freshly ground nutmeg
Salt and white pepper to taste
1 pound vermicelli, cooked *al dente*
6 egg yolks, lightly beaten
3 ounces freshly grated Parmesan cheese
1/2 teaspoon chopped parsley

Melt 1/4 cup butter in medium sauté pan over moderate heat, add shallots, and sauté until limp. Add broccoli flowerets and mushrooms and stir-fry 2 minutes.

Increase heat until mixture gets very hot (don't let it burn); add wine and deglaze pan.

Reduce heat, add half-and-half, heavy cream, remaining butter, nutmeg, salt, and pepper and bring to very light boil. Add cooked vermicelli and, stirring constantly, add egg yolks. Stir until eggs are completely incorporated into hot cream and mixture sticks to pasta. Add Parmesan cheese and stir. Divide evenly among warmed serving plates, sprinkle with chopped parsley; and serve immediately.

BLENDER PESTO
SERVES 4

To preserve your precious crop of basil for all year round, place whole basil leaves in a large jar and pack tightly. (Basil begins to lose flavor, I think, the moment it's cut or torn into the necessary size pieces for pesto or sauces.) Add fresh, light, really good olive oil to cover and store in refrigerator. Just before using, drain off excess oil; pat dry gently and use just about as you would the freshly grown gems.

2 cups whole fresh basil (handle carefully as
  they lose essence and flavor when torn or
  chopped too soon before use)
1/3 cup olive oil
3 tablespoons pine nuts
2 cloves garlic, lightly crushed and peeled

1 teaspoon salt
1/2 cup very finely grated Parmesan cheese
3 tablespoons very finely grated pecorino
  Romano cheese
3 tablespoons butter, softened

Place basil, olive oil, pine nuts, garlic cloves, and salt in blender and mix at high speed. Stop from time to time and scrape ingredients down toward bottom of blender cup with spatula.

When evenly blended, pour into bowl and by hand, beat in finely grated cheeses. (This results in more interesting texture and better flavor than when you mix cheeses in blender.) When cheeses have been evenly incorporated, beat in softened butter.

1/2 pound spaghettini or linguine, cooked
  just *al dente*

2–3 tablespoons hot water in which pasta
  was cooked

Before spooning pesto over pasta, add 2–3 tablespoons hot water in which pasta was cooked.

TUSCAN TORTELLINI

SERVES 4–6

FILLING

MAKES 1 1/2 CUPS

1/3 cup plus 3 tablespoons quality olive oil
  (not virgin olive oil—too heavy taste)
1 onion, peeled and chopped
2 garlic cloves, peeled and chopped
1/4 cup chopped fresh sage *or* 2 teaspoons
  dried sage
2 tablespoons chopped parsley
1 sprig fresh rosemary *or* 1 teaspoon dried
1/2 pound raw lean meat, half pork, half
  beef

1/2 cup red wine
Salt and pepper to taste
2 ounces mortadella or *cooked* ham (mortadella ham is available at Italian markets)
1 egg
1/3 cup freshly grated Parmesan cheese
1/4 teaspoon freshly grated nutmeg
10 leaves fresh sage *or* 1 1/2 teaspoons
  dried

In medium sauté pan, heat 3 tablespoons oil over medium heat.

Add onions and garlic and sauté until soft (about 3 minutes). Add sage, parsley, rosemary; stirring, sauté another 2 minutes. Add meat and brown lightly about 4 minutes. Pour in wine, add salt and pepper to taste. Cook, uncovered, over low heat 30 minutes or until all liquid has evaporated.

Transfer meat mixture to meat grinder or food processor fitted with steel blade. Add mortadella, egg, Parmesan, and nutmeg. Process or grind mixture thoroughly. Set aside.

In 1-quart saucepan, heat remaining oil over low heat, add sage leaves, and cook 5 minutes to release aromatic qualities of sage in oil. Set aside.

3 cups flour
3 eggs
1 tablespoon olive oil

1 tablespoon salt
Parsley and cherry tomatoes for garnish

Place flour on board, making well in center of flour. Break eggs in center of well. Add oil and salt. Using fork, mix eggs into flour until all liquid has been absorbed and dough is easy to handle.

Lightly flour board. Knead dough until it comes away easily from surface of board. Cut into four parts and roll out to about 1/16 of an inch thick. With cookie cutter (1 1/2-inch diameter), cut rounds out of each sheet of dough. Place about 3/4 teaspoon filling in center of each round. Fold dough over and press sides tightly so no filling can escape during cooking.

In 6-quart saucepan, bring 4 quarts of salted water to boil; add tortellinis and return water to boil. Cook 2 minutes. Strain and place tortellinis in medium pasta bowl and toss with sage-seasoned olive oil. Garnish with parsley and cherry tomatoes.

BLACK PASTA

SERVES 6–8

Maybe this isn't a new one to you, but it certainly was to me. I was introduced to it by a remarkably talented career chef and party maker named Randy Fuhrman. The ideas for combinations of foods and menus and decorations and all forms of entertaining just roll out of him in a steady non-stop stream. One evening at one of our larger taste-testing go-rounds, he volunteered not only to do the tables and generally help out in setting up the 27-some odd dishes we were trying, but also to bring over this special, most unusual almost exotic cold pasta. He's generous and open and honest about recipes. You'll find the Asparagus Oriental on page 264. Try it, that's his too.

P.S. For your oyster mushrooms, have your favorite specialty grocer order them ahead for you. If he can't, substitute 8 ounces Chinese mushrooms (soaked in hot water 20 minutes, stems removed) and 8 ounces regular mushrooms, medium size, cut into quarters including stems.

2 pounds oyster mushrooms (funny-looking but great unusual taste and texture)
1 1/3 cups plus 3 tablespoons olive oil
2 cups black olive paste (Olivia)
1/2 cup chopped fresh basil

2 teaspoons minced garlic
2 cups pine nuts
2 pounds angel-hair pasta
Fresh basil leaves and cherry tomatoes for garnish

Slice off ends of mushrooms to separate clusters. Heat 1 1/3 cups olive oil in large skillet until light haze forms over it. Add mushrooms and sauté until limp, about 5 minutes. Stir in olive paste, basil, and garlic. Blend thoroughly. Cook over medium heat about 3 minutes. Set aside.

Heat 3 tablespoons olive oil in medium skillet. Add pine nuts and sauté until golden brown, about 3–4 minutes. Set aside.

Cook pasta *al dente* in boiling water 2–3 minutes. Drain in colander and rinse with cold water. Stir into olive paste mixture. Stir in half of pine nuts. Serve hot or at room temperature garnished with remaining pine nuts, basil leaves, and cherry tomato halves.

BAKED MACARONI RED DEVIL SERVES 4

When I first wangled that chance to spend an extended time in New York in pursuit of that career I knew was going to be mine, it was on condition that I'd come home as soon as that limited store of funds ran out. I sang anywhere for everything, pay or no pay, sure somebody would hear me and say the magic words, "This broadcast is going on the network to Nashville." Never mind coast to coast—how they thought I was doing down home was all that mattered. The money was not rolling in any faster than the opportunities.

There was a restaurant called the Red Devil that was kind of a musicians' hangout for a lot of reasons. Almost everybody was broke and the management didn't seem to mind when three of us shared the same dish. The food was delicious and the whole place smelled heavenly. It had hot, spicy dishes—nothing like the macaroni and cheese from Mr. Oliver's boarding house, nor was it anything like Petrone's, our Italian restaurant in Nashville which had great chili and barbecue, but the only pasta I remember was the spaghetti in the chili.

This may not rival that first experience with real Southern Italian pasta, but it's delicious and uncomplicated. This is the one we had our twelve-year-old friend, Katie Korshak, test very successfully. This story may seem like a far-fetched way of getting you to try a simple pasta, but I think the best tastes and smells and sensations we experience in food have as much to do with the warm memories, ambiance, and the people with whom we shared it as the expertise of the cook.

1/2 pound ziti macaroni (small tubular pasta)	1 tablespoon oil
1 quart boiling salted water	1 teaspoon red pepper flakes
1 large eggplant, peeled, soaked in salt water, drained and patted dry, and diced	1 1/2 cups Italian Tomato Sauce
	1/2 pound mozzarella cheese, cut into thin slices
2 tablespoons butter	1/4 cup grated Parmesan cheese

Boil macaroni or pasta in salted water until just tender or *al dente.* Drain and set aside.

Sauté eggplant in butter and oil. Drain and set aside.

Preheat oven to 350°F.

Place drained pasta in a buttered 8-inch baking dish. Layer eggplant over pasta and sprinkle with red pepper flakes. Spread tomato sauce over it and then layer with slices of mozzarella cheese. Sprinkle Parmesan cheese over all and bake 15 minutes or until cheese bubbles.

ITALIAN TOMATO SAUCE MAKES 3 CUPS

1 onion, minced	1 8-ounce can tomato sauce
2 stalks celery, minced	1/2 teaspoon sugar
1 carrot, minced	1 bay leaf
3 tablespoons oil	1/4 teaspoon oregano
3 tablespoons minced parsley	1/2 teaspoon basil
1 16-ounce can Italian tomatoes with juice, broken up	Salt and freshly ground black pepper

In medium saucepan, sauté onions, celery, and carrots in oil until tender but not brown (10–15 minutes). Add parsley, tomatoes, tomato sauce, sugar, bay leaf, oregano, and basil.

Bring sauce to boil, lower heat, and simmer 10 minutes. Add salt and pepper to taste and simmer 15 more minutes until sauce is thoroughly blended and slightly thickened. Remove bay leaf.

SPAGHETTI CARBONARA

SERVES 6 AS A SIDE DISH

10 strips bacon
3/4 cup diced ham or prosciutto
1 pound spaghettini (thin spaghetti)
1/4 pound butter
Freshly ground black pepper

Pinch of oregano
1/2–3/4 cup freshly grated Parmesan cheese, or to taste
3 eggs, beaten
Parsley, chopped

Fry bacon until crisp. Drain on paper towels. When cool, crumble. Remove all but 1 tablespoon of bacon fat, add diced ham or prosciutto, and sauté until heated through. Set aside and keep warm.

Cook spaghettini *al dente*. Drain and place in warmed serving bowl. Add butter, pepper, and oregano and mix gently.

Sprinkle bacon, ham, and cheese over and toss. Add eggs and mix in quickly and thoroughly. Garnish with parsley and serve immediately.

STIR-FRIED NOODLES

SERVES 6

Seasoning is the big trick with this recipe. It's so good you can serve it after a full menu and they'll come back for seconds. If there ever is any left over (there usually isn't) I have it for breakfast and lunch.

1 head Chinese cabbage
3/4 pound spaghetti or thick Chinese noodles
4 tablespoons oil
3 ounces lean uncooked pork, shredded

2 teaspoons salt
1 1/2 cups chicken broth
4 tablespoons dark soy sauce
1/2 teaspoon sesame seed oil
1/4 teaspoon white pepper

Wash cabbage thoroughly, shake out excess water, and chop coarsely. Blanch in boiling water for 30 seconds. Drain well. Rinse with cold water and drain again. Set aside. (This can be done in morning.)

Drop spaghetti or noodles in boiling water. When water returns to boil, add 4–5 tablespoons cold water. When it returns to boil again, test—spaghetti or noodles should be almost done, not even *al dente*. Rinse with cold water immediately. Spread in shallow baking tin to dry until ready to use. (This may also be done in the morning.)

Heat wok. When very hot add 3 tablespoons oil and stir-fry pork with cabbage about 1 1/2 minutes. Remove and set aside.

Add noodles and salt to wok, adding more oil if necessary. Stir-fry until lightly colored, about 1 minute. Add chicken broth, cover, and simmer 5 minutes.

Add pork and cabbage and soy sauce. Stir-fry until sauce has completely evaporated. Taste for seasoning. Add 1 tablespoon oil, stir in lightly.

Transfer to hot serving plate and sprinkle with sesame seed oil and white pepper. Serve immediately or for breakfast or lunch.

FRESH TOMATO PASTA

SERVES 6

A combination of cold vegetables and herbs and hot pasta that is a perfect summer dish when the tomatoes are at their peak and the basil is as high as a hound dog's eye. The basil must be fresh and the tomatoes small and beautifully ripe to be at its best.

2/3 cup light olive oil
5–6 ripe tomatoes, peeled, seeded, and
   chopped
1 large clove garlic, very finely chopped

1 cup loosely packed fresh basil, coarsely
   chopped
Salt and fresh ground pepper to taste
1 pound linguine or spaghettini

Mix olive oil, tomatoes, garlic, basil, salt, and pepper and set aside.

Cook pasta in boiling salted water until *al dente.* Drain. Pour over sauce and toss. Adjust seasonings.

COLD PASTA SALAD

SERVES 4–6

Le Dome is an informal friendly bistro in L.A.; it's one of TV and movie folks' favorite watering holes. We catch up with each other over great new creations by the executive chef, J. C. Bourlier. I've pigged out on this one, days at a time, and when I was dieting, on their Isabelle Salad (page 108). On one of those "you owe it to yourself" days, I might have both.

4 fresh tomatoes, peeled and quartered
1/4 cup vinegar
1/4 teaspoon finely chopped fresh basil
1 pound fresh Italian egg noodles
6 tablespoons olive oil
1/2 onion, finely chopped
1/3 green pepper, finely chopped
1 clove garlic, finely chopped
2 sprigs fresh tarragon, finely chopped

1/3 cup fresh oregano, finely chopped
1 cup finely chopped fresh basil
2 tablespoons finely chopped or grated fresh
   peeled ginger root
4 thin slices prosciutto, cut into strips
10 black olives, pitted
Salt and pepper to taste
1 teaspoon soy sauce

Marinate tomatoes in vinegar and basil 6–8 hours.

Cook noodles in boiling salted water 3–4 minutes or until just *al dente.* Drain under cold water until they are completely cool.

Heat olive oil in sauté pan. Sauté onions and green pepper over high heat for 4 minutes. Add garlic, tarragon, oregano, basil, and ginger and sauté an additional 5 minutes, stirring often. Remove to mixing bowl and let cool.

When cold, mix with noodles. Add prosciutto and black olives. Season with salt and pepper and soy sauce. Mix ingredients thoroughly and serve.

Drain tomatoes and serve as a garnish with the salad.

BREAD DUMPLINGS
SERVES 4–6

The recommendations at the tail end of the instructions are the way these dumplings are served at the fine restaurant Le Bistro in the Marc Plaza Hotel in Milwaukee, Wisconsin. Venison may be just roaming around there and the geese may be flying overhead, but they're a little tougher to come by in other parts of the country, so rather than miss the experience, try them with roast pork, lamb, chicken, pot roast—anything with a light, smooth gravy or, as we say, "in the altogether."

4 cups dried bread, cut into 1-inch cubes
3/4 cup whole milk, scalded
3 eggs, slightly beaten
1/2 cup finely chopped onions

1 tablespoon chopped parsley
Pinch nutmeg
Salt and pepper to taste
1 quart chicken stock

Place dried bread cubes in mixing bowl; add scalded milk. Mix gently but thoroughly. Let stand 3 minutes.

Add beaten eggs, onions, parsley, nutmeg, salt, and pepper. Mix gently but thoroughly. Bring chicken stock to simmer in saucepan.

Roll dumpling mixture by hand into 1 or 2-inch balls; they should have a sticky texture. Drop dumplings, one at a time, into simmering chicken stock and cook 5–8 minutes until dumplings are firm. Serve immediately with roast pork, venison, or goose.

SPAETZLE
SERVES 4–6

This is a perfect spaetzle recipe. I didn't happen to have a spaetzle maker, so John Schumacher's tin can method worked great for me. This is a light, dumpling-like noodle, wonderful with roasts, veal, chicken, anything that has a sauce; or just with butter and fried bread crumbs as a side dish.

4 eggs
1/4 cup cold water
1/4 teaspoon salt

1/4 teaspoon nutmeg
1 1/2 cups flour
3 quarts boiling, salted water for cooking

In medium-sized bowl, break 4 eggs. Add cold water, salt, and nutmeg. Beat with wire whip until frothy. Add flour slowly until mixture is stiff and gathers around whip, and comes off sides of bowl.

Bring salted water to boil. Put mix in spaetzle machine (see below) and drop into water. Bring water back to boil; simmer 5 minutes. Rinse in strainer and serve with butter or pan gravy.

How to make homemade spaetzle machine: Clean and wash medium-sized tin can. Punch holes in bottom, the size of a pencil. Put mix in can and pour through holes with ladle.

Punch holes in bottom of medium-sized tin can with screwdriver or ice pick.

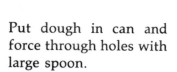

Put dough in can and force through holes with large spoon.

RISOTTO

It's hard to find even in the best Italian restaurants because, as they warn you, risotto takes longer than pasta. It takes patience and a real feel for when each grain is coated and cooked, so settle in—it's worth it! You need Italian rice. Arborio is best.

Marcella Hazen suggested burying a whole truffle in the uncooked rice to give it the proper, true risotto feel. I'd love to, Marcella, but fresh truffles are hard to come by and expensive. If I had one I don't think I could bear to bury it after what that pig had to go through just to find it and dig it up in some forest.

6 tablespoons unsalted butter
1 small onion, finely chopped
1 1/2 cups short-grain Arborio Italian rice

3–4 cups chicken or beef stock (page 7)
1/2 cup freshly grated Parmesan cheese

Melt 4 tablespoons butter in heavy skillet. Add onions and cook over medium heat, stirring, until light gold in color. Add 2 more tablespoons butter. When it has melted, add rice. Stir rice in melted butter until grains are well coated and almost translucent.

Have chicken or beef stock heating on another burner. Pour 1 cup of hot stock onto rice and stir with fork, then let rice cook over medium-high heat until liquid is almost absorbed, stirring now and then so it doesn't stick to the pan.

Add another cup of stock and continue to cook and stir until liquid is almost absorbed. As rice gradually softens and becomes creamy, add stock more sparingly, 1/2 cup at a time, stirring until absorbed. Add only as much as rice can absorb—it should not be drowned with liquid. Keep tasting a grain or two. After 25–30 minutes rice should be creamy and tender, but a little firm in center, not mushy. Stir well during final cooking to prevent sticking.

Sprinkle with grated Parmesan cheese and serve at once on hot plates.

RICE PILAF

Julie Dannenbaum of Philadelphia has a way of reducing the mystery of cooking to its simplest level. One day while we were testing, I turned this over to Liliana of Liliana's Guatemalan Chiles Rellenos on page 233, who understands and speaks English very well. I wasn't sure she had read much English. The Spanish newspapers must be a relief after a long day of coping with English. She not only read it, she followed it to the delicious letter. Ms. Dannenbaum would have approved.

1/4 cup butter (1/2 stick)
1 onion, finely chopped
1 1/2 cups long-grain rice

3 cups chicken or veal stock
Salt and pepper to taste

Melt butter in pan and sauté onions. Add rice and cook 1 minute. Pour in chicken or veal stock, salt and pepper to taste, and bring to boil. Turn to simmer and cover with a heavy lid. Simmer 23 minutes.

Remove lid and fluff up rice with two forks. Pack rice into buttered timbale molds and unmold.

CHINESE OR JAPANESE RICE SERVES 4–6

2 cups Chinese or Japanese rice   2/3 teaspoon salt
Water

Wash rice many, many times until water is clear.

Put rice in heavy saucepan for which you have a well-fitting lid. (I prefer an enamel pan.) Pour in enough water to cover rice up to first joint of your index finger. Add salt.

Let water come to full boil. Lower heat and simmer until water appears to disappear. Cover, remove from heat, and let rice sit 15–20 minutes. *Do not peek.*

If you plan to use it for fried rice it is better, for some reason, if you cook the rice the day before.

GLORIA'S MEXICAN RICE SERVES 10–12

Gloria does rice as simply and purely as her Mexican Pork Roast on page 207 is complicated. Since the starch has been washed away, you can eat as much of this as you like—almost.

5 cups rice
3 medium tomatoes, quartered
1/2 cup finely chopped onions
1/4 cup water
2 cups corn oil
2 cloves garlic, left whole

5 cups water
5 cups chicken broth
5 teaspoons salt
2 sprigs parsley
1 10-ounce package frozen peas
2 hard-cooked eggs, sliced for garnish

Wash rice many times. Soak 15 minutes in hot water. Drain and set aside.

Place tomatoes, onions, and water in blender or food processor. Blend 30 seconds and set aside.

In heavy saucepan, put corn oil, garlic, and rice. Fry rice until brown, then remove garlic and remaining oil.

Add tomato-onion mixture. Bring to boil, lower heat, and cook over moderate heat, stirring constantly, until rice becomes dry.

Add water, chicken broth, salt, parsley, and peas. Bring to boil, reduce heat, cover, and simmer 30–35 minutes or until all liquid has been absorbed.

Garnish with hard-cooked eggs before serving.

SPANISH RICE EL DORADO

SERVES 6–8

Spanish rice with Italian tomatoes and American pickling spices shows you how homogeneous we've really become, but that's what this whole book is about—and this dish is really a treat. Served with New Zealand lamb chops or Iowa pork chops, it'll still be Spanish rice—arroz! If you like, serve it all by itself for a vegetarian main dish, as can be done with the Special Bulgur Pilaf on page 260.

1 tablespoon mixed whole pickling spices
4 cups chicken broth
1 cup tomato sauce
1 teaspoon salt
1/2 teaspoon cayenne pepper
2 cups long-grain rice
1 tablespoon oil

1 tablespoon softened butter
1/2 cup Italian tomatoes, sliced into small wedges (if Italian tomatoes are not available, use peeled fresh tomatoes, seasoned with a little salt and pepper)
1/2 cup chopped green pepper

Wrap pickling spices in cheesecloth and tie securely.

Combine chicken broth, tomato sauce, salt, cayenne, and pickling spices in large saucepan. Bring to boil, reduce heat, and simmer 10 minutes.

Sauté rice in hot oil in skillet until coated and light beige.

Add to broth mixture. Bring to boil. Cover, lower heat and simmer 25 minutes or until rice is tender. Leave rice covered (don't remove lid) until ready to serve. If anybody is really late and you have held rice longer than 1 hour, turn heat to low, set rice over asbestos pad or in a larger skillet filled with hot water, and heat through. Don't let it burn.

Remove spice bag. Add 1 tablespoon softened butter. Sprinkle cold tomatoes and peppers over all.

VEGETABLE WILD RICE SALAD

SERVES 4–6

3 cups cooked wild rice
1 8-ounce can water chestnuts, drained and sliced
1 small green pepper, diced
1 tomato, peeled, seeded, and diced

1 tablespoon minced cilantro
Honey-Yogurt Dressing
Lettuce
1 cup bean sprouts (optional)

Combine wild rice, water chestnuts, green peppers, tomatoes, and cilantro in bowl. Add enough dressing to moisten and toss lightly but thoroughly. (Reserve remaining dressing for passing at the table.) Cover and chill well.

To serve, mound on individual lettuce-lined plates and surround with bean sprouts if desired.

HONEY-YOGURT DRESSING

1 cup plain yogurt
1 teaspoon prepared mustard
2 tablespoons honey

1/2 teaspoon garlic salt
1/4 teaspoon salt
1 tablespoon toasted sesame seeds

Combine all ingredients and mix well.

TANGY RICE SALAD

SERVES 6

4 cups fluffy just-cooked rice
1 tablespoon vinegar
1 teaspoon lemon juice
1 tablespoon salad oil
2 teaspoons curry powder or more to taste
1/4 teaspoon turmeric

1/2 teaspoon cayenne pepper (optional)
3/4 cup raisins
1/3 cup chopped green pepper
2 tablespoons chopped chutney
2/3 cup yogurt or sour cream
2/3 cup mayonnaise

Sprinkle hot rice with vinegar, lemon juice, and oil. Mix lightly; add curry, turmeric, and cayenne and blend. Stir in raisins, green peppers, and chutney.

Add yogurt or sour cream and mayonnaise; mix well. Place in 6-cup buttered mold or Pyrex dish, or in individual lightly buttered molds, or small teacups, and chill. To serve, either unmold or heap on lettuce-lined plate.

POTATOES GRAND-MÈRE

SERVES 6

This is written proof of the fact that Grand-mère and Momma could prepare all those favorite creamy dishes without a single smidgen of conscience about the consequences. I suppose it was because dinner was in the middle of the day, was the main meal, and everybody had to walk back to work. Le Bistro in the Marc Plaza Hotel in Milwaukee, Wisconsin, serves this quite often, mostly in the winter I'll bet.

6 unpeeled potatoes, cut into 1/8-inch slices
Salt and white pepper
2 cups heavy cream
2 tablespoons Dijon mustard

2 garlic cloves, crushed and finely chopped
1 tablespoon softened butter
1/4 cup grated Parmesan cheese

Preheat oven to 350°F.

Layer sliced potatoes in casserole and season with salt and white pepper.

Combine cream, mustard, garlic, and butter and heat to just under boiling point. Pour cream mixture over potatoes.

Cover and bake 1 hour.

Remove lid and top with Parmesan cheese. Bake 30 minutes longer until cheese is golden brown and potatoes are tender. Serve immediately.

STEAMED CRISP POTATOES

4 new potatoes, thinly sliced
Salt and pepper

1 cup chicken broth
2 tablespoons butter

Arrange potatoes in single layer on bottom of large, heavy skillet. Season with salt and pepper. Pour 3/4 cup chicken broth over all; cover and simmer 10 minutes or until broth is absorbed.

Remove potatoes from skillet. Deglaze pan with remaining chicken broth. Add butter to skillet; return potatoes to skillet. Brown potatoes until crisp.

CHILE PAPA

SERVES 4

You wouldn't believe you could diet on potatoes—but you almost can with this one.

If you're grilling outdoors on a warm day, grill these along with your meat, fowl, or fish. Just allow plenty of time, as the potatoes will require more time than your meat unless it's a large roast beef, pork, or lamb.

4 large baking potatoes, unpeeled and each
    cut lengthwise into 4 slices. Don't cut all
    the way through to bottom.
1 large onion, cut into thin slices

1 4-ounce can whole green chilies sliced into
    2-inch widths
Green chile salsa, mild or picante style
Melted butter

Preheat oven to 400°F.

Place each potato on square of heavy-duty aluminum foil. Insert onion slices and green chile slices between potato slices. Wrap potatoes in foil and seal tightly. Bake 45–60 minutes until tender. Open foil to let potatoes crisp a little the last 15 minutes.

Just before serving, place 1 tablespoon of green chile salsa (which is usually red) and a little melted butter (if you're thin) over potatoes. If you're not thin you won't miss it—and neither will they.

SCALLOPED POTATOES

SERVES 4–6

The mustard makes these scalloped potatoes different from just ordinary scalloped potatoes. You can use half-and-half or even cream, but I've come to believe they are just as good the milky way. I've even done them with a good chicken broth instead of milk and they're delicious. A little extra butter and a sprinkle of Parmesan on top if you go the broth route adds a little something.

This recipe is one of those comfortable side dishes that does not, like a soufflé, have to be served immediately. It will stay warm 20 minutes or so before serving but not much longer. Scalloped potatoes are better hot and bubbly.

PASTA, RICE, POTATOES, AND BEANS

257

6 medium potatoes, peeled or unpeeled,
   thinly sliced
1/4 cup butter
1/4 cup flour
3 cups milk

1 teaspoon salt
1/4 teaspoon pepper
1 medium onion, minced
1/4 cup Dijon mustard
2 tablespoons chopped fresh parsley

Preheat oven to 350°F.

Cover sliced potatoes with cold water until ready to use, then drain and pat dry.

In medium saucepan, melt butter, blend in flour, and cook 2 minutes over low heat. Add milk and cook, stirring constantly, until thickened. Season to taste with salt and pepper. Mix in onion and mustard.

In shallow 2-quart baking dish layer potatoes and sauce, ending with sauce. Top with chopped parsley. Bake 1 1/2 hours or until potatoes are tender.

VARIATION   Instead of onion, use 1 large clove of garlic slivered thin, sprinkled throughout dish.

OLIVER'S POTATOES

SERVES 8–10

Bob Oliver is the Oliver of these potatoes. He's one of our Malibu permanents, and his New Year's Eve dinners are special. He and Hazel make them seem easy. Not all dishes are, but this one is truly simple and simply great.

8 unpeeled baking potatoes, sliced 1/2 inch
   thick
1 cup (2 sticks) sweet butter, melted

2 bunches scallions, cut into 1/4-inch pieces
   including green tops
Coarse salt

Preheat oven to 450°F.

Stand sliced potatoes on end in a casserole and sprinkle with salt. Scatter onions on top and pour melted butter over all. Bake uncovered 30 minutes. Reduce heat to 400° and bake 1 1/2 hours longer.

BAKED SWEET POTATOES AND BANANAS

SERVES 6

Sweet potatoes are a very cooperative, friendly tuber. They will blend with almost any fruit or nut or spice (except maybe Tabasco) and keep their individuality. Christmas and Thanksgiving dinners in Nashville were complete only when mashed sweet potatoes were layered with pineapple chunks and fresh pecans and topped with marshmallows. I love them with brown sugar and butter—baked so they are crisp on the outside and meltingly soft on the inside. Here they are mingling with bananas (maybe I ought to reconsider the Tabasco!).

This is only good the first time around; after that the bananas look yucky, so just this once forget the leftovers. Unless you want to whip the whole thing in a food processor with a couple of eggs, a little cinnamon, 2 tablespoons butter, and 2 tablespoons cream and bake in a piecrust—just a suggestion, mind you, 'cause I can't bear to waste anything.

6 medium-sized sweet potatoes
6 ripe bananas, sliced
1/2 cup butter, softened
Salt and freshly ground white pepper

2/3 cup brown sugar
1/4 cup lemon juice
Scant 1/2 cup pineapple or orange juice

Boil sweet potatoes in their jackets until just done. (Do not overcook or they will become too mushy to slice and layer.)

Let cool, peel, and slice.

Preheat oven to 350°F.

Arrange sweet potatoes and bananas in alternate layers in a well-buttered shallow, rectangular baking dish. Start with potatoes and end with bananas. Dot each layer of potato with butter and sprinkle with salt and pepper. Sprinkle banana layer with brown sugar and a little lemon juice. Dot top with more butter and add pineapple or orange juice. Bake, uncovered, 30 minutes.

GOLDEN SWEET POTATO PUFF   SERVES 6

This comes from a pen friend of many, many years—Mrs. Clark Allen.

Did you know that sweet potatoes are one of the most nutritious tubers grown? The onions and herbs give this dish a most unusual flavor.

3 large sweet potatoes
1/4 cup plus 1 tablespoon butter, softened
1/3 cup orange juice
1/3 cup chopped fresh onions

1/2 teaspoon salt
1/8 teaspoon pepper
1/4 teaspoon dried leaf tarragon
4 eggs, separated

Bake sweet potatoes in 350°F. oven, or cook in boiling water until tender, about 20 minutes. Cool and peel.

Preheat oven to 350°F.

Beat sweet potatoes until smooth. Beat in 1/4 cup butter and orange juice.

In small skillet melt 1 tablespoon butter, add onions and sauté until translucent. Add to sweet potatoes with salt, pepper, and tarragon. Beat in egg yolks.

In large mixing bowl, beat egg whites until stiff but not dry. Spoon a tablespoon of egg white into sweet potato mixture to soften them, then fold in remaining egg whites. Place in buttered 1 1/2-quart baking dish. Bake 50 minutes or until mixture puffs and is lightly browned.

SPECIAL BULGUR PILAF

This is so easy—and if you're not familiar with bulgur, you're in for a treat. Serve it with something that has a good sauce on it—a pot roast, roast chicken or lamb, something that's been simmering in some kind of wonderful juices for a while. Or if you want it with just a simple green salad, bulgur can handle it.

3 tablespoons butter
1 scallion, chopped
1/2 green pepper, chopped
1 stalk celery, chopped
2 tablespoons chopped unpeeled zucchini
1 cup rice
1 cup bulgur (cracked wheat)

Scant teaspoon salt
2 tablespoons chopped parsley
3 mushrooms, chopped
4 cups chicken broth
1/2 teaspoon dill weed
1/4 teaspoon dried oregano
1/2 teaspoon freshly ground black pepper

Melt 2 tablespoons butter in heavy 3-quart saucepan and sauté until just tender all vegetables except mushrooms.

Add rice and bulgur and blend until each grain is coated with butter and mixed in with vegetables. Sprinkle salt over mixture, add remaining ingredients, and let come to a boil.

Cover, lower heat, and let simmer 15–20 minutes. *Do not peek.* Just before serving, add scant tablespoon butter.

KASHA VARNISHKAS

One fine Saturday evening I sang at Brown's Hotel in Loch Sheldrake, New York. The audience was great, the orchestra the same, and I sang like a well-fed bird. Mrs. Lillian Brown and her superb staff saw to that. This was one of my favorites, and Mrs. Lillian sent me the recipe—I have a feeling she's got a million of 'em. I'd have been willing to sample them all, but it was a one-nighter.

1 pound bow-ties (macaroni)
10 tablespoons margarine
1/2 cup flour
Maggi seasoning (optional)
1 pound fresh mushrooms, sliced
1 large onion, chopped

Salt, pepper, and paprika to taste
1 quart hot milk
2 cups kasha
1 egg, slightly beaten
4 cups chicken broth

Cook bow ties in boiling salted water according to package directions; drain and cool.

In skillet over medium heat, melt 8 tablespoons margarine. Add flour and brown very slowly, stirring constantly, until it is a rich light-brown color. You may need Maggi to color your roux.

In separate skillet, while roux is cooking, lightly brown mushrooms and onions in 2 tablespoons margarine.

When roux is golden brown, add mushroom-onion mixture. Add salt, pepper, and paprika. Slowly pour in hot milk, stirring constantly.

Preheat oven to 350°F.

Place kasha in heavy skillet; blend in egg until well mixed. Cook until kasha is well dried and very hot, then carefully add chicken broth and cook slowly until kasha is done (soft).

Mix kasha and bow ties together in casserole. Pour mushroom sauce over all. This can be prepared ahead, in the morning, in three steps—cooking the bow ties, making your sauce, and cooking the kasha—and assembled an hour or so before baking.

Bake 30–40 minutes or until heated through.

FRIJOLES RANCHEROS (SPICY BEANS)

SERVES 4–6

Ethnically we play no favorites in this book. In the vegetables alone, we have Middle Eastern, North American, Chinese, Italian, German, French, East Indian, and here's a little Mexican goody. You've had a lot of great Mexican specialties throughout this book. In Southern California, as well as Texas and other parts of the Southwest, it's kind of an addiction.

1 cup dried red kidney beans
2 cups cold water
1/2 onion, sliced
1 tablespoon shortening or bacon fat
2 cups boiling water
1 1/2 teaspoons salt
1/2 onion, chopped
1 clove garlic, minced

1 tablespoon vegetable oil
1 tomato, peeled, seeded, and chopped
1 jalapeño pepper, seeded and chopped
1 1/2 tablespoons lemon juice
1 teaspoon salt
1/4 teaspoon cinnamon
1/8 teaspoon ground cloves

Wash kidney beans and place in flameproof earthenware pot or heavy kettle with tightly fitting lid. Add cold water and sliced onion and bring to a boil. Add shortening and simmer, covered, over low heat for 30 minutes or until most of liquid is absorbed.

Add boiling water and continue cooking, covered, for 1 hour.

Season beans with salt and continue cooking 5 minutes more or until very soft. Add more boiling water, if necessary; there should be 2 1/2 to 3 cups of beans and a little thick bean liquid.

In skillet, sauté onions and garlic in oil 3–4 minutes until soft. Add tomato, jalapeño pepper, lemon juice, salt, cinnamon, and cloves.

Stir into bean mixture and simmer, covered, 20 minutes.

LIMA POT

This is an old-fashioned dish (old-timey, we said down home). It is nourishing, filling, and economical. I can't resist beans in any form, so I'm probably prejudiced; but it's like a good pot roast, and people forget how satisfying some of the basics can be.

1 1/2 cups dried lima beans	1 pound canned tomatoes, drained
1/2 cup chopped onions	1/2 teaspoon hot pepper sauce, or to taste
1/2 teaspoon salt	3/4 cup fresh bread crumbs
1 cup chopped celery	3/4 cup freshly grated Parmesan cheese
1/4 cup chopped green peppers	4 slices crisply fried bacon, crumbled

Soak limas in cold water to cover 8 hours or overnight. Drain well. Place in large pot, cover with water, and bring to a boil. Add onions and salt. Lower heat and simmer slowly 45 minutes until beans are tender. Drain beans well, reserving 1/4 cup liquid.

Preheat oven to 350°F.

Combine limas, celery, green peppers, tomatoes, reserved lima liquid, and hot pepper sauce in 2 1/2-quart casserole. Top with bread crumbs and grated cheese and bake uncovered 40 minutes.

Sprinkle crumbled bacon on top of casserole before serving.

Chapter 11

VEGETABLES

It's no longer just meat and potatoes. Folks are eating vegetables—but not simply because their parents or mates tell them to. It's because we're beginning to love them and learn how to handle them as skillfully and tastily as any other food. It's the difference between watercolor and oil paintings. The latter's mistakes can be handled with a bit of overpainting. A watercolor has to be right the first time. It takes a lighter touch, a real feel, and a little imagination.

I really don't plan my whole meal until I've shopped those beautiful produce shelves at the market to see what's fresh and new. Experiment with new vegetables. If you've never seen or heard of them before, ask someone who is in there buying them what they're used with and how to cook them.

We have some great combinations and variations on combinations in these pages, as well as some simple, pure, quickly prepared and served ones such as Mollie's Zucchini, Broccoli and Friend with cauliflower, Chinese Jade Broccoli, Wilted Cabbage with Bacon, plus a guaranteed surprise and the Piselli Famiglia Capozzi a few pages farther on. It doesn't use fresh vegetables, but it is one of my pets. Probably because of some peculiarity in my upbringing.

Vegetables don't need a lot of garnishes. They're beautiful unto themselves if properly selected and carefully prepared. Treat them well in cleaning and storing when you get them home. Buy in season for the peak in flavor and the pit in price.

Some of the best restaurants save a lot of time in last-minute preparation by blanching the heavier vegetables—string beans, broccoli, cauliflower, carrots, etc.—ten to twelve seconds in boiling salted water early in the day and setting aside until final serving. You lose nothing in color and flavor and you can save the blanching broth and its vitamins for use in broths and sauces.

ASPARAGUS ORIENTAL

SERVES 6

1 tablespoon sesame seed oil
1 tablespoon Chili Oil
1 pound asparagus, peeled and cut on an
  angle into 1 1/2-inch lengths
1 whole red pepper, cut into 1/2-inch strips
  (if not available, use 1/2 pound cherry to-

matoes)
1/2 teaspoon salt
1 8-ounce can pitted black olives
2 tablespoons oyster sauce
1 tablespoon soy sauce
Sesame seeds for garnish

In large skillet heat sesame seed and Chili Oil. When oil is hot, sauté asparagus 2 minutes. Add red peppers and sauté 1 minute. Add salt.

Add olives just to warm through. Stir in oyster and soy sauce. Sprinkle with sesame seeds.

CHILI OIL

1 pint vegetable oil

4–5 dried red chili peppers

Cook chili peppers in oil until they smoke. Let chilies steep in cooling oil. Store in refrigerator.

ASPARAGUS PIZZA PIE

This is the pie that almost swallowed the house.

I wanted to prepare the yeast dough ahead of time instead of just before the guests came, so I made the dough early the day before, right up through the butter mixture and into the pizza pan, and put it in the freezer. It must have scared the poor thing to death, because after I took it out and followed the rest of the steps it began to rise and rise and rise. I put it in the oven and it rose up over the pizza pan onto the oven racks and floor—almost to the coils. The oven was one big, bubbling, beautiful pizza pie and was it ever good.

I used fresh asparagus (in season), cooked until almost tender. I only tested it once, so I don't know if you'll have the same result—but it's worth any kind of try.

CRUST

1 package (1/4 ounce) active dry yeast
1/2 teaspoon sugar
1 cup warm milk (110°–115°F.)
3 1/2 cups flour

1/2 teaspoon salt
3 eggs
1/2 cup butter, softened

FILLING

1/2 pound soft cheese, sliced (Port Salut, Gruyère, etc.)
2 tablespoons butter
1 package (10 ounces) frozen asparagus, thawed

3 eggs, lightly beaten
1 cup heavy cream
Dash of salt, pepper, and nutmeg
2 limes, thinly sliced

In a warm bowl, proof yeast with sugar in warm milk and let stand 5 minutes or until yeast is dissolved.

In large mixing bowl, place 2 cups flour and salt. Make a well in center and pour in yeast mixture and eggs.

Beat with wooden spoon by hand or with electric mixer, gradually working in flour until you have a stiff but workable dough.

Turn out on floured board and knead 5 minutes or until dough is elastic and smooth. Roll into ball and place in buttered bowl, seam side down, turning to grease dough on all sides. Cover with plastic wrap and large tea towel and place in warm, draft-free place to let rise until doubled in bulk, about 1 1/2 hours.

Keeping dough in bowl, work butter in with fingers, a tablespoon at a time. Pat dough out to line a buttered 14-inch pizza pan, pushing dough up side of pan to form edge. Cover dough with cheese slices, then dot with butter.

Drop asparagus into boiling water for 1 minute, then arrange spoke fashion on cheese.

Mix eggs, cream, salt, pepper and nutmeg; pour over all.

Preheat oven to 400°F.

Garnish top with 6–8 thin slices of lime. Let rise 15 minutes in warm, draft-free place.

Bake 25–30 minutes until custard is set and crust is golden. Cut into wedges. Serve at once with wedge of lime.

BROCCOLI AND FRIEND

This lovely vegetable is so available and lends itself to so many variations that it is unlikely it will suffer the fate of the little, ever available string bean. Here are just a few broccoli dishes that can make your simple dinner look like a party.

1 bunch broccoli	1/2 teaspoon dried tarragon
1 head cauliflower	Salt and pepper to taste
4 tablespoons butter or margarine	Dash of nutmeg
1/2 cup fresh bread crumbs	2 tablespoons pimiento strips

Wash and trim broccoli, cut off and peel stems, and cut into julienne strips. Break flowerets into even pieces. Wash and core cauliflower and cut into flowerets approximately same size as broccoli.

Plunge broccoli stems into boiling salted water for 1 minute to blanch; add flowerets and blanch until tender and very bright green—about 2 minutes; don't overcook. Remove to colander. (I use sieve of a deep-fat fryer for this so that it can be removed quickly; removing with slotted spoon may let some of it cook too long.)

Return water to boiling and repeat process with cauliflower. It will have to cook a little longer (3–4 minutes). Again, don't overcook; when underpart is almost tender, remove to colander with broccoli.

In large skillet, melt butter and allow to brown a little but not burn. Add bread crumbs and tarragon and allow to cook about 1 minute over medium heat. Toss in broccoli and cauliflower, salt, pepper, nutmeg, and pimiento strips. Lift and stir gently to coat thoroughly. Taste for seasoning, correct if necessary. Turn into warmed platter or bowl.

BROCCOLI AND MORE FRIENDS

1 large bunch broccoli, broken into flowerets	1/4 cup grated Parmesan cheese
1 large head cauliflower, broken into flowerets	1/4 cup Dijon mustard
	1/2 teaspoon salt
2 tablespoons butter	1/4 teaspoon pepper
2 tablespoons flour	3/4 cup fresh bread crumbs
1 cup milk	1 tablespoon butter, melted
1 cup grated Cheddar cheese	1/4 cup slivered roasted almonds

Preheat oven to 350°F.

Cook broccoli and cauliflower in boiling salted water until just tender, 2–3 minutes. Drain. Place in 2-quart casserole.

In medium saucepan, melt butter, blend in flour, and cook 2 minutes over low heat. Stir in milk. Cook, stirring constantly, until thickened. Mix in cheeses and mustard. Add salt and pepper. Taste for seasoning.

Pour cheese sauce over vegetables. Mix bread crumbs and melted butter and sprinkle over cheese sauce. Top with almonds. Bake 15 minutes or until bubbly.

VARIATION

3 slices bread including crusts	3 tablespoons butter or margarine
1/2 cup grated Cheddar cheese	1/4 teaspoon red pepper flakes
3 large tomatoes, sliced	

In food processor, using metal blade, process bread and Cheddar cheese until fine and well mixed.

Line bottom of baking dish with layer of sliced tomatoes.

Add half of broccoli and cauliflower and sprinkle with 1/3 of cheese-bread crumb mixture; dot with half of butter. Sprinkle red pepper flakes over all. Add remaining broccoli and cauliflower. Cover with remaining crumb-cheese mixture; dot with remaining butter. Bake at 350°F. until warmed through and cheese is melted and bubbling.

STILL ANOTHER VARIATION

To the original recipe, add 1/2 pound Brussels sprouts, cooked until just tender.

CHINESE JADE BROCCOLI   SERVES 4

This is bright green in color, aromatic and spicy. It is basically a side dish, but is so delicious it shouldn't be relegated to those seven-course Chinese banquets. It's a great first course or side dish for a simple, unsauced main course like broiled chicken, steak, lamb chops, or fish.

1 pound fresh broccoli, stems peeled and cut into finger-sized pieces, flowerets separated into bite-sized pieces	quarter
	3 cloves garlic, peeled and crushed
3 tablespoons peanut oil	Sauce
2 slices fresh ginger root, about the size of a	1 teaspoon cornstarch dissolved in 2 tablespoons water

SAUCE

2 tablespoons light soy sauce	1 teaspoon sesame seed oil
2 tablespoons dark soy sauce	1/4 cup Chinese rice wine or dry sherry
2 tablespoons brown sugar	

Combine all ingredients and set aside.

Blanch broccoli stems first, by plunging into boiling water for 30 seconds. Add flowerets and blanch another 30 seconds. Remove to colander and run cold water over broccoli to stop cooking.

Heat wok over high heat. Add oil. When oil is hot, brown ginger and garlic. When essence is released, remove from oil and discard. Add blanched broccoli to hot oil. Stir in sauce and mix well. Cover and cook 20 seconds.

Stir in dissolved cornstarch and cook 15 seconds, stir-frying and scooping gently and continuously from bottom. Place on warmed serving platter and serve hot.

MARINATED BROCCOLI GREEK STYLE   SERVES 6

MARINADE

2 cups chicken broth
3/4 cup dry white wine
3/4 cup olive oil
1/2 cup lemon juice
4 sprigs parsley

1 clove garlic, finely chopped
1/2 teaspoon dried thyme
8 crushed peppercorns
1 teaspoon salt

Stir all marinade ingredients in enamel or stainless-steel pan and bring to boil. Lower heat and simmer 45 minutes. Strain.

3 pounds fresh broccoli, stalks peeled, cut in
    half lengthwise through flowerets
1 lemon, thinly sliced

1 or 2 hard-cooked eggs, chopped
1 2-ounce jar pimiento pieces
Anchovies

In large pot, bring strained marinade to boil, add broccoli, and cook 10–12 minutes until just tender.

Place broccoli in shallow glass dish, pour marinade over, cover with foil, and chill at least 4 hours or overnight—the longer the better.

To serve, arrange broccoli attractively on serving platter. Pour a little marinade over all and garnish with thin lemon slices, chopped egg and pimiento pieces, and an anchovy strip or two.

SICILIAN BROCCOLI   SERVES 4–6

1 large bunch broccoli (approximately 2
    pounds)
2 tablespoons butter
3 tablespoons finely chopped shallots or
    scallions including tops
1 clove garlic, finely minced
1 tablespoon flour

1 cup chicken stock
4 anchovies, finely chopped
1/2 cup sliced black olives, preferably im-
    ported
Freshly ground black pepper
2 cups shredded mozzarella cheese

Wash broccoli carefully. Remove leaves; peel stems and cut to shorten. Cut length-wise through stems to flowerets into 2-inch pieces, drop in boiling salted water to cover, and cook until just tender.

While broccoli cooks, melt butter in saucepan; add shallots and garlic. Cook, stirring, about 3 minutes. Do not brown.

Sprinkle with flour and add stock, stirring vigorously with wire whisk. When mixture is thickened, continue to simmer over low heat for 5 minutes.

Add anchovies, olives, pepper to taste, and cheese; stir until cheese melts. Serve over hot, well-drained broccoli.

CABBAGE BÉCHAMEL

Cinderella cabbage dresses up for the party. I didn't think it could be done but Jackie Desmarais did. Here's her creamy, smooth beauty that helped make me a believer.

There are good things that have happened in my relationship with my onetime anathema, cabbage. Several appear in this chapter and there's one that is simply so special I'd set it to music if I thought it would work in concert. Try the Shrimp and Cabbage with Caviar, on page 51 in the Openers chapter. If it inspires a melody we'll share the royalties on our hit. I'll let Swifty Lazar handle my deal. He was one of the first to taste this one at dinner one night, and was convinced it had a world market just waiting out there breathlessly.

SAUCE

4 tablespoons butter
1/2 onion, finely chopped
1 stalk celery, finely chopped
3 tablespoons flour
3 cups hot milk
Salt to taste

2 ounces uncooked veal or ham *or* 1 ounce
   of each, finely chopped
1/2 bay leaf
1 small sprig thyme
White pepper
Freshly grated nutmeg

In double boiler, melt 3 tablespoons butter and cook onions and celery until onions are transparent. Add flour, stirring constantly. Cook for 2 or 3 minutes, then add hot milk and salt.

In another small saucepan, simmer veal or ham in 1 tablespoon butter over low heat. Season with bay leaf, thyme, and pepper to taste. Cook only 5 minutes so as not to brown meat. Add this mixture to white sauce and cook in double boiler 20–25 minutes, stirring occasionally.

Add nutmeg about 10 minutes before serving. Strain sauce, pressing on meat to extract all juices.

If you reheat sauce, be sure to reheat very slowly and gradually. It does not have to be very hot, as dish will be placed under broiler.

CABBAGE

1 large head green cabbage, cut into julienned strips
1/4 pound (1 stick) butter

Freshly grated Parmesan cheese
Freshly grated nutmeg

Place cabbage in ice water for 30 minutes. Drain and dry carefully in a tea towel.

In large skillet, melt butter and add cabbage, stirring gently until just tender—no longer. Remove from heat. All of this can be done ahead of time, but it's better to assemble just before serving.

Line heatproof casserole or gratinée dish with layer of cabbage and then cover with sauce. Repeat until casserole is filled, finishing with sauce. Add layer of Parmesan cheese. Sprinkle nutmeg over top and place under broiler until cheese is brown.

RED CABBAGE WITH APPLES

SERVES 4

Everybody has a favorite red cabbage and apple recipe. I must have tried ten before I hit on this one. It's a lovely balance of sweet, sour, and crunch.

1/2 cup cider vinegar
2 tablespoons brown sugar
1/4 teaspoon nutmeg
1 teaspoon salt
2 tablespoons lemon juice
1 small head of red cabbage, washed, cored,

and shredded
1 onion, finely chopped
3 small apples, chopped
2 tablespoons butter
1 cup boiling water

Mix vinegar, brown sugar, nutmeg, salt, and lemon juice and pour over shredded cabbage.

In a large saucepan sauté onions and apples in butter until transparent—don't brown. Cook about 5 minutes, stirring frequently. Add cabbage mixture and pour boiling water over all. Let come to boil again, reduce heat, and cook 1 1/2 hours or until done. Check from time to time to be sure cabbage is not too dry; add 1 or 2 tablespoons of boiling water if needed. It shouldn't be soupy.

WILTED CABBAGE WITH BACON

SERVES 4

I always had this thing about cabbage. Maybe it's because the pungent smell of cabbage permeated the whole house in early cooking stages; but with the era of fans and ventilation, it's a whole new story. This is a particularly delectable way to serve my new best friend.

10 strips of bacon
1 large head green cabbage, washed, cored,
  and finely shredded

1/2 cup heavy cream
Salt and pepper
1 tablespoon lemon juice or to taste

In a skillet, cook bacon until crisp. Drain in paper towel. When cool, crumble.

Pour off all but 2 tablespoons of fat, add cabbage and sauté 5 minutes until just wilted. Stir in heavy cream. Salt and pepper to taste and cook 2 minutes, stirring gently. Add lemon juice, transfer cabbage to a very warm serving bowl, and sprinkle reserved bacon over it.

BRAISED CARROTS IN DILLED CREAM

SERVES 6

Start this one the day before. The Crème Fraîche, which is really so good with it, takes time to set and gather itself. There are several Crème Fraîche variations; this one is easier than most. You would have to send to France for the real thing.

3 tablespoons unsalted butter
8–10 medium carrots (1 pound), peeled and
  cut into 1 1/2-inch matchsticks
1/2 teaspoon sugar
Pinch of salt
Freshly ground white pepper

2–3 tablespoons chicken stock
Sprig of fresh thyme or a pinch of dried
  thyme
3/4 cup Crème Fraîche
3 tablespoons minced fresh dill

Melt butter in 10-inch skillet over moderate heat. Add carrots, sugar, salt, and a good grinding of white pepper. Sauté carrots, stirring, 1–2 minutes until they begin to brown.

Add stock, lower heat, and bury thyme in carrots. Cover skillet and simmer carrots until just tender, about 5 minutes.

Uncover skillet, raise heat to moderate, and cook until liquid is reduced and glazes bottom of pan.

Stir in Crème Fraîche and boil down liquid, stirring occasionally, until it thickens and coats carrots. Correct seasoning and stir in minced dill.

CRÈME FRAÎCHE

MAKES 3/4 CUP

1/2 cup heavy cream

1/4 cup sour cream

Put sour cream in 1-quart mixing bowl. Gradually whisk in heavy cream until it is blended with sour cream. Cover with plastic wrap and let stand at room temperature 8–24 hours or until mixture has thickened.

CARROTS WITH GINGER, GARLIC, AND CUMIN

SERVES 4

This has an Asian feel to it and could be served with either an Oriental or Occidental meal, but with plain broiled chicken and a smooth starch like mashed potatoes or steamed rice, it's a bit of a kicker.

1 tablespoon peeled and chopped ginger root
1 tablespoon chopped garlic
2 tablespoons water
1 1/2 tablespoons olive oil
2 teaspoons cumin seed

1 pound carrots, cut into 2 × 1/4-inch julienne strips
1/2 cup water
2 tablespoons lemon juice
Salt and pepper

In food processor or in blender, puree ginger root and garlic; with motor running, add 2 tablespoons water and blend until smooth.

In stainless-steel or enamel skillet, heat olive oil over moderately high heat until hot. Add cumin seed and sauté 30 seconds or until fragrance is released. Add ginger-garlic puree and cook mixture over moderate heat, stirring, for 1 minute.

Add carrots and cook mixture, stirring, for 3 minutes until the carrots are thoroughly coated with spice mixture.

Add water and lemon juice, cover immediately and simmer, stirring occasionally. If necessary, add more water, 1 tablespoon at a time, to keep carrots from sticking, for about 10 minutes or until carrots are just tender. Add salt and pepper to taste; raise heat to moderate and cook mixture, stirring gently, until liquid has evaporated. Transfer carrots to heated serving dish and serve immediately.

BAKED CAULIFLOWER WITH HERB SAUCE

SERVES 6

Don't let anybody tell you they won't touch cauliflower until they've tasted this one.

1 large head cauliflower *or* 2 small, cut into flowerets	1 tablespoon butter
	1/4 teaspoon salt
Salt	1/4 teaspoon white pepper
1 cup milk for each 3 quarts of boiling water (to keep cauliflower white)	Pinch of nutmeg
	1/2 cup grated Swiss cheese
Salad oil	5 eggs
1 cup stale white bread crumbs or English muffin crumbs	1 cup milk, scalded with 1/4 cup butter
	Herb Sauce
1/2 cup finely chopped onions	

In large kettle, bring to rapid boil enough water to cover cauliflowerets. Salt to taste and add milk. Drop cauliflowerets into rapidly boiling water and bring back to a boil as quickly as possible. Boil, uncovered, 9–12 minutes. Don't overcook. Cauliflowerets are done when knife easily pierces stems. With skimmer or slotted spoon, carefully remove cauliflowerets when done, and drain in colander. Set aside.

Preheat oven to 325°F.

Oil 1 1/2-quart soufflé dish or 6 individual molds with salad oil. Dust with 1/3 cup bread crumbs, covering entire surface. Knock out excess crumbs. Set aside.

In covered saucepan, cook onions in butter slowly until just translucent, not allowing them to color. Transfer to mixing bowl. Stir in salt, pepper, and nutmeg. Add cheese and remaining bread crumbs. Beat in eggs. Add hot milk-butter mixture in a thin stream, beating constantly. Fold cauliflowerets into custard mixture. Taste for seasoning. (May be prepared in advance up to this point.)

Spoon custard into prepared soufflé dish or molds and set in a shallow pan of boiling water. Place in lower third of oven and bake 35–40 minutes, regulating heat so water remains just below boiling point. Custard is done when knife inserted in center comes out clean (small individual molds will need only 17–20 minutes).

Remove soufflé dish or molds from water and allow to settle 5 minutes. Run knife around edge of custard and reverse on warm serving platter. Surround with Herb Sauce. Serve immediately.

NOTE If custard is not served immediately, do not unmold but leave in pan of hot water, adding a little boiling water from time to time if necessary. Unmold when ready to serve.

HERB SAUCE

2 tablespoons butter
3 tablespoons flour
2 cups milk and 1/4 teaspoon salt, heated to boiling point
Salt and white pepper to taste
1 cup dry white wine *or* 2/3 cup dry white vermouth

4 tablespoons minced fresh chervil, tarragon, and parsley, mixed, *or* 2 tablespoons mixed dried herbs
2 tablespoons minced shallots or scallions
4 tablespoons minced fresh chervil, tarragon, and parsley, mixed, *or* just minced parsley
1–2 tablespoons softened butter

In heavy saucepan melt butter over low heat. Blend in flour and cook slowly, stirring, until butter and flour are well blended. Remove from heat.

Slowly add hot milk, beating vigorously with whisk to blend thoroughly. Set saucepan over moderately high heat and stir with whisk until sauce comes to boil. Boil 1 minute, stirring constantly. Remove from heat, taste, and add white pepper and salt if necessary. Set aside.

In small saucepan combine wine, minced fresh herbs or dried herbs, and shallots or scallions; boil slowly 10 minutes, allowing mixture to reduce to about 3 tablespoons. Watch carefully so it doesn't boil away.

Strain herb-wine mixture into white sauce, pressing juice out of herbs. Simmer 2–3 minutes, then remove from heat.

Just before serving, stir in 4 tablespoons fresh herbs or parsley and softened butter.

SPICY CAULIFLOWER AND POTATOES   SERVES 4

Shakira (Mrs. Michael) Caine is one of the most beautiful vegetarians walking around today. One evening a group of us were at Sue Mengers' for dinner having a rich, succulent roast something or other, and the cook brought in this entrée for Shakira. I could turn vegetarian if I thought it all tasted like this and I would end up looking like Shakira.

2 tablespoons oil
1 clove garlic, minced
1 teaspoon minced fresh ginger root
1 chopped scallion *or* 1 tablespoon minced onion
3/4 teaspoon turmeric
1/4 teaspoon cayenne pepper

1 head cauliflower, flowerets separated and cut in half
1 large potato, peeled and cut into thick french-fry shapes
1/2 cup chicken broth
Salt to taste

Heat oil in large skillet with lid and sauté garlic, ginger, and scallion or onion until garlic and ginger fragrance is released and onion is just translucent.

Add turmeric, cayenne, then cauliflowerets and potatoes. Mix well and gently. Cover and cook slowly about 5 minutes, shaking frequently to prevent sticking.

When vegetables begin to dry, add broth, 1/4 cup at a time. Continue cooking, shaking frequently to prevent sticking, until potatoes and cauliflowerets are tender. Add salt. Taste for seasoning. Serve hot.

BRAISED CELERY WITH PUREE OF MUSHROOMS

SERVES 4

Celery is almost always available and plentiful, thank heaven. Usually it's used to accompany or bolster some other dish. Here's a nice way to give celery its own solo on the bill of fare.

4 hearts of celery	1 pound fresh mushrooms
1 cup chicken stock	2 tablespoons minced shallots
4 tablespoons butter (softened)	Pinch of nutmeg
1 1/4 teaspoons salt	2/3 cup cream
1/4 teaspoon white pepper	

Remove outer leaves from hearts of celery. Cut each heart lengthwise into 4 sections.

Arrange celery in flameproof serving casserole; add chicken stock and 3 tablespoons butter. Sprinkle with 1/2 teaspoon salt and 1/8 teaspoon white pepper. Bring to boil, cover and braise over low heat 20 minutes until tender. Drain off all but 1/4 cup liquid.

While celery is cooking, mince mushrooms in food processor (do not puree). Sauté shallots in 1 tablespoon butter, add mushrooms, and cook over low heat 10 minutes or until moisture in mushrooms has cooked away. Stir occasionally.

Sprinkle with 3/4 teaspoon salt, 1/8 teaspoon pepper, and nutmeg. Add cream and cook over low heat 5 minutes, stirring frequently. Pour over hot braised celery. Serve hot in casserole in which celery was cooked.

CORN PUDDING

SERVES 6–8

3 tablespoons butter	Salt, pepper, and cayenne pepper to taste
2 generous cups fresh corn cut from cob (8 medium ears), *or* 2 boxes frozen corn, thawed and drained	2 tablespoons sugar
	1 1/2 cups scalded milk or cream
	3 eggs, separated

Preheat oven to 375°F.

In large skillet, melt butter, add corn, and sauté about 5 minutes. Add salt, pepper, and cayenne to taste and then sugar. Add milk or cream. Cover and heat through. Let cool.

Beat egg whites until stiff but not dry. In separate bowl, beat yolks until thick and lemon-colored. Gradually add yolks to cooled corn mixture, stirring constantly. Carefully fold in egg whites.

Pour into greased 1 1/2-quart soufflé dish and bake 1 hour.

CORN AND TOMATO STEW

SERVES 6–8

This is a true summer Southern dish, but I'm easy if you want to do it in the winter. Just use frozen corn and, after you combine the two mixtures, reduce the simmering time to 2 minutes.

1/4 cup bacon or chicken fat
2 onions, minced
1 green pepper, minced
1 clove garlic, minced
4 cups fresh corn (16–18 medium ears)
2 large fresh tomatoes, peeled and chopped

with their juice
1/4 cup chicken broth
1/2 teaspoon sugar
Salt and pepper to taste
Cayenne pepper to taste

Heat bacon or chicken fat in large skillet. Sauté onions, green peppers, and garlic until soft; add corn.

Simmer tomatoes in chicken broth with sugar until blended. Salt and pepper to taste and add to onion-green pepper mixture. Bring liquid to boil over moderate heat and simmer, covered, 5 minutes until corn is just tender.

HOT AND SOUR CUCUMBERS
SERVES 4

2 firm slender cucumbers, unpeeled and
   preferably unwaxed (a little over a pound)
1 tablespoon light soy sauce
2 tablespoons sugar
1/2 teaspoon salt

3 tablespoons oil
1 large clove garlic, peeled and lightly
   crushed
2–4 dried chili peppers
2 tablespoons white vinegar

Wash and dry cucumbers; trim off ends and cut in half lengthwise. Remove seeds with a small spoon and cut each half to make 4 strips, then crosswise. Set aside.

Have ready soy sauce in one cup; in another cup, combine sugar and salt.

Heat skillet or wok over high heat until hot; add oil and lower heat. Add garlic and chili peppers (2 for mild dish; 4 for hot) and press them against pan with spatula. Stir-fry until garlic is light brown and peppers have darkened. Turn heat high, add cucumbers, and stir immediately in fast, sweeping turns to tumble and roll in hot oil—about 25 seconds, or until skin is bright green.

Sprinkle in soy sauce and scatter sugar-salt mixture over top. Stir-fry briskly from bottom for 5 seconds to blend all ingredients thoroughly and to melt but not darken sugar. Pour immediately into bowl. Let cucumbers cool, cover, and then refrigerate until thoroughly chilled, stirring a few times for even marinating.

With slotted spoon, remove cucumber from marinade and place on serving dish. Add vinegar, toss to mix well, and serve.

BAKED EGGPLANT WITH TOMATO SAUCE
SERVES 6–8

There are more than two ways to prepare this dish. This is the low-calorie way and quite delicious. If anyone in your family has suddenly turned vegetarian on you, this is a perfect main dish. The other, slightly more caloric, way is to sauté the eggplant in oil before assembling. For still another, see Joe's Mother's Rolled Stuffed Eggplant (page 278). I love them all!

1 eggplant, peeled and sliced 1/4 inch thick   may need less)

2 tablespoons olive oil or vegetable oil (you   Salt and pepper to taste

Soak eggplant in salted cold water 30 minutes or more (a plate weighted with a full can on top will hold slices under water). Remove from water and pat dry.

Brush small amount of oil over surface of each slice. Salt and pepper lightly. Place under preheated broiler and broil on each side until lightly browned.

TOMATO SAUCE

1/3 onion, finely chopped

1 stalk celery, finely chopped

2 tablespoons finely chopped green pepper

1 clove garlic, finely chopped

1 tablespoon olive oil

1 16-ounce can of whole tomatoes, pureed in blender

1 bay leaf

1 tablespoon fresh oregano *or* 1 1/2 teaspoons dried

1 tablespoon fresh basil *or* 1 1/2 teaspoons dried

1 tablespoon finely chopped fresh parsley

Salt and pepper to taste

Sauté onions, celery, green peppers, and garlic in oil until soft. Add tomatoes, bay leaf, oregano, and basil. Let come to full boil over high heat. Add parsley and salt and pepper to taste. Reduce heat and let simmer until well blended and thickened. Remove bay leaf.

8 ounces mozzarella cheese, sliced   1/2 cup freshly grated Parmesan cheese

ASSEMBLY

Preheat oven to 350°F.

Cover bottom of 9 × 13-inch baking dish with small amount of Tomato Sauce. Place eggplant slices on top of Tomato Sauce. Place slices of mozzarella over eggplant, reserving a few thin slices. Pour remaining Tomato Sauce over all and top with thin slices of mozzarella. Sprinkle Parmesan cheese over all and bake 30–40 minutes until done. Serve hot.

EGGPLANT RELISH

MAKES ABOUT 2 CUPS

1 1-pound eggplant, peeled

2 teaspoons salt

1/2 cup soy sauce

1 tablespoon sake or dry sherry

1 tablespoon sugar

1 piece ginger root 2 × 1 × 1/8 inches, finely shredded

Cut eggplant into 1 × 1/4-inch strips. Place in colander set over bowl; toss with salt. Let eggplant drain 2–3 hours or overnight; pat dry with paper towels.

In glass jar with a tightly fitting lid, combine eggplant, soy sauce, sake or sherry, sugar, and ginger. Cover jar and shake to combine ingredients. Let mixture marinate in refrigerator overnight. It will keep for a couple of weeks.

BAKED TOMATO-STUFFED EGGPLANT   SERVES 8

Try this one. The look of it, the flavor, and the fact that it's easy and fun to do make it a must.

3 tablespoons olive oil
2 cups thinly sliced onions
3 cloves garlic, minced
Salt and pepper
8 Chinese eggplants *or* the smallest you can find

8 small tomatoes, cut into 4 slices
1/4 cup oil
Italian parsley *or* fresh basil, minced
Italian parsley sprigs *or* fresh basil for garnish

Preheat oven to 400°F.

Oil shallow baking dish with olive oil, distribute onions and garlic over bottom, and sprinkle with salt and pepper.

Starting just below stem, make four lengthwise cuts in each unpeeled eggplant, leaving cut slices attached to stem. Place one slice of tomato in each cut.

Arrange eggplants in dish, spreading slices slightly apart, and pour oil over all. Sprinkle with Italian parsley or fresh basil, and salt and pepper to taste.

Bake, covered, for 15 minutes, then uncover and bake 15 minutes more until vegetables are soft. Let eggplants cool to room temperature and serve garnished with sprigs of Italian parsley or fresh basil.

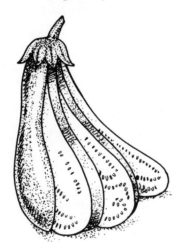

Starting just below stem, make four lengthwise cuts into each Chinese eggplant.

EGGPLANT-ZUCCHINI SOUFFLÉ   SERVES 12–16

This is a party dish. It's beautiful when unmolded—but much more than that, it's absolutely delicious. I first tasted it when Jeremiah Tower served it in Napa Valley. This is close (and maybe a cigar!). It's a few more steps than most dishes, but well worth it—remember, it's a party.

3 large eggplants
Olive oil
1 cup flour
8 eggs
1/2 cup freshly grated Parmesan cheese
1/2 cup (1 stick) butter
4 pounds zucchini, coarsely shredded, salted, placed in colander to drain, and tightly squeezed in tea towel to dry completely
Salt and freshly ground black pepper
1 1/2 cups ricotta cheese
1/2 cup mixed Parmesan and Gruyère cheese, freshly grated
3 tablespoons finely chopped fresh marjoram *or* 1 1/2 tablespoons dried

Carefully peel eggplants as uniformly as you can, so that skins will be about 1/4 inch thick with some of eggplant meat attached. This is for lining your mold. Slice remaining eggplant lengthwise 1/4 inch thick.

Fry all slices of eggplant in olive oil over medium heat about 10 minutes until tender. Lightly coat inner slices with flour, then dip in mixture of 2 eggs beaten with 1/2 cup grated Parmesan cheese and fry them again. Let drain on paper towels and cool.

Generously butter (you'll need almost 1/2 stick for this) 4-quart round-bottomed casserole or two 2-quart soufflé dishes.

Line mold or soufflé dishes with outer slices of eggplant, starting by putting circle of eggplant in center. Lay three quarters of remaining slices in an overlapping radial pattern so that they completely cover bottom and sides of mold.

PREPARING THE STUFFING

Preheat oven to 375°F.

Salt and pepper zucchini. Heat 1/2 stick butter in large skillet and sauté zucchini over medium heat 6–8 minutes, tossing often and spreading mass out again and again with spoon until lightly colored.

Let cool and mix well with ricotta cheese and mixed Parmesan and Gruyère. Taste for seasoning; add 6 well-beaten eggs and marjoram. Mix well. Fill lined mold with zucchini-cheese stuffing and arrange remaining eggplant slices in overlapping slices on top. Cover dish and bake 30 minutes.

Remove mold from oven and let sit 15 minutes in a warm place. If soufflé is still wobbly, leave it in dish until it sets more. Then unmold onto a large round platter. Jeremiah recommends serving with Fresh Tomato Basil Sauce (page 4) or a light tomato sauce. Or serve at room temperature with fresh olive oil sprinkled over it. It really doesn't need anything!

JOE'S MOTHER'S ROLLED STUFFED EGGPLANT
SERVES 4

I've said many times, you never know where you'll find some wonderful, unusual way of turning an old familiar into a brand-new treat. Joe Acquafreda has a security service in Palm Springs. He's very helpful to us during our Nabisco–Dinah Shore Invitational golf tournament each year at Mission Hills Country Club in Rancho Mirage. One day during the tournament, Joe's assignment was to handle the golf cart with my clubs on it to be sure I didn't run over somebody, into the lake, onto the greens, or over somebody's ball. We started talking food and he promised to have his mother, Mary, send me her special way with eggplant and Parmesan cheese. She did. In her letter, with explicit hand-written instructions, she kept referring to the gravy. I kept reading it over to see if a page was missing. The "gravy" was the tomato sauce. It's better than Joe said it was—and he was practically licking his chops just describing it to me.

1 large eggplant, about 1 1/2 pounds
1 cup flour
9 eggs
1/4 cup mixed coarsely grated Parmesan and Romano cheese
Salt and pepper to taste
Oil
1/2 pound (1 cup) mozzarella cheese, coarsely grated
1/4 pound (1/2 cup) Parmesan cheese, coarsely grated
1/4 cup fine bread crumbs
2 to 2 1/2 cups Italian Tomato Sauce (page 248)
3/4 cup mixed coarsely grated mozzarella and Parmesan cheese

Peel eggplant and slice about 1/8 inch thick. Set slices upright in colander and sprinkle liberally with salt. Let stand at least 30 minutes. Dry eggplant slices well. Place flour in shallow bowl and flour each slice. Set aside.

In bowl, beat 3 eggs lightly. Add 1/4 cup mixed Parmesan and Romano cheese and sprinkle of salt and pepper. Add enough oil to a skillet to come 1 inch up sides. Heat until oil is hot. Dip eggplant slices into egg-cheese mixture and fry slices until golden brown, not stiff. Drain on paper towels.

In large bowl, beat remaining 6 eggs with 1/2 pound mozzarella cheese and 1/4 pound Parmesan cheese. Add bread crumbs and a sprinkle of salt and pepper. Place some of mixture on top of each eggplant slice and roll up jelly-roll fashion.

Preheat oven to 350°F.

Line bottom of buttered 8 1/2 × 11-inch casserole with tomato sauce and place rolled eggplant slices one after the other in casserole. Pour Italian Tomato Sauce over eggplant slices. Sprinkle 3/4 cup mixed mozzarella and Parmesan cheese over top. Bake 35–45 minutes until top is golden brown.

SPICY EGGPLANT

SERVES 4–6

An Oriental vegetable variation—it's great either hot or cold. Make a lot and serve it hot for dinner, then cold the next day for lunch.

1 pound eggplant
4 tablespoons oil
1/4 cup chicken stock (if needed)
2 cloves garlic, minced
1 1/2 teaspoons minced ginger root
2 scallions, finely chopped
1/4 pound ground pork
2 tablespoons dark soy sauce
1 teaspoon red wine vinegar
1/2 teaspoon sugar
2 teaspoons chili paste with garlic
1/4 cup chicken stock
1 teaspoon sesame seed oil

Slice unpeeled eggplant diagonally, if using the Chinese variety. If using American eggplant, peel and cut into thick 1/2-inch strips. Heat 2 tablespoons oil in wok. Stir-fry eggplant 5 minutes until almost soft. (If wok becomes dry and eggplant begins to stick, add 1/4 cup chicken broth.) Cover and steam until soft, 3–4 minutes. Lift eggplant from wok and place on paper towels.

Turn off wok and clean with paper towels. Reheat wok and heat 2 tablespoons oil. Stir-fry garlic, ginger, and half of scallions on low heat until aroma is released, about 30 seconds. Add pork; turn heat to high. Stir-fry until pork is no longer pink.

Mix together soy sauce, vinegar, sugar, and chili paste with garlic. Add to wok and stir-fry 30 seconds. Add eggplant, remaining scallions, and chicken stock. Cook 3 minutes. Stir in sesame seed oil.

A RATATOUILLE

SERVES 6–8

This is not only party-pretty but marvelously delicious. It can be done ahead—each vegetable separated until that moment when you finally assemble the whole wonderful concoction. Season it generously, that's important.

2 medium carrots slant-cut in 1/4-inch pieces
1/2 pound young string beans slant-cut in 1/4-inch pieces
3 tablespoons butter
2 tablespoons vegetable oil
2 cloves garlic
1 medium onion, peeled and thinly sliced
1 small eggplant, peeled and slant-cut in 1/4-inch pieces

2 medium zucchini slant-cut in 1/4-inch pieces
2 medium summer squash slant-cut in 1/4-inch pieces
1 medium green pepper cut in 1/2-inch pieces
1/2 cup fresh corn
2 medium tomatoes, sliced
1/4 cup bread crumbs
Salt and pepper

Blanch the carrots, then the string beans in boiling salted water 30 seconds. Set aside in separate bowls.

Heat 1 tablespoon oil with 1 tablespoon butter and add 2 whole cloves of garlic (don't let the garlic brown—just let it flavor the oils).

Sauté each of the vegetables separately beginning with the onions, then eggplant, zucchini, squash, green pepper, carrots, string beans, corn. (Add a little more oil and butter as needed, just enough to flavor each vegetable.) Save 1 tablespoon butter for dotting top of the Ratatouille. After each vegetable has been sautéed, drain and place in separate piles (discarding the garlic). It can all be done ahead up to this point.

Preheat oven to 350°F. Take a pretty, oblong shallow baking and serving dish and line it with eggplant. Salt and pepper, then layer in overlapping rows: carrots, zucchini, squash, green pepper, string beans. Season each vegetable generously with salt and pepper. Add a row of tomatoes slightly overlapping the other layers. Place two neat rows of corn the length of the dish. Sprinkle the onion rings and bread crumbs over all the vegetables. Dot with butter.

Bake 20 minutes before serving to heat through and blend the flavors.

DRY SAUTÉED GREEN BEANS
YUNNAN YUAN SERVES 2–3 AS MAIN DISH, 4–6 AS PART OF FULL DINNER

A beautiful, spicy Chinese vegetable that will give a lift to your everyday simple All-American dinner or do the same to your favorite Chinese menu.

3/4 pound young green beans, trimmed
1 3/4 cups oil for deep-frying
1 tablespoon chicken broth
1 tablespoon minced scallions
1 teaspoon crushed and minced garlic
1 teaspoon fresh peeled and minced ginger
  root
1/2 teaspoon hot chili paste
1/2 teaspoon sesame seed oil

2 teaspoons soy sauce
1 teaspoon vinegar
1/2 teaspoon salt
Pinch of sugar
1/2 teaspoon peanut oil
2 tablespoons ground pork
2 tablespoons minced preserved Szechwan
  vegetable (available in Oriental markets)

Rinse green beans under running cold water and dry thoroughly with paper towels.

Pour oil into deep fryer or wok to a depth of 3 inches and heat to 375°F. Fry beans in 2 batches 1 minute until skins are wrinkled. With skimmer or slotted spoon transfer to paper towels to drain.

In small bowl combine chicken broth, scallions, garlic, ginger, chili paste, sesame seed oil, soy sauce, vinegar, salt, and sugar and stir until well combined. Recipe may be done ahead of time up to this point.

Heat wok or deep heavy skillet over high heat until hot. Add peanut oil and heat until oil is hot. Add pork and Szechwan vegetable and stir-fry mixture 30–45 seconds until pork is no longer pink. Add beans and stir-fry 30 seconds.

Mash beans lightly with back of metal spatula, add sauce, and stir-fry 30 seconds. Taste for seasoning. You may need more soy sauce and chili paste. Transfer mixture to heated platter to serve.

GREEN BEANS WITH NUTMEG SERVES 4–5

When I was growing up I thought string beans—or snap beans, as we called them—were a gray-green, stewy taste treat that had been cooked half the day with a red pepper, a piece of side meat or lean bacon, and onion, then sopped up with fresh hot corn bread. Maybe our soul food wasn't all that great. The string beans were tough, had strings no matter how you strung them, and large white beans inside the gray-green part.

Imagine my surprise when I first saw those bright green, skinny, small french-cut jobs that everybody was serving with toasted almonds—I went into ecstasy. I still do when they come in to my garden or my grocery store. I'll have them for breakfast, lunch, and dinner.

1 1/4 pounds fresh green beans
Salt
3 tablespoons butter

1/8 teaspoon freshly grated nutmeg
Freshly ground pepper

Cut or break off ends of green beans. Bring to boil enough water to cover beans when they are added. Add salt to taste and then beans. Simmer 10 minutes or until beans are tender. Drain well in colander.

Combine beans, butter, nutmeg, and salt and pepper to taste in saucepan and cook, stirring, until beans are just piping hot.

BRAISED LEEKS WITH RICE SERVES 4–6

I always used to wonder what you did with those beautiful, silvery-fading-into-delicate-green long vegetables that looked like large scallions. I knew they were the base for soups and vichyssoise and complemented many other dishes but I'd rarely heard of a way to serve them on their very own. You may know dozens of variations. So do I, now; these are two of my favorites.

2 pounds firm, fresh leeks approximately
  1 1/2 inches across
Scant 1/4 cup olive oil
1 cup finely chopped onion
1 teaspoon flour
1 teaspoon salt

1/2 teaspoon sugar
1 1/4 cups water
6 tablespoons uncooked long- or medium-grain white rice
2 lemons, each cut lengthwise into 6–8
  wedges

With sharp knife, cut roots from leeks. Strip away any withered leaves and cut off and discard all but about 2 inches of green tops. Wash leeks under cold running water, spreading leaves apart to rid them of sand. Slice leeks into 1-inch lengths and set aside.

In a heavy 3 to 4-quart casserole, heat oil over moderate heat until a light haze forms above it. Add onions and cook 5 minutes, stirring frequently, until limp and transparent but not brown. Stir in flour, salt, and sugar and cook a minute or so; add water and raise heat to high. Stir constantly until mixture comes to a boil and thickens slightly.

Add rice and leeks and stir to coat evenly with sauce. Cover tightly, reduce heat to low, and simmer 30 minutes until leeks and rice are tender but still intact. Taste for seasoning.

Cool to room temperature and serve directly from the casserole, accompanied by lemon wedges.

LEEKS IN CREAM SERVES 4–6

2 pounds leeks, including green tops
1/4 cup (1/2 stick) unsalted butter
1 cup heavy cream or half-and-half

1 teaspoon salt
Freshly ground black pepper

With sharp knife, split leeks lengthwise to within 1/2 inch of root. Under cold running water, separate each leaf to remove sand wedged between leaves.

Trim roots and wedge leeks vertically in feed tube of your food processor. With medium slicing disc, slice leeks, using medium pressure.

Melt butter in 2-quart saucepan over moderate heat. Add leeks and cook about 10 minutes, stirring occasionally, until soft. Do not let brown. Stir in cream or half-and-half. Raise heat to moderately high and continue to cook, uncovered, until mixture has thickened. Add salt and pepper to taste.

The mixture may be reheated, but it will lose its bright green color.

PISELLI FAMIGLIA CAPOZZI   SERVES 4

I love petit pois. I've never had them fresh. I've had big pois fresh and could eat my weight (!) in them if I could get somebody to shell that many. But of all the canned petit pois recipes I've ever tasted, Irene Montague's is the best. (Also taste her Scallops Vittorio on page 160.)

1 16-ounce can tiny peas, drained
2 tablespoons olive oil
1 small clove garlic, finely minced

1/4 cup freshly grated Parmesan cheese, plus some for sprinkling on top

Preheat oven to 350°F.

Place peas in ovenproof dish. Drizzle with olive oil, sprinkle with garlic, then cheese. Stir thoroughly with wooden spoon (carefully, lest you break skin on peas). Sprinkle with additional cheese and bake 15–20 minutes until cheese is melted and top has begun to brown slightly.

NOTE Mrs. Montague has tried this recipe with frozen and with fresh peas, and claims it is not as good as it is with canned peas, especially the tiny LeSueur peas.

CHEESE-TOPPED SPINACH   SERVES 6–8

1 6-ounce jar marinated artichokes or marinated artichoke bottoms
2 10-ounce packages frozen chopped spinach, thawed
Salt and pepper to taste

1 8-ounce package cream cheese, softened
2 tablespoons butter, softened
4 tablespoons milk
1/2 cup freshly grated Parmesan cheese

Preheat oven to 350°F.

Place drained artichokes over bottom of greased 1-quart baking dish. Drain spinach well and spread over artichokes. Season to taste with salt and pepper.

With an electric mixer, blend cream cheese with butter until fluffy, then mix in milk. Spread over spinach. Sprinkle top with Parmesan cheese. Cover and bake 30 minutes. Remove cover and bake 10 minutes longer.

SPANAKOPITA (SPINACH PIE)

This may be served hot or cold, as an appetizer in small squares, as a vegetable side dish in larger squares, even after meals with a chilled white Greek wine. Or for breakfast with coffee—ummmmm!

2 bunches scallions, finely chopped
1 cup olive oil
3 pounds fresh spinach, stemmed, washed, dried, and chopped
1/2 cup minced parsley
2 tablespoons finely chopped dill

8 eggs, beaten
1 pound crumbled feta cheese
Salt
1/2 pound phyllo pastry sheets
1 cup melted butter

Preheat oven to 350°F.

Cook scallions in 1/2 cup olive oil until tender.

Combine spinach, parsley, dill, beaten eggs, and cheese. Add cooked scallions, season lightly with salt, and mix well.

Grease a 9 × 13-inch baking pan and line with 5 phyllo pastry sheets, brushing each sheet with melted butter combined with 1/2 cup olive oil. Spread spinach mixture over phyllo and top with remaining sheets of pastry, brushing each with butter and oil. Brush top sheet and bake 45 minutes.

Cool and cut into squares (for best results cut through phyllo dough with single-edged razor blade).

NOTE Phyllo pastry leaves (sheets) are found in the frozen food section of your supermarket or in your best deli or specialty food shop. They are easy to handle once you get the hang of it. Remove from box, unroll, and cover with damp (not wet) tea towel until ready to use. When ready, brush each sheet with butter and oil mixture. Keep remaining sheets covered with towel until you're ready to use them.

STIR-FRIED SPINACH

This soft, shiny dish is delicious hot or cold.

2 pounds fresh spinach
1/4 cup peanut oil
2 large cloves garlic, peeled and lightly crushed

3/4 teaspoon salt
1 teaspoon sugar
2 teaspoons sesame seed oil

Wash spinach leaves well. If they have roots, separate them and cut into 2 or 4 pieces. They are extremely sweet and succulent. Chop stems, if long.

Bring a large pot of water to a rolling boil and submerge spinach. One minute after water begins to boil again, remove spinach to colander and spray with cold water to stop cooking. Press down lightly to remove excess water.

Heat wok or large, heavy skillet over high heat until hot; add oil, swirl, and heat about 30 seconds till hot. Toss in garlic cloves and press them against the pan a few times.

Add spinach; poke and shake to separate the mass, then stir, in fast turning motions, to coat it all with oil. Sprinkle in salt and sugar and stir briskly for 1 minute. Add sesame seed oil, give a few fast turns, and pour into hot serving dish, discarding the garlic.

CROOKNECK SQUASH RELLENOS   SERVES 8–10

This is fun, attractive, and a surprise. Be careful not to fry too long or your cheese will melt right through the coating. Also, they're easier to handle if the crook in the crookneck is not too crooked.

Make your salsa in the morning; parboil your squash and slice, scoop out, and season it at the same time.

12 crookneck squash, parboiled
Salt and pepper to taste
1 1/2 cups Monterey Jack cheese, grated

6 large *or* 8 small eggs, separated
4 cups oil for deep frying
Salsa

Cut squash in half as evenly as possible. Scoop out seeds. Season cavity well with salt and pepper. Fill cavity with grated Monterey Jack cheese.

Beat egg whites until stiff. Beat yolks. Fold whites into yolks.

Dip each squash in egg mixture and coat heavily.

Fry in hot oil (400°F.). Drain on paper towels. Serve with Salsa.

SALSA

3 tomatoes, cut into chunks
2 serrano chilies, seeded and cut up
1/2 onion, cut into chunks

6–8 sprigs cilantro
1 teaspoon salt

Place all ingredients in food processor or blender and blend well. Let stand for 1 1/2 hours before serving.

SUMMER SQUASH IN A SUMMER WAY   SERVES 6–8

My friend Betty Rule claims she's not all that crazy about cooking. I don't believe her for one minute. She comes up with some of the most delightfully simple and unusual recipes, and her kitchen is always neat. I don't know how she does it, but as an incurable tornado-making menace, I'm envious.

8 uniform green pattypan (summer) squash, unpeeled
Salt and pepper to taste
1 tablespoon oil
1 tablespoon butter

2 small onions *or* 1 medium, thinly sliced
2/3 cup sour cream
1/2 cup Cheddar cheese, grated (more if desired)

Cut tops off each squash and remove seeds. Season with salt and pepper.

Heat oil and butter in large skillet. Sauté squash until lightly browned on one side. Add sliced onions and turn squash. When squash and onions are lightly browned on both sides, reduce heat, cover and cook until squash are just tender and still keep their shape.

Lift out squash carefully. Fill cavity of each with cooked onions and generous tablespoon of sour cream. Sprinkle grated cheese over sour cream. This can be done well ahead of serving. Just before serving, preheat oven to 350°F. Place squash on cookie sheet and bake until heated through and cheese melts.

WINTER SQUASH WITH NUTS AND MADEIRA WINE
SERVES 4–6

This is a very tasty vegetable that can be prepared ahead and refrigerated. Remember to let it sit for 30 minutes or so to reach room temperature, then bake 45–55 minutes until squash is tender when tested with a fork. Don't overcook it or the squash will get too mushy.

2 acorn squash *or* 1 butternut squash, approximately 1 1/4 pounds (enough to make 3 cups of 1/4-inch slices)
2 tablespoons butter
2 tablespoons oil
Salt and freshly ground black pepper to taste

1 cup heavy cream
1/4 cup Madeira
1/2 cup bread crumbs
1/2 cup walnuts or pecans, coarsely chopped
2 tablespoons melted butter

Preheat oven to 325°F.

Peel, quarter, and seed squash. Slice 1/4 inch thick. Sauté slices in butter and oil until lightly browned, 2–3 minutes.

Butter a 1-quart baking dish. Place half of squash in baking dish. Sprinkle with salt and pepper. Combine cream and Madeira and pour half this mixture over squash. Top with remaining squash; season and pour remaining cream mixture over all.

Combine bread crumbs and nuts with melted butter and sprinkle over top. Bake 45–55 minutes until squash is done.

BAKED TOMATO BALLS
SERVES 6

This sounds like nothing and tastes like something. *It's Julie Dannenbaum again with her succinct, unique, and no-nonsense delicacies.*

6 ripe tomatoes, skinned and seeded
3 tablespoons butter, melted

Salt and pepper to taste
Chopped parsley

Preheat oven to 350°F.

Cut tomatoes in half. Squeeze halves in towel to form round ball. Place in buttered baking dish, sprinkle with salt and pepper, and pour melted butter on each. Bake 5–10 minutes. Top with chopped parsley.

BROCCOLI-STUFFED TOMATOES   SERVES 12

This can be done partially ahead of time. The broccoli should be bright, shimmering green, so do it just before serving; but your tomatoes and sauce can be prepared ahead. Keep tomatoes cold. Keep sauce warm (but not hot or it will curdle).

6 large tomatoes
Salt
3 pounds broccoli
3 tablespoons tarragon vinegar
3 tablespoons dry white wine
3 tablespoons minced shallots
1 tablespoon heavy cream

3 large egg yolks, lightly beaten
1 cup clarified butter
Lemon juice
White pepper
Fresh parsley, minced
Fresh parsley sprigs or watercress

Halve tomatoes attractively (in points). With small teaspoon, remove seeds, core, and juice tomatoes without squeezing them. Sprinkle tomatoes with salt, invert, and let drain on paper towels 30 minutes.

Trim broccoli and separate into flowerets. In large pot of boiling salted water, cook flowerets 4–5 minutes until just tender. Drain and keep warm, covered.

In small heavy stainless-steel or enamel saucepan combine vinegar, wine, and shallots and carefully reduce liquid over high heat to about 1 tablespoon. Remove pan from heat and add heavy cream. Add egg yolks and cook mixture over low heat, whisking until thick.

Whisk in clarified butter, 2 tablespoons at a time, removing pan occasionally from heat to cool mixture. Whisk until thick. Strain sauce through fine sieve into another saucepan and add lemon juice and salt and white pepper to taste. Cover surface of sauce with buttered round of waxed paper and keep warm in shallow pan of warm water.

Arrange tomato cups on platter and divide broccoli flowerets, then sauce, evenly in them. Sprinkle minced parsley over all, and garnish platter with sprigs of parsley or watercress.

ITALIAN PLUM TOMATOES AND FRESH BASIL   SERVES 6

When the little 1 1/2 to 2-inch Italian plum tomatoes come in so plentifully all through the summer and fall, they're perfect for the sauces, canned in large batches, but I use them individually in a most simple way. They dress up a whole dinner and provide a colorful, low-cal solution to the vegetable problem.

2 pounds Italian plum tomatoes, peeled
2 tablespoons butter
Salt and pepper to taste

1/2 cup fresh basil leaves, chopped at the last minute

Plunge tomatoes into boiling water for 1 minute or less. Drain and rinse in cool water to peel easily. This can be done early in the day.

Just before serving, melt butter in skillet and add tomatoes, stirring to coat with butter and warm through. Add salt, pepper, and half of basil. Continue to shake pan and stir until tomatoes are softened but still whole. Add remaining basil and serve on warm platter or as pretty, tasty complement to your main course.

TOMATO-ZUCCHINI CASSEROLE

SERVES 4–6

Butter
2 small zucchini, scrubbed and sliced diagonally into ovals
1 small onion, sliced
2 large tomatoes, sliced
2 anchovy fillets, cut up

2 teaspoons capers
1 small clove garlic, minced
1/2 teaspoon salt
Freshly ground black pepper to taste
1 teaspoon dried basil
1/4 cup freshly grated Parmesan cheese

Rub shallow ovenproof casserole with butter. Line with half of sliced zucchini, onions, and tomatoes. Top with half of anchovies, capers, garlic, salt, pepper, basil, and cheese. Dot with butter. Repeat layers. Dot with butter. Can be done ahead up to this point and refrigerated until ready to bake.

Let come to room temperature and bake, uncovered, at 375°F. 30–45 minutes until zucchini is tender.

MOLLIE'S ZUCCHINI

SERVES 4

My friend Mollie Chappellet and her kitchen—the atmosphere around it and the food it produces—are a constant pleasure. There's no limit to her experiments in food and no equal in her artistry in presenting it.

4 medium zucchini, grated in food processor
1 teaspoon salt
1 clove garlic, minced
1/4 cup sliced scallions, including tops
1/4 cup butter

1/2 pound mushrooms (whole if small, quartered if large)
1/2 cup sour cream
1 tablespoon chopped fresh basil

Sprinkle zucchini with salt and let stand until moisture is gone; rinse and pat dry.

Sauté garlic and scallions in butter. Add mushrooms and then zucchini. Stir-fry 5 minutes. Stir in sour cream and basil.

SAUTÉED ZUCCHINI AND ASPARAGUS SERVES 4

2 zucchinis, diagonally cut into 1 1/2-inch
  lengths
1/2 pound asparagus, diagonally cut into 1
  1/2-inch lengths
Milk
Flour
Oil for frying

1 onion, thinly sliced
1 1/2 tomatoes, peeled and diced
1 clove garlic, finely minced
Salt and pepper to taste
3 tablespoons freshly grated Parmesan
  cheese

Place sliced zucchini and asparagus in shallow pan and cover with milk.

Drain and dust lightly with flour. Heat 1/4 inch of oil in skillet; add zucchini, asparagus, and onions, and sauté until slightly wilted. Add tomatoes, garlic, salt, pepper, and cheese.

Toss together and place in shallow buttered casserole. Cover and place in warm (200°F.) oven until serving time.

ZUCCHINI SAUTÉ WITH CAYENNE SERVES 4

It's so simple and so delicious. Chef Eldridge recommends a finger pinch. I don't know how big his fingers are, so I suggest a scant 1/8 teaspoon of oregano and a full 1/8 teaspoon of cayenne. See page 232 for his Alsatian Meat Pie and page 161 for Shrimps and Scallops Bengalese.

1/4 cup (1/2 stick) butter, softened
1 tablespoon minced garlic
1 tablespoon minced shallots
2 medium-sized zucchini, julienned

1/8 teaspoon oregano
1/8 teaspoon cayenne pepper
1/4 cup chicken stock or bouillon
Salt and pepper

Heat sauté pan. Add butter, garlic, and shallots; sauté until golden brown. Add zucchini, oregano, cayenne, and chicken stock; sauté until tender. Season to taste with salt and pepper.

MID-EASTERN STUFFED VEGETABLES SERVES 6–8

We did a few television shows of which I am rather proud in Israel and Egypt one summer. Not the optimum time to visit there climatically—110° in the shade (if you could find it)—but we hardly noticed, we interviewed so many fascinating world figures, from Aliza Begin to Jehann Sadat to almost all of the political and military figures who were making the front pages at that time. One night in Jerusalem, after a really heavy schedule, my Israeli guides (two charming young ex-soldiers who had been born and raised under the most spartan conditions, and had done their tour of duty and were wounded in the process) took me to their favorite restaurant. It was called Philadelphia.

The restaurant was owned and operated by an enthusiastic young Arab who served us the most unusual combinations of foods that melded into one of the best meals I remember anywhere. After he had shown me around his spotless, tiny, perfectly equipped kitchen and carefully had shown me how to prepare the vegetable dish below, I asked him about the name of his restaurant—Philadelphia. He said, "Well, if I'd called it America, as I wanted to, tourists would have expected hamburgers and hot dogs. I want to go to America one day to live so I picked the name of the perfect, typical American city, the one I intend to raise my children in someday—Philadelphia!" I didn't quote W. C. Fields; I happen to love the place myself.

1 cup Japanese or Chinese rice
4 carrots
4 medium zucchini
4 small green or red peppers, tops cut off
    and seeded (do not cut off bottoms)
1 1/3 cups freshly ground pork or lamb
1 1/2 teaspoons salt
1/2 teaspoon freshly ground pepper
1 tablespoon coarsely chopped fresh marjo-

ram *or* 1 teaspoon dried
4 cups water
2 cups chicken broth
Salt
Pinch of marjoram
4 fresh tomatoes, coarsely chopped *or* 1
    16-ounce can whole tomatoes, coarsely
    chopped

Wash rice many times, until all milky starch has disappeared and water runs clear. Place rice in saucepan and pour boiling water over it; let stand 5 minutes.

Meanwhile cut off ends of carrots and hollow them out all the way through with corer. (There is a special slender corer that does this job beautifully. It's longer and narrower than your apple corer. I found mine in the hardware store nearby.) Cut off ends of zucchinis and hollow out all the way through. Have prepared green or red peppers.

Drain rice. It will now measure about 1 1/3 cups.

Mix pork or lamb with salt, pepper, and marjoram. Add rice to meat mixture and mix well. Stuff meat-rice mixture into vegetables.

Boil water and chicken broth to which you have added salt, pinch of marjoram, and tomatoes.

Place carrots in bottom of 3-quart saucepan. Pour chicken broth-tomato mixture over carrots to just cover. Simmer on low heat 5 minutes. Add zucchinis and more chicken broth-tomato mixture to cover. Circle pot with green peppers so that they stand up. Add water-chicken broth to cover. Simmer until vegetables are tender.

Hollow out vegetables with long-bladed zucchini corer. Carrots will be easier to core if precooked 5 to 6 minutes. Stuff hollowed vegetables with rice-meat mixture.

Chapter 12

BREADS

Breads—ah! Your own home-baked, aromatic, crisp, hot bread, with a small chunk of butter when it's fresh—sandwiches the next day—toasted the day after that—and then bread crumbs (you don't even have to toast them anymore). Place bread in food processor with the metal blade and you have perfect, even, constantly useful fresh coatings, fillings, toppings; and then there are bread puddings.

Yet so many of my friends who venture into all kinds of unexplored ground with other culinary combinations are scared witless at the idea of yeast breads—the rising, kneading, rising again, baking, and so forth. Well, ol' buddies, it's a cinch and satisfying. It has other uses too. I once sold a house during a difficult house-selling time by insisting that the prospective buyers come at 4:00 in the afternoon (we're at our hungriest then). As insurance, I had a pot roast in one oven, bread baking in the other, and was casually icing a German Chocolate Cake on the counter as the agent took the prospective buyers through the house. The house was beautiful—too big, but smelled divine. After they made the tour, I served the bread just out of the oven with chunks of cold sweet butter. I think they took the first asking price by 5:15. So, whether you want to sell a house or get to know a reasonably attractive fellow better, bread smells better than perfume. Learn how to bake it.

A few simple rules. Always have plenty of flour on hand. I use all-purpose unbleached flour—wheat flour, rye, even soybean. There's a little attachment on my big mixer that lets me mill my own so easily. I buy winter wheat at health food stores, mill it fine. The degree of fineness depends on the number of times you run it through your little flour mill. I like leaving some coarse for cracked-wheat or health breads.

Be sure your yeast is fresh. I use good old Fleischmann's powdered. It's dated accurately and I buy extra to keep it in the refrigerator so I don't have to run to the store for the one or two packages I need. Yeast must be proofed, which means making sure it's not too old to leaven as it should. If they have leveled with you on the date, usually your bread can't fail, but test it anyway, as it's important. You'll need a thermometer—the finger or the elbow test that you did for the temperature of the baby's bottle isn't always reliable. The warm water must be 110 to 115°F., no more. Put sugar and warm water in a bowl or cup. Check the temperature, then sprinkle yeast over the top and stir, being sure to remove all excess yeast from the scraper you've used. Let it sit until it begins to form, get bubbly, and then doubles in size. It is ready to use.

This step may not be necessary, but since I have gone to that much trouble to ensure the temperature of the water, and yeast is temperamental, I don't want it to change its mind. I warm the bowl of my big mixer by just running warm water in it for a minute or two, then dry it and it's ready for adding the other ingredients. I will have repeated this yeast-proofing bit so often in this chapter, you'll say "Yeah, yeah, I know. Let's get on with it." But I'm taking no chances.

I use the large mixing bowl that came with my electric mixer and the dough hook attachment to get my bread started. That business of beating the flour in by hand gets so laborious it isn't even fun. After the dough attains the consistency needed for the recipe you're following, turn it out on a floured board and knead. There is something about the temperature of your palms and the yeast and the flour that brings the whole thing into happy focus. The kneading of the bread is illustrated in pictures below. The palms and the fingers are cupped together like one unit; pulling over with the fingers cupped and pushing with the heel of your hand in one direction is usually the best process. Kneading only takes 10 to 12 minutes maximum, if that long, so listen to the radio, hum a tune or two, or think of the exercise in tightening your arms.

Lightly butter a bowl into which you will place the dough so that it can rise. I mark my "rising bowl" with a small piece of masking tape at level of dough when first placed in bowl.

When it passes well over the mark, it's doubled, and I'm on my way! Place dough, which you have formed into a ball, in the bowl seam side down and turn to coat with butter on all sides, leaving pretty side up. Cover with plastic wrap or aluminum foil, and cover this with a large tea towel (Mother wrapped the bowl in a bath towel) to ensure that it is draft-free, and set it in a corner that doesn't get too much traffic in and out the door. There are plastic rising bowls on the market that are inexpensive. They're marked at various rising levels and have a clear, draft-free plastic cover which eliminates the need for plastic wrap and the tea towel. Some people say the oven with the pilot light is perfect. I don't agree. It makes the dough rise too fast and disturbs the chemical balance of yeast and flour. A warm, draft-free place is the answer.

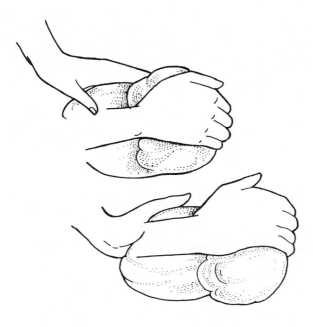

Knead dough by pushing forward with the palm of the hand
and pulling back with the fingers cupped.

After the prescribed rising time, usually 1 1/2 to 2 hours, depending on the heaviness of the dough and bread you are preparing, punch down firmly with your fist. This releases extra bubbles and air pockets in dough. The first couple of times, I literally did punch and met too little resistance and almost fractured my fist on the bottom of the bowl. It's somewhere between a push and a punch. For the last rising, most recipes suggest that same draft-free place and tell you to cover the bread pans with tea towels. That doesn't work for me because tea towels leave unsightly marks on my beautiful up-to-here-now-ready-to-bake bread loaves. I place loaves or loaf pans close to one another on the counter and cover with the largest roasting pan or roasting pan lid I can find. It's certainly draft-free and won't inhibit or mark my loaves. The slashes are performed after this rising to release extra air pockets, and the egg wash or cold-water wash for crispier crust should be done at this point.

In this chapter you'll find recipes for your own sourdough starter, the uses for it, and how to replenish to keep it going. Do try it.

The great James Beard was one of the first to come on my TV show to initiate the public to the intricacies—and at the same time, the basic simplicity—of bread baking. Imagine our chagrin, his and mine, when our time ran out before we barely got past incorporating the flour. I stayed after school and so did teacher, and I learned a little about bread baking. I tell you, it was a happy, well-fed crew that set up for the next show.

Almost the first things I learned to make were baking-powder biscuits, corn bread, and all sorts of other quick breads. You'll find some of those in here too. I've done the baking-powder buttermilk biscuits and corn bread so often that I'm embarrassed to repeat them, but I have. They're still my hurry-up, fall-back, stand-by, truly reliable meal makers.

BUTTERMILK WHITE BREAD   MAKES 1 LOAF OR 6 ROLLS

This is a light, buttery all-purpose bread. It has a smooth texture and for toast it is superb. I prefer the loaf; however, the rolls are lovely and keep well, and heated and split three fourths of the way through and filled with your favorite tuna, chicken, or crab meat salad are great for a party luncheon. They are definitely fork food—not a sandwich.

1/2 cup warm water (110–115°F., approximately)	4 cups unbleached flour
1 tablespoon granulated sugar	1 tablespoon salt
2 packages active dry yeast	3 tablespoons melted butter
	1 to 1 1/2 cups buttermilk

In small bowl, combine water, sugar, and yeast and allow to proof until bubbly and doubled in size.

In large mixing bowl, mix flour, salt, melted butter, and buttermilk together. Work into smooth dough and then add yeast mixture. Beat well for 2 minutes.

Remove to well-floured board and knead for approximately 10 minutes, or until dough is supple, smooth, and satiny. (Dough can also be prepared in electric mixer equipped with dough hook. Combine all ingredients, knead with dough hook for approximately 5–6 minutes, and then remove dough to floured board for about 4 minutes of kneading by hand.)

Place dough in buttered bowl and turn to coat with butter. Place seam side down in bowl. Cover well with plastic wrap and large tea towel and set in warm, draft-free place to let rise until more than doubled in bulk.

Punch down dough. Remove to floured board, and knead for 2 minutes to remove air and extra bubbles.

Form into loaf about 9 × 5 inches by patting flat to a rather rough rectangle, folding in ends, and then folding in sides. Pinch seams together well. Place in buttered 9 × 5 × 3-inch loaf pan, seam side down. Make 3 evenly spaced diagonal slashes on top of loaf with sharp knife. Cover and place in warm, draft-free place to let rise until more than doubled in bulk. I cover my pans with lid of large roasting pan.

Preheat oven to 375°F. Bake in center of oven for about 40 minutes, or until brown and hollow-sounding when rapped with knuckles on top and bottom. If not completely hollow-sounding on bottom, remove from pan and place loaf on oven rack for approximately 5 minutes to brown sides and bottom of loaf.

For rolls, cut dough into 6 even pieces and roll into shape by hand as with bread. Place on buttered cookie sheet and bake 18–20 minutes. Remove from baking sheet and bake on oven rack for another 5–8 minutes to give a crisp brown crust all over. Cool on a rack before slicing.

For an even crispier crust on bread and rolls, place a pan of boiling water under bread while baking.

LIGHT AS A FEATHER BREAD   MAKES 2 FREE-FORM LOAVES

This bread is easier than most because it takes only one rising.

2 packages active dry yeast
1 tablespoon sugar
1 cup warm water (110–115°F.)
1/3 cup butter, cut into small pieces
3/4 cup hot water

2 teaspoons salt
5 1/2–6 cups flour
Cornmeal
1 egg, lightly beaten with 2 tablespoons water

In large bowl of your mixer, proof yeast with sugar and warm water until bubbly and double in size, while your yeast is proofing, melt butter *in* hot water and let cool to lukewarm. Add salt and combine with yeast mixture. Add cooled butter-water mixture to yeast mixture. Stirring vigorously with wooden spoon or dough hook, add flour, 1 cup at a time, until dough almost comes away from sides of bowl. It will be a little sticky.

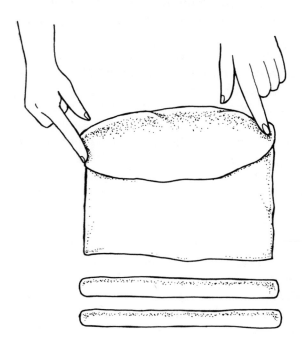

Roll each half of dough into rectangle about 12 × 8 inches. Cut two 1/2-inch strips from long side. Starting from wide end, roll rectangle loosely, pinching ends as you roll.

Place strip of dough across top of each loaf, pressing gently on underside to hold in place.

Turn dough out onto lightly floured board. Using baker's scraper or large spatula, scrape under flour and dough, fold dough over, and press it with your free hand. Continue until dough has absorbed enough flour from board and is easy to handle. Knead 2–4 minutes, being sure to keep your hands well floured, because it is still sticky dough. When dough is soft and smooth, let rest for 5–6 minutes.

Divide dough into two pieces. With rolling pin, roll each half into a rectangle about 12 × 8 inches. Cut two 1/2-inch strips from long side of dough and set aside. Starting from wide end, roll rectangle up gently, pinching seams at end of each loaf as you roll.

Roll each 1/2-inch strip of dough in your hands until it is slightly longer than each loaf. Place them on top and in center of each loaf of bread, pulling over each end and pressing gently on underside of loaf to hold in place while dough is rising.

Butter two baking sheets well and sprinkle with cornmeal. Place loaves on sheets. Cover with plastic wrap and large tea towel and place in warm, draft-free place to let rise until more than doubled in bulk, 50–60 minutes. I cover my loaves with lid of large roasting pan to give dough plenty of room to rise.

Preheat oven to 425°F. Brush lightly and thoroughly top and sides of each loaf with beaten egg wash and bake 40 minutes, or until loaves are a rich, golden color and make a hollow sound when you tap crust, top and bottom, with your knuckles. Cool on rack. Serve warm with cold butter.

SALLY LUNN HOT BREAD   MAKES 10 CAKES

This beautiful hunk of bread—really early American—can be made, except for baking, completely in the food processor, that is, the mixing, the rising, the punching down, and rising again. If you bake it earlier than you plan to serve it, place it on a cookie sheet for 10 minutes in a preheated 350°F. oven to heat through and crisp outside a little. Drizzle a couple of tablespoons of melted butter over all just before serving. Just a little added craziness.

1 package dry yeast
1/4 cup plus 1 teaspoon sugar
1/4 cup warm water (110–115°F.)
3 cups flour
1 1/2 teaspoons salt
4 tablespoons unsalted butter, at room

temperature, cut into pieces
1/4 cup vegetable shortening or fresh
  chicken fat, at room temperature
3 eggs
2/3 cup cold milk

Proof yeast with 1 teaspoon sugar and water in small bowl until bubbly and doubled in bulk.

Use metal blade of food processor to process flour, remaining 1/4 cup sugar, salt, butter, and shortening until well mixed, about 20 seconds.

Add yeast mixture. With machine running, add eggs one at a time. Continue to process while pouring milk through feed tube in steady stream. Dough will be very sticky. Continue processing for 15–20 seconds to knead.

The 3 to 4-hour rising and punching down are most easily done by leaving dough in food processor bowl with cover and pusher on but not locked into place. Cover with towel. After dough has risen for 30 minutes, turn machine on and off 3 times to punch down dough; scrape down side of bowl. (CAUTION: If you wait too long to punch down dough, you'll see your processor top and towel rising like the table at a seance—yeast gets pushy.) Continue to let rise, punching down every 30 minutes for 3 hours at least, and preferably 4 hours.

Punch dough down again at end of rising period and spoon dough evenly into well-greased 10-cup fluted pan. Cover with oiled plastic wrap and allow to rise again until doubled, 35–45 minutes. Preheat oven to 350°F.

Bake 45–50 minutes, or until ring is nicely browned and sounds hollow when tapped. Turn out immediately onto wire rack to cool slightly. Serve warm with lots of butter. If not for immediate use, cool completely, put into tightly sealed plastic bag and freeze. Let return to room temperature before unwrapping.

NOTE Your food processor may slow down and stall when you knead this heavy sticky dough with metal blade. Don't be concerned because the numerous risings and "punching downs" ensure a completely kneaded dough and a loaf with a lovely light texture.

If you need to use processor bowl during rising time, transfer dough to a well-buttered mixing bowl. Cover with plastic wrap and allow to rise 3–4 hours, punching dough down every 30 minutes. Since dough is sticky, you will need to sprinkle top lightly with flour each time before punching down.

BRIOCHE IN THE FOOD PROCESSOR

MAKES 1 RING MOLD OR 10 INDIVIDUAL BRIOCHES

This is so luscious I serve it as a dessert still warm or reheated with cold butter and a favorite jam.

1 package active dry yeast
1/4 cup warm water (110–115°F.)
1/3 cup sugar
2 1/3 cups flour

3/4 cup butter (1 1/2 sticks), very cold, cut
   into small pieces
3 eggs
1 egg yolk, beaten with 2 tablespoons water

In small bowl, proof yeast with 1/2 teaspoon sugar in warm water until bubbly and double in size. While yeast is proofing, place remaining sugar, flour, and butter in bowl of food processor and blend until mixture resembles cornmeal. Add yeast mixture and blend by turning the machine on and immediately off. With machine running, add eggs through feed tube and process for 1 1/2 minutes. If motor stops, consider dough ready.

Remove spongy dough and place in floured bowl. Cover with plastic wrap, then with large tea towel and let dough rise in warm, draft-free place. When tripled in bulk, punch down and let rise again, covered, in refrigerator 6 hours or overnight.

Take two thirds of dough and form ball to fit buttered round charlotte mold or ring mold. Cut a deep cross, about 1 inch deep, in center of ball. With remaining dough, form smaller, pear-shaped knob; fit pointed end of knob into cross, pressing it firmly in place. Let brioche rise uncovered in warm, draft-free place until dough has doubled in bulk.

Preheat oven to 375°F. Glaze brioche with egg-yolk wash. Bake 40 minutes or until nicely browned. If it browns too rapidly, cover tops loosely with foil.

I have often removed brioche from pan and placed on baking sheet and placed in oven for 10 minutes or longer so that it will crisp a little on the bottom.

If you have small brioche tins or regular-sized muffin tins, make individual brioches by using same procedure through chilling process. Then take two thirds of dough and cut into 10 pieces. Roll into balls to fit bottom of brioche tins or muffin tins. Cut cross 3/4-inch deep in center of each ball. With remaining dough, form small pear-shaped knobs; fit pointed ends of knobs into crosses, pressing them firmly in place.

Let rise in warm, draft-free place until doubled in bulk. Glaze with egg-yolk wash and bake 20 minutes, or until nicely browned.

ENGLISH MUFFINS IN A LOAF

MAKES TWO 8 × 4 × 2-INCH LOAF PANS

I found a couple of rounded loaf pans with indentations indicating the slices. It's great for this bread.

6 cups unsifted unbleached flour
1 package active dry yeast
2 teaspoons sugar
2 teaspoons salt
1/4 teaspoon soda

2 cups milk
1/2 cup water
1 cup Sourdough Starter (page 308)
Cornmeal

Combine in bowl of your mixer with dough hook, 3 cups flour, undissolved yeast, sugar, salt, and soda.

Heat milk and water until very warm (120–130°F.). Add to dry ingredients and beat well. Add sourdough starter and beat well again. Stir in remaining 3 cups flour to make a stiff batter.

Spoon into two 8 × 4 × 2-inch loaf pans that have been buttered and sprinkled with cornmeal. Cover with plastic wrap and large tea towel and place in warm, draft-free place to let rise until doubled in bulk, about 45 minutes. Preheat oven to 400°F. Bake 25 minutes. Remove from pan and cool. To serve, slice, toast, and slather with butter.

CRUMPETS

These are really what I keep hoping English muffins will taste like. I served them one testing afternoon to my crusty publisher. He melted!

I used to use my 3-inch biscuit cutter or any and every size I had until I found some circular cutters with a little wooden handle on top. Now my crumpets are all the same size.

1/2 cup milk
1/2 cup boiling water
1 teaspoon sugar
1 package active dry yeast

1 1/2 teaspoons salt
1 3/4 cups sifted flour
1/4 teaspoon soda, dissolved in 1 tablespoon
   water

In small bowl, combine milk and boiling water and cool to lukewarm. Add sugar and yeast and allow to proof until bubbly and double in size.

In large mixing bowl, blend salt and sifted flour and combine with proofed yeast mixture. Beat thoroughly for several minutes with wooden spoon.

Cover bowl with foil and tea towel to keep out drafts. Let batter rise in warm place until almost doubled in bulk and bubbly. Add dissolved soda and beat into batter. Allow to rise again until doubled in bulk.

Heat griddle to moderate, 325°–350°F. Spoon batter into buttered rings placed on hot griddle to depth of about 1/2 inch. Cook until dry and bubbly on top. Remove rings, turn crumpets and brown lightly on other side. Let cool. To serve, toast and drench with butter.

CORNMEAL BREAD

This bread helped me lose my first nervousness about baking yeast breads. The house smelled wonderful. We hardly got it out of the oven before slicing, buttering, and serving it with tea. I don't know about you, but I find it hard to resist anything with cornmeal in or around it. It toasts well too.

1/2 cup cornmeal
1 cup boiling water
1 teaspoon salt
2 packages active dry yeast
1/2 cup warm water (110–115°F., approximately)

1 tablespoon granulated sugar
1 cup warm milk
1 1/2 tablespoons salt
1/4 cup dark brown sugar
4 1/2 to 5 cups unbleached flour

Pour cornmeal into boiling water with teaspoon salt; cook and and stir vigorously until it thickens, about 4 minutes. Place in large bowl of mixer with dough hook and let cool.

Proof the yeast with sugar and water in a medium bowl. When bubbly and double in size, pour into mixing bowl with cooled cornmeal mixture. Mix well. Add milk, salt, brown sugar and flour, 1 cup at a time, stirring very well after each addition of flour.

When mixture is well blended and begins to pull away from sides of bowl, turn out on lightly floured board and knead until smooth and elastic, 10–12 minutes, adding more flour as needed.

Butter a large bowl. Place dough in bowl and turn to coat with butter on all sides. Cover with plastic wrap and a large tea towel and set in warm, draft-free place to double in bulk.

Punch dough down and turn out on lightly floured board. Cut in half, shape into two loaves, and let rest while you butter two 9 × 5 × 3-inch loaf pans. Preheat oven to 425°F.

Place dough in pans, cover, and let rise until almost doubled in bulk, or just level with tops of baking pans. Bake in oven for 10 minutes, then lower temperature to 350° and continue baking 20–25 minutes, or until bread is nicely browned and sounds hollow when removed from pans and rapped with knuckles on top and bottom. Place loaves, without pans, on oven rack for a few minutes to crisp the crust. Remove from oven and cool on racks.

BOLILLOS (MEXICAN HARD ROLLS) MAKES 3 DOZEN

I've been to Mexico only a few wonderful times, but I have fond memories of tennis and golf and water skiing around the bay, friendly people who actually understood my Spanish, and every morning freshly baked Bolillos for breakfast.

2 packages active dry yeast
1 tablespoon sugar
1 3/4 cups warm water (110–115°F.)

1 teaspoon salt
6 cups sifted unbleached flour

In large mixing bowl of electric mixer, proof yeast with sugar in warm water until bubbly and doubled in size. Add salt, flour, 2 cups at a time, beating well with dough hook or by hand with wooden spoon after each addition. After adding fifth cup of flour, add flour slowly, 1 tablespoon at a time, until dough becomes firm but workable. Turn out on lightly floured board and knead until dough becomes smooth and elastic.

Shape into ball and place in buttered bowl, turning to coat with butter on all sides. Place seam side down. Cover with plastic wrap and large tea towel and let rise in warm, draft-free place until doubled in bulk. When doubled, punch down and allow to double again.

Remove to lightly floured board and form into long, slender rolls, 3–4 inches long, twisting each end. The easiest way to ensure uniformity in size and shape is to roll dough into a very long rope about 2 inches in diameter and snip off 3- to 4-inch pieces of dough, twisting each end. For authentic-looking rolls they should be rather flat with twisted ends. Lay rolls about 2 inches apart on lightly floured baking sheet.

After shaping rolls, slash tops 1/2-inch deep with sharp knife or razor blade (single-edge please!). Cover with towel (I use the old roasting-pan-lid trick here as referred to in previous recipes, since I found the towel was leaving marks on top of my rolls) and let rise again in warm, draft-free place until doubled in bulk. When nearly doubled, lightly brush top of rolls with oil.

Preheat oven to 400°F. Bake 20–30 minutes or until rolls are lightly browned. Serve piping hot with lots of butter.

CHALLAH (BRAIDED EGG BREAD)

This is a heavenly holiday bread to behold and to taste. It can be baked in a loaf pan for ease in slicing. When it begins to dry out a little (it hardly ever lasts that long) use it for the best French Toast you ever tasted. Page 88.

1 cup lukewarm water (110–115°F.)
4 teaspoons sugar
3 packages active dry yeast
5–6 cups flour
2 teaspoons salt

3 eggs
1/4 cup plus 1 teaspoon vegetable shortening
1 egg yolk combined with 2 tablespoons water

Pour 1/2 cup lukewarm water into small, shallow bowl and sprinkle it with 1 teaspoon sugar and yeast. Let mixture stand 2–3 minutes, then stir to dissolve yeast completely. Set bowl in warm, draft-free place about 5 minutes, or until mixture almost doubles in volume.

In deep mixing bowl, combine 4 cups flour, remaining sugar, and salt. Make a well in center, pour in yeast and remaining 1/2 cup lukewarm water, add eggs and 1/4 cup vegetable shortening. Gently stir center ingredients together with large spoon by hand or with dough hook. Beat vigorously until all flour is absorbed. Add up to 2 cups more flour, beating it in 1/4 cup at a time and using as much as necessary to form dough that can be gathered into soft ball. If dough becomes difficult to stir, work in flour with your fingers.

Place dough on lightly floured surface and knead about 15 minutes, or until dough is smooth and elastic. Sprinkle it from time to time with a little flour to prevent its sticking to the board.

Shape dough into a ball and place it in lightly greased bowl, turning to coat dough with butter. Place seam side down in bowl. Drape loosely with kitchen towel and set aside in warm, draft-free place for 45 minutes, or until dough doubles in bulk. Punch dough down with your fist and place on board. Knead it again for 2 to 3 minutes. Set aside to rest for 10 minutes.

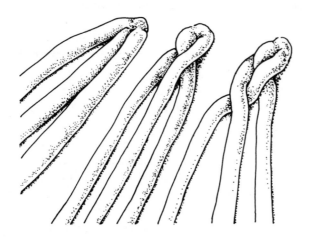

Pinch one end of the ropes together, then interweave strips of dough into 3-part braid, pinching both ends to seal.

Preheat oven to 400°F. With pastry brush, coat large baking sheet with remaining teaspoon vegetable shortening. Divide dough into 3 equal pieces. On lightly floured surface, roll each piece into a rope about 22 inches long. The ropes should be thicker at center and taper at both ends. Pinch one end of ropes together and interweave in a 3-part braid, pinching end to seal. (I keep remembering how I used to braid my daughter's lovely long hair to keep it from tangling.) Carefully place challah on baking sheet and let it rise in warm place for about 30 minutes. I cover challah with top of a large roasting pan to keep out drafts.

Brush top of loaf thoroughly with egg-yolk-and-water mixture and bake in middle of oven for 15 minutes, then reduce heat to 375° and continue baking 45 minutes longer, or until golden brown and crusty. Cool on cake rack.

CHEESE BREAD

MAKES TWO 8 × 4 × 2-INCH LOAVES

1 package active dry yeast
1 tablespoon granulated sugar
1 3/4 cups warm water (110–115°F.)
5–6 cups flour
1 tablespoon salt

1/4 cup softened butter
1 generous teaspoon Tabasco
1/4 cup freshly grated Parmesan cheese
1/2 cup grated Cheddar cheese
1/4 cup grated Monterey Jack cheese

Dissolve yeast with sugar in 1/4 cup warm water and allow to proof.

In large bowl, mix 5 cups of flour and salt. Make a well in center and add remaining 1 1/2 cups warm water, butter, Tabasco, and proofed yeast mixture. Stir with wooden spoon or spatula or with your floured hands until dough is well amalgamated.

Turn out on heavily floured board (use about 1/2 cup flour) and knead 10–12 minutes or until dough is smooth and elastic and rather satiny in texture and all flour on board is absorbed; add flour if you need it.

Place dough in buttered or oiled bowl and turn to coat on all sides. Cover with towel and let rise in warm, draft-free place until doubled in bulk, 1 1/2–2 hours. Punch down dough, turn it out on lightly floured board, and knead in cheeses. When thoroughly blended, cut dough in half and let rest 10 minutes. Then roll out each half into a rectangle about 11 × 6 inches and let rest 2–3 minutes more. Roll each rectangle up, pinching the edges as you do so, and tucking in ends so that loaf measures about 4 1/2 × 7 1/2 inches.

Place dough in 2 well-buttered 8 × 4 × 2-inch loaf pans, cover, and let rise in warm, draft-free place until bread has reached top of pan or higher, or has more or less doubled in size.

Preheat oven to 375°F. Bake in center of middle rack of oven for approximately 30 minutes, or until loaves sound hollow when removed from pans and rapped with knuckles on both top and bottom. After removing loaves from pans, place directly on oven rack for a few minutes to firm crust. Cool on bread racks before slicing.

OLD FASHIONED HONEY WHEAT BREAD

MAKES TWO 8 × 4 × 2-INCH LOAVES

This bread is crunchy, chewy, and has an unusual texture. It keeps moist and is great for toasting.

1 1/2 cups water	2 packages active dry yeast
1 cup low-fat cottage cheese	5 cups unbleached flour
Scant 1/2 cup honey	1 1/2 cups whole wheat flour
1/4 cup butter or margarine	3 teaspoons salt
1/3 cup warm water (110–115°F.)	1 egg
1 1/2 tablespoons sugar	

Heat 1 1/2 cups water, cottage cheese, honey, and butter in medium saucepan until very warm (120–130°F.). In small bowl, combine warm water, sugar, and yeast and allow to proof until bubbly and double in bulk.

Measure flour into large bowl. Combine 2 cups flour with salt and cottage-cheese mixture in large bowl of mixer with dough hook. Beat with dough hook or by hand and gradually add 2 more cups flour, then proofed yeast, and then egg. Keep adding flour, 1 cup at a time, until you have a fairly stiff but workable dough.

Remove from bowl and place on floured board. Knead until smooth and elastic, 6–8 minutes and then shape into ball.

Place in buttered bowl, turning to coat dough with butter on all sides. Place seam side down in bowl. Cover well with plastic wrap and large tea towel and set in warm, draft-free place to let rise until doubled in bulk, at least 1 hour. Punch down dough with fist 3–4 times. Remove to lightly floured board and knead slightly to remove air and extra bubbles.

Cut into 2 even pieces. Form each piece into loaves about 8 × 4 inches by patting flat to a rather rough rectangle, folding in ends, and then folding sides. Pinch seams together well. Place in buttered 8 × 4 × 2-inch loaf pans, seam side down. Cover with plastic wrap and large tea towel and place in warm, draft-free place to let rise until doubled in bulk. I also cover my pans with lid of large roasting pan.

Preheat oven to 350°F. Bake in center of oven for 35 to 40 minutes. Carefully remove loaves from pans and place on tiles if you have them or tins if you don't, and bake for an additional 10 minutes. They are done if they sound hollow when rapped with knuckles on top and bottom.

Turn off heat and let loaves sit in oven for 10 more minutes to crisp a little on the bottom. Place on racks on sides to cool.

CRACKED WHEAT BREAD MAKES TWO 9 × 5 × 3-INCH LOAVES

I bake this bread so often I keep thinking I'll run out of customers. I haven't so far! It's crunchy and even better toasted the next day. If you believe in natural health foods, this one is loaded with goodies.

1/2 cup fine cracked wheat (bulgur)	1 1/2 tablespoons salt
1 1/2 cups boiling water	2 tablespoons molasses
1 package active dry yeast	2 tablespoons honey
1 teaspoon sugar	1 cup milk
1/3 cup warm water (110–115°F.)	1 cup whole wheat flour
1/4 cup softened butter or shortening	4 cups all-purpose flour

Cook cracked wheat in boiling water about 10 minutes or until all water is absorbed, stirring occasionally to prevent sticking.

In large mixing bowl, proof yeast with sugar in warm water until bubbly and double in size.

While yeast is proofing, stir butter, salt, molasses, honey, and milk into cooked cracked wheat. Cool to lukewarm and then add to yeast mixture.

Start stirring in flours, 1 cup at a time, either with large spoon by hand or with dough hook. When dough is stiff enough to work, turn out on floured board and knead 10–12 minutes, working in as little of the remaining flour as necessary. (Dough should have a slightly tacky but not sticky texture.) When dough is smooth and elastic, shape into ball and place in buttered bowl, turning to coat with butter. Place seam side down and allow to rise. Cover, place in warm, draft-free place, and let rise until doubled in bulk, about 1 1/2 hours.

Punch down and remove to lightly floured board. Cut in half and let rest while you butter two 9 × 5 × 3-inch loaf pans. Roll out each piece of dough into rectangles, approximately 6 × 9 inches. Roll dough up from wide end, jelly-roll fashion and place in loaf pans seam side down. Cover and let rise again until doubled in bulk, or until dough reaches tops of pans.

Preheat oven to 375°F. Bake in oven 30 to 35 minutes, or until loaves sound hollow when tapped on top and bottom. Cool on racks.

CASHEW WHOLE WHEAT BREAD

MAKES TWO 9 × 5 × 3-INCH LOAVES

1/2 cup Potato Sourdough Starter (page 308)	2 tablespoons molasses
2 cups freshly milled whole wheat flour	1 tablespoon honey
1 1/4 cups warm water (110–115°F.)	3 tablespoons soft butter or shortening
1/2 cup bulgur	1 tablespoon salt
1 cup boiling water	2 cups all-purpose flour
1/2 package active dry yeast	3/4 cup raw cashews, chopped fairly fine
1 scant teaspoon sugar	

Place starter, 1 cup whole wheat flour, and 1 cup warm water in large bowl. Cover with plastic wrap and let stand overnight on counter. The next day, stir down and place in bowl of electric mixer with dough hook.

Cook bulgur in boiling water until water is absorbed, about 10 minutes. Proof yeast with sugar in 1/4 cup warm water until bubbly and doubled in size.

While yeast is proofing, warm molasses, honey, and salt. Add remaining cup of whole wheat flour to bowl of mixer. Then add proofed yeast and the slightly warmed molasses mixture. Add all-purpose flour, 1 cup at a time, mixing with dough hook until dough is of a sticky consistency and clings to dough hook. (It usually requires 1 3/4–2 cups flour.)

Remove and place on floured board. Knead in chopped cashews about 10 minutes, making sure nuts are thoroughly mixed into dough. Continue kneading 10–12 minutes until dough is smooth and elastic. Roll into ball. Place in buttered bowl, seam side down, turning to coat on all sides with butter. Cover with plastic wrap and large tea towel and let rise in warm, draft-free place until doubled in bulk, about 1 1/2 hours.

Remove from bowl and punch down firmly. Cut into two equal portions and shape into two loaves. Place in well-buttered 9 × 5 × 3-inch loaf pans, cover, and let rise again until doubled in bulk, about 1 hour.

Preheat oven to 375°F. Place pan of water in bottom of oven to create steam. Bake for 30 minutes or until lightly browned. Cool on rack.

BRAN AND WHOLE WHEAT BREAD WITH MOZZARELLA AND PROSCIUTTO LOAF

MAKES 1 FREE-FORM LOAF

This is an easy, moist, crunchy loaf that toasts delicious. I happen to like it freshly baked and warm. A good trick is to bake it about 10 minutes less than indicated and just before serving, pop it in your pre-heated oven for the final 10–15 minutes of baking preceding the knuckle rapping number.

2 tablespoons active dry yeast
1 tablespoon sugar
2 cups warm water (110–115°F.)
1 cup all-bran
3 1/2 cups unbleached flour
1 cup whole wheat flour
1 tablespoon salt

2 tablespoons brown sugar
6 ounces mozzarella, diced into 1/4-inch pieces
1/4 pound prosciutto, diced into 1/4-inch pieces
Cornmeal
Cold water

In large bowl of electric mixer with dough hook, proof yeast with sugar in 1/2 cup of warm water until bubbly and doubled in size.

In another bowl, soak bran in 3/4 cup warm water to soften, 10–15 minutes. When softened, stir bran into bowl with proofed yeast.

Add unbleached flour and whole wheat flour and remaining 3/4 cup warm water to proofed yeast mixture. Add salt and brown sugar and combine mixture well with dough hook or by hand with wooden spoon. Add more unbleached flour, 2 tablespoons at a time, if necessary, to make soft but not sticky dough.

Transfer dough to lightly floured board and knead, incorporating more unbleached flour if dough is too sticky, 8–10 minutes, until dough is smooth and elastic.

Shape into ball and place in buttered bowl, seam side down, turning to coat with butter on all sides. Cover with plastic wrap and large tea towel and set in warm, draft-free place to let rise for about 1 1/2 hours, or until tripled in bulk.

Punch down dough and let rise again, covered with plastic wrap and large tea towel, 1 hour, or until doubled in bulk. Remove to lightly floured board and knead mozzarella and prosciutto into dough. Form dough into large round loaf and transfer to baking sheet sprinkled with cornmeal. Let rise again, uncovered, for 1 hour, or until doubled in bulk.

Preheat oven to 425°F. Brush loaf with water, sprinkle with cornmeal, and bake in center rack in oven. Splash oven door with water to create steam. After 10 minutes, brush loaf with cold water for crisp crust. Ten minutes later repeat cold water wash. Reduce oven heat to 350° and bake bread for 25 minutes more, or until it sounds hollow when top and bottom are rapped with knuckles. Transfer to rack and let cool.

CRUSTY FRENCH BREAD   MAKES 3–4 FREE-FORM LOAVES

Those marvelous crusty French baguettes are hard to duplicate because their flour is quite a different texture from ours. When I was in Paris last summer I noticed that a few of the finer French restaurants were serving whole wheat rolls as well as baguettes. For the following recipe just for fun—try it with 2 cups of whole wheat flour mixed with your unbleached white but do this the second or third time you make it. The recipe is as they say "a bit of all right."

1 package active dry yeast
3 cups warm water (110–115°F.)
1 tablespoon sugar
1 tablespoon salt
2 tablespoons Sourdough Starter (page 308)
   at room temperature
6–8 cups unbleached flour

2 tablespoons butter, softened
Cornmeal
1/2 cup water
1/2 teaspoon salt
1 1/2 teaspoons cornstarch
Sesame seeds

In large bowl of electric mixer with dough hook, combine yeast, warm water, sugar, salt and starter, stirring enough to dissolve yeast; let stand 5 minutes to proof yeast.

Stir in butter; then slowly stir in flour, either by hand or with dough hook, 1 cup at a time, until dough is fairly stiff, but workable. Turn out on lightly floured board and knead until dough is smooth and elastic and then shape into ball.

Place in buttered bowl, seam side down, turning to coat dough with butter on all sides. Cover tightly with plastic wrap and large tea towel and let rise in warm, draft-free place until doubled in bulk.

Cut dough into 3–4 pieces. Let dough rest 15 minutes. Shape each piece into a roll 12–15 inches long, tapered like a boat at each end. Place on buttered baking sheet, sprinkle sparsely with cornmeal. Cover with large roasting pan and let rise again in warm, draft-free place until doubled in bulk, about 1 hour.

Meanwhile, combine water, salt, and cornstarch. Cook and stir until clear but thick. Brush mixture over loaves; sprinkle tops of loaves with sesame seed. With sharp knife, make 3 evenly spaced diagonal slashes on top of each loaf, 1/3 to 3/4 inch deep.

Preheat oven to 450°F. Place loaves on upper shelf and splash water in oven to create steam. Bake 5–10 minutes; lower temperature to 350° and bake 50–60 minutes longer. Cool on racks. A small, shallow pan of water on shelf below loaves will help keep them crusty.

SOURDOUGH STARTER

This starter takes a little longer to ferment than does the flour-yeast starter, but once it does it has a nutty, yeasty, unmistakable sourdough flavor.

1 package dry yeast	2 cups warm water (110–115°F.)
1 teaspoon sugar	2 cups flour

In medium bowl, proof yeast with sugar and water until bubbly and double in size. When yeast has proofed, add flour and mix well. Pour into jar, cover tightly, and let stand at room temperature 2 days. Then refrigerate 1 day.

Whenever you use starter, replenish with 1/2 cup flour, 1/2 cup warm water, and 1/2 teaspoon sugar. Let stand at room temperature 12–24 hours and then place in refrigerator. To nourish your starter, stir with wooden spoon every 5–6 days.

POTATO SOURDOUGH STARTER

6 potatoes, peeled	1 cup warm water (110–115°F.)
2 quarts boiling water	1/3 cup sugar
1 package active dry yeast	3 tablespoons salt

Cook potatoes in boiling water until very tender. Drain and save water. Puree potatoes and set aside.

Proof yeast in warm water until bubbly and double in size in large mixing bowl. When yeast is proofed, add pureed potatoes, sugar, salt, and reserved potato water. Stir until creamy and place in large jar or crock. Cover and let stand at room temperature 48 hours. Store in refrigerator in jar or crock and use as needed.

Whenever you use starter, replenish with 1/2 cup flour, 1/2 cup warm water, and 1/2 teaspoon sugar. Let stand at room temperature 12–24 hours and then place in refrigerator. To nourish your starter, stir with wooden spoon every 5–6 days.

SOURDOUGH FRENCH BREAD

MAKES 4 SMALL FREE-FORM LOAVES

1 package active dry yeast
1 tablespoon sugar
1 1/2 cups lukewarm water (110–115°F.)
1 cup Sourdough Starter (page 308)
1 tablespoon shortening (butter, margarine,

or oil)
1 1/2 teaspoons salt
1/8 teaspoon soda
4 cups flour
Cornmeal

Proof yeast with sugar and 1/2 cup lukewarm water in a medium bowl until bubbly and double in bulk.

In a large mixing bowl, combine starter, remaining lukewarm water, proofed yeast mixture, shortening, and salt. Stir this mixture until it is dissolved and completely blended. Add soda and flour and mix well with dough hook or by hand.

Remove to well-floured board and knead 8–10 minutes, or until dough is supple, smooth, and elastic. Place dough in buttered bowl and turn to coat with butter. Place seam side down in bowl. Cover well with plastic wrap and large tea towel, set in warm, draft-free place, and let rise for about 2 hours.

Punch dough down and knead about 20 times. Cut into 4 pieces. Use rolling pin to press out all air. Now roll each portion of dough into an oblong shape, preferably 9 × 14 inches. Take the long side and "jelly-roll" dough, sealing edges. Seal very well and gently stretch loaves into desired length. Place on greased baking sheet, sprinkled with cornmeal. With sharp knife, make 3 evenly spaced diagonal slashes on top of each loaf. Again, let rise for about 90 minutes in warm, draft-free place. I cover my dough with roasting pan lid to ensure it is draft free.

Preheat oven to 450°F. Brush top of loaves with cold water and place in upper third of oven. Splash oven door with water to create steam and bake for 10 minutes. Lower temperature to 400° and bake for 20 minutes more. Remove from oven to cooling rack.

SOURDOUGH RYE BREAD

This bread takes a couple of days' preparation, but when you have casually mentioned you're serving your own homemade Sourdough Rye—something magical happens. The bread is wonderful and is worth the extra days.

2 packages active dry yeast
3 1/4 cups warm water (110–115°F.)
6 cups all-purpose flour (approximately)
2 cups rye flour
3 tablespoons sugar
2 teaspoons salt

2 tablespoons caraway seeds
2 tablespoons melted butter
Cornmeal
1 egg, lightly beaten with 1 tablespoon
    water

Four days ahead of making bread, prepare starter. Combine 1 package of yeast, 2 cups warm water, and 2 cups all-purpose flour in plastic bowl or container. Cover tightly and let stand at room temperature for 2 days. Then refrigerate for at least another day.

The day before preparing dough, combine 1 cup starter, rye flour, and 1 cup warm water in bowl. Cover with plastic wrap and let stand at room temperature overnight.

The next day proof second package of yeast with sugar and 1/4 cup warm water until bubbly and double in size. Stir down dough and add salt, caraway seeds, and butter. Then add proofed yeast mixture. Place in large bowl of mixer with dough hook; add up to 4 cups all-purpose flour, 1 cup at a time, to make stiff but workable dough.

Knead 10–12 minutes; then shape into ball. Place in buttered bowl, turning to coat with butter. Cover with plastic wrap and let stand in warm, draft-free place 1 1/2 hours or until dough has doubled in bulk.

Remove from bowl and punch down firmly. Cut into 2–3 equal portions and roll into smooth balls. Place on buttered cookie sheet generously sprinkled with cornmeal. Cover with roasting pan to keep draft-free and let rise again until doubled in bulk, about 1 hour.

Preheat oven to 375°F. Brush with egg wash for crisp, shiny crust. Place pan of water in bottom of oven to create steam. Bake 30 minutes or until lightly browned.

PORTUGUESE SWEET BREAD MAKES 2 ROUND LOAVES

2 packages active dry yeast
1 cup sugar
1/4 cup warm water (110–115°F.)
3 tablespoons butter, cut into small chunks
1 cup milk

5 1/2–6 cups unbleached flour
1 teaspoon salt
3 eggs, room temperature
1 egg, lightly beaten with 1 tablespoon water

In small bowl, proof yeast with 1 teaspoon sugar in warm water until bubbly and double in size.

Add butter to milk and scald milk. Let cool to room temperature. In large mixing bowl, combine remaining sugar, 4 cups flour, and salt. Make a well in center of flour mixture and pour in yeast mixture and cooled milk. Add eggs and stir mixture until ingredients are combined. Then add more flour until dough forms soft ball. When it becomes difficult to stir dough, work in flour with your fingers. Turn dough out onto floured board and knead it with heel of your hand until it is smooth and elastic.

Shape dough into ball and place in buttered bowl seam side down, turning to coat with butter. Cover with plastic wrap and large tea towel and let rise in warm, draft-free place until doubled in bulk, about 1 hour. Dough is ready when dent remains in it after it has been poked with a finger. Punch dough down; divide in half and let rest for 10 minutes.

Butter two 9-inch aluminum pie tins. Pat each half of dough into an 8-inch round in each tin. Cover and let rise again in warm, draft-free place until doubled in bulk, about 40 minutes.

Preheat oven to 350°F. Brush top of each loaf with beaten egg and bake 45–55 minutes. Loaves are done when wooden toothpick inserted in center comes out clean. If tops brown too much before loaves are baked, cover lightly with aluminum foil. Cool loaves on wire rack. Serve warm with sweet butter.

WALNUT RAISIN FILLED BREAD

MAKES TWO 9 × 5 × 3-INCH LOAVES

2 packages active dry yeast
2 tablespoons sugar
1 cup warm water (110–115°F.)
1 cup milk, scalded
1/4 cup shortening (butter, margarine, or oil), melted

2 1/2 teaspoons salt
7 cups unbleached flour *or* 5 cups unbleached flour, 1 cup wheat flour, and 1 cup rye flour
1/2 cup butter, melted
1 egg, beaten

FILLINGS

1/4 cup cinnamon and 1/4 cup sugar, mixed
1/2 cup walnuts, coarsely chopped

1/4 cup chopped raisins and 1/4 cup dates (if you want a sweet bread)

In large bowl of mixer, proof yeast with sugar in warm water until bubbly and double in size.

In small bowl, mix milk, shortening, and salt and cool to lukewarm. Slowly pour milk mixture into proofed yeast mixture and stir. Slowly stir in flour, either by hand or with dough hook, 1 cup at a time, until dough is stiff but workable, or wraps around dough hook. Turn out on lightly floured board and knead for 12 minutes. When dough is smooth and elastic, shape into ball.

Place in buttered bowl, seam side down, turning to coat with butter on all sides. Cover with plastic wrap and large tea towel and set in warm, draft-free place to let rise 45 minutes or until doubled in bulk.

Punch down dough and remove to lightly floured board. Let dough rest while you butter two 9 × 5 × 3-inch loaf pans. Cut dough in half and roll into balls. Roll out each piece of dough into rectangle, approximately 7 × 9 inches and 1/4 to 1/2 inch thick.

Brush with melted butter and beaten egg. Spread desired filling over rectangle, roll up from wide end, jelly-roll fashion, and place in loaf pans seam side down. Brush tops with melted butter and cover and let rise again in warm, draft-free place for approximately 1 hour.

Preheat oven to 400°F. Bake in center of oven 1 hour, or until loaves sound hollow when tapped on top and bottom. Cool on racks or serve warm.

CHEESE PECAN COFFEE CAKE

This is beautiful! It's a coffee or tea cake that isn't too rich and, if eaten in proper quantities at late tea or coffee time, will dull your appetite pangs for that large lunch or dinner. It's kind of like the Ayds diet plan. (Do you believe me?)

DOUGH

1/4 cup warm water (110–115°F.)
1 teaspoon sugar
2 packages active dry yeast
4 1/2 cups unbleached flour
2 teaspoons salt
2 tablespoons melted butter

1 egg
3 tablespoons sugar
1 cup buttermilk
1/2 cup sour cream
1 egg, slightly beaten with 2 tablespoons of water

In small bowl, mix water, sugar, and yeast together and set aside to proof until bubbly and double in size.

Mix flour, salt, butter, egg, sugar, buttermilk, and sour cream in bowl of food processor or electric mixer with dough hook. Add yeast mixture and process 2–3 minutes. Leave in processor with cover on but unlocked. Cover with large towel or several dish towels and let rise in warm, draft-free place until doubled in bulk, about 45 minutes. Turn machine on and off 2 or 3 times to punch down dough. If you have time, let it rise again. If not, remove from processor bowl (it will be sticky) to lightly floured board. Knead almost 5 minutes, absorbing some flour, 1/2 to 3/4 cup at most. You want a light, soft, but elastic dough.

Roll out in large circle (14–15 inches in diameter) on lightly floured board. Let rest while you butter generously an 8- or 9-inch cake pan. Lay center of dough in center of pan, letting extra dough hang over sides.

Add filling (see below), pull sides, overlapping slightly to center of cake. There will be large ridges where dough overlaps, but don't flatten them. Pinch dough together by pushing and pulling up slightly to emphasize ridges. Allow to rest uncovered in warm, draft-free place 30 minutes or more.

Preheat oven to 350°F. Glaze all over with egg wash and sprinkle with brown sugar and pecans. Bake on center rack in oven 20 minutes. Lower heat to 275°, and bake 20 minutes longer. If it starts to brown too quickly, cover lightly with foil. Let cool on rack in cake pan. Remove carefully to serving platter. If you have trouble removing it (you won't), serve it right in pan in which it was baked.

FILLING

8-ounce carton fine cottage cheese, whipped
   in food processor
1 tablespoon cream or half-and-half
2 tablespoons honey
1 tablespoon lemon rind

1 teaspoon vanilla
4 eggs
3/4 cup chopped pecans
2/3 cup brown sugar
2 tablespoons butter, or more if needed

Blend well all of above ingredients (except pecans, brown sugar, and butter). Pour cheese mixture over bottom of coffee cake; then cover with chopped pecans, reserving a small amount to sprinkle on top. Sprinkle brown sugar over all, reserving small amount to sprinkle on top, and dot with little chunks of butter.

Pull dough over cheese filling, overlapping slightly toward center but not completely covering filling.

RICH SOUR CREAM COFFEE CAKE

MAKES TWO 10-INCH RING LOAVES

DOUGH

3 packages active dry yeast
1/2 cup sugar
1/2 cup warm water (110–115°F.)
1 teaspoon salt
1/2 cup cold milk
1 cup sour cream

2 teaspoons lemon juice
1 teaspoon vanilla
3 egg yolks
5–6 cups flour
1 cup (2 sticks) sweet butter, softened

FILLING

2 tablespoons sweet butter, melted
1/4 cup brown or white sugar mixed with 1 teaspoon ground cinnamon

1/4 to 1/2 cup currants or raisins, presoaked, preferably in brandy
1/2 cup finely chopped nuts

APRICOT GLAZE

1 pound jar of apricot jam or preserves (preferably without pectin)

1 tablespoon brandy, Cointreau, or Grand Marnier

Proof yeast with 1/4 cup sugar in warm water in medium bowl until bubbly and double in size. When yeast has proofed, stir in remaining 1/4 cup sugar, salt, milk, sour cream, lemon juice, and vanilla and mix well. Add egg yolks and blend.

Place 5 cups flour and butter in large bowl of mixer with dough hook. Rapidly work butter into flour to produce a dry, mealy consistency. Add yeast mixture to flour-butter mixture and knead with dough hook, adding more flour by table-spoonfuls if necessary until you have a fairly stiff, but workable, dough.

Turn out on lightly floured board and knead 5–10 minutes until dough is smooth and elastic and then shape into ball. Place in buttered bowl, seam side down, turning to coat dough with butter on all sides. Cover tightly with plastic wrap and large tea towel and refrigerate to let rise for at least 4 hours or overnight or until doubled in bulk. Remove from refrigerator, punch dough down with fist, and turn out on lightly floured board.

Divide dough in half and roll out each piece into a rectangle, about 12 × 20 inches. Brush rectangles with melted butter and sprinkle with brown or white sugar and cinnamon. Over this sprinkle drained currants or raisins and then chopped nuts. Gently press filling into dough with rolling pin. Roll up from wide end, jelly-roll fashion. Let rest while you butter generously two 10-inch tube pans. Carefully fit rolls into pans so that ends of dough join. Cover with plastic wrap and large tea towel and let rise in warm, draft-free place until doubled in bulk.

Preheat oven to 375°F. Bake on middle rack of oven 45–55 minutes or until they are golden brown and give a hollow sound when rapped with knuckles. Let cool for 15 minutes in pans; then invert on rack.

Meanwhile melt apricot jam over low heat. Add brandy, Cointreau, or Grand Marnier and blend. Strain and coat sides and top of cakes with glaze while cakes are still warm. Cool thoroughly before slicing.

BEER BREAD

MAKES ONE 9 × 5 × 3-INCH LOAF

3 cups self-rising flour
3 tablespoons sugar

12-ounce can of beer at room temperature
1/4 cup butter or margarine, melted

Preheat oven to 375°F. Combine flour, sugar and beer in large bowl. Mix just enough to blend. Pour into buttered 9 × 5 × 3-inch loaf pan. Pour butter or margarine on top and bake 45–50 minutes or until bread sounds hollow when rapped with knuckles on top, or if cake tester or toothpick inserted in center of loaf comes out clean. Do not overbake. This bread is better the next day toasted for breakfast.

VARIATION You may add 1 teaspoon cinnamon, scant cup of raisins, and 3/4 cup chopped nuts mixed together and added after blending in ingredients.

BISCUITS

2 cups sifted flour
2 teaspoons baking powder
1/2 teaspoon salt

1/2 cup shortening
1 cup plus 2 tablespoons milk
2 tablespoons cream

Preheat oven to 400°F. Sift dry ingredients together into medium-sized mixing bowl. Add shortening. Cut shortening into flour mixture coarsely with 2 knives. Stir mixture gently while adding milk sparingly until dough is sticky and not dry.

Lift dough out to floured board. Knead lightly a few seconds. Pat or roll to 1/2-inch-thick large circle. Then cut with 1 1/2-inch biscuit cutter. After first batch is cut, pinch dough together, trying not to mix too much flour into it during process.

Place on greased cookie sheet so that biscuits don't touch. Bake for 10 minutes until nice and brown. Brush top of biscuits with cream to give them a gloss.

For Buttermilk Biscuits substitute buttermilk for regular milk. You may need a little more. Two tablespoons should do it. Add 1/2 teaspoon baking soda and proceed as for regular biscuits.

LEAVENWORTH BISCUITS

Along with Merle Haggard, his great band, Jonathan Winters, and a few other people, I was a guest on a TV show Burt Reynolds hosted at Leavenworth Prison. During one of the rehearsal breaks, the warden's wife and a few of her friends invited me to lunch. These spicy biscuits were a big hit with me. I subsequently cooked them for Howard Cosell on my TV show, hoping to elicit an encouraging word from the mighty one. He sampled one and then another and suggested that my biscuits and I should serve a long sentence in solitary. Are you going to take my word or Howard's? They're delicious.

2 cups flour
1 teaspoon salt
2 1/2 teaspoons baking powder
1/2 cup shortening
1/3 cup margarine (or 1/2 cup if desired)
3/4 pound spicy bulk sausage (uncooked)

1 1/2 cups (or more) very sharp cheese, grated
Dash of cayenne (optional)
Dash of Tabasco (optional)
1/3 cup milk

Preheat oven to 450°F. Combine flour, salt and baking powder. Add shortening and margarine. Cut in with two knives or pastry blender until mixture is in pieces size of small peas. Add sausage and mix together thoroughly, preferably with hands. Add cheese and blend in well. Add cayenne and Tabasco if desired. Sprinkle milk over top and mix in gently.

Form mixture into patties about 2 inches across and 3/4 inch thick. Place on greased cookie sheet and bake for about 15 minutes or until browned. Serve immediately.

BUTTERMILK CORN BREAD SERVES 8

This is the most popular quick bread (outside of biscuits) where I come from. Corn bread really has to be served hot. Do not prepare until you are just about ready to serve dinner. If the others are not ready, go ahead and eat yours anyway; somebody should be able to appreciate this nutlike delicacy at its peak and that's when it's hot!

1 cup cornmeal, yellow or white
1 cup unbleached flour
3 teaspoons baking powder
1 tablespoon sugar
1/2 teaspoon salt
1 1/2 cups buttermilk
2 eggs

1/2 cup butter, melted
1/2 generous teaspoon baking soda
1 tablespoon butter for baking dish
1/4 cup chopped jalapeño peppers (optional)
1 tablespoon chopped and drained pimiento
　(optional)

In large bowl, mix cornmeal, flour, baking powder, sugar, and salt and set aside. Pour buttermilk into 1-quart measuring cup. Add eggs and beat lightly with fork. Add melted butter and soda.

Preheat oven to 425°F. Just before you are ready to bake corn bread, put lump of butter in 8-inch-square baking dish. (I use 9-inch quiche pan.) Place baking dish with butter in oven and let it heat through, butter will coat pan. Or you can grease baking dish with butter or margarine. (I prefer the former method.)

Combine dry ingredients with egg-buttermilk mixture and mix until just blended. Do not overmix. The mixture should be of a fluid consistency to pour into preheated baking dish. Add more buttermilk if necessary. Add peppers and pimiento at this point if you are using them. Pour mixture into heated baking dish. Bake for about 15–20 minutes or until just done.

Drizzle with a little melted butter and cut into wedges. Serve in same dish in which it was baked, or lift out and serve in a linen napkin. I warm the serving dish and the napkin.

POPOVERS

You may not be aware of it but there is a raging controversy about popovers. It has to do with preheating or not preheating your oven and heating the ovenproof custard cups in which you bake them or not heating them. I heat and preheat! Craig Claiborne—dear friend! That's the way momma taught me.

1 cup flour, sifted
1/2 teaspoon salt
2 eggs

1 cup milk
1 tablespoon salad oil

316   BREADS

Preheat oven to 425°F. Grease aluminum popover pans or large muffin tins. (If you have an old iron popover pan, all the better.) I use ovenproof custard cups, grease them well, and place on baking sheet in oven to heat thoroughly just before filling.

Measure all ingredients into a bowl and beat with rotary beater until mixture is very smooth. It is a thin batter. Fill cups a little less than half full and bake 30 minutes without peeking, or until sides are rigid to the touch. If drier popovers are desired, pierce each one with knife and bake 5 minutes longer.

The three tricks here are the preheated custard cups or muffin tins, filling them less than half full of batter so the popovers will have room to grow, and *not peeking*.

I use popovers instead of Yorkshire pudding with roast beef.

CUCUMBER DILL MUFFINS
MAKES 12–14 MUFFINS

2 cups unbleached flour
3 tablespoons sugar
1/2 teaspoon salt
1/2 teaspoon soda
3 teaspoons baking powder

1/2 cup grated unpeeled cucumber
2 teaspoons finely chopped fresh dill
1 1/3 cups buttermilk
2 eggs
1/3 cup butter, melted

Preheat oven to 400°F. Combine dry ingredients and add cucumber and dill in large mixing bowl. In another bowl, mix buttermilk and eggs together with wire whisk. Add butter and whisk again. Pour milk-egg-butter mixture into dry ingredients. Mix just enough to blend, but do not overmix.

Spoon mixture into paper-lined or well-buttered muffin tins, filling cups about two-thirds full. Place muffin tin in center of oven and bake 25 minutes.

HOTEL PEABODY VANILLA MUFFINS
MAKES 36 MUFFINS

To us teenagers in Nashville, the Peabody Hotel in Memphis was one of the most glamorous palaces in Tennessee and completely remote unless you happened to be invited to a prom. I never quite made it to a prom at the Peabody, nor was I ever at the Peabody long enough to have their vanilla muffins. For the rest of you who missed this treat too, here they are exactly as they were prepared in a no-nonsense way in the old days. It sounds perfect for adaptation to the new processor methods.

2 cups sugar
4 eggs
4 cups flour
2 cups sweet milk

1 tablespoon baking powder
1/2 cup (1 stick) butter, melted
1 tablespoon vanilla

Preheat oven to 400°F. In large bowl, beat sugar and eggs together; add flour, milk, baking powder, butter, and vanilla and mix thoroughly.

Spoon mixture into well-buttered muffin tins, filling cups about two-thirds full. Bake 25–30 minutes or until golden brown.

LEMON BREAD MAKES FIVE 5 3/4 × 3 1/4 × 2 1/4-INCH MINI-LOAVES

This is a lemony, buttery cake bread that is as simple to make as it is delicious. Like most baking-powder breads, it's better the first couple of days. The small loaves make welcome house gifts.

3 cups sugar
1 cup plus 2 tablespoons softened butter
6 eggs
1 1/2 cups milk
4 1/2 cups flour

1 1/2 tablespoons baking powder
1 1/2 teaspoons salt
Rind of 3 lemons, finely grated
Lemon Glaze

Preheat oven to 350°F. Combine all the ingredients in mixer bowl or food processor, except lemon rind and glaze. Blend well. Stir in lemon rind. Pour into well-buttered loaf pans. Bake on center rack of oven approximately 1 hour, or until toothpick inserted in center of loaf comes out clean. *Do not overbake.* Remove from pans and set on large platter right side up and while hot pour Lemon Glaze over all.

LEMON GLAZE
1 1/2 cups sugar   Juice of 3 lemons

In heavy saucepan, combine sugar and lemons. Cook over medium heat for about 2 minutes or until sugar is completely dissolved.

WHOLE WHEAT BANANA BREAD
MAKES ONE 9 × 5 × 3-INCH LOAF

Joanne Woodward stays in great shape. She runs, goes to regular ballet classes and takes care of her handsome, talented family in thoughtful, healthy ways. She baked this bread on our TV show one day, using ingredients carefully assembled from the health-food section of her grocery store. It's good and good for you.

1/2 cup butter, cut into chunks
3/4 cup brown or raw sugar
1 egg
1 1/4 cups mashed ripe bananas (2 large or 3 small)
1/4 cup yogurt

1 cup unsifted stoneground whole wheat flour
1/2 cup unsifted unbleached flour
1 teaspoon soda
3/4 teaspoon sea salt

Preheat oven to 350°F. Place butter and sugar in bowl of food processor and process until light and creamy, stopping once or twice to scrape down bowl. With machine running, add egg through feed tube and blend. Add bananas and yogurt, turning machine on and off just long enough to blend.

Sift together whole wheat flour, unbleached flour, soda, and salt. Add to mixture in processor bowl. Turn machine on and off 2–3 times, or just long enough to mix batter.

Pour mixture into oiled 9 × 5 × 3-inch loaf pan and bake 50–55 minutes, or until toothpick inserted in center comes out clean. *Do not overbake.* Cool in pan 10 minutes. Remove from pan and finish cooling on rack.

AUNT GUSTY'S CARROT BREAD

MAKES THREE 9 × 5 × 3-INCH LOAVES

I never met Aunt Gusty, but she sure knows how to make a carrot bread. Some friendly niece or nephew passed it on to me. I pass it on to you and make you an honorary niece or nephew.

3 eggs
3 cups sugar
1 cup oil
3 cups flour, sifted
1 teaspoon soda
1 teaspoon cinnamon

1 teaspoon salt
2 cups carrots, grated
1 cup walnuts, coarsely chopped
1 cup crushed pineapple
1/2 teaspoon vanilla

Preheat oven to 375°F. In large mixing bowl, beat eggs well with electric beater. Add sugar and oil and blend. Add dry ingredients and beat until well blended. Add carrots, walnuts and pineapple and blend well. Stir in vanilla and mix gently.

Butter or oil three 9 × 5 × 3-inch loaf pans. Pour mixture into loaf pans and bake on center rack in oven for 1 hour, or until toothpick inserted in center comes out clean. Let cool in pans for about 5 minutes. Remove from pans and cool on rack.

BRAN BREAD

Self-explanatory. It's moist and crunchy and nutritious.

1/3 cup butter or margarine
1/2 cup dark brown sugar, packed, *or* scant
  1/2 cup honey
1 egg
1 1/2 cups sifted unbleached flour
1 scant teaspoon salt
1 1/2 teaspoons soda
1/2 teaspoon baking powder

2 tablespoons wheat germ
1/2 cup black coffee
1 cup water plus 2 tablespoons
1/4 cup dark molasses
1 heaping cup all-bran cereal (soaked in
  water for 15 minutes)
1 cup raisins
1/2 cup coarsely chopped walnuts (optional)

In bowl of food processor or with hand beater in large mixing bowl, cream butter, and then add sugar or honey and mix well. Add egg. Preheat oven to 350°F. Sift flour, salt, soda, and baking powder together; then add wheat germ. Mix together coffee, water, molasses, and bran. Alternately add flour mixture and water mixture to creamed butter-sugar mixture. Combine thoroughly and then add raisins and walnuts. Turn food processor on and off 2–3 times to mix. Bake in well-buttered 9 × 5 × 3-inch loaf pan 45 minutes. Serve hot for breakfast or tea.

BUTTERMILK BRAN MUFFINS
MAKES 12 MUFFINS

A luscious breakfast treat. Step up and sit down—get your health food and fiber right here, folks!

1 1/4 cups all-bran cereal
1 cup buttermilk
1 cup flour
2 1/2 teaspoons baking powder
1/4 cup sugar or 3 tablespoons honey*
1/2 teaspoon soda

1 egg
1/3 cup melted butter or oil
2 tablespoons white raisins
2 tablespoons chopped walnuts
12 teaspoons melted butter or oil for muffin
  tins

Preheat oven to 400°F. Combine all-bran and buttermilk in bowl. Set aside to soak for 5 minutes. Mix flour, baking powder, sugar, and soda together in large bowl. Mix egg and melted butter together in large measuring cup. Add to buttermilk and all-bran. Combine with dry ingredients and mix well. Add raisins and walnuts.

    Place scant teaspoon of butter or oil in each muffin tin. Place in oven and heat tins until butter or oil is sizzling. Carefully remove muffin tin from oven and fill each cup half full. Bake 20 minutes. Eat while hot with butter and honey.

    *If using honey instead of sugar, mix with melted butter and egg instead of dry ingredients. It makes for easier handling.

DATE-BRAN-NUT BREAD

MAKES TWO 5 3/4 × 3 1/4 × 2 1/4 LOAVES

I had all these little goodies around one wintry afternoon at the beach and a new set of small loaf pans. With Christmas holidays just around the corner, I couldn't resist. I'm not a big coffee drinker, but I love its flavor in quick breads and puddings and it was left over from breakfast. The bread is healthy and keeps neighbors and relatives the same.

1/2 cup strong coffee (if you don't like coffee, use boiling water)
1/4 cup water (or substitute 3/4 cup medium-strong coffee for coffee and water)
1 cup dates, pitted and cut in half
1/2 cup coarsely broken walnuts
1/2 cup all-bran cereal
1/2 cup buttermilk
1/2 teaspoon soda
2 eggs, lightly beaten

1/4 cup honey
4 tablespoons vegetable oil
1 1/2 cups whole wheat flour
2 teaspoons baking powder
1/2 teaspoon salt
1/2 cup brown sugar
1/4 teaspoon coriander
1/4 teaspoon cinnamon
1/4 teaspoon nutmeg
1/4 teaspoon coarsely ground black pepper

Boil coffee and water. Add dates, continue boiling for 2 minutes, then add walnuts. Turn off heat and let stand. In large bowl, combine bran and buttermilk. Add soda, eggs, and honey. Then add coffee-date-walnut mixture and oil. Mix lightly until well blended.

Combine remaining ingredients and add to mixture. Stir lightly to blend, but do not overmix. Let stand 15–20 minutes.

Preheat oven to 325°F. Butter or grease two 5 3/4 × 3 1/4 × 2 1/4-inch loaf pans. Fill each loaf pan about two-thirds full with batter. Bake about 30 minutes. Check at 20 minutes with cake tester or toothpick inserted in center of loaf. If it comes out clean, bread is done or if it starts to draw away from sides of pan, take out immediately and remove from pan carefully so it won't continue to bake. Set out on rack.

Bread is much better 24–48 hours later. To reheat lightly wrap in foil and warm in preheated 325° oven 5 minutes.

SOUR CREAM COFFEE CAKE

MAKES 1 COFFEE CAKE 10 3/4 × 7 × 1 1/2 INCHES

1/2 cup butter or margarine
1 cup sugar
2 eggs
1 teaspoon vanilla
2 cups sifted flour

1 teaspoon baking powder
1 teaspoon soda
1/2 teaspoon salt
1 cup sour cream
Nut Topping

Preheat oven to 350°F. Cream butter and sugar thoroughly in large mixing bowl. Beat in eggs, 1 at a time; add vanilla. Sift flour with baking powder, soda, and salt. Add to creamed mixture, alternately with sour cream.

Pour half of batter in greased 10 3/4 × 7 × 1 1/2-inch baking pan. Sprinkle with half of topping mixture; add remaining batter and sprinkle with remaining topping mixture. Bake 45 minutes or until cake tester or toothpick inserted in center of cake comes out clean.

NUT TOPPING

1/4 cup sugar
1/4 cup packed brown sugar

1/4 cup walnuts, coarsely chopped
2 teaspoons cinnamon

Mix all ingredients well. P.S. This works great in the food processor too.

KATHY'S NUT BREAD   MAKES FIVE 8 × 4 × 2-INCH LOAVES

Kathy is the guiding charmer of the Los Posas Country Club dining room. About the fifteenth hole, you begin to salivate, anticipating what Kathy and her associates in the kitchen will have prepared as the special treat of the day. This was one little specialty she brought in from home for me to try. Obviously, the best way to handle Kathy's marvelous and personal recipe and those specials for lunch she and her associates devise is to jog between shots around the course. This is one of my better ideas (which I have not followed so far) because, for the regulation number of shots on each hole, I generally have an extra one or two. They are called bogies or double bogies if you're interested.

This bread makes a lovely gift for holidays. But it also keeps well for a week or more in the refrigerator or wrapped securely in aluminum foil in the bread box.

5 cups flour
4 1/2 cups sugar
3/4 teaspoon baking powder
3 teaspoons soda
2 1/4 teaspoons salt
3 teaspoons cloves
3 teaspoons cinnamon
1 1/2 teaspoons nutmeg

1 1/2 cups vegetable oil
1 1/2 cups water
3 cups canned pumpkin or applesauce or mashed bananas
6 eggs
1 1/2 cups coarsely chopped walnuts, pecans, or almonds

Preheat oven to 325°F. In large bowl, mix together the first 8 ingredients listed above. Stir in oil, water, and pumpkin or applesauce or mashed bananas. Beat eggs lightly and stir into mixture. Add nuts.

Butter or grease five 8 × 4 × 2-inch loaf pans. Fill each loaf pan two-thirds full of batter. Bake 1 1/2 hours.

Chapter 13
CAKES, COOKIES, AND PIES

I can ad lib or improvise to my heart's content in almost any area of cooking except baking. There are just certain basic rules to follow:

Use the correct amount and type of flour in proportion to the liquids and the leavening agents—baking powder, soda, yeast, and egg whites.

Follow directions about liquid ingredients, the amount of mixing time, and the blending with other ingredients.

Add a little soda as well as baking powder when making quick breads or cakes with sour cream or butter.

Bake in the proper-sized pan: too big and your cake is thinner—unless you cook it for less time than prescribed, and it could dry out on you in that large a pan; too small and it rises up over your pan onto the oven floor or doesn't cook completely in the middle.

Bake at the right temperature and for the right length of time.

Keep an oven thermometer handy, the kind that hangs on the rack of your oven and indicates whether or not the temperature is registering accurately when the light goes on or off. If the oven is not working properly, get that expert out to check it and fix it. One common problem is an oven door that doesn't seal in the heat.

All of these rules are basic, and, if followed, make you a good baker. When you're good, you can move on to great by perfecting a few almost intuitive techniques: the folding in of egg whites and the final blending of the ingredients before baking. Some recipes call for 3 to 6 minutes' beating time; others, such as corn bread and biscuits, minimum handling.

Read the recipe and then keep it close by for instant reference. Set out the ingredients, preferably in the order in which you will be using them. Of course, baking procedures have changed and completely simplified since the introduction of the food processor; shortenings and sugars cream effortlessly and quickly. Sometimes you pour the whole thing into the processor instead of 4 or 5 bowls. Stiffly Beaten Egg Whites the New Way, in the Basics chapter, is a precious time and bowl saver.

There are as many cookie formulas as there are vegetables or flowers. I always admire and wonder about an original cookie recipe. The originals, or a version of them, seem to have been around almost forever. There are family favorites, your mother's favorite cookie recipe, her mother's best friend's recipe, and Minnie Sue's special. They came from someplace, and if they sound familiar, it's because they are. Mom probably found them in the old *Settlement House Cook Book* or *The Joy of Cooking,* or in those spiral-bound local ladies' aid community cookbooks. If she added her special touch and passed it on to you, you're lucky. Anyway, whatever you found in the cookie jar after school was so satisfying and terrific, it was unforgettable. You were hungrier then.

Mother and our housekeeper, Lillian, were great cookie bakers, but for the longest time I thought Mother made Oreos or Fig Newtons because when she'd run out of her homemades, or was on her beloved golf course, they'd be there as a little something before or after I'd had my after-school snack—usually crisp fried potatoes or sandwiches of some sort. They were trying to fatten me up a little (oh, glorious day). "Don't forget," her favorite phrase was, "save a little something to take the sweet taste out"—which meant don't eat every bit of your favorite dinner food; save one or two bites for after dessert. Sweets were not the premium we've made them today by holding back the luscious sweet thing till you've "finished every bite on that dinner plate."

There's a gracious custom on the Continent that we've begun to adopt—afternoon tea. When my children were smaller, it was a real treat to break up the afternoon homework regimen with a "tea party"—choice of hot cocoa or milk with a drop of tea in it, served in front of the fireplace in my prettiest teacups and saucers with a plate of little sandwiches and their favorite cookies: the Quality Coconut Cookies in Quantity, the Butterscotch Nuggets (Jody's favorite), and if adult company came by, Mother's Pecan Rum Cakes (page 332)—wow! One to a customer. The idea was not to spoil dinner, but to fill that little hunger gap at about four in the afternoon, so that we didn't have to have dinner at 5:30 or 6 o'clock when they were "starving" but could all eat together when everybody in the family was home and comfortable and ready.

If hot dogs and hamburgers are the All-American favorites, how about apple pie? Pies are splendid cappers for light or heavy meals, but I used to steer clear of them—I was terrified of piecrusts. They either came out thin, fork-resistant soles of slippers, or fell apart like a pile of fish scales in a windstorm. I remember standing across the kitchen staring at the enemy in a bowl and saying softly, "Are we going to be nice to each other today or is it the same old routine?" My crust would roll out smooth and pretty and lie perfectly on the lightly floured board, waiting for my rolling pin (lightly floured) to lift its "perfectness" onto the pie plate, and *then* it would stick, split, hole, and tear. It was never like those in the books I read or the pictures I saw. It still isn't, but I make one of the best piecrusts around. I decided who's boss. If it tears, it doesn't matter—it can be patched and no one will ever know but my crust and me.

It's flaky, crisp, and meltingly tender because of a few tricks I've learned. First, don't work it too long; the shortening and butter and other ingredients have to stay cold. Next, add ice water, a tablespoon at a time, and when it forms a ball wrap loosely in waxed paper and flatten slightly with the palm of your hand. Then place it in the refrigerator to chill 30 minutes or an hour or even a day before using. This lets the gluten in the flour get used to its companions. Some people roll out crusts the minute they're mixed. It's easier, but it never seems as buttery or crunchy to me.

When your dough comes out of the refrigerator, it's hard as a rock; place it on your lightly floured board. Get a firm grip on the rolling pin and give it a few whacks to flatten it so it can be rolled quickly, making sure it doesn't get too warm in the process. Turn it on your board from time to time, checking the flour underneath. If necessary, sprinkle a little more flour on the board and rub a little on your rolling pin. Keep turning and rolling quickly and lightly but firmly until the dough is the right size, about an inch larger than the pie pan you'll be using.

There are piecrusts listed here and also in the Basics chapter. Simply put all your ingredients, except the water, into the bowl of your food processor. Using the metal blade, blend until the mixture resembles coarse cornmeal. Have a little measuring cup of ice water handy (I even have an ice cube floating in the cup). With the motor running, pour the water, 1 tablespoon at a time, through the feed tube until the dough wraps itself around the blade in a ball. No more mixing—it's ready! The number of possible fillings is infinite—fruits to ice creams. I've got a million of them and so will you, once you start letting those creative juices flow.

You may be confused by the terms "piecrust" and "pie shell"—they are interchangeable. Some recipes may call for a baked pie shell; others call for unbaked. In the latter case, the piecrust bakes right along with your filling, and if the edges begin to brown before your center is done, roll a little band of aluminum foil around the edges to cover and protect your hard-come-by "perfectness."

GÂTEAU AU CHOCOLAT
SERVES 8–10

There is a superb restaurant in Wheeling, just outside of Chicago. It is called Le Français and it is very Français. The chef is an artist named Jean Banchet. This is his chocolate cake. Serve it in thin slices as it is really rich and you'll have a little left over the next day for you—you—you.

Incidentally, that cooking time—3, count 'em, 3—hours is correct as is the low baking temperature. If cake begins to get a little crusty and dark on top, place a circle of aluminum foil over the top.

CAKE

14 ounces semisweet baking chocolate	10 eggs, separated
14 tablespoons unsalted butter	1 tablespoon Grand Marnier
1 1/2 cups sugar	1 teaspoon pure vanilla extract

CRÈME ANGLAISE

4 cups milk	2 whole vanilla beans (split beans and use
8 egg yolks, beaten	inside scrapings)
1 1/4 cups sugar	Powdered sugar

Preheat oven to 250°F. Butter and flour 12-inch springform pan. Break chocolate into chunks. Place in top of double boiler along with butter. Melt over simmering water, stirring occasionally. Stir 1 1/4 cups sugar into chocolate-and-butter mixture. Continue heating until sugar is dissolved. Beat egg yolks in separate bowl. Beat some of hot chocolate mixture into yolks. Combine all together in saucepan.

Cook over simmering water, stirring constantly, until slightly thickened; stir in Grand Marnier and vanilla. Beat egg whites until they stand in soft peaks. Continue beating, gradually adding remaining 1/4 cup sugar until whites stand upright in stiff peaks when beater is removed. Carefully fold egg whites into chocolate mixture.

Pour mixture into prepared pan. Bake 3 hours. Remove from oven. Let cool to room temperature, cover, and chill.

While cake cools, make Crème Anglaise. Bring milk to boil in medium saucepan. Mix egg yolks and sugar in bowl and whisk hot milk into mixture. Return mixture to saucepan.

Add vanilla-bean scrapings, heat and stir over low heat until custard coats spoon (this can take up to 10 minutes). Do not allow to boil or it will curdle. Immediately place Crème Anglaise into bowl and set in pan of ice water to cool. Stir occasionally. When cool, remove the vanilla beans.

Transfer cake to serving platter. Cut cake into very thin wedges (it is extremely rich) and serve with a few spoonfuls of Crème Anglaise.

GLAZED FUDGE CAKE

SERVES 10

3/4 cup plus 2 tablespoons cake flour
1 teaspoon baking powder
1/2 teaspoon soda
1/2 teaspoon salt
1 1/4 cups sugar
2 squares unsweetened baking chocolate (2 ounces total), broken into pieces
1 tablespoon cocoa

1/3 cup boiling water
2 large eggs
1 1/2 stick unsalted butter (6 ounces), at room temperature and cut into 6 pieces
1/2 cup sour cream
1 tablespoon dark rum
Chocolate Rum Glaze

Preheat oven to 325°F. Cut round of parchment or waxed paper to fit bottom of an 8-inch springform pan. Place in pan and butter paper and sides of pan. Insert metal blade in food processor and add flour, baking powder, soda, and salt. Process 5 seconds to blend. Set aside.

Put 1/4 cup sugar, chocolate, and cocoa in processor; process 1 minute, or until chocolate is finely minced. With machine running, pour boiling water through feed tube. Process until chocolate is melted. Add eggs and process for 1 minute. Add remaining sugar and process for 1 minute, stopping once to scrape down bowl. Add butter and process 1 minute more. Add sour cream and rum and process 5 seconds. Add reserved dry ingredients and turn machine on and off 3 or 4 times, just until flour disappears. Do not overprocess.

Transfer batter to prepared pan and spread it evenly with a spatula. Bake 50–55 minutes on center rack in oven or until cake begins to withdraw slightly from sides of pan. Let cake cool in pan on cake rack. Meanwhile, prepare the Chocolate Rum Glaze. When cake is cool, remove from pan and spread glaze over top and sides with flexible spatula.

NOTE If using hand or other electric mixer:

Mix flour, baking powder, soda, and salt well in separate bowl. Melt chocolate in boiling water. Add sugar, chocolate mixture, and cocoa and blend well together. Then follow remaining instructions, folding in dry ingredients until flour disappears into batter.

CHOCOLATE RUM GLAZE

MAKES ABOUT ½ CUP

3 ounces sweet chocolate
2 tablespoons water
2 tablespoons unsalted butter

4 tablespoons sifted powdered sugar
Pinch of salt
1 teaspoon dark rum

Put all glaze ingredients, except rum, in top of double boiler. Cook slowly until heated through and chocolate is melted. Add rum, and refrigerate glaze until it begins to thicken.

BATICA (COCONUT CAKE)

SERVES 6–8

Try this. It's perfect for tea, coffee time, and just plain nibbling.

2 2/3 cups sugar
1/2 cup water
6 tablespoons butter (well softened)
2 small eggs plus 3 egg yolks

1 1/2 cups semolina
4 cups loosely packed freshly grated coconut
1/2 teaspoon freshly grated nutmeg

In heavy saucepan combine sugar and water; bring liquid to boil over moderate heat, stirring and brushing down any sugar crystals clinging to sides of pan with brush dipped in cold water. Simmer syrup 5 minutes. Remove from heat and let cool.

Preheat oven to 350°F. In bowl of electric mixer beat syrup at moderate speed 1 minute. Beat in butter, 1 tablespoon at a time. Add whole eggs and egg yolks, one at a time, beating well after each addition. Add semolina, beating mixture until it is smooth. Stir in freshly grated coconut and nutmeg. Spoon mixture into buttered and floured 1 1/2-quart ring mold and bake 45 minutes or until golden. Let cake cool in pan 25 minutes. Turn out on rack to cool completely and serve it cut into very thin slices.

THE JUDGE'S CHOCOLATE CAKE

Shaw's Restaurant in Lancaster, Ohio, generously sent me this recipe. I don't know the name of the judge for whom this cake was named, but he can handle my cake case any day.

1 cup sifted cake flour
1/4 cup unsweetened cocoa
1 1/2 cups superfine sugar
1 1/4 cups egg whites at room temperature

1 1/4 teaspoons cream of tartar
1/4 teaspoon salt
1 teaspoon vanilla

Preheat oven to 325°F. Sift flour with cocoa and 1/2 cup of sugar. Set aside. Beat egg whites until frothy and add cream of tartar, salt, and vanilla. Gradually add remaining sugar and beat until stiff. Fold into flour mixture. Put into 10-inch tube pan and bake 1 hour. Turn pan upside down to cool 1 hour before removing cake.

FROSTING

1 cup unsalted butter

2 cups powdered sugar

4 eggs

2 1-ounce squares unsweetened chocolate

2 teaspoons vanilla

Beat butter in electric mixer until light and fluffy; add sugar. Separate eggs and add yolks to butter. Melt chocolate and add it to butter mixture. Add vanilla. Beat egg whites until glossy but not too stiff. Fold into butter mixture.

TO ASSEMBLE CAKE

Split cake into two layers horizontally. Spread generous amount of frosting on cut edge of bottom half. Place top half in place and frost whole cake. This is not too much frosting—just pile it on! (If it gets too runny put it in the fridge for a bit.) Refrigerate cake for at least 2 hours or overnight if possible.

CHOCOLATE MOCHA CAKE

4 squares (1 ounce) unsweetened chocolate

1 cup hot water

1/4 pound (1 stick) butter, melted

2 cups flour

2 cups sugar

Pinch of salt

1/2 cup buttermilk

1 1/4 teaspoons soda

2 eggs

1 teaspoon vanilla

Preheat oven to 350°F. Grease bottom of two 9-inch layer-cake pans, line with waxed paper and grease paper. Melt chocolate with water in top of double boiler. Bring to boil and then add butter.

Sift together in large mixing bowl flour, sugar, and salt. Add chocolate-butter mixture and beat by hand or with electric mixer until mixture is smooth. Add buttermilk and soda and beat until well blended. Add eggs, one at a time, beating well after each. Add vanilla and blend. Pour into prepared cake pans and bake for almost 30 minutes, or until cake tester or toothpick inserted in center comes out clean.

Cool in pans for 5 minutes. Turn out on rack and remove paper. Cool.

MERINGUE

6 egg whites

1/2 teaspoon cream of tartar

1/4 teaspoon salt

1 cup sugar

Preheat oven to 275°F. Combine egg whites, cream of tartar, and salt in large mixing bowl. Beat with electric mixer until foamy. Add sugar, 3 tablespoons at a time, beating after each addition until sugar is blended. Continue beating until mixture stands in very stiff peaks.

Spoon mixture into three 9-inch-round cake pans lined with brown wrapping paper, spreading meringue just over bottom of pan. Bake 1 1/2 hours. Turn off oven. Let sit in oven for another hour. Cool and remove meringue.

FILLING AND ICING

5 cups whipping cream
1/3 cup powdered sugar
1/3 cup instant coffee

1 teaspoon vanilla
Slivered almonds for garnish

In large mixing bowl, beat cream until soft peaks form. Add sugar and instant coffee and beat until stiff peaks form. Add vanilla. Toast almonds and set aside.

TO ASSEMBLE CAKE

Take each layer of cake and cut in half. Starting with a layer of cake, place a layer of meringue over it, cover meringue with filling and then a layer of cake. Repeat until all layers are used, ending with cake layer. Frost top and sides with icing and decorate with toasted slivered almonds.

TOFFEE COFFEE ICE CREAM CAKE   SERVES 6–8

If there's a candymaker in your ara who will sell you bits and pieces of his broken-up English toffee, fine—if not, use the great recipe cousin Selma sent me from Memphis on page 331.

10-inch angel-food cake (a store-bought one
  will do if you're in a hurry)
1 pint coffee ice cream
2 cups whipping cream

1 teaspoon sugar
1 teaspoon instant coffee
1 pound Double Almond Toffee (page 331)
  or English Toffee

Slice cake crosswise twice, making 3 layers. Spread generous layer of coffee ice cream an inch or more thick on the lower two layers. Replace top layer.

Whip cream; add sugar and taste. Whip in instant coffee. Frost entire cake with it. Crush toffee into small bits and sprinkle it generously over entire cake. Chill in refrigerator until ready to serve.

TART APPLE CAKE   SERVES 6–8

5–6 tart apples
1/4 cup lemon juice, plus 2 tablespoons
1 cup sugar
3 tablespoons melted butter
1 egg

Scant teaspoon vanilla
A few drops almond extract
1 cup flour
1 teaspoon baking powder

Preheat oven to 350°F. Peel, seed, and slice apples about 1/8 inch thick. Pour 1/4 cup lemon juice over and set aside. Cream together sugar and butter. Add egg, vanilla, almond extract, and remaining lemon juice. Sift together flour and baking powder. Add to butter-sugar mixture. It will be like a thick cookie dough.

Spread mixture in bottom of 9-inch springform pan. Arrange sliced apples in a neat, thickly layered pinwheel design on top of cake. Bake 30–35 minutes.

TOPPING

1 egg
1/2 cup sugar

3 tablespoons melted butter

Mix all ingredients together. Spread over top of cake and bake an additional 15 minutes, or until brown.

BAKEWELL CAKE   SERVES 6–8

The Bakewell Cake is famous in England but it was brand new to me when I was first served it by "Choosy" (see page 75 for her Tomato and Orange Soup) at Bo Sutherland's Brotherton's restaurant in Oxfordshire. Over here we'd call this a tart or a pie, but she's the chef and I wasn't about to argue the point with her—especially since it's about as good a cake, pie, tart, whatever, as I've tasted.

CRUST

1 cup flour
1/2 cup butter or margarine

Pinch of salt
4 tablespoons water

Preheat oven to 400°F. Mix flour and butter or margarine together to a crumblike consistency. Add salt and water. Grease and flour 8-inch flan pan. Roll out pastry to line flan pan. Bake 15 minutes. Let cool before adding filling.

FILLING

3/4 cup butter
2/3 cup granulated sugar
3 eggs
1/3 cup ground almonds

1/4 cup flour
1/4 teaspoon almond extract
1 cup strawberry or raspberry jam

Cream butter and sugar together. Add eggs one by one, beating after each addition. Then add almonds, flour, and almond extract. Mix well. Line baked pastry with jam and add filling. Reduce heat to 325°, and bake 20–25 minutes.

DOUBLE ALMOND TOFFEE   MAKES ABOUT 3 POUNDS

My cousin Selma Lewis from Memphis contributed this great recipe. It's the only candy in the book—but it's so good I just couldn't leave it out. She and her husband, Marshall, brought about a bushel, so we could all share when they visited the family out here in the fall. It didn't last too long. Make it by itself, for yourself, as a gift, and if those aren't enough excuses, use it for the Coffee Toffee Ice Cream Cake preceding it.

1 pound butter

2 cups sugar

1/2 cup water

1 1/2 cups (8 ounces) whole unblanched

almonds

1 1/2 cups semisweet chocolate chips

1 1/2 cups chopped almonds, lightly toasted
(10 ounces)

In large, deep saucepan melt butter over medium heat. Grease sides of pan with some of butter. Stir in sugar and water. Cook over medium-high heat, stirring constantly, until sugar dissolves and mixture starts to boil. Cover saucepan with lid 2–3 minutes to ensure that all sugar is melted down from sides of pan.

Remove lid. Boil, stirring syrup until it changes to golden caramel color, 10–12 minutes. Add almonds, increase heat to high, and cook until almonds pop, about 2 minutes. Pour into well-greased 15 × 10 × 1-inch jelly-roll pan and cool.

Melt chocolate over hot water in double boiler. Spread half of chocolate over candy and sprinkle immediately with half of almonds; cool. Loosen edges of candy with sharp knife. Turn over on waxed paper. Spread other side with remaining chocolate. Sprinkle with remaining almonds. Allow to set. Break into pieces. Store in covered tin lined with waxed paper.

MOTHER'S PECAN RUM CAKES

MAKES ABOUT 40 LITTLE CAKES

These are something special! In the good old days in Winchester, Tennessee, when all mothers were plump and forced everybody to eat a little more, Mother used to serve, at her ladies' bridge-club luncheons, her special chicken or crab meat salad with piping hot homemade rolls—and then these—probably with homemade ice cream. Just a little something to keep body and soul together until they went home to cook dinner.

2 1/4 cups cake flour, sifted

1 1/2 cups sugar

1 teaspoon salt

3 1/2 teaspoons baking powder

1/2 cup softened butter, margarine, or shortening

3/4 cup milk

1 1/2 teaspoons vanilla

4 egg whites, at room temperature

1/2 teaspoon rum extract

1/4 cup rum

Pecan Icing

Preheat oven to 350°F. Sift flour, sugar, salt, and baking powder into large bowl of mixer. Add butter, milk, and vanilla. Beat on slow speed until blended. Then beat at medium speed for 2 minutes, occasionally scraping sides of bowl with rubber spatula. Add unbeaten egg whites, rum extract, and rum. Beat 2 minutes longer at medium speed.

Pour batter into one long 13 × 9 × 2 1/2-inch pan or two 8-inch pans greased and floured and lined with waxed paper. Bake 35–40 minutes or until surface springs back when gently pressed with finger tips. Let cake cool and prepare Pecan Icing.

PECAN ICING

1/2 cup butter (1 stick)
3 scant cups powdered sugar, sifted
Pinch of salt
4 tablespoons milk

1 1/2 teaspoons vanilla
1 cup rum
1 cup chopped fresh pecans

Cream butter and sugar with electric beater until fluffy. Add salt and stir in milk. Keep beating until very fluffy. Add vanilla.

Cut cake into 1 1/2-inch squares. Pour a generous teaspoon of rum on each cake square. Spread icing on all sides and roll in chopped fresh pecans. The icing part is pretty messy, but it all comes out beautifully as you roll it around in chopped nuts. I use a chopping bowl for this.

VARIATION You can substitute moist coconut for nuts and have Snow Rum Balls instead of Pecan Rum Cakes. Or, if you omit rum, you have plain Snow Balls, which are great too. Make them 2 1/2 inches square and you have a dessert dish instead of an accompaniment.

ALMOND AND PINE NUT TART   SERVES 8–10

Mollie Chappellet and her big, beautiful family sent me a cookbook one Christmas with recipes and enchanting illustrations of every family member's contribution to that gem of a collection. I don't know when I've ever appreciated anything more. I treasure it not only because of the loving effort that went into getting it together but because the recipes were truly terrific. Here's one.

PASTRY DOUGH

1 cup flour
6 tablespoons (3/4 stick) cold butter, cut into bits

2 tablespoons sugar
1 egg, lightly beaten

In bowl, blend flour, butter, and sugar until mixture resembles meal. Stir in egg, toss mixture until egg is absorbed, and form dough into ball. Chill dough, wrapped in waxed paper, 30 minutes.

Roll dough into a round, 1/8 inch thick, on floured surface. Fit it into 11-inch shallow flan pan with removable fluted ring, and trim edges. Prick bottom of shell with fork and chill for 30 minutes. Preheat oven to 425°F.

Line shell with waxed paper; fill paper with raw rice, and bake in lower third of oven 10 minutes. Carefully remove rice and paper; bake shell 10 minutes more, and let cool on rack.

FILLING

1/2 cup apricot preserve
1 cup almond paste, crumbled
1/4 cup (1/2 stick) butter, softened
1/3 cup sugar
1/4 teaspoon almond extract

4 eggs
1/4 cup flour
1/2 teaspoon double-acting baking powder
1/2 cup pine nuts
Sweetened whipped cream

In small saucepan, melt apricot preserve over moderately low heat, force through sieve into bowl and brush shell with it. In another bowl, beat almond paste, butter, sugar, and almond extract until mixture is smooth; beat in eggs, one at a time, beating well after each egg. Add flour and baking powder, and continue to beat mixture until it is smooth.

Transfer filling to shell, smooth top, and sprinkle it with pine nuts. Preheat oven to 425°F. Bake tart 10 minutes, reduce heat to 375°, and bake another 10 minutes, or until filling is just set. Transfer tart to rack, let it cool, and serve it with lightly sweetened whipped cream.

APRICOT TART

SERVES 14

PÂTE SUCRE II (PAGE 21)

8 tablespoons unsalted butter (1 stick), *or* 6 tablespoons (3/4-stick) unsalted butter and 2 tablespoons chicken fat

1 1/2 cups cake flour (if you don't have cake flour, sift regular flour and remove 2 tablespoons of it)

1/4 cup sugar

1 whole egg

4 egg yolks

Place flour and shortening in bowl of food processor. Using metal blade, blend until it becomes a crumbly mixture. Add whole egg and egg yolks and blend again until ball forms on blade. Chill in waxed paper for a minimum of 1 hour.

Remove and roll into 1/8-inch thick rectangle, at least 17 × 8 inches, on lightly floured surface. Drape dough over rolling pin and unroll it on 14 × 4 1/2-inch flan pan with removable bottom. Fit dough firmly into pan and cut off excess dough, leaving 1/2-inch overhang. Fold dough inward, push it up 1/4 inch over edge, and crimp edge decoratively. Prick bottom of shell with fork and chill for 1 hour.

Preheat oven to 400°F. Line shell with waxed paper, fill paper with raw rice, and bake in lower third of oven 10–15 minutes, or until it begins to set. Carefully remove rice and wax paper and bake shell for 5 minutes more, or until it is lightly colored. Carefully remove from pan, transfer to rack using large spatula, and let cool.

FILLING

1 pound apricots, dried

1/2 cup sugar

6 tablespoons (3/4 stick) butter, chilled and sliced

Apricot Glaze

Blanched almonds, halved

Sweetened whipped cream

In saucepan, combine apricots with enough water to cover them by 1/2 inch and bring water to boil over moderately high heat. Reduce heat to low, simmer 20 minutes, and let cool in water. Preheat oven to 375°F.

Transfer shell to baking sheet. Drain apricots, and arrange them slightly overlapping in crosswise rows in shell. Sprinkle with sugar, dot with butter, and bake tart in upper third of oven 30 minutes. (If apricots have not become richly colored, put tart under preheated broiler for 3 minutes). Brush hot tart with Apricot Glaze (page 313), transfer it to rack, and let it cool slightly. Decorate center of tart with halved blanched almonds, transfer tart to serving board, and serve it slightly warm with whipped cream.

UNAUTHENTIC FRENCH APPLE TART   SERVES 4

The conventional French apple tart or Tarte aux Pommes is a classic—an elegant array of perfectly overlapping, matched apple slices glazed gorgeously on a crisp, flaky, buttery crust. Obviously, this is nothing like that, but the friend who volunteered it as authentic has my gratitude for a whole new ballgame in apple tarts. It's as easy to do as it is to eat.

4 tart apples
Juice of 1 lemon
3 tablespoons butter
1/4 cup sugar
2 whole eggs, plus 2 egg yolks
2 tablespoons flour

1/2 cup sweetened condensed milk
1 teaspoon vanilla
1 teaspoon cinnamon
1/2 pint heavy cream, whipped
1 tablespoon apple liqueur (optional—I use Calvados)

Peel and seed apples. Cut 3 apples into 1/4-inch slices and 1 apple into 1/2-inch slices lengthwise. Sprinkle 2 tablespoons lemon juice over apples to prevent discoloration. Preheat oven to 350°F.

Butter a small soufflé dish (6 inches diameter × 2 1/4 inches deep) with about 1 tablespoon butter. Sprinkle about 2 tablespoons sugar on sides and bottom, coating evenly. Stand and slant large apple slices on sides of soufflé dish. (They will cling because of butter and sugar.) Fill and pack center of soufflé dish with 1/4-inch slices of apple and continue to press in and around sides of center, sprinkling remaining 2 tablespoons sugar and lemon juice on apple slices. Dot with remaining butter.

Mix well eggs, flour, condensed milk, vanilla, and cinnamon. Carefully pour mixture over apples so as not to disturb form. Bake on center rack of oven 40–55 minutes, or until apples are tender. (Pierce apples with fork.) Place soufflé dish on lower rack of oven and bake 15 minutes more. Cover with foil if apple tips get too brown. Remove soufflé from oven.

When soufflé is cool, run sharp, long-bladed knife around side to loosen. Firmly place serving platter over soufflé dish. Turn upside down. Serve at once with whipped cream flavored with apple liqueur, if desired.

REALLY LETHAL PECAN PIE   SERVES 8–10

This is truly a down-home specialty and there's no holiday around here that's real unless I bake one. A small note: it's loaded with nuts and if by any chance it falls on your toe without bruising or breaking it, then you'll know you haven't used enough pecans.

1 1/4 cups dark corn syrup
1 cup firmly packed light brown sugar
4 tablespoons unsalted butter
4 large eggs
1 teaspoon vanilla
2 1/2 cups pecans (some versions use pecan

halves, but I prefer the nuts broken into
coarse pieces)
1/4 teaspoon salt
9-inch unbaked pie shell
(Pâte Brisée I, page 19)

Preheat oven to 350°F. Combine corn syrup and sugar in 1-quart saucepan and stir over moderate heat until sugar has dissolved. Let mixture boil 2–3 minutes, remove from heat, and stir in butter.

In 2-quart mixing bowl, beat eggs well with wire whisk or electric mixer. Continue to beat while slowly pouring in syrup. Stir in vanilla, pecans, and salt.

Pour half of mixture into unbaked pie shell; place on center rack of oven. Pour in remaining mixture and bake 45–50 minutes, or until filling has set. You may have to cover crust with foil to prevent burning.

MACADAMIA NUT CREAM PIE

SERVES 6–8

1/3 cup cornstarch
3 tablespoons sugar
1 whole large egg plus 1 large egg yolk
2 cups milk
1/2 cup sugar
1 teaspoon unflavored gelatin

1/4 cup brandy
2 1/2 cups heavy cream
1 1/4 cups coarsely chopped macadamia nuts
6 ounces semisweet chocolate, melted
9 macadamia nuts, whole
9-inch baked piecrust (Pâte Sucre I, page 21)

Combine cornstarch, sugar, whole egg, and egg yolk in bowl. In saucepan, combine milk and sugar; bring just to boil over moderate heat, and add to cornstarch mixture in stream, beating until ingredients are thoroughly mixed.

Transfer mixture to saucepan, bring to simmer over low heat, and cook, stirring, for 5 minutes. This is your pastry cream. Transfer to bowl and chill, covered, for 30 minutes.

In small bowl, sprinkle gelatin over brandy to soften for 5 minutes, set bowl in pan of hot water, and stir gelatin until it is dissolved. In chilled bowl beat heavy cream until it holds a shape. Beat pastry cream with electric mixer until it is completely smooth. In large bowl, combine with gelatin mixture, 2 cups of the whipped cream and 1/2 cup chopped nuts.

In small saucepan melt chocolate over low heat. Dip whole nuts in chocolate, and let them dry on waxed paper. Brush bottom of pie shell with *thin* layer of chocolate, pour in filling, and chill pie, covered, for 1 hour, or until it is completely set.

Sprinkle remaining 3/4 cup chopped nuts around edge of pie, transfer remaining whipped cream to pastry bag fitted with star tip, and pipe 9 rosettes of cream over top of pie. Top each rosette with a chocolate-covered nut and chill pie 2 hours.

MYSTERY PECAN PIE

SERVES 6–8

Quite different from most pecan pies and a mysterious beauty, as Mrs. Kafadar says. If you haven't tasted her Hummus (page 44), you're missing a treat.

9-inch pie shell, unbaked (Pâte Brisée II, page 20)	1 egg
	1/3 cup sugar
8-ounce package cream cheese, softened	1 teaspoon vanilla

Preheat oven to 350°F. Cream together cream cheese, egg, sugar, and vanilla in mixing bowl. Spread mixture on bottom of prepared pie shell.

1 1/4 cups chopped pecans	1/4 cup sugar
3 eggs	1 teaspoon vanilla
1 cup light corn syrup	1/4 teaspoon salt

Sprinkle chopped pecans over cream cheese mixture. Beat eggs in mixing bowl until mixed but not foamy. Do not overbeat. Add corn syrup, sugar, vanilla, and salt. Mix well. Pour over pecans. Bake for 40 minutes or until nuts are lightly browned. Top will rise like a soufflé and sink when it cools—not to worry!

FRESH PEACH PIE

SERVES 6

This was in my first book. I had to repeat it here by popular request—mine. Actually, it's a summer madness; it must be made with fresh peaches. I will never forget the first two summers after the book came out. There was never a dinner party I attended where they didn't serve it out of deference to me—and to show they were using the book. I was flattered; it was really great. But even I began to wince after the first fifteen such occasions. You won't and your guests will eat it up.

COCONUT ALMOND PIECRUST

1 cup blanched almonds	1/4 cup sugar
1 cup canned moist-style flaked coconut	1/4 cup butter or margarine

Preheat oven to 375°F. Grind almonds medium fine. Mix with coconut. Work in sugar and butter with fingers or spoon. Press evenly in bottom and sides of 9-inch glass pie plate, reserving 3 tablespoons crumbly mixture for top. Bake 10–12 minutes or until light golden brown. If edges get too brown, cover with aluminum foil, leaving center uncovered. Place remaining crumb mixture in shallow pan and toast in oven at same time as pie shell, about 5 minutes.

FILLING

1 cup sour cream	1 teaspoon shredded orange rind
Dash of salt	1 teaspoon vanilla
6 tablespoons powdered sugar	3 cups fresh peaches, peeled and sliced
1 teaspoon orange juice	1 cup whipping cream

Beat sour cream. Add salt, 4 tablespoons powdered sugar, orange juice, orange rind, and vanilla. Spread on bottom and sides of shell. Cover with peaches arranged in an attractive manner in pie shell. Whip cream; fold in remaining 2 tablespoons powdered sugar. Cover peaches with whipped cream. Sprinkle top with toasted coconut mixture reserved from pie shell. Chill.

COCO-RUM CUSTARD PIE

SERVES 6–8

CRUST

1 cup chocolate wafer crumbs   1/3 cup melted butter

Mix together. Reserve 3–4 tablespoons for topping. Press remainder into bottom and sides of 9-inch pie pan. Bake in preheated 350°F. oven for 5 minutes. Let cool.

FILLING

1/4 cup sugar   2 tablespoons dark rum
5 tablespoons flour   1 1/3 cups coconut
1/4 teaspoon salt   3 egg whites
2 cups milk   2 teaspoons sugar
3 egg yolks, slightly beaten   1 teaspoon rum flavoring (optional)

In double boiler, combine 1/4 cup sugar, flour, and salt. Add milk gradually, stirring until smooth. Cook over rapidly boiling water 10 minutes, stirring constantly. Mix 1–2 tablespoons of custard mixture to egg yolks so that egg yolks are warmed slightly. Add egg yolks to double boiler slowly, stirring constantly, and cook 2 minutes longer, or until custard starts to thicken and coats back of spoon. Add rum and coconut. Let cool.

Preheat oven to 400°F. Meanwhile, beat egg whites with 2 teaspoons sugar until stiff but not dry. Add rum flavoring if desired. Fold egg whites into cooled custard. Pour into pie crust. Bake 5 minutes. Lower heat to 325° and continue baking 10 minutes or until custard is set. While pie is still hot, sprinkle reserved crumbs on top. Let cool and place in refrigerator. This pie is better served cold.

VARIATION   You can eliminate egg whites and cover top of pie with sweetened whipped cream to which you have added 2 teaspoons of rum. Sprinkle reserved crumbs on top of whipped cream.

PARISIAN STRAWBERRY TARTS

MAKES 8 TARTS

Make recipe for Pâte Sucre I on page 21. Preheat oven to 375°F. Roll dough out on floured board to about 1/8 inch thick. Cut in circles large enough to place over backs of little pie pans or large muffin tins. Bake 10–15 minutes. Cool before filling.

FILLING

4 cups strawberries

2 tablespoons cornstarch

1 cup sugar

1 teaspoon lemon juice

Heavy cream, whipped (optional)

1/2 cup sugar (optional)

1 teaspoon vanilla extract (optional)

Hull, wash, and dry strawberries, reserving largest, most perfect ones. Fill tarts with reserved strawberries.

Mash remaining smaller berries until you have 1 cup pulp. If cup is not full, add a little water. Combine cornstarch and sugar, and stir into berry juice. When well blended, add lemon juice. Place over medium heat and cook until mixture thickens, about 5 minutes. Cool.

Pour this prepared glaze over strawberries in tart shells until they are completely covered. Serve with or without whipped cream. If whipped cream is used, sweeten with 1/2 cup sugar, or to taste, and flavor with vanilla.

GRAPEFRUIT CUSTARD PIE   SERVES 6–8

This is unlike any other fruit dessert I've ever tasted. The only difficult part was peeling and sectioning the grapefruit into perfect pieces. That became much easier when my sister, Bessie, gave me a great tip on peeling a grapefruit. Let the whole grapefruit stand in very hot water about a minute, then run a little cold water over it. It will then peel and section easily, with hardly a pith to pull.

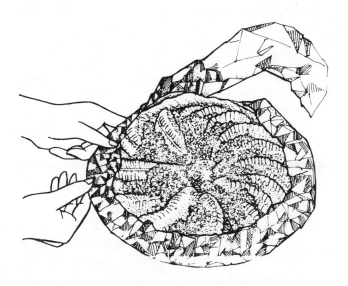

To prevent overbrowning, wrap exposed edge of piecrust with long strip of foil.

1 cup sugar
1/2 cup sifted flour
1/2 teaspoon salt
2 eggs, lightly beaten
1 1/4 cups milk
1/2 cup fresh grapefruit juice
1 tablespoon zest of grapefruit rind

3/4 teaspoon vanilla
1/8 teaspoon freshly grated nutmeg
2 large grapefruit
1/3 cup firmly packed dark brown sugar
9-inch pie shell, baked (Pâte Sucre I, page 21
  or Pâte Brisée II, page 20)

Into bowl sift together sugar, flour, and salt. Beat in eggs. In top of double boiler scald milk. Stir 1/2 cup of milk into sugar mixture. Stir mixture into remaining milk, and cook custard over hot water on moderate heat, stirring, until it is thickened. Add fresh grapefruit juice and grapefruit zest and cook mixture, stirring, for 10 minutes. Stir in vanilla and nutmeg. Let mixture cool, and pour it into shell.

Pour boiling water over grapefruit. Let sit about 1 minute; drain and rinse with cold water. Now you are ready to peel your fruit. With sharp knife remove peel and pith from grapefruit and cut enough sections, slicing between membranes, to measure 1 1/2 cups. Arrange grapefruit in decorative pattern on custard and sprinkle with brown sugar.

Cover exposed crust with strip of foil and put pie under preheated broiler 6 inches from heat until sugar is melted. Remove foil and let pie cool.

TART AU CITRON (LEMON PIE)   SERVES 6–8

I fell in love with this at Saint-Germain Restaurant here in Los Angeles. It was before we got into this book and I couldn't muster up enough nerve to ask the owner or the chef for the recipe. I still feel kind of funny about it. I mean, suppose somebody liked a number I was singing in my show, that we'd labored over to create and made our very own, and wanted to use my arrangement!

Great chefs and restaurateurs are generous, but instead of asking Saint-Germain—the easy way—I wrote to Gourmet Magazine and they got it for me, in grams, kilos, milligrams, liters, etc. We did a lot of transposition and translations and here it is. It is truly a tart tart. No meringue or whipped cream or other distractions . . . the real thing.

1 cup sugar
5 eggs
1/2 cup melted butter
2 teaspoons grated lemon rind
1/2 cup lemon juice

5 tablespoons orange juice
9-inch unbaked pie shell (Pâte Sucre II, page
  21)
Powdered sugar

Preheat oven to 300°F. In medium-sized mixing bowl, beat sugar with eggs. Add butter, grated lemon rind, lemon juice, and orange juice. Pour into unbaked pie shell. Bake 30 minutes. Cover with powdered sugar. The pie should be eaten slightly warm.

LIME CUSTARD PIE

4 large eggs
1 1/2 cups sugar
Zest or rind of 1/2 large orange, removed
   with zester or grater
1/2 cup fresh lime juice
1/2 cup fresh orange juice

1/4 cup heavy cream
9-inch baked pastry shell, Pâte Sucre I (page
   21)
1 1/2 tablespoons powdered sugar
1 lime, rind and membrane removed, flesh
   cut into segments

In food processor, mix eggs, sugar, and zest or rind for about 1 minute, or until light yellow and fluffy. Pour fruit juices and cream through feed tube with machine still running. Preheat oven to 375°F.

Pour filling into crust. Bake 10 minutes; then reduce temperature to 350° and bake 12–14 minutes longer. If crust edges darken too quickly, cover with foil. When filling is browned and moves only slightly when pan is shaken, remove pie from oven.

Preheat broiler and adjust rack 4 inches from heat. Sprinkle powdered sugar through sieve uniformly over pie's surface. Arrange lime segments on top in circular pattern. Place pie under broiler. Check every few seconds, turning pie so it browns evenly. When entire surface is browned, after 1–1 1/2 minutes, remove pie. Let it cool to room temperature before serving.

FRESH PLUM TART

Do try this one. It too is very seasonal and when the fresh tart plums are in we serve it once or twice a week. It's truly easy and needs no help. I have mentioned whipped cream, but that's only if you can't live without it. A warm thank you to the fine British writer Edana Romney, who introduced me to this tart at one of her Sunday afternoon high teas.

9-inch unbaked pie shell
(Pâte Sucre II, page 21 or Pâte Brisée II, page
   20)
3/4 cup coarsely ground almonds
6 heaping tablespoons sugar

8 medium-sized fresh plums, halved and pitted
1/4 pound (1 stick) butter, softened
Sweetened whipped cream for garnish (optional)

Preheat oven to 375°F.

Sprinkle bottom of unbaked pie crust with about 3 tablespoons almonds and 2 heaping tablespoons sugar. Place plums, cut side up, over almonds and sugar. Sprinkle over plums 1/2 cup almonds and remaining sugar. Dot generously with butter.

Bake 20 minutes or until crust is nicely browned. Toast remaining almonds by placing in 400° oven for a few minutes, or until they just start to brown. Remove immediately. Sprinkle toasted almonds on baked tart and serve with or without whipped cream.

SHAKER SUGAR PIE

SERVES 6–8

Also known as Sister Lizzie's Shaker Sugar Pie at the famous, historic Lion's Head Inn, which is near King's Island, which is near Cincinnati. It's simple and easy and, surprise!—while it's baking, the flour and sugar rise right through the cream, flavoring it all the way up.

1 cup brown sugar
1/3 cup flour
9-inch unbaked pie shell
   (Pâte Brisée I, page 19)

2 cups light cream (half-and-half)
1 teaspoon vanilla
1/4 cup butter
Nutmeg

Thoroughly mix sugar and flour. Spread evenly in bottom of unbaked shell. Add cream and vanilla. Slice butter into pieces and distribute evenly over top of pie. Sprinkle with nutmeg. Bake in 350°F. oven 40–45 minutes or until firm.

BOURBON BALLS

MAKES 24 BALLS

My sister, Bessie, gave me this recipe—I got the buck teeth—she got the sweet tooth—and she really knows a good thing when she tastes it.

1/2 cup bourbon
1 1/2 tablespoons white corn syrup
1 cup finely rolled vanilla wafers

1 cup pecans, finely chopped
2 tablespoons cocoa
1/4 cup powdered sugar

Mix bourbon and syrup. Add remaining ingredients. Dust hands with powdered sugar. Make balls the size of walnuts and roll in powdered sugar. Store in refrigerator between layers of waxed paper.

GRANDMA'S WOOCHIES

MAKES ABOUT 30 COOKIES

Linda Sanfilippo is a beautiful cellist who was happily playing away with the San Diego Symphony until we had a concert with that fine orchestra. When she met my percussionist, Mark Stevens, it was thunderous drum rolls and soulful cello strings and, I guess, lightning flashes. I was just singing my songs in front of the whole drama. They haven't been apart since. Her grandmother makes these unusual-sounding cookies. They're sort of homemade date newtons with a romantic history.

DATE FILLING

2 12-ounce packages pitted dates, chopped
4 3/8-ounce package chopped pecans or walnuts

1 tablespoon plus 1 teaspoon cinnamon
3 tablespoons orange juice

Combine all filling ingredients.

PASTRY

3 cups flour
1/2 cup butter
1/2 cup oil

Grated peel from 1 orange
1/4 cup orange juice

Preheat oven to 300°F. Place flour in bowl. Add butter, oil, and orange peel and mix well. Gradually add orange juice to make soft dough.

Divide into parts. Pat or roll each part into rectangles (approximately 6 × 2 1/2 inches). Place date filling 1 inch wide down length of center. Pull edges of dough together, sealing with fingertips. Flatten slightly.

Cut into 1-inch shapes and place on greased baking sheets. Bake 15 minutes.

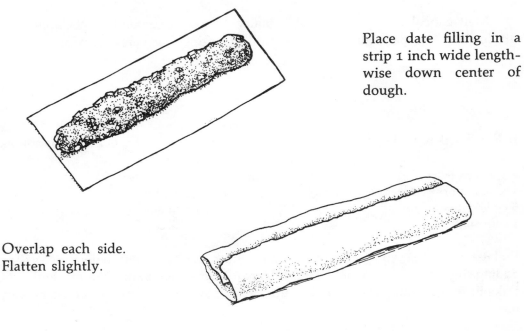

Place date filling in a strip 1 inch wide lengthwise down center of dough.

Overlap each side. Flatten slightly.

Cut each bar into 1-inch pieces.

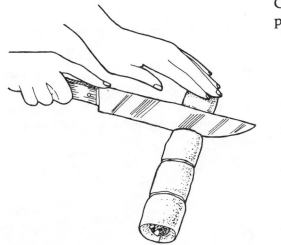

FLORENTINES

This is a gem of a recipe. I had a delicious meeting with the manager of the Beverly Hilton one day. We conducted our business as we lunched, and afterward, I went home with an extra box of these and the recipe for all of us from their great chef pâtissier, Harold Nightlinger.

A generous 3/4 cup (1/4 pound) sliced almonds
Rind from 2 large oranges, grated
1 tablespoon flour

1/2 cup sugar
1 tablespoon grated lemon rind
1/2 cup milk
2-ounce square sweet chocolate

Preheat oven to 350°F. Combine almonds, orange rind, flour, sugar, lemon rind, and milk. Mix until well blended. Drop by tablespoons on greased cookie sheet. Flatten into 2-inch rounds with back of spoon. Bake for 15 minutes. Cool on wire rack.

Melt chocolate in top of double boiler. Dip each cookie into chocolate. Let dry on waxed paper right side up or chill in refrigerator before serving.

BEST BROWNIES

1 1/2 cups butter
1/2 pound unsweetened chocolate
6 eggs, beaten
3 cups sugar

1 1/2 cups flour, sifted
3 teaspoons vanilla
1 cup chopped nuts

Preheat oven to 350°F. Melt butter and chocolate in double boiler. Beat eggs, adding sugar slowly; add melted chocolate and butter. Add flour, vanilla, and nuts. Bake in two 8-inch pans 20–25 minutes. Don't overcook. Centers should be very moist.

BROWNIE DROPS

Shirley, my secretary, and her sister, Wanda, are both great cooks. They both love sweets and why Wanda doesn't weigh a ton is a wonder. She's always coming through with some irresistible cookie-jar filler like these—she's got a million of 'em.

2 bars, 4-ounces each, German's Sweet
  Chocolate
1 tablespoon butter
2 eggs
3/4 cup sugar
1/4 cup unsifted flour

1/4 teaspoon baking powder
1/4 teaspoon cinnamon
1/8 teaspoon salt
1/2 teaspoon vanilla
3/4 cup finely chopped pecans

Preheat oven to 350°F. In double boiler melt chocolate and butter over hot water. Stir. Cool.

Beat eggs until foamy, then add sugar, two tablespoons at a time. Beat until thickened (5 minutes with electric mixer). Blend in chocolate. Add flour, baking powder, cinnamon, and salt. Blend. Stir in vanilla and nuts.

Drop by small teaspoonfuls onto greased baking sheet. Bake until cookies feel "set" when lightly touched—8–10 minutes.

PECAN NUT BALLS

MAKES ABOUT 60 COOKIES

1/2 pound butter
4 tablespoons sugar
2 teaspoons vanilla

2 cups flour, less 2 tablespoons
2 cups chopped pecans
Powdered sugar

Cream butter and sugar and vanilla. Sift and add flour. Add nuts. Cream well until dough cleans bowl, adding a little more flour if necessary.

Form dough into small balls about 3/4 inch in diameter, or roll into finger shapes. Place on ungreased cookie sheet 1/4 inch apart. Bake in preheated 300°F. oven until light straw color (25–30 minutes depending on oven). Immediately roll hot cookies in powdered sugar and repeat when cold. These will keep well in an airtight tin.

PECAN AND WALNUT SLICES

MAKES ABOUT 24 SLICES

PASTRY DOUGH

1/4 cup butter
1/4 cup sugar
1 egg

1/2 teaspoon vanilla
1 1/4 cups flour, sifted
1/2 teaspoon salt

Preheat oven to 350°F. In food processor cream butter and sugar. With motor running, add egg and vanilla. In three stages, add flour sifted with salt. Mixture will form ball. Press evenly into 8 × 12-inch pan, covering bottom and sides, pressing with thumbs in corners so dough won't be too thick. Bake 15 minutes.

FILLING

1 1/4 cups pecans *or* 1 1/4 cups pecans and
    walnuts mixed
1/2 cup coconut (or another 1/2 cup nuts)
2 eggs
1 1/2 cups brown sugar
2 tablespoons flour

1/2 teaspoon baking powder
1/2 teaspoon salt
1 teaspoon vanilla
3 tablespoons semisweet chocolate (grated or
    chocolate chips)

Place nuts in food-processor bowl (no need to wash), chop, and set aside. Add co-
conut if you are using it or 1/2 cup nuts, eggs, and brown sugar. Turn on motor.
Add flour, baking powder, salt and vanilla. Blend well. Press into half-baked crust.
Return to oven and bake 20 minutes more.

    During last five minutes of baking sprinkle with grated chocolate or chocolate
chips. When cool cut into thin oblong slices.

CARL REINER'S CREAM CHEESE COOKIES

MAKES ABOUT 3 DOZEN COOKIES

*Carl Reiner is one of my favorite people. Never mind how talented he is; he's funny, warm and
a great delineator of his mother's recipes. He came on my TV show several times. I remember him
carrying an eggplant through an entire segment of the show, discussing the marvelous properties of
the vegetable, as a relish, eggplant caviar, and an infinite variety of other uses. Then he decided
to make these cookies. I don't think I ever got those great eggplant recipes.*

3-ounce package cream cheese, softened
1/4 pound butter (1 stick)
9 tablespoons sugar

9 walnut halves, very finely chopped
1 cup flour

Preheat oven to 350°F. Cream together cheese and butter. Add sugar gradually,
creaming after each addition. Add walnuts. Fold in flour and blend until smooth.
Drop dough by teaspoonfuls onto ungreased cookie sheet. Flatten dough with wet
finger until wafer thin. Bake 10 minutes.

MACADAMIA NUT BARS

MAKES ABOUT 2 DOZEN BARS

*A friend who had made several trips to Hawaii sent me lots of macadamia nuts. They're rich and
rare and not as expensive as they used to be. I baked these for him and he loved them. You will
too!*

    *They are so complete and rich you almost don't need the frosting, but for that finishing touch,
we've included it.*

PASTRY CRUST

1 cup sifted flour

1/2 cup butter or margarine, cut into pieces

1/4 cup granulated sugar

2–3 tablespoons ice water

Put all ingredients except ice water in bowl of food processor. Using metal or plastic blade, blend well until mixture becomes crumbly, almost like cornmeal. With motor running, pour 1 tablespoon of ice water through feed tube in steady stream. Continue adding ice water, 1 tablespoon at a time, until dough begins to form ball around blade. Don't overmix. Chill for 30 minutes.

Preheat oven to 350°F. Pat mixture into bottom of greased 9 × 9 × 1 3/4-inch pan. Bake 20 minutes or until golden brown.

While crust is baking prepare filling.

MACADAMIA NUT FILLING

1 cup macadamia nuts

1 1/2 cups light brown sugar, firmly packed

2 eggs

1/2 cup flaked coconut plus 1 tablespoon for garnish

2 tablespoons flour

1 teaspoon vanilla extract

1/2 teaspoon salt

1/4 teaspoon baking powder

In food-processor bowl, using metal blade, chop macadamia nuts. Set aside. In same food processor, add brown sugar, eggs, coconut, flour, vanilla, salt, and baking powder. Mix until well blended. Add nuts, reserving 1 tablespoon for garnish, and mix well. Spread filling over baked cookie crust; bake 20 minutes or until browned and firm to touch. Let cool in pan on wire rack.

FROSTING

1 1/4 cups powdered sugar

2 tablespoons soft butter or margarine

1 1/2–2 tablespoons milk

In medium bowl, with spoon, beat powdered sugar, butter, and milk until smooth. Spread evenly over filling. Garnish with reserved chopped nuts and coconut. Cut into bars.

QUALITY COCONUT COOKIES IN QUANTITY

MAKES ABOUT 8 DOZEN COOKIES

2 cups flour, sifted

1/2 teaspoon baking soda

1 cup butter or margarine

1/2 teaspoon vanilla extract

1 cup sugar

1 egg, well beaten

3 1/2 cups shredded and chopped moist coconut

1 egg yolk

1 tablespoon cream

1 1/2 cups pecan halves

1/2 cup white corn syrup

Sift together flour and baking soda. Set aside. Cream butter or margarine until softened. Gradually add vanilla, creaming until fluffy. Add sugar in thirds, beating thoroughly after each addition. Blend egg and 2 cups coconut in bowl. Mix thoroughly. Stir in dry ingredients. Knead lightly with fingertips 5–10 times, or until mixture holds together.

Spread remaining coconut onto waxed paper. Form dough into 6 rolls about 1 inch in diameter. Roll in coconut. Wrap in waxed paper and place in refrigerator for at least 3 hours. Preheat oven to 325°F. Meanwhile, lightly grease cookie sheets. Remove rolls from refrigerator and with a sharp knife slice crosswise in half-inch slices. Place on cookie sheets 3/4 inch apart. Mix egg yolk and cream together and brush cookie tops with mixture. Press pecan half on top of each cookie. Bake about 20 minutes or until very lightly browned. Remove to cooling rack. Heat syrup until warm. Glaze pecans and cookies by brushing with syrup.

LEMON SQUARES

MAKES ABOUT 20 SQUARES

I love this one; it's lemony and keeps very well.

1 cup flour	2 eggs
1/2 cup cold butter (1 stick) cut into chunks	2 tablespoons flour
1/4 cup powdered sugar	1/4 cup lemon juice
1/2 teaspoon vanilla	Rind of 1 lemon
2 scant tablespoons ice water	1 cup sugar

Preheat oven to 350°F. In food processor, using steel blade, combine flour, butter, powdered sugar, and vanilla and blend. With motor running, gradually add water through tube to form dough ball around blade. Pat into 9 × 9-inch pie or cake pan with raised sides. Pat well up sides using spatula. Bake 15 minutes.

Place eggs, flour, lemon juice, rind of lemon, and sugar in food-processor bowl. Blend until well mixed, using steel blade. Pour into baked pie shell and bake 25 minutes. Sprinkle top with powdered sugar. Cool. Slice into squares with sharp knife, taking out center square first and then remaining squares. (If you baked it in pie pan, slice into wedges.)

WANDA'S BUTTER COOKIES

MAKES ABOUT 4 1/2–5 DOZEN SMALL COOKIES

Wanda is Shirley Schroer's sister, who lives in Minnesota. For more about Wanda and her wonders, see page 349 for Butter Pecan Turtle Cookies. This one came from Wanda's husband's brother's wife, Millie. His name is Russell and they live in San Diego. I just didn't want you to think we mined any one particular area for our lode—our sources are nationwide, *folks.*

1 cup butter (2 sticks)
2/3 cup sugar
1 egg, beaten
2 1/2 cups cake flour

3/4 teaspoon baking powder
1/4 teaspoon salt
1 teaspoon vanilla

Preheat oven to 400°F. Cream butter. Add sugar slowly, creaming thoroughly. Add beaten egg. Mix and sift flour, baking powder and salt together and add to first mixture. Add vanilla. Put cookie mixture through cookie press. Place on lightly greased cookie sheet and bake immediately about 10 minutes. *Do not chill dough.*

NOTE If you would like smaller and flatter cookies, eliminate the baking powder.

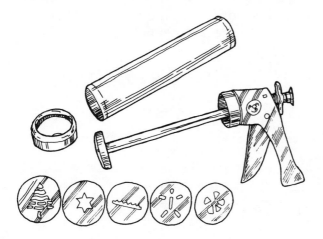

For decorative cookies, force dough through cookie press.

BUTTER PECAN TURTLE COOKIES

MAKES ABOUT 3 DOZEN COOKIES

I love pecans. I'd put them in chili con carne if other people would eat it, but this is a better way.

CRUST

2 cups all-purpose flour
1 cup firmly packed brown sugar

1/2 cup sweet butter, softened
1 cup whole pecan halves

TOPPING

2/3 cup sweet butter
1/2 cup firmly packed brown sugar

1 cup semisweet chocolate chips

Preheat oven to 350°F. In 3-quart bowl, combine flour, 1 cup brown sugar, and 1/2 cup butter. Mix with electric beater at medium speed, scraping sides of bowl often, 2–3 minutes or until well mixed and particles are fine. Pat firmly into ungreased 13 × 9 × 2-inch baking dish. Sprinkle pecan halves evenly over unbaked crust.

In heavy 1-quart saucepan, combine 2/3 cup butter and 1/2 cup brown sugar. Cook over medium heat, stirring constantly, until entire surface of mixture begins to boil. Boil 30 seconds to 1 minute, stirring constantly. Pour brown sugar-butter mixture evenly over pecans and crust.

Bake in center of oven 18–22 minutes, or until entire top layer is bubbly and crust is light golden brown. Remove from oven and immediately sprinkle with chocolate chips. Allow chips to melt slightly 2–3 minutes. Slightly swirl chips as they melt; leave some whole for a marbled effect. Do not spread chips. Cool completely. Cut into squares.

LACE COOKIES

MAKES ABOUT 3 DOZEN COOKIES

1/2 cup butter (1 stick)
1 cup sugar
1 egg, beaten
1 cup old-fashioned oats
2 rounded tablespoons flour

1/4 teaspoon salt
1 teaspoon vanilla
1/2 teaspoon baking powder
1/3 cup walnuts

Preheat oven to 350°F. Line cookie sheet with foil. Grease well. Mix together all ingredients except walnuts in bowl of food processor or electric mixer. Add walnuts for 1–2 seconds at the last moment. Drop by small teaspoons onto cookie sheet. Leave ample space as they spread. Bake 8–10 minutes. When cookies are done, peel off foil.

ALMOND GINGER SNAPS

MAKES 3 1/2 DOZEN COOKIES

Mr. Julius is Swedish. He is my hairdresser, but not mine exclusively. I can only get him between his trips to the White House, New York, and around the world. Yet he faithfully appeared every time I had to tape those hour-and-a-half Dinah shows. If we were lucky, he would just have paid a visit to his mother, Queenie, and would bring us beautiful samples of her cookies. This was my favorite.

1/2 pound butter (2 sticks), softened
1 cup sugar
1/2 cup dark corn syrup
3 1/2 cups flour
1 tablespoon ginger

2 teaspoons cinnamon
2 teaspoons cloves
1 teaspoon baking soda
1 cup blanched almonds, finely chopped

Cream butter in bowl of electric mixer. Add sugar and syrup; beat until light and fluffy. In large bowl, sift flour, spices, and baking soda. Add dry ingredients to butter mixture and beat only long enough to combine ingredients (beating too much will toughen dough). Stir in almonds. Turn onto floured board, and knead until smooth.

Divide in half. Shape into rolls 1 1/2 inch in diameter, flattening both ends so there is no waste. Wrap each roll in waxed paper. Chill 2 hours or overnight.

Preheat oven to 350°F. Cut cold dough into 1/16-inch slices with sharp knife. Place on greased baking sheet. Bake 10–12 minutes.

TIP If extra-spicy cookies are desired, add 1/2 teaspoon of mace and 1/2 teaspoon nutmeg.

For a creative look, place a blanched almond on each cookie before baking.

BUTTERSCOTCH NUGGETS   MAKES ABOUT 36 SQUARES

1 cup walnuts
1/4 cup cold butter
1 cup brown sugar, packed
1 scant cup flour less a tablespoon
1/2 teaspoon salt

1 teaspoon baking powder
1 egg
1 teaspoon vanilla
1/2 cup flaked coconut

Preheat oven to 350°F.

Place walnuts in bowl of food processor. Using metal blade, chop coarsely. Remove and set aside.

Place butter in bowl of processor and process until creamy, add brown sugar and blend until creamy. Mix in flour, salt, and baking powder. Blend well. Gradually, with motor running, add egg and vanilla. When blended, add chopped nuts and coconut.

Butter a 9 × 9-inch pan and pour cookie mixture into it. Bake about 20 minutes. Cookies are done when toothpick inserted in center comes out clean. Do not overcook. Cookies should be chewy and moist. When cool, cut into small squares. They're very rich.

Chapter 14

DESSERTS

I have never been all that hung up on sweets and desserts. But there are some that I find absolutely irresistible. They're in this chapter.

They range from the simple to the more complicated. By complicated, I mean they'll take a little more of your time to prepare, but since most people look forward to that part of dinner and don't consider they've really dined without it, it's really worth the little extra effort. As with almost every other recipe in the book, most of them can be done ahead, in part or completely.

Prepare two or three extra portions of some of the individual ones for safety's sake, an extra guest, a slight bungle in preparing—I'm thinking of the Chocolate Wrapped Pears or the Poached Peaches, each with its own little crust. They're a little hard to split without somebody noticing. The big, generous, rich ones, the bread puddings, and mousses all keep well and can be served in small or generous portions, depending on how lavishly you've fed your guests earlier.

A good rule of thumb—and if I sound as if I'm repeating myself it's because I am—when you plan that menu is, consider the balance. A cheesecake won't be nearly as enthusiastically received if it has followed a cream soup, a big roast, potatoes or pasta, and vegetables—the works—as it would be if it were following a light fish, chicken, or veal dish. Don't bring out all the big guns on your first shot. They'll come back. Believe me, they'll think about you more fondly on the way home if they haven't had to undo buckles, buttons, and hooks just to sit comfortably in the car. If they looked stuffed, offer a "sweetie bag"—a nice portion of whatever it is they would have had—to be enjoyed the next day or while watching "The Late Late Show."

Another piece of advice. Except for apple, the fruit desserts—strawberry, pear, grape, peach, plum—are really only good in season. Canned or frozen substitutes just aren't as good in the ones I've specified. Not to worry, however: when fruit is not in season, look up the any-time-of-the-year tempters—Gingerbread with Caramel Sauce, Chocolate Cheesecake, the mousses, the soufflés, and so on.

If I haven't exactly found proof of the adage, "The road to a man's heart is through his stomach," these little numbers have certainly dug some garden paths from time to time.

LEMON CRÊPES
MAKES ABOUT 24 CRÊPES (USE 12 AND FREEZE THE REST)
SERVES 6 (2 PER SERVING)

New Orleans is a lot of wonderful things—jazz, history, Mardi Gras, fun, and food. Here's one of the best of the last one. They sent it to me from the famous Commander's Palace. Miss Adelaide Brennan and your ever inventive chef, Gerhardt Brill—Thank you!!!!

GREAT CRÊPES

1 cup cold water	1/2 teaspoon salt
1 cup milk	2 cups flour, sifted
4 eggs	1/4 cup clarified butter
2 teaspoons sugar	

In food-processor bowl, place water, milk, eggs, sugar, and salt; then add flour. Process 3 minutes or so, until really smooth. Let sit for a minimum of 30 minutes at room temperature, 2 hours if you have time.

Brush crêpe pan with clarified butter. Heat. Ladle 1/4 cup batter at a time into skillet. Tilt until bottom and sides are covered. Cook 1–2 minutes, shaking pan; then loosen gently with spatula. Flip over and cook other side. Crêpes do not have to be brown, just cooked. Slip out onto a clean dish towel. Wrap in foil and freeze in packages of 4 or 8. Crêpes thaw out quickly.

NOTE Crêpe pan should be a special heavyweight 6–8-inch pan. Don't use it for anything else and don't wash it. Wipe after using and hide so nobody will use it for bacon and eggs, etc.

FILLING

1 pound cream cheese, softened
2/3 cup sugar
Juice of 1 lemon

1 tablespoon rum
1 tablespoon grated lemon peel

Using electric mixer, beat cream cheese until fluffy. Gradually add sugar while continuing to beat. Add all other ingredients; beat until well blended.

LEMON BUTTER SAUCE

MAKES 1 1/2 CUPS

1 cup butter
1/4 cup sugar

1/2 cup lemon juice
1 tablespoon grated lemon peel

In small saucepan, over low heat, melt butter, add sugar, and stir until dissolved. Stir in lemon juice and peel; heat through.

TO ASSEMBLE

3 ounces brandy

Fill center of each crêpe with 3 tablespoons of filling, using either pastry tube or spooning in long strip down center. Roll up.

In large skillet or chafing dish, warm lemon butter sauce. Add crêpes, side by side, seam up. Heat 1–2 minutes. Turn so seam is now down.

Add brandy and swirl around to front of pan, evenly coating crêpes. Ignite (if using a gas range, brandy should ignite by itself). Place two crêpes on each individual dessert dish, and spoon on sauce.

CRÊPES PAPAYA

SERVES 8

Crêpes are all the things you want them to be. I remember one occasion in Paris when Simone Signoret and Yves Montand took me to dine in their favorite little French restaurant. I ordered some wild, creamy spécialité de la maison *that had sent the* maître d' *into ecstasies just describing it. Simone and Yves ordered crêpes over which they simply spread a thin layer of their favorite* confiture *(jelly or jam to us peasants). I liked theirs better and you'll love this one.*

1/2 cup (1 stick) butter
1 1/2 cups brown sugar
2 tablespoons orange rind
2 tablespoons lime rind
Juice of 1 lime
Juice of 1 orange

2 tablespoons Grand Marnier
1 teaspoon ground cinnamon
2 papayas, thinly sliced into 16 slices
1 tablespoon butter
8 Great Crêpes (page 18)
Vanilla ice cream for topping

Place butter and brown sugar in bowl of food processor and process until creamy. Add remaining ingredients, except papaya, and blend. Set aside.

Sauté papaya slices in butter until soft. Divide sauce among warmed crêpes, and place 2 slices of papaya on top. Roll up crêpes, and serve with ice cream on top.

GINGER ORANGE PEARS

SERVES 4

3/4 cup orange juice
1/3 cup orange marmalade
2 tablespoons chopped preserved ginger in syrup
1 teaspoon lemon juice

Pinch of salt
4 fresh pears, peeled, cored and halved
1 tablespoon orange liqueur
1/2 teaspoon vanilla

Combine orange juice, marmalade, ginger, lemon juice, and salt in saucepan. Cook, stirring, until marmalade has melted. Add pear halves, bring to boil, lower heat, cover, and simmer until just tender. Remove pears to serving dish.

Boil liquid down to about 1/2 cup. Remove liquid from heat; stir in orange liqueur and vanilla; pour mixture over pear halves. Cool. Cover and chill well.

CHOCOLATE WRAPPED PEARS

SERVES 6

Fortunately pears have a nice long season. When one variety goes out, another comes in—different, but just as subtly and delicately flavored, so you can do this pretty thing many weeks out of the year. It's easy.

1 cup sugar
4 cups water
Juice of 1 lemon
2 tablespoons crème de menthe
2 cinnamon sticks
4 whole cloves

6 firm, ripe pears with stems
4 ounces semisweet chocolate squares
4 tablespoons sweet butter, softened
Fresh or crystallized mint
Crème Fraîche (page 271)

Dissolve sugar in water. Add lemon juice, crème de menthe, and spices and simmer, tightly covered, 10–15 minutes.

Peel pears carefully, leaving stems intact, and cut a slice off bottoms so they will stand upright. Poach pears gently in boiling syrup until tender, 30–40 minutes. Cool in syrup and chill thoroughly overnight.

Melt chocolate in bowl over warm water. Add butter, and stir until melted and mixture is smooth. Remove pears from syrup and dry carefully with paper towels. Dip in melted chocolate to coat evenly. Use spoon, if necessary, to fill in uncoated spots. Lift pears to drain off excess chocolate; arrange on a serving dish. Decorate top of each with a sprig of fresh or crystallized mint. Chill until ready to serve. Serve with Crème Fraîche.

POACHED PEACHES   SERVES 6

The peaches were in Napa Valley all over Mollie and Donn Chappellet's orchards surrounding their magnificent vineyard. Mollie and I decided we wanted to make fresh peach cobbler without all that crust and without so much cooking the peaches would lose their shapes and fresh taste. This is the result. We never had any idea how many there'd be for dinner, so while she poached peaches, I made pie crusts and cut out little circles and big circles—enough to cover the Napa and Sonoma Wine country.

Pâte Brisée II (page 20)

Preheat oven to 450°F. Separate dough into 2 pieces. Whack with rolling pin a couple of times. Roll dough out to a thin sheet on lightly floured board. Cut dough with 2 fluted round pastry cutters: one to fit inside bottom and one to fit top of your prettiest crystal stemware. (You will need 6 of each size.) Place on buttered cookie sheet and brush with egg-white wash. Place pastry circles in oven; then reduce temperature to 375°. Bake 15 minutes or until done.

6 whole fresh peaches	2 tablespoons apricot brandy
1 cup water	Juice of 1/2 lemon
5 tablespoons sugar	1 cinnamon stick
1 cup orange juice	Whipped cream, sweetened with 1/4 tea-
Peel of 1 whole orange, cut into slices	spoon sugar
1 small orange, peeled	

To peel peaches, blanch in boiling water 20–40 seconds, depending on ripeness. The skin should slip off easily. Reserve any juices that run off as you peel.

In saucepan combine all ingredients except peaches and whipped cream. Bring to boil. When sugar dissolves, add whole peaches and any reserved juice. Simmer peaches, turning carefully, and basting from time to time until peaches are tender but not mushy. With slotted spoon, remove peaches to sieve placed over bowl to catch juices. Cover peaches with plastic wrap and refrigerate until chilled.

Pour juices from bowl into saucepan with liquid. Boil over moderate heat until liquid is reduced to 3–4 tablespoons. Cover and refrigerate until chilled. Then remove orange, orange peel and cinnamon stick. Add 1 tablespoon of syrup to whipped cream. Before serving, place one baked pastry shell on bottom of each of 6 large crystal goblets or stemware. Arrange whole peaches over shell. Pour remaining syrup over peaches. Place fluted shell on top. Add dollop of whipped cream.

NOTE If you have any leftover pastry dough, freeze it for another occasion.

Cut two circles of dough for each glass, one to sit on the bottom and one to fit over the top of the fruit.

ARCHBISHOP FULTON J. SHEEN'S SWEET CHRISTMAS APPLE SURPRISE
SERVES 6

The Archbishop made several visits to our TV show. He was as much fun as he was wise. This was his favorite dessert—I brought it out for the doubting Thomases or Mabels who weren't sure it was as good as I assured them it was. We served it during that testing party, the big one. It was one of those unusual California dewy evenings that have been known to bring your mountaintop aerie down to the beach. The lady who valiantly brought in this dish had already prepared it three times that day with little success—the phone rang at the wrong time, the kids had to be picked up in the middle of a crucial step. When she finally got them together and brought them over, the wind took hold of her, her umbrella and her platter of Archbishop Sheen's Apples and dumped them all into the mud that was gathering all over the driveway. She was practically in tears—never mind her hairdo, her rain-soaked, mud-covered clothes and her shoes—but her APPLES!!!! Making a long story short, they were delicious and a big hit; and if I'd known the exact proportion of rainwater to mud, I'd have added it to the recipe. You have the original. Do you suppose the good Archbishop looked down and protested our daring to test his pretested specialty?

3 cups water
2 cups sugar
1 stick cinnamon

Juice of 1/2 lemon
6 red cooking apples, cored (Rome Beauties or McIntosh)

PASTE

1 cup almonds, finely ground
2 tablespoons sugar

3 to 4 tablespoons syrup from cooking apples

In large pot or Dutch oven, combine water, sugar, cinnamon stick, and lemon juice. Stir and cook over very low heat until mixture is syrupy. Add apples and simmer in syrup, over low heat, for 1/2 to 3/4 hour. Keep spooning mixture over apples, to cook evenly and prevent discoloration. Cook just until inside is done but skin doesn't slip off.

Lift apples out very gently with slotted spoon and place on heatproof plate to cool. Spoon more syrup over apples before placing them in refrigerator to chill.

While apples are cooling, make almond paste. Mix almonds with sugar and add syrup, little at a time. Blend into paste. If desired, add a little ground cinnamon and few drops lemon juice. When ready to serve, fill center of each apple with almond paste. Spoon more syrup over, and decorate with fresh mint leaves.

RICH PASTRY STRAWBERRY SHORTCAKE

MAKES ONE 8-INCH SHORTCAKE

This is the genuine article. The honest-to-pete strawberry shortcake. There are other versions. Mother used to make the lightest white cake and cut it into three layers and slather each with whipped cream and loads of slightly sweetened strawberries. Then she'd ice the whole thing with gobs of whipped cream decorated with the biggest and prettiest berries of the lot. It was the prettiest thing for picnics, Fourth of July parties, and so on. But this was the one we had at home—I liked and like it the best of all.

3/4 cup unbleached flour
1/4 teaspoon salt
6 tablespoons (3/4 stick) unsalted butter, chilled and cut into 12 pieces

2 tablespoons ice water
1 pint fresh strawberries, hulled
1 1/2 cups heavy cream, whipped and sweetened to taste

Use metal blade of food processor to mix flour and salt, turning machine on and off 2–3 times. Add butter, and turn machine on and off 3–4 times or until it is coarsely chopped. Remove top and drizzle ice water over mixture. Turn machine on and off 3–4 times or until mixture just holds together. Carefully remove dough from work bowl and divide it in half. Shape each portion into a disk. Cover with plastic wrap, and chill in refrigerator for at least 2 hours.

On lightly floured surface, roll each disk out into a circle, about 1/8-inch thick and a little more than 8 inches in diameter. Place 8-inch lid or cake pan on dough and cut around it with sharp knife to ensure even circles. Place dough circles on ungreased cookie sheet and prick with fork. Refrigerate for 30 minutes.

Preheat oven to 400°F. Bake 8–10 minutes or until edges are lightly browned. Transfer pastry round to wire rack and let cool.

Use medium slicing blade to process strawberries. Reserve a few for garnish and fold sliced strawberries into whipped cream. Place 1 pastry round on serving dish and cover with half strawberry mixture; place other pastry layer on top and cover with remaining strawberry mixture. Garnish with reserved sliced strawberries.

GRAPES IN SOUR CREAM WITH BROWN SUGAR

SERVES 6

5 heaping cups seedless grapes   1/2 cup brown sugar
1 1/2 cups sour cream

Wash and chill grapes. Pluck grapes from stems so that all used are perfect. Have both grapes and cream very cold.

Mix grapes with cream and place in silver or glass bowl. Chill again. Sprinkle sugar over entire top just before serving. Sugar may be sieved or dropped in lumps if you like that effect and taste. A thin, crisp spice cookie is a good accompaniment.

DINAH'S CHEESECAKE

SERVES 12

Some friends of mine aren't too crazy about sugar. I use a cup and a quarter of honey instead, and I think I like it better than the original.

CRUST

1 3/4 cups honey graham cracker crumbs   1/2 teaspoon cinnamon
1/4 cup finely chopped walnuts   1/2 cup melted butter

Mix ingredients together. Reserve 3 tablespoons for topping. Press remainder into bottom and sides of 9-inch springform pan.

FILLING

6 eggs   1/4 cup lemon juice
4 8-ounce packages of cream cheese   2 tablespoons grated lemon rind
1 1/2 cups sugar or 1 1/4 cups honey   6 cups sour cream
4 teaspoons vanilla extract

Preheat oven to 375°F. Combine eggs, cheese, sugar or honey, and flavorings. Beat until smooth. Blend in sour cream. Pour into crust. Top with reserved crumbs. Bake 1 hour. Chill 4–5 hours before serving.

CHOCOLATE CHEESECAKE

SERVES 10–12

CRUST

18–20 chocolate wafers, rolled into crumbs   1/3 cup melted butter

Combine crumbs and melted butter. Press into bottom and completely up the sides of 8-inch springform pan. Chill.

FILLING

8 ounces semisweet chocolate

3 ounces unsweetened chocolate

1 tablespoon butter

1 1/2 pounds cream cheese at room temperature

1/2 cup sugar

1/4 teaspoon cinnamon

1 teaspoon vanilla

2 cups sour cream

6 eggs

Slowly melt chocolate with butter in double boiler. Beat softened cream cheese until fluffy in food processor fitted with metal blade or with electric beater. Blend in sugar and cinnamon. Add melted chocolate, vanilla, and sour cream. Add eggs, one at a time, beating after each addition.

Pour into chilled crust and bake in preheated 350°F. oven 1 hour and 10 minutes. Filling may still be runny but will firm up as it chills. Chill 3–5 hours. If cracks develop, shave semisweet chocolate over the top.

GINGERBREAD WITH CARAMEL SAUCE SERVES 8

Pauline makes this better than anybody. Anybody.

GINGERBREAD

1 cup molasses

2 teaspoons baking soda

1 teaspoon cinnamon

1 teaspoon ginger

1/4 teaspoon nutmeg

1/2 cup sugar

1/2 cup butter, melted

2 scant cups flour

1 cup boiling water

2 egg yolks

2 egg whites

Caramel Sauce

Preheat oven to 350°F. Mix molasses, soda, and spices. Add sugar, butter, flour, and water; beat well. Beat egg whites until stiff and fold into slightly beaten egg yolks. Add to batter. Pour in greased 6-cup ring mold and bake 35–40 minutes. (Don't worry if batter seems thin, it's supposed to be.) Serve with Caramel Sauce.

CARAMEL SAUCE

2 egg yolks, slightly beaten	1 tablespoon butter
1 cup cream	1 teaspoon vanilla
1 pound light brown sugar	1/8 teaspoon salt

Place egg yolks, cream, and sugar in double boiler. Cook until creamy and mixture coats the back of a spoon. Add butter. When cool, add vanilla and salt.

Serve on large round platter. I have a little silver bowl that fits in center of ring after gingerbread has been unmolded. Gingerbread and sauce are even nicer when served a little warm.

SOUFFLÉ ''RUE PEKING''

SERVES 6–8

The Culinary Olympics is exactly what the name implies. It doesn't receive quite the coverage of the sports variety, but in the world of culinary artistry it is the sum and substance of achievement in the field. We hosted our American team on the TV show before they took off for the event in Frankfurt, Germany, one year. This masterpiece was created by a member of our team, chef Lutz Olkiewitz of the Drake Hotel in Chicago. I hope he got a gold medal. This recipe alone entitles its creator to four forks, seven spoons, the Croix de Guerre—and five pounds on the diner.

3 ounces pitted dates, coarsely chopped	2 ounces pecans, coarsely chopped
3 ounces pitted prunes, coarsely chopped	3–4 ounces brandy

Soak dates, prunes, and nuts in brandy for 3 hours.

YELLOW MIX

2 tablespoons butter	4 egg yolks, beaten
1 tablespoon flour	5 egg whites
1 cup milk	2 tablespoons sugar
1/2 tablespoon Grand Marnier	1 tablespoon cornstarch
Pinch of salt	

CHOCOLATE MIX

2 tablespoons butter	4 egg yolks
1 tablespoon flour	5 egg whites
1 cup milk	2 tablespoons sugar
1/2 tablespoon cognac	3/4 tablespoon cornstarch
1 tablespoon cocoa powder	1/4 cup powdered sugar and cinnamon
Pinch of salt	Sauce Taipang

Prepare Yellow Mix by melting butter in small saucepan (do not brown); add flour and remove from heat. Bring milk, Grand Marnier, and salt to boil and remove from heat. Stir egg yolks into milk mixture. Add butter mixture to milk-egg mixture and cook over low heat, stirring constantly, until thick and smooth. Beat egg whites and sugar until stiff but not dry; then gradually fold in cornstarch. Fold egg whites into egg-milk mixture. Set aside.

To prepare Chocolate Mix, melt butter in small saucepan; add flour and remove from heat. Bring milk, cognac, cocoa powder, and salt to a boil and remove from heat. Stir egg yolks into milk mixture. Add butter mixture to milk-egg yolk mixture and cook over low heat, stirring constantly, until it is thick and smooth. Preheat oven to 375°F.

Beat egg whites and sugar until stiff but not dry; then gradually fold in cornstarch. Fold egg whites into egg-milk mixture. Set aside. Drain fruit mixture and place in bottom of buttered 2-quart soufflé dish sprinkled with sugar, to which buttered collar has been attached.

Pour yellow and chocolate soufflé mixtures alternately in layers (like marble cake) to top of soufflé dish. Place soufflé dish in pan containing 1 inch of hot water and bake 35–45 minutes. After removing soufflé from oven, dust with cinnamon powdered sugar and serve piping hot with Sauce Taipang.

SAUCE TAIPANG

1 tablespoon butter
1/4 cup sugar
2 egg yolks, beaten
Pinch of salt
1 tablespoon cornstarch (if desired to thicken)

1 cup white wine or champagne
1/2 cup orange juice
1 cup chopped tangerine slices
Grated rind from 1/2 orange
1/4 cup Cointreau liqueur

Melt butter in saucepan and add sugar, egg yolks, salt, and, if desired, cornstarch, stirring constantly over moderate heat until thickened. Add remaining ingredients, mixing well. Serve hot or cold.

APRICOT SOUFFLÉ

SERVES 9

My friend Barbara Sinatra, after we'd played a round of golf, a few sets of tennis, and a few hands of gin rummy (not my best sport, that last one—I think they cut the cards to see who had to take me as a partner), would sometimes take on lunch too. (See her Sea Sandwich, page 227.) This is a terrific dessert she'd serve every once in a while.

The ice cream sauce is a beautiful complement to this, but it's a lily-gilder. Another possibility is a generous gob of whipped cream, to which you have added sugar to taste, and a tablespoon of apricot liqueur or cognac on top of each serving.

1 1/2 cups dried apricots
Sherry
1 1/2 cups sugar
3/4 teaspoon salt

6 tablespoons cognac or apricot liqueur
8 egg yolks
10 egg whites

Soak apricots in glass jar with sherry to cover for at least a week. (You can soak them for a month, if you'd like.)

Preheat oven to 400°F. Drain apricots. (Save the sherry, of course!) Combine with sugar, salt, cognac or apricot liqueur, and egg yolks in blender or food processor. Beat egg whites until stiff but not dry, and fold into mixture.

Pour into buttered and sugared 2-quart soufflé dish, fitted with collar 2 1/2 inches wide and tied with kitchen string. Bake 25–30 minutes. You can serve this with sauce made by melting ice cream and blending in a little of same liqueur used in soufflé.

SOPAIPILLAS

MAKES 48 SOPAIPILLAS

Don and Susan Meredith are dear friends who moved to Santa Fe. I hated to see them leave their home down the street from me, but there are some compensations. I visit them occasionally in Santa Fe, where I learned all about glowing sunsets, clear air, hand-knit fabrics, and sopaipillas. It's a dessert here, but plain, unsauced sopaipillas, just crisp little pillows, are perfect along with your meal instead of bread or tortillas.

1 package active dry yeast
1 teaspoon sugar
1/4 cup warm water (110–115°F.)
1 1/4 cups (approximately) scalded milk
4 cups sifted flour

1 1/2 teaspoons salt
1 teaspoon baking powder
1 tablespoon butter
1 quart peanut oil
Sherry Sauce

Stir yeast, sugar, and warm water together in large mixing bowl; let sit until yeast dissolves and starts to proof. Let scalded milk cool to room temperature. Add to yeast mixture.

Meanwhile, combine dry ingredients and cut in butter. Make a well in center of dry ingredients. Add about 1 1/4 cups liquid to dry ingredients and work into dough. Add more liquid until dough is firm and springy and holds its shape, similar to a yeast dough. Knead dough 15–20 times, invert bowl over dough, and set aside approximately 10 minutes.

Heat oil to 375–400°F. in deep-fryer. Roll one fourth of dough to 1/4-inch thickness or slightly thinner, then cut into squares or triangles, about 3 inches; do not reroll any of the dough. Cover cut dough with towel as you fry sopaipillas, a few at a time, in hot oil. They should puff up and become hollow very soon after being dropped into oil. To assure puffing, slightly stretch each piece of dough before lowering it into oil, then place rolled or top side of dough into oil first, so it will be bottom side. Hold each piece of dough down until it puffs. Drain sopaipillas on paper towels. Dust with powdered sugar and dip in Sherry Sauce.

SHERRY SAUCE

6 tablespoons brown sugar
1/2 cup water
1/2 cup dry sherry

1/2 cup raisins
1/2 teaspoon maple flavoring, optional

In saucepan, bring brown sugar and water to boil, stirring constantly, until sugar is dissolved. Lower heat and simmer until slightly thickened. Add dry sherry, raisins, and maple flavoring. Serve hot.

FRENCH BREAD PUDDING WITH RUM SAUCE

SERVES 8–10

Bread puddings seem to be coming back. I came across so many preparing for this book. Maybe the bread is better—and like me, most people can't bear to waste anything. I tested dozens and found each one so delectably different, I couldn't resist passing them on to you.

You might as well be as intrigued and confused as I was—try them all!

In the next volume, I'll give you the ones that we deferred, not eliminated, in the interest of space.

This one is from Commander's Palace in New Orleans. How can you go wrong?

BREAD PUDDING

5 eggs
1 pint whipping cream
1 cup sugar
Dash of cinnamon
1 tablespoon vanilla

1/4 cup raisins
1/4 cup butter
12 1-inch slices french bread (the long-loaf size)

Preheat oven to 350°F. In large bowl combine eggs, cream, sugar, cinnamon, vanilla, and raisins. Mix well. Use a little butter to grease bottom of pan 9 inches square by 1 3/4 inches deep. Pour mixture into pan.

Lay slices of french bread flat in above mixture; let stand for 5 minutes, to soak up custard mixture; then turn bread over. Let stand 10 minutes, then push bread down so most of it is covered by custard mixture. Do not break the bread. Dot top with remaining butter.

Put pan into larger pan filled with water up to a half inch from top. Cover with aluminum foil. Bake 45–50 minutes, uncovering pudding for last 10 minutes so top browns nicely. When done, custard mixture should be somewhat liquid, rather than very firm.

RUM SAUCE

2 cups water
1 cup sugar
1 cinnamon stick or dash of cinnamon
1 tablespoon butter

1/2 teaspoon cornstarch
Additional water
1/2 ounce rum

Bring water, sugar, cinnamon, and butter to boil. When mixture is boiling, whip into it cornstarch which has been mixed with water to make 1/4 cup. Take mixture off heat, add rum. Sauce will be thin.

NEW ORLEANS BREAD PUDDING WITH WHISKEY SAUCE

12 slices french bread (not sourdough)
1 quart milk, slightly warmed, not hot
3 large eggs, slightly beaten
2 cups sugar

2 tablespoons vanilla
1 cup pecans
1/3 cup seedless raisins

Preheat oven to 350°F. Cut bread into large cubes and place in bowl of food processor. Process a second or so—don't let it get too fine. Put bread in large bowl. Mix together milk, eggs, sugar, and vanilla. Pour over bread and mix lightly with wooden spoons. Add pecans to processor bowl and dice coarsely. Add raisins, one more quick on and off of processor, using work blade.

Add to bread mix. Generously butter large-sized soufflé dish. Pour pudding in. Bake 55 minutes. Let cool slightly. Cut carefully with sharp knife and loosen sides. Unmold on flat platter.

WHISKEY SAUCE

1 1/2 cups sugar
3/4 cup butter or margarine (1 1/2 sticks),
   cut into about 12 pieces

1/2 cup bourbon
1/3 cup water
1 teaspoon cornstarch

Combine all ingredients in saucepan. Simmer, stirring constantly, until slightly thickened. Pour half of sauce over pudding after it has been unmolded and serve remainder warm in sauceboat with pudding.

BERTHA ANN'S BREAD PUDDING   SERVES 6–8

Yes, ma'am!! Canned fruit cocktail in this one. I tried it both ways and it's infinitely better this way. Those fine, busy people at Pichon Catering in New Orleans know exactly what they're doing.

It begins to look as though I've spent a large portion of my food life these last few months seeking out bread puddings in New Orleans—not so—it's just one of those delightful coincidences. I think I could have filled a chapter or maybe two with bread puddings alone. I haven't even told you about what happens at home in Tennessee when there's a half a loaf left over—wonders, that's all!!!

6 slices stale french bread
2 16-ounce cans evaporated milk
2 1/2 cups water
2 1/2 cups sugar
3 teaspoons vanilla

2 cups raisins
2 cups fruit cocktail
1 cup coconut (optional)
1 stick margarine, melted
6 eggs

Soak bread in milk, water, sugar, and vanilla. Let stand 1 hour, mixing occasionally.

Preheat oven to 350°F. Add raisins, fruit cocktail, coconut, and melted margarine. Beat eggs well by hand or at low speed in mixer, add to mixture, blend well by hand. Pour pudding mixture into well buttered 3-quart Pyrex bowl. Bake for 1 hour.

ORANGE SAUCE

1/2 cup sugar
1 tablespoon cornstarch
1 cup orange juice
2 tablespoons butter

1 teaspoon vanilla
1/8 teaspoon nutmeg (optional)
Pinch of salt

In small saucepan mix together sugar, cornstarch, and orange juice. Place over low heat and boil 5 minutes, stirring constantly. Remove from heat. Stir in butter, vanilla, nutmeg, and salt. Serve over bread pudding.

GINGER MOUSSE   SERVES 6

Steve Raichlen of Boston Magazine *in Cambridge, Massachusetts, sent me this glorious light-as-a-whisper confection. Don't miss a bit of it—use those regular and optional garnishes, and wonder of wonders, you can and have to do it ahead. No trip back to the kitchen for a long assembling session just when the conversation gets good.*

2 cups milk
6 tablespoons sugar, plus 2 tablespoons for
  egg whites
6 egg yolks
1 envelope unflavored gelatin softened over
  4 tablespoons water
2-inch piece fresh ginger root, grated with
  fine grater
2 tablespoons cognac

3/4 cup heavy whipping cream
4 tablespoons candied ginger, chopped, plus
  1 tablespoon for sprinkling on top of
  mousse
3 egg whites
Optional garnish: julienned lemon zest simmered in a little green chartreuse and/or
  grenadine

In heavy saucepan scald milk. Whisk sugar and egg yolks together. Melt gelatin in small pan over boiling water.

Pour milk over yolk mixture in thin stream, whisking constantly. Return this mixture to milk pan and cook over low heat, stirring constantly with wooden spoon, until foam subsides and milk thickens enough to thickly coat back of wooden spoon. (Do not let mixture boil or go above 165°F. or egg yolks will scramble.) Pour custard mixture through a fine-meshed strainer into a bowl. Whisk in gelatin, let mixture cool slightly, and whisk in grated ginger and cognac.

Place mixture over ice and stir with rubber spatula to cool. Meanwhile, whip cream to stiff peaks. When mixture starts to set (about 1 hour) gently fold in whipped cream, reserving a few tablespoons for garnish, and four tablespoons candied ginger. Beat egg whites to stiff peaks, adding remaining sugar to make them firm and glossy. When mixture begins to set again, carefully fold in stiffly beaten egg whites. Spoon mixture into 6-cup soufflé dish and let set for at least 2 hours in refrigerator before serving.

Just before serving, decorate mousse with rosettes made of remaining whipped cream. Sprinkle top with remaining candied ginger and lemon julienne.

LEMON PUDDING

A lemon custard pie without the crust. One of Shirley Secretary's (also known as Schroer) contributions. Remember, I told you everybody who works around here cooks and cooks. I haven't checked out Johnny, who takes care of the pool, but I'll bet you after all the testings he's had to go through—along with the milkman, the mailman, the United Parcel people—he'd come up with something.

2 cups milk
2 cups sugar
1/2 cup flour
Juice of 4 lemons

Grated rind of 2 lemons
4 eggs, separated
Lemon knots for garnish

Preheat oven to 350°F. Mix all ingredients except egg whites and beat until smooth. Beat egg whites until stiff and fold into mixture.

Place in greased 12 × 8 × 2-inch casserole dish. Place casserole, uncovered, in pan containing 1 inch of hot water and bake 50 minutes. Cool and garnish with lemon knots.

BESSIE'S PERSIMMON PUDDING

This is one of sister Bessie's specialties. It's a must around the holiday season, which jibes perfectly with the persimmon season out here. Bessie has a tree of the beautiful golden things in her front yard. The number and size of her puddings is in direct ratio to the number she has been able to rescue from the winged birds, four-legged squirrels, and two-legged neighbors and passersby, who find them irresistible. I think she slips out in the dead of night to salvage what's left for our puddings. Naturally she does it "by the feel" but this year I made her measure every step of the way. It almost made her decide to "leave it for the birds."

3–4 persimmons, to make 1 cup puree
2 teaspoons baking soda
1 1/2 cups sugar
1/2 cup (1 stick) butter or margarine
2 eggs
2 tablespoons brandy
2 teaspoons vanilla

1 teaspoon lemon juice
1 cup flour, unsifted
1 teaspoon cinnamon
1/4 teaspoon salt
1 cup raisins
1/2 cup pecans, chopped
Brandied Hard Sauce

Scoop flesh out of persimmons. Discard stems, seeds, and skins. Blend in food processor. Makes 1 cup of puree. Stir in soda. Set aside. (Puree will get black on top.)

Cream sugar and butter until fluffy. Beat in eggs, brandy, vanilla, lemon juice, and puree. Sift flour, cinnamon, and salt. Add to mixture and stir well. Add raisins and nuts.

Thoroughly grease 2-quart pudding mold and lid. Spoon mixture into mold and secure lid. Place on rack above boiling water in steamer kettle. Cover. Steam 2 1/2 hours. Add more water if needed. Remove and allow to cool 10 minutes and unmold. Wrap in foil. It will keep. Serve with Brandied Hard Sauce.

Beat eggs; add hot milk and sugar. Cook over boiling water in top half of double boiler until back of wooden spoon is generously coated. Add dissolved cornstarch to about 2–3 tablespoons of egg-milk mixture, return to mixture, and blend well. On no account allow it to boil (no higher than 165°) or custard will curdle. Stir until cool.

Add liqueur to taste. Arrange the "islands" in serving dish and pour Diet Crème Anglaise around them.

CARAMEL

1/2 cup sugar   2–3 tablespoons boiling water

In saucepan, dissolve sugar in water over low heat, brushing sides of pan with water until sugar is dissolved. Raise heat and cook without stirring until dark amber (don't let it get too brown). Carefully pour over islands. The dish may be refrigerated 3–4 hours, but no longer.

FRENCH VANILLA ICE CREAM   MAKES 1 QUART

1/2 cup granulated sugar   2 cups whole milk or half-and-half, scalded
1/8 generous teaspoon salt   1 cup heavy cream, unwhipped
4 egg yolks, slightly beaten   1 generous teaspoon vanilla extract

Combine sugar and salt, add egg yolks, beating gently until sugar is dissolved and mixture is thoroughly blended. Pour scalded milk or half-and-half over slowly, while stirring briskly and constantly.

Turn creamy custard into top of double boiler and cook over simmering water, stirring constantly, until mixture coats spoon. Strain through double cheesecloth, cool, then chill. Add cream and vanilla. Freeze according to directions that come with your ice cream maker.

COCONUT PINEAPPLE ICE CREAM   MAKES 2 QUARTS

4 cups milk   1/2 teaspoon salt
4 eggs, separated   2 cups whipping cream
1 1/2 cups sugar   1 cup fresh coconut, grated or 1 cup canned
2 teaspoons vanilla   flaked coconut
1 teaspoon lemon juice   1 cup crushed pineapple, drained

Combine milk, egg yolks, and sugar over medium heat in double boiler until mixture forms soft custard. Add vanilla, lemon juice, and salt. Beat egg whites and fold into custard. Whip cream and fold into custard. Add coconut and pineapple. Pour mixture into freezer can and freeze by following instructions that come with your ice cream maker.

BITTERSWEET CHOCOLATE ICE CREAM

MAKES 2 QUARTS

2 tablespoons instant coffee
1/2 cup boiling water
6 ounces (6 squares) semisweet chocolate
5 egg yolks
1/4 cup water, at room temperature

1/2 cup sugar
1/4 teaspoon cream of tartar
1/3 cup bittersweet chocolate liqueur (I use Droste's)
3 cups heavy cream

Dissolve coffee in boiling water. Combine with chocolate in small, heavy saucepan, or in top of small double boiler over hot water on moderate heat. Stir occasionally to melt chocolate. Remove from heat and set aside to cool.

Beat yolks in small bowl of electric mixer at high speed for several minutes until thick and pale-lemon-colored.

Meanwhile, in small saucepan, mix 1/4 cup water with sugar and cream of tartar. With small wooden spatula or spoon, stir over high heat until sugar is dissolved and mixture comes to boil. Let boil without stirring about 3 minutes until the syrup reaches 230°F. on a candy thermometer (light-thread stage).

Gradually, in thin stream, add hot syrup to egg yolks, still beating at high speed. Continue to beat about 5 minutes or until mixture is cool. Stir chocolate liqueur into chocolate mixture. Then add to cooled egg-yolk mixture, beating only until blended. Remove from mixer.

In chilled large bowl of electric mixer, with chilled beaters, beat cream only until it holds a very soft shape. Fold 1 cup cream into chocolate mixture and then fold chocolate mixture into remaining cream. Pour mixture into freezer can and freeze according to directions that come with your ice cream maker.

LEMON DE MENTHE ICE CREAM

MAKES 1 QUART

1 cup heavy cream
1 cup milk
1 cup sugar
Juice and rind of 2 lemons

2 teaspoons crème de menthe
Oranges and lemons (optional)
Sprigs of fresh mint for garnish

Heat cream, milk, and sugar in heavy-bottomed saucepan, stirring occasionally, until sugar is dissolved and mixture is hot. Cool.

Add lemon juice and lemon rind and crème de menthe. Pour mixture into freezer can and freeze by following instructions that come with your ice cream maker.

To serve, hollow out an orange or a large lemon. Place lemon ice cream inside and add a sprig of fresh mint.

BROWN SUGAR PECAN ICE CREAM

MAKES ABOUT 5 CUPS

3 cups heavy cream
1 cup milk
1 scant packed cup brown sugar

4 egg yolks
1 cup pecan pieces

Heat cream, milk, and sugar in heavy-bottomed saucepan, stirring occasionally until sugar is dissolved and mixture is hot. Place egg yolks in bowl and whisk briefly. Still whisking, slowly pour in about 1 cup of hot liquid. When mixture is blended, slowly pour it into liquid in saucepan, whisking constantly. Cook over medium heat, stirring constantly, until mixture thickens slightly and coats back of spoon, about 8 minutes. Be sure not to let mixture boil at any time or it will curdle.

Strain into clean bowl and cool thoroughly. Stir in nuts. Pour mixture into freezer can of your ice cream maker and follow instructions that come with your ice cream maker.

STRAWBERRY SORBET

MAKES 1 QUART

2 10-ounce packages frozen strawberries
 packed in syrup

1 cup Simple Syrup (page 18)
3 tablespoons fresh lemon juice

Puree strawberries with their syrup in food processor. Stir in Simple Syrup and lemon juice.

Pour mixture into freezer can of your ice cream maker and freeze according to instructions that come with your ice cream maker.

FRESH PINEAPPLE SORBET

MAKES ABOUT 1 QUART

1 small ripe pineapple, peeled, cored, and
 cubed

1 cup Simple Syrup (page 18)
2 tablespoons fresh lemon juice

Place pineapple cubes in food processor and process until very smooth and frothy. You should have 2 1/2 cups. Stir in Simple Syrup and lemon juice. Taste and add more syrup or juice if needed.

Pour mixture into freezer can of your ice cream maker and freeze according to instructions that come with your ice cream maker.

INDEX